SECOND EDITION

AMERICA SINCE 1941

a history

SECOND EDITION

AMERICA SINCE 1941

a history

JAMES T. PATTERSON
Brown University

Harcourt College Publishers

Fort Worth   Philadelphia   San Diego   New York   Orlando   Austin   San Antonio
Toronto   Montreal   London   Sydney   Tokyo

Publisher	Earl McPeek
Executive Editor	David Tatom
Market Strategist	Laura M. Brennan
Project Editor	Laura Therese Miley
Art Director	Burl Sloan
Production Manager	Linda McMillan

ISBN: 0-15-507859-3
Library of Congress Catalog Card Number: 99-61319

Address for Domestic Orders
Harcourt College Publishers, 6277 Sea Harbor Drive, Orlando, FL 32887-6777
800-782-4479

Address for International Orders
International Customer Service
Harcourt, Inc., 6277 Sea Harbor Drive, Orlando, FL 32887-6777
407-345-3800
(fax)407-345-4060
(e-mail) hbintl@hartcourtbrace.com

Address for Editorial Correspondence
Harcourt College Publishers, 301 Commerce Street, Suite 3700, Forth Worth, TX 76102
Web Site Address
http://www.harcourtcollege.com

Printed in the United States of America

9 0 1 2 3 4 5 6 7 8 016 9 8 7 6 5 4 3 2 1

Harcourt College Publishers

Preface

This fifth edition of *America in the Twentieth Century* revises my thoughts concerning United States history from about 1900 to the present, a subject I have taught for nearly forty years. As with the first four editions, this one pays due attention to political and diplomatic events. It also devotes considerable space to areas of special interest to many students today: black history, women's history, urbanization, the role of ethnic groups, the rise of presidential power and of the federal bureaucracy, the power of corporations and the conflict of economic groups, changing sexual mores, and trends in regional and national values.

I have tried to give pace to the narrative by including anecdotes and quotations, by describing key personalities, and by setting aside selections from primary sources that illuminate passages in the text. I hope, however, that readers will not conclude that my purpose is to entertain or to avoid serious issues. On the contrary, I have tried to offer up-to-date interpretations and to state my conclusions about major questions. Without sacrificing my own viewpoint, I have also tried to present various sides of controversial issues. My aim is to stimulate the thinking of college-level students in survey courses and in courses dealing with twentieth-century American history.

Thanks for help with this edition go to my colleagues at Brown University, Howard Chudacoff, Charles Neu, Luther Spoehr, and John Thomas; to graduate students Jeffrey Reiser and Joshua Zeitz; and to John Snyder, my undergraduate research assistant. I also thank my wife, Cynthia Patterson, for her help in many ways.

James T. Patterson

A NOTE ON THIS EDITION

This volume is a reprinting of chapters ten through seventeen of *America in the Twentieth Century: A History,* Fifth Edition. While this book exactly reproduces the text found in the larger book, the pages and chapters have been renumbered and a separate index is provided. Publishing the book in this form is a response to the significant increase in courses on postwar America, and the publisher hopes that instructors and students will find this edition a useful and convenient alternative for a variety of courses.

Contents

Maps and Graphs

SECOND EDITION

AMERICA SINCE 1941

a history

A Great Divide: Internment of Japanese-Americans

CHAPTER 1

World War II: A Great Divide

Around 1939, the social historian John Brooks concluded, America began a "Great Leap" toward the future. The critic Irving Kristol added that the 1930s were governmentally the "last amateur decade." Both writers accurately stressed the almost incalculable impact of World War II on American life. In every area—military and diplomatic affairs, politics, social and economic relations—the war greatly accelerated the processes of economic change, political centralization, and international involvement that have been grand themes of American history in the twentieth century.

The Military Effort

America's primary task after the attack on Pearl Harbor was of course to settle on the quickest, most effective way of defeating the enemy. This problem, in turn, ultimately raised four major questions, all of which had profound long-range implications.

Which adversary, Germany or Japan, was to be dealt with first? Should the enemy be totally defeated or, as in 1918, be permitted to reach an armistice? What emphasis should Britain and the United States place on strategic bombing, thought by some to be a way of avoiding the bloodbath of trench warfare in World War I? Where, and when, should Allied ground forces actually attack Germany and Japan?

The answer to the first question aroused little controversy at the time. Roosevelt always considered Germany the number one enemy, and in March 1941 British and American military leaders secretly agreed. After the attack on Pearl Harbor, Prime Minister Winston Churchill came to the United States for the first of many summit conferences, and the agreement became official policy.

At times during the war Roosevelt appeared to depart from this position. In mid-1942, American naval forces scored an unexpectedly quick victory at the battle

3

of Midway, and Admiral Chester Nimitz, commander in the central Pacific, was authorized to mount offensives against Japanese-held islands. By the spring of 1943 Nimitz's forces had captured the Solomon Islands; by late summer of 1944 they had taken Tinian, Guam, and Saipan in the Marianas; and by October 1944, after desperate island battles, American soldiers were invading the Philippines. Dramatic military progress in the Pacific caused a few critics to argue later that America should have concentrated its efforts against Japan, thereby leaving Hitler and Stalin to destroy each other in the West.

Roosevelt refused to do that. He recognized that any American invasion of Japan's home islands would encounter fanatical resistance. He also had to respond to the incessant pleas of Josef Stalin, his wartime ally, for aid against Germany. And like most of his contemporaries, the President wanted to destroy the scourge of Hitler first and forever. For all these reasons he paid little attention to the "Asia-firsters" (whose counsel might have left Stalin free to overrun all of Europe).

The second question—should the enemy be allowed to sue for peace?—was answered formally at the Casablanca conference in January 1943, at which Roosevelt proclaimed a policy of unconditional surrender. Later, America deviated slightly from it: Italy was permitted to lay down its arms in late 1943, and Japan was ultimately allowed to retain its emperor. But the total defeat of the enemy remained at the heart of Roosevelt's thinking. "I do not want them to starve to death," he said of the Germans, "but, as an example, if they need food to keep body and soul together, they should be fed three times a day with soup from army soup kitchens." In late 1944 he initialed the so-called Morgenthau Plan aimed at "converting Germany into a country primarily agricultural and pastoral in character." Though he later dropped the plan, he adhered consistently to the central goal, that of beating the enemies so thoroughly that they could never again threaten the peace.

First Person

Whether nations live in prosperity or starve to death interests me only so far as we need them for slaves for our Kultur; otherwise it is of no interest to me. Whether 10,000 Russian females fall down from exhaustion while digging an anti-tank ditch interests me only in so far as the anti-tank ditch for Germany is finished. We shall never be rough and heartless when it is not necessary, that is clear. We Germans, who are the only people in the world who have a decent attitude toward animals, will also assume a decent attitude toward these human animals. But it is a crime against our blood to worry about them and giving them ideals, thus causing our sons and grandsons to have a more difficult time with them. When someone comes to me and says: "I cannot dig the anti-tank ditch with women and children, it is inhuman, for it will kill them," then I have to say "You are the murderer of your own blood, because if the anti-tank ditch is not dug German soldiers will die, and they are the sons of German mothers. They are our own blood."

Heinrich Himmler, head of the Nazi SS, explains the nature of modern war.

To many postwar critics the policy of unconditional surrender seemed a tragic mistake. They asserted that it steeled the resolve of the enemies, discouraged leaders of the resistance in Germany and Japan, and left power vacuums in central Europe and Manchuria—vacuums filled by the Soviets. Roosevelt, it appeared, forgot the fundamental maxim that wars are fought for political as well as military objectives.

Some of these criticisms were convincing. American insistence on Japan's unconditional surrender proved a major stumbling block to peace in July 1945, before the dropping of the atomic bombs on Hiroshima and Nagasaki. Otherwise, however, the critics were unfair. No policy, no matter how generous, could have swayed the leaders of Germany and Japan from their destructive course. The demand for unconditional surrender did not prevent dissidents in Germany from attempting to overthrow Hitler—an officers' plot almost succeeded in 1944. And Russia charged into central Europe mainly because its armies were powerful, not because of the policy of unconditional surrender. If Roosevelt had shown the slightest tendency to negotiate a truce with Hitler—which he did not—Stalin would probably have kept on fighting—and have ended up with more territory than he did.

The critics of unconditional surrender also forgot the ruthless nature of modern war. In 1917 it was possible for "Yanks" to believe that they were fighting a war to save democracy; there were ideals to be achieved. In World War II, American soldiers were "GIs"—"government issued" machines sent abroad by a much more organized society that remembered Pearl Harbor and loathed Hitler. Like Willie and Joe, cartoonist Bill Mauldin's dirty, unshaven infantrymen, they fought because they had to, and they had few aims save destroying the enemy and coming home. General Lesley J. McNair, director of the training program for all American ground forces, put it this way to a radio audience in 1942: "We must lust for battle; our object in life must be to kill; we must scheme and plan night and day to kill." What McNair meant, and what every American understood, was that Germany and Japan must be totally defeated. No Allied leader in World War II could have pursued a policy that promised otherwise.

The quest for total victory helps explain Roosevelt's support of scientific research into the development of atomic weaponry. This effort began in October 1939, when Leo Szilard, Enrico Fermi, and other emigré scientists, worried about Nazi progress in the field of atomic physics, persuaded Albert Einstein to write a letter to Roosevelt. The letter urged the President to engage the United States in the race to harness atomic energy. Though responsive to the scientists' pleas, the President moved slowly, and it was not until the summer of 1941 that the administration established a "uranium section" in the National Defense Research Committee.

The attack on Pearl Harbor gave renewed urgency to the program, and in 1942 Secretary of War Henry Stimson placed General Leslie Groves, a tough, secretive administrator, in charge of the Manhattan District Project, code name for bomb development. The project's purpose was to beat the Nazis in the race for atomic weaponry. Japan, concentrating on more conventional weapons, was never seriously engaged in the race.

From 1942 on, American and emigré scientists working on the program received more than $2 billion in federal funds. All of it was appropriated for unspecified military purposes by a Congress that heeded Stimson's requests not to probe closely into how it was going to be used. Top military leaders, including Generals Douglas MacArthur and Dwight Eisenhower, America's army commanders in the Pacific and Atlantic, were kept almost as much in the dark. Meanwhile, some 540,000 people worked on the project during the war. This incredibly vast, secret operation enabled the United States to pass Germany, which diverted much of its expertise to jet planes and rocketry. The Manhattan Project testified amply to America's desire to win the war by whatever means necessary, and to the willingness of the nation's elected representatives to turn over authority, no questions asked, to the executive branch.

As the United States entered the war, the nation was mass-producing planes for the armed forces.

The passion for total victory also helped to sustain the argument for strategic bombing—mass raids against enemy cities, factories, storage facilities, military bases, and transportation complexes. Theoretically, these raids could do such a thorough job of weakening enemy strength (and morale) that ground forces could complete the job with minimal loss of American life. "Strategic air power," General Henry ("Hap") Arnold claimed, "is a war-winning weapon in its own right, and is capable of striking decisive blows far behind the battle line, thereby destroying the enemy's capacity to wage war."

Though Arnold did not get all the planes he wanted until late in the war, he could hardly complain. As early as 1940 Roosevelt astounded Congress by asking for production of 50,000 planes per year. By 1942, B-17s and B-24s were already being flown over to Great Britain; by 1943 they were taking off on steady raids against the enemy; and by late 1944 they were smashing the Japanese home cities. Before the end of the war the strategic bombing attacks had leveled many industrial cities in both enemy nations.

Whether strategic bombing was as effective as Arnold claimed was another matter. Undoubtedly, it forced the enemy nations to divert manpower and equipment to reconstruction. In crowded, urban Japan it was so destructive that neither the atomic bombs nor an invasion may have been necessary. But until late 1944 it was also costly to the United States. Only 28 of 120 bombers that took off for a raid on Berlin in July 1943 made it to the target. Between February 20 and 26, 1944, America lost 226 bombers, 28 fighter planes, and 2,600 crewmen. Only in the last year of the war, when American fighter planes finally gained air supremacy, did these raids become reasonably safe for planes and crew.

Strategic bombing enthusiasts were also far too optimistic about the possibility of "pinpoint" bombing. The British bombed mostly at night and could not be too precise about their targets. Americans were scarcely more accurate. Often it was too overcast to see much; often German fighters or antiaircraft artillery forced American pilots to hurry in and off. Either way, the bombs frequently blasted civilian areas. And the British and Americans sometimes resorted to indiscriminate firebombing. One raid against Tokyo killed an estimated 84,000 people and left a million homeless. The city, said one observer, was a "midden of smoking flesh." Another attack by the British and Americans, against nonindustrial Dresden in 1945, killed tens of thousands of civilians.

Even when the bombs hit their targets, they caused much less disruption than many strategists supposed. Against Japan in 1945 they were often devastating, for by then many key targets were defenseless. Germany, however, always maintained surplus factory space and labor, and the bombers caused more inconvenience than crisis. Die-hard enthusiasts of bombing argued later that America's mistake was only in not staging enough raids against German oil reserves, necessary for most forms of production. Perhaps so. But because that was not done, it cannot be proved that bombing the oil reserves would have made a significant difference. What is known is that Germany's productive capacity increased until the last weeks of the war.

These limitations of bombing should have suggested to military leaders that modern war requires great flexibility in response, that not only bombers but also fighters, tanks, and—as ever—infantry are essential to victory. Strategic bombing

Dresden, Germany, after Allied bombing

nonetheless continued to offer great allure after the war. To many people anxious for quick solutions to complex international problems, it seemed a "surgical" way to dispose of troublesome opponents.

The fourth military question—where and when to attack the enemy—was partially avoided in the Asian theater, where a land invasion of Japan's home islands proved unnecessary. Regarding Europe, however, it sparked heated debate.

At first it was assumed that Britain and the United States would attack Germany's western front as soon as possible. Stalin, whose people were suffering horribly, insisted on help right away. He was supported by American army leaders like Marshall and Dwight D. Eisenhower, commander of the war plans division. "We've got to go to Europe and fight," Eisenhower said in January 1942, "and quit wasting resources all over the world—and still worse, wasting time."

With men like Marshall so optimistic, Roosevelt led Stalin to believe that America might stage a second front before the end of 1942. But he had to confront Churchill, whose cooperation was essential to the success of a cross-Channel invasion. Churchill vividly remembered the frightful British losses in World War I. He was also persuaded, probably correctly, that the Allies lacked sufficient men and equipment, especially landing ships for vehicles. Accordingly, he insisted on smaller attacks against Germany's periphery in the Mediterranean. Churchill's stand infuriated some American leaders. But FDR, needing British cooperation before undertaking a cross-Channel invasion, relented and accepted the British plan for an allied offensive in North Africa in late 1942.

When the North African campaign proved successful, Marshall and Eisenhower hoped for a cross-Channel invasion in 1943. Churchill, however, still posed objections, and at Casablanca in January he persuaded Roosevelt to agree to assaults against Sicily and Italy. Marshall observed angrily that "we lost our shirts . . . we came, we listened, and we were conquered." Moreover, the Italian campaign proved costly: at war's end in 1945 Allied troops were still battling their way up the peninsula. So the months slipped by without the long-anticipated invasion. Not until the Teheran summit conference of November 1943 did the Russians receive a guarantee for an attack in 1944.

Churchill was probably right in arguing that a second front in 1943, when the Allies lacked full control of the air, would have been costly. But the political ramifications of postponing "D day" to June 1944 were unfortunate, for Stalin, having hoped for aid in 1942 and again in 1943, grew ever more suspicious of his English-speaking allies. During this time the Soviet Union suffered catastrophic damage and lost millions of its people (perhaps 20 million by the end of the war). Moreover, when the second front finally materialized, his armies were already

Eisenhower talking to American paratroopers, 1944

poised on Germany's eastern borders. By the end of the war he mistrusted the "friends" who had been slow to help in his time of trial.

Roosevelt's handling of these military questions subjected him later to complaints that he was a short-sighted opportunist during the war. If he had thought more often about the postwar world, critics argued, he would have insisted on a second front in 1943 and done all he could to build up ground forces capable of getting into eastern Europe before the Russians. Barring that, he should have agreed to a conditional surrender before the Russians moved into Germany. These arguments ask the impossible. Neither the American public nor Roosevelt's allies would have tolerated such a conditional surrender, and Churchill stood in the way of a harmoniously organized invasion prior to 1944. In acting to safeguard the anti-Axis alliance and to keep the voters behind him in a long and bloody struggle, FDR did what he had to do.

Wartime Diplomacy

Complaints about Roosevelt's military leadership were but part of the broader attacks on his diplomacy. Left-wing critics later charged him with refusing to stand up to imperialists like Churchill and with cooperating with decadent forces in China and France. Right-wingers countered by accusing him of naiveté concerning the Soviet Union. Whatever he did, it seemed he was criticized.

The liberal critics focused first on Roosevelt's dealings with Vichy France, the pro-Nazi collaborators who controlled most of central and southern France following Hitler's victory in 1940. First he recognized the puppet regime. Then he worked out a controversial deal with Vichy Admiral Jean Darlan, a notorious collaborator with the Nazis, in order to secure Darlan's noninterference with Allied forces fighting in North Africa. These dealings outraged General Charles de Gaulle, the extremely sensitive leader of the French resistance forces, and it antagonized many American progressives. The United States, they thought, was tainted by association with fascists.

The American Left also disliked Roosevelt's handling of China. During the war Chiang Kaishek, the Nationalist leader, angered American officials by fighting harder against the communist Chinese than against the Japanese. Corruption and mismanagement within Chiang's regime were undermining what little hold he retained on the peasantry. By 1943, General Joseph ("Vinegar Joe") Stilwell, America's military commander in China, was so disgusted that he referred to Chiang as "Peanut." Roosevelt urged Chiang to mend his ways. Chiang, however, ultimately responded by demanding Stilwell's recall. Roosevelt acceded. When he named General Patrick Hurley, a Republican anticommunist with little knowledge of China, as ambassador in 1944, he played further into Chiang's hands.

Other liberals grumbled that FDR failed to appreciate the anticolonial stirrings of the nonwhite world. Why didn't the President make it clear to Churchill, who had been so anxious for American aid in 1941, that the price was surrender of India, Malaya, and other colonial possessions? Roosevelt did not, his biographer James MacGregor Burns concluded, because he was too "soft and pasty" to risk unpleasantness in negotiations, and because he was content to let occasional rhetorical outbursts against colonialism substitute for the effective use of American power.

These critics agreed with spokesmen of the Right (and the center) that Roosevelt possessed many traits ill-suited for the business of diplomacy. One of these was his legendary reliance on his own charm. This led him, critics charged, to jolly his way through conferences instead of standing up to Stalin or Churchill. Worst of all, FDR's detractors pointed out, it caused him to rely on summit meetings and on personal emissaries like Hopkins instead of on briefings by experts. "I know you will not mind my being brutally frank," he told Churchill in 1944, "when I tell you that I think I can personally handle Stalin better than you or your Foreign Office or my State Department. Stalin hates the guts of all your top people. He thinks he likes me better, and I hope he will continue to do so."

These habits appeared to make Roosevelt into a Great Procrastinator who preferred to keep everyone happy by committing himself to nothing. Unlike Wilson, he gave only cautious encouragement before 1945 to supporters of a United Nations organization. He refused to be specific about America's postwar commitments, except to imply that the United States would go home after the war. At the Teheran conference he told Stalin that the American people would chafe at stationing soldiers in Europe after 1947. And in early 1944 he wrote, "I do not want the United States to have the post-war burden of reconstituting France, Italy, and the Balkans. This is not our natural task at a distance of 3,500 miles." Attitudes such as these caused some observers to wonder if the President had any purposeful postwar goals at all.

Critics on the Right insisted that Roosevelt's desire to avoid unpleasantness led him to be "soft on the Soviets." If Roosevelt had not been such a procrastinator, they argued, he could have exacted promises from the Russians in 1942, when they were calling anxiously for American assistance. If he had understood the peculiar ruthlessness of Stalin, he would have been more hardheaded in dealing with him. If he had not been so eager to win friends at the conference table, he would have refused to make damaging and unnecessary concessions.

The culmination of this foolish approach, critics grumbled, was at the Yalta Conference of February 1945. There, Roosevelt allegedly betrayed American interests by permitting Russia three seats in the UN General Assembly, by settling for a vague agreement on reparations (which later permitted Russia to paralyze eastern Germany), by doing nothing to assist Polish boundary claims, and by failing to secure a noncommunist Polish government. Without consulting China, Roosevelt also reached a secret accord with Stalin that gave the Soviets Southern Sakhalin, the Kurile Islands, and joint operation of the Chinese-Eastern and Southern Manchurian railways, and which recognized Russia's "preeminent interests" in Manchuria. In return for these concessions Roosevelt secured only the vague Soviet promise to hold free elections in eastern Europe and the assurance that Russia would enter the war against Japan within three months of Germany's surrender.

Many of these complaints, from both the Left and the Right, were partly justified. Roosevelt placed far too much faith in Chiang Kaishek, and he overestimated the value of personal diplomacy. His hopes for democratic governments in eastern Europe were misplaced: by 1948 all of them had fallen under the thumb of the Kremlin. His failure to secure precise guarantees of access routes to western zones in postwar Berlin caused no end of conflict later on. And successful development of atomic energy later made the Asian deal at Yalta unnecessary.

Critics have also pointed to flaws in the Roosevelt administration's policies affecting European Jews. After the war it became clear that the Nazis, pursuing a deliberate racist policy of extermination, had killed an estimated 6 million Jews, many of them in gas chambers. The Holocaust represented systematic barbarism on an incredible scale. Though news of Hitler's "final solution" was slow to be confirmed by the Allies, it was widely rumored in 1941–42. But American officials, including Hull, doubted the feasibility in wartime of trying to transport large numbers of Jews to safety. Latin American nations, too, would not accept many of the Jews seeking to escape. The British controlling Palestine refused to open it to refugees. By 1944 the United States had aerial photographs of the extermination camp at Auschwitz, but refused to bomb the gas chambers. Bombing, they argued, might lead the Germans to accelerate their slaughter of the Jews. Creation of a War Refugee Board by FDR in 1944 led to erection of refugee centers in Europe and to the salvation of thousands late in the war. In retrospect, however, it is clear that Western nations, the United States included, pursued highly insensitive policies with regard to European Jewry in the 1930s and 1940s.

But in many of these matters FDR's options were restricted. As commander-in-chief his first concern was to win the war with as little suffering to America as possible. The deal with Darlan, therefore, seemed necessary; the alternative might have subjected Allied forces to substantial fighting against the Vichy French. Playing along with Chiang was less wise. But cutting off aid to Chiang, who threatened to quit the war unless America kept the dollars flowing, was politically hazardous. And in combating colonialism what was the President to do with Churchill, who proudly proclaimed, "I did not become the King's first minister in order to preside over the liquidation of the British empire"? With the preservation of wartime unity as the primary goal, it was hard for America to issue demands to such an important ally. In assuming that the United States could have forced its will, Roosevelt's detractors presumed an omnipotence that America has never possessed.

Survivors liberated from concentration camp in Flossenberg, Germany

Complaints about the President's approach to Stalin falsely assumed that Soviet designs were both evil and clear at the time. In fact, FDR's advisers included men like Hopkins, Hull, and Eisenhower, who reported that "nothing guides Russian policy so much as a desire for friendship with the United States." The critics also exaggerated America's potential to influence postwar eastern Europe. The Soviets overran the area by force of arms, just as the United States and Great Britain took France and the Benelux countries. Recognizing the American sphere of influence, Stalin expected the United States, which had historically shown little concern for the fate of eastern Europe (witness the Munich accord, or the division of Poland in 1939), to leave him alone in his sphere of interest. This meant letting Russia protect itself against unfriendly governments on its borders. In this sense Roosevelt did well to get any Soviet "assurances" whatever about eastern Europe. Americans at the time applauded his "success" at Yalta.

Churchill, Roosevelt, and Stalin at Yalta in 1945, where the "Big Three" worked out international distribution ot power

Roosevelt was right also in recognizing that force, which he had neither the will nor the power to apply, was probably necessary to secure free elections in eastern Europe. His attitude was best expressed in an exchange with Admiral William Leahy, a top military aide. Leahy complained that the Polish accord was so vague that Russia could "stretch it all the way from Yalta to Washington without ever technically breaking it." Roosevelt nodded, but replied, "I know it, Bill—I know it. But it's the best I can do for Poland at this time." This was not naiveté, but an accurate appreciation of military reality in Europe. It was therefore unfortunate that Roosevelt, seeking political credit for a "victory" at Yalta, did not explain to Americans the limitations of the accord. Stalin, he implied, had agreed to promote democracy in eastern Europe. When that did not happen, Americans were quick to cry that the Russians had broken a promise.

Roosevelt could even be forgiven his concessions to the Soviet Union in Asia. In February 1945 the Japanese were obviously headed for defeat, with or without Russian intervention. But no one could be sure at the time that the atomic bomb, untested until July 1945, would work. What Roosevelt did know was that Japan was fighting fanatically to hold all its possessions. He was further advised (probably wrongly) that America might suffer as many as a million casualties in an invasion of the home islands. To avoid such a catastrophe, he determined to secure Russian

First Person

We really believed in our hearts, that this was the dawn of a new day we had all been praying for and talking about for so many years. We were absolutely certain that we had won the first great victory of the peace, and by "we" I mean ALL of us—the whole civilized human race. The Russians had proved that they could be reasonable and farseeing, and there wasn't any doubt in the minds of the President or any of us that we could live with them and get along with them peacefully for as far into the future as any of us could imagine.

Harry Hopkins reflects American hopes for postwar cooperation, after Yalta (1945).

help, which Stalin might have given only grudgingly, if at all, without securing concessions for himself.

In these ways Roosevelt's Russian diplomacy revealed not softness but perceived political and military necessity. Despite strains over the second front, his policies managed to sustain Allied cooperation. Roosevelt may also have been correct in assuming that Stalin was more interested in protecting his nation's security than in fomenting worldwide communist revolution. Stalin gave little support to communist forces under Marshal Tito of Yugoslavia; he recognized Chiang in China (then, as always, Stalin was ambivalent about Mao Zedong); and he kept a bargain made with Churchill in the fall of 1944, by which Britain recognized Russia's paramount interests in much of southeastern Europe in return for a Soviet hands-off policy in Greece (which became scarcely more "democratic" than Poland). Stalin also cruelly disappointed the communist parties in Italy and France, which had hoped for Russian postwar aid.

All these Soviet actions suggested to some moderates in America that Stalin's territorial ambitions—at least to 1945—were limited, and that postwar coopera-

First Person

The reality was that of a fantastically cruel and crafty political personality, viewing with deadly enmity everything, whether within Russia or without it, which did not submit absolutely to his own authority; a personality the suspiciousness of which assumed forms positively pathoglogical; a personality informed by the most profound cynicism and contempt for human nature, dominated by an insatiable ambition, driven by a burning envy for all qualities it did not itself possess, intolerant of every sort of rival, or even independent, authority or influence.

George Kennan, top American diplomat and expert on Russia, offers a view of Stalin that was widespread among Americans in the 1940s and 1950s.

tion with the Soviet Union was possible. In making these assumptions Roosevelt took risks, and he exaggerated, for political effect at home, his diplomatic "triumphs" at Yalta. But he also perceived that some form of Soviet-American détente in the postwar world was indispensable for world peace. Compared to Wilson's millennial visions, Roosevelt's view struck anticommunist Americans as amoral. But given the realities of military power in 1945—the Soviets, after all, already occupied eastern Europe—Roosevelt's options were limited.

The Expansion of Government

FROM WELFARE PROGRAMS TO WARTIME POWERS

In December 1943 Roosevelt explained that he was no longer "Dr. New Deal," but "Dr. Win the War."

His remark confirmed that the exciting days of domestic reform were past. Though Roosevelt continued to work for his programs, he was necessarily preoccupied with military problems. And Congress grew even more obstructive than it had been in his second term, especially after the Republicans made further inroads in 1942. The conservative coalition of Republicans and rural Democrats killed the WPA, the CCC, and the National Resources Planning Board. It defeated bills for federal aid to education, national health insurance, and public power development, and it ignored groups crusading for civil rights. As responsive as ever to well-organized interest groups, it approved legislation granting farmers 110 percent of parity and exempting many agricultural laborers from the draft.

The conservatism of the wartime Congresses was most pronounced in the areas of labor legislation and taxation. In 1943 Congress approved, over Roosevelt's veto, the Smith-Connally Act, which authorized the president to seize strike-bound defense plants and to impose thirty-day "cooling off" periods before workers could go on strike. In the same year it enacted a plan that introduced the principle of federal tax withholding, but at the cost of forgiving taxpayers an estimated 75 percent of 1942 taxes. The plan especially benefited high-income people. Then in 1944 Congress passed a tax bill that raised only $2 billion more than before. FDR, who had called for an increase of $10 billion, snapped publicly that it was "not a tax bill, but a tax relief bill providing relief not for the needy but for the greedy." His blunt remark angered even his congressional supporters, who helped to pass the bill over his veto. Long before FDR's death in 1945, relations between Capitol Hill and the White House were cold indeed.

The balance of power within the parties also shifted toward the Right during the war. In 1944 the GOP nominated New York Governor Thomas E. Dewey as its presidential candidate. Though Dewey accepted much of the New Deal, he waged an abrasive campaign. Other Republican orators engaged in a demagogic effort to link the Roosevelt administration with communism. The Democrats, meanwhile, refused to renominate the liberal Henry Wallace for the vice-presidency. Instead, Harry Truman, a dependable middle-of-the-roader from Missouri, received the prize. Thanks to the power of the Democratic voting coalition, and especially to the efforts of organized labor (which provided $2 million to party funds), Roosevelt and Truman won handily. But their margin of 3.6 million votes fell well short of the Democratic lead of 5 million votes in 1940 and 11 million in 1936. Republicans understandably looked forward to 1948, when they expected to triumph at last.

Despite these blows against the New Deal, the war years did not witness a triumph for reaction. Many of the defeated programs, such as the WPA or the CCC, truly seemed unnecessary in the midst of a revived wartime economy. More important reforms — TVA, social security, the minimum wage, even the NLRB — emerged intact. Federal nondefense spending actually increased during the war from $7.2 billion to $17 billion, thus remaining at about 8 percent of the gross national product. Having helped to build a partial welfare state, Congress was not about to dismantle it.

The growth in domestic expenditures was but one manifestation of a virtual explosion in the size of government during the war. Thanks primarily to defense spending, the federal budget jumped from $9 billion in fiscal 1940 to $98 billion in 1945, or from 9 percent to 46 percent of the GNP. The number of civilian employees of the federal government increased during the same period from 1 to 3.8 million. Federal taxes leaped ahead from $5 billion to $44.5 billion, and millions of Americans felt the bite of the Internal Revenue Service for the first time. With so much money at its command, and with virtual armies of bureaucrats staffing such new agencies as the Office of Price Administration, the War Production Board, the War Labor Board and the Selective Service, the federal government enjoyed more reach than the most avid New Dealers ever envisioned in the 1930s.

The impact of this expansive fiscal policy was little short of revolutionary. By increasing federal spending more than tenfold within six years, the government ran up deficits averaging more than $30 billion per year, or ten times the average deficits during the New Deal. Chiefly because of this spending, the economy finally surged back. Unemployment virtually disappeared (thanks in part to the draft), and the GNP (in 1929 prices) shot forward from $121 billion in 1940 to $181 billion in 1945. Few politicians dared to endorse this Keynesian approach as a matter of regular policy, and deficits became modest (except during war) from 1946 through 1963. Still, the power of public spending had been demonstrated beyond doubt. Thereafter all but the most hardened fiscal conservatives admitted that a little pump priming in times of recession was desirable.

The war witnessed an almost equally revolutionary growth in the power of the presidency. Only the White House seemed able to carry on the war and manage the nation's more complex international responsibilities. As Professor Edward Corwin noted ruefully, phrases describing the presidency as the "great engine of democracy" and "the American people's one authentic prophet" began appearing in textbooks. The diplomatic historian Thomas Bailey spoke for many scholars in 1948 by stressing the need for a strong presidency. "Just as the yielding of some of our national sovereignty is the price we must pay for effective international organization," he wrote, "so the yielding of some of our democratic control of foreign affairs is the price we may have to pay for greater physical security." If TR began the twentieth-century American infatuation with the presidency, World War II transformed it into a long-lived affair.

Economic Growth, 1939–47, Compared to Select Years before and after This Period

| | NATIONAL PRODUCT AND PER CAPITA INCOME | | | | |
| | CURRENT PRICES | | 1958 PRICES | | |
	GNP (in billions of dollars	PER CAPITA (in dollars)	GNP (in billions of dollars	PER CAPITA (in dollars)	IMPLICIT PRICE INDEX (1958 = 100)
1929	103.1	847	203.6	1,671	50.6
1933	55.6	442	141.5	1,126	39.3
1939	90.5	691	209.4	1,598	43.2
1940	99.7	754	227.2	1,720	43.9
1943	191.6	1,401	337.1	2,465	56.8
1945	211.9	1,515	355.2	2,538	59.7
1947	231.3	1,605	309.9	2,150	74.6
1960	503.7	2,788	487.7	2,699	103.3
1970	977.1	4,803	722.5	3,555	135.2

SOURCE: Adapted from *Statistical History of the U.S.* (New York: Basic Books, 1976), p. 224.

BIG GOVERNMENT: BLESSING OR CURSE?

Most reformers welcomed this explosion in the power of the presidency. Congress, after all, was in the hands of conservatives, and the Supreme Court had until 1937 stood in the way of social legislation. By 1945 belief in an activist central administration was a cardinal tenet of modern American liberalism.

Even during the war, however, some people worried about the concentration of enormous power in the hands of a few. One concern was the Office of War Information, which was formed to apprise the public of the course of the war. *The New York Times* observed that the office was "feeding us bad news when it was thought we could stand it and good news when it was thought we needed it." Even Elmer Davis, the experienced newsman who headed the agency, fought regularly with military brass who refused to give him accurate, up-to-date information. Admiral King's idea of war information, Davis complained, "was that there should be just *one* communique. Some morning we would announce that the war was over and that we won it." These charges were accurate in recognizing the government's close-mouthed monopoly on many sources of important news.

The administration's handling of civil liberties during the war was equally unsettling. The 12,000-odd conscientious objectors who refused to accept noncombatant military service were placed in so-called Civilian Public Service camps, where the courts refused to extend the protection of the First and Fifth Amendments. They did not receive pay. The administration imprisoned some 5,500 other conscientious objectors, including Jehovah's Witnesses, who claimed exemptions as ministers. Roosevelt was especially harsh in handling allegedly profascist dissenters. In 1942 the Justice Department charged twenty-six "native fascists" with conspiring against the government. The accusations were based in part on the arbi-trary Smith Act of 1940, which made it an offense even to advocate the overthrow of the government. After much legal wrangling, which revealed no evidence of con-spiracy, the government finally had to drop the cases in 1944.

Defenders of the administration rightly pointed out that Roosevelt treated dissenters more even-handedly than Wilson had in World War I. But this improve-ment did not necessarily signify that America was growing more tolerant or more ma-ture. Rather, it reflected the relative absence of dissent in a war precipitated by the "sneak attack" on Pearl Harbor. As one congressman phrased it a week after the attack, "This war had to come. It is a war of purification in which the forces of Christ-ian peace and freedom and justice and decency and morality are arrayed against the evil pagan forces of strife, injustice, treachery, immorality, and slavery. . . ."

This kind of superpatriotism erupted quickly in open racism against Japanese-Americans. A California barber advertised "free shave for Japs," but "not responsi-ble for accidents." A funeral parlor proclaimed, "I'd rather do business with a Jap than with an American." In a 1944 poll that asked Americans to say which enemy, Germany or Japan, the United States could "get along with better after the war" only 8 percent picked Japan.

Popular thinking such as this reinforced flagrantly unconstitutional policies. In 1942 Roosevelt authorized the army to round up Japanese-Americans in the West

Mealtime at a Japanese-American internment camp, 1942

and to place them in detention centers. These were really concentration camps guarded by soldiers and mostly situated in remote and desolate areas of the West. In all, they contained some 112,000 people for the duration of the war. Most of these (perhaps 70,000) were second-generation Nisei who were American citizens. Virtually all were given forty-eight hours or less to pack their belongings and to sell or otherwise dispose of their property. In the camps they lived in tar-papered wooden barracks behind barbed wire. Facilities were primitive, services (such as education) poor, privacy virtually nonexistent. Losses of Japanese-American property have been officially estimated to have been as high as $2 billion.

The internment of the Japanese-Americans did not rest on evidence of sabotage; nobody was ever indicted for treason or sedition. The pretext for the internments, disloyalty, was not against the law. In fact, racist feelings on the West Coast—Japanese-Americans in Hawaii were not affected—lay behind the relocations. Still, the Supreme Court approved the internments. With three judges dissenting, it ruled in the *Korematsu* case (1944) that the removal was justified by the exigencies of war. One of the dissenters, Justice Frank Murphy, labeled the treatment of the Japanese-Americans as "one of the most sweeping and complete deprivations of constitutional rights in the history of the nation."

Within a few years of the war many Americans came to recognize the truth of Murphy's judgment. But the government was slow to think about compensation. Only in 1982 did a special Commission on Wartime Relocation and Internment of Civilians conclude that the Japanese-Americans had been victimized by "race prejudice, war hysteria and a failure of political leadership." It recommended compensation of $20,000 to each surviving internee. A year later a federal judge ruled that Fred Korematsu, and by implication all the detainees, had suffered from application of "unsubstantiated facts, distortions and misrepresentations of at least one military commander whose views were affected by racism."

Ominous wartime developments like the Office of War Information and detention centers were temporary phenomena. The administration's handling of defense contracting, however, led first to bureaucratic confusion and then to the develop-

First Person

The Japanese, because they are unassimilable, because the aliens have been denied the right to own real property in California, because of the marked differences in appearance between Japanese and Caucasians, because of the generations of training and philosophy that makes them Japanese and nothing else—all of these contributing factors set the Japanese apart as a race, regardless of how many generations have been born in America. Undoubtedly many of them intend to be loyal, but only each individual can know his own intentions, and when the final test comes, who can say but that "blood will tell"?

Los Angeles Mayor Fletcher Bowron arouses passions against Japanese-Americans, February 1942.

ment of a military-industrial complex. Together these exposed long-run dangers of governmental expansion produced by modern war.

Bureaucratic confusion began as early as 1939, when Roosevelt created the War Resources Board to oversee defense needs. It received only limited support from the administration before being replaced after the fall of France by the Advisory Commission of the Council of National Defense. This, in turn, gave way in 1941 to the Office of Production Management. All these agencies had to contend with other sources of power, such as Secretary of the Interior Harold Ickes, who was also oil administrator, and Jesse Jones, the imperious banker who headed the Reconstruction Finance Corporation. Critics demanded that Roosevelt create a more permanent agency and give it real authority.

When the President established the War Production Board in January 1942, it appeared that he recognized the need for centralization. But he still refused to make Donald Nelson, the WPB chief, a "czar" over production. His stand was deliberate. As he told Labor Secretary Frances Perkins, "There is something to be said . . . for having a little conflict between agencies. A little rivalry is stimulating. . . . the fact that there is somebody else in the field who knows what you are doing is a strong incentive to strict honesty." Moreover, the President did not want to turn over power to a potential rival to himself. So he gave only sporadic support to Nelson's efforts at concentrating authority in the WPB. From the beginning Nelson, like almost all later civilian officials in charge of defense planning, was unable to prevent interagency fighting or to override the military, which Roosevelt permitted to control the crucially important matter of procurement.

Despite these problems, American production leaped ahead with astonishing speed. After procrastinating in 1940 and 1941 to assure themselves of markets, American manufacturers converted rapidly to war production. Many assumed direction of plants built almost overnight with public funds. The enormous airplane manufacturing facilities at Willow Run, Michigan, were larger than the combined prewar plants of Boeing, Douglas and Consolidated Aircraft. More than a mile long, they included 1,600 machine tools and 7,500 jigs and fixtures. The story of rubber production was equally amazing. The government built fifty-one synthetic rubber-making plants, which by 1944 made close to a million tons per year. (The German

---

First Person

The President is the poorest administrator I have ever worked under in respect to the orderly procedure and routine of his performance. He is not a good chooser of men and he does not know how to use them in coordination.

The inevitable result is that the Washington atmosphere is full of acrimonious disputes over matters of jurisdiction. In my own case a very large percent of my time and strength, particularly of recent months, has been taken up in trying to smooth out and settle the differences which have thus been created.

Secretary of War Henry Stimson, March 1943, complains of FDR's administrative habits.

peak, in 1943, was 109,000 tons). These fantastic increases in output created a virtual overabundance of weaponry by late 1943. Thereafter many contractors began scrambling for the privilege of reconverting to civilian production.

The production miracle encouraged business leaders to praise themselves for accomplishing so much. Conveniently overlooking the role of government spending, they extolled the virtues of capitalistic free enterprise. They also rejected arguments that more rigorous government direction of their efforts might have secured still better results. Their claim had some merit, for even a "czar" might have found it impossible to fine-tune an economy so huge and complex as America's. Businessmen may have been equally correct in asserting (Roosevelt agreed) that a degree of voluntarism was necessary for morale in such a long war. For social reformers, however, the self-assured hostility of many businessmen to government "interference" proved a formidable obstacle to change in the 1940s and 1950s.

Liberal reformers worried especially about the lasting connections developed in wartime between big business and the military. For it was the big operators to whom the army, the navy, and the newly created Office for Scientific Research and Development turned for help. These large corporations had the capital, the research potential, and the equipment to produce quickly. They could afford to employ middle-management specialists and white-collar workers to handle government red tape. Above all, big institutions could be dealt with quickly. Government officials liked to work with a handful of experienced operators instead of with a host of smaller entrepreneurs.

Top government officials made sure that big business was at home in its developing relationship with Washington. Many of these officials had been recruited from corporations, and they agreed that producing for defense ought to bring a handsome profit. "If you are going to . . . go to war, . . . in a capitalist country," Stimson observed, "you have got to let business make money out of the process." Stimson and others offered contractors cost-plus contracts and generously renegotiated deals when businesses complained. The government also provided low-interest federal loans for plant expansion and easy tax writeoffs. Patents for processes developed with government aid generally reverted to private hands. Such massive assistance assured big corporations of commanding positions in areas formerly handled by subcontractors.

There was no easy way for government to reverse the long-range movement toward concentration in business. Still, progressives not surprisingly complained about government's enthusiastic hand on the tiller. They observed that big business and the military, eclipsed by other contenders for federal favor in the 1930s, used the war to enhance their political and economic power. They prophesied also that the military-industrial complex, as it came to be known, could lock the nation on a martial course. Among the baneful results of political centralization, the military-industrial nexus perhaps was for them the most frightening of all.

The War and American Society

Stuart Chase, a liberal economist, surveyed American society at the end of the war and concluded that prosperity had worked wonders undreamed of during the New

First Person

This is the last time
This time we will all make certain
That this time is the last time!
For this time we are out to finish
The job we started then
Clear it up for all time this time
So we won't have to do it again

The words to a wartime song by Irving Berlin suggest the no-nonsense thoroughness with which Americans approached the war.

Deal. "The facts," he said, "show a better break for the common man than liberals in 1938 could have expected for a generation."

Almost every economic indicator supported Chase's conclusion. Despite rationing of gasoline, coffee, tin, and other goods, few Americans suffered much at home. National income jumped from $81 billion in 1940 to $181 billion five years later, or from $573 to $1,074 per capita. Improvements in diets and health care during the same period caused life expectancy to increase by three years to sixty-six. (However, poor teeth and eyes, symptoms of malnutrition, still caused more than 50 percent of young men in some regions to fail preinduction physicals.) Thanks in part to the GI Bill, 8 million young people learned a trade or attended college after the war, while bonuses for American veterans totaled more than $2 billion.

The war even slightly improved the distribution of income. This was not because the rich were getting poorer, but because more workers were regularly employed and drawing pay for overtime. The average wages of workers employed full-time in manufacturing rose from $28 per week in 1940 to $48 in 1944. These were unprecedented advances. Accordingly, the share of income owned by the richest 5 percent declined from 23.7 to 16.8 percent. As these figures suggest, the United States remained a country with sharp disparities in wealth. Still, World War II did much to accelerate one of the major trends of modern American society: the development of a large middle class. It was the only time in modern American history that income distribution improved.

Important social changes accompanied this return to prosperity. One was even greater movement of an already mobile people. Those who moved included 12 million men in uniform, dependents who pulled up roots to follow them to training *Migration* bases, and millions more who left their homes to work in war plants. The migrations slightly increased urbanization, which had slowed during the depression years. The number of people living in towns with populations of 25,000 or more increased from 53 million in 1940 to 63 million ten years later, or 42 percent of the total 1950 population of 152 million.

The total classified as "rural farm" decreased during the decade, from 30 to 23 million. A few states, well-favored in the granting of war contracts, virtually exploded in population. California alone gained 2 million people during the four years of war.

First Person

Saturday night is the loneliest night of the week,
Cause that's the night my baby and I
Used to dance cheek to cheek.
I don't mind Sunday night at all,
Cause that's the night friends come to call,
And Monday to Friday go fast
Then another week is past.

A popular song expresses the loneliness of many American women during the war.

The lives of women also changed considerably during the war. In 1940 only 14 million American women (26 percent of the total work force) were employed; by 1945, 19 million (or 36 percent) were. A total of 22 percent of these working women in 1945 were married, as opposed to 15 percent five years earlier. Most of these married workers were mothers. Contemporaries thought these trends were temporary, for the numbers of regularly employed women dipped in 1946. Polls also suggested that Americans still considered it unnatural for women to enter the labor force: a woman's place, the ladies' magazines added, was at home. Moreover,

Women left home for the factory during World War II

wartime ads for women workers made it clear that they were expected to resume their "true" roles—as wives and mothers—when the war was over. Even while working, they were often segregated from men and sometimes paid less for similar work. But increasing numbers of women disagreed, and by 1951 the number of women in the work force was already higher than at any time in World War II.

The jobs that they took during the war presaged a sharp departure from traditional patterns of women's work. Abandoning jobs as domestics, waitresses, and laundresses, they headed for aircraft plants and shipyards. Hundreds of laundries had to close for lack of female help. Some 400,000 women dropped domestic service to labor in the factories. The percentage of black women who did paid housework declined from 69 to 35 percent; for the first time, many found work in industrial occupations, which (despite pay scales lower than those for men) paid about 40 percent more than the traditional jobs for women workers. The public seemed to welcome this great change. A popular symbol of female patriotism, Rosie the Riveter, appeared on magazine covers and in newspapers.

These trends in female employment were significant. In the short run, the working women contributed much to the war effort. As in the depression years, when they had been forced into the job market, their wages enlarged the budgets of working-class people, who began to put aside money for wartime (and postwar) purchases of consumer goods, including houses. Consumption of household furniture, equipment, and supplies jumped from $4.9 million in 1940 to $16.6 million in 1950. In the long run, the growth of female employment widened the public sphere of women and challenged older notions relegating women to the home. As women ventured into the working world in ever-increasing numbers, they provided an economic and ideological underpinning to later movements for women's liberation.

Wartime developments had many other effects, especially on young people. Homosexuals, for instance, began for the first time to develop their own institutions when they found significant numbers of other gay people in large military camps and defense plants. Other young people who had postponed marriage or family in the depression refused to wait in the 1940s. Thousands more, confronted with the draft and overseas service, did the same. The result was a trend toward younger marriages and a baby boom that began in 1940 and continued irregularly throughout the war. Demographers who assumed the increase in birthrates would end with the war were wrong, for the baby boom lasted until the early 1960s. Rising birthrates stimulated demand in a host of consumer-goods industries; they prompted great growth in postwar home building and in suburban development; and they all but swamped educational institutions until the 1970s. By 1965, when the early boom babies had reached their late teens or early 20s, the baby boom helped make visible the growth of a "youth culture," which baffled and frightened older generations.

To many observers during the war (and since) these developments were unfortunate. Young people, it seemed, were hurrying irresponsibly into marriage and parenthood. They were pulling up roots to live in ill-constructed housing developments without proper socializing institutions for children. Some women were "abandoning" their children in order to enter the work force, while others—"allotment Annies"—deserted their soldier husbands as soon as their dependents' allowances stopped coming. A rapidly increasing divorce rate appeared to be one unhappy result of these patterns of behavior. Juvenile delinquency involving "wolf packs" in housing developments and "zoot suit" gangs in large cities appeared to be another. Some people foresaw a new "Lost Generation."

Above all, the war prompted anxieties about the future. Having survived ten years of depression, Americans entered the 1940s already searching for security. With regular employment, they seemed at last to have found it. But could it endure? Many felt certain that depression would recur, that hard-earned gains would be wiped out, that the status of other groups would rise at the expense of their own. The writer Bernard de Voto observed that this anxiety rarely received "public expression, and little direct expression even in private." But "it exists and it may well be the most truly terrifying phenomenon of the war. It is a fear of the coming of the peace."

One group that clearly displayed this anxiety was organized labor—in part because it gained so much. In a strong bargaining position at the start of the war, unions received government support of "maintenance of membership" clauses in contracts. These required members to stay in the union for the duration of the war. Unions then drove ahead to recruit the millions of new workers who found jobs between 1940 and 1945, Accordingly, union membership increased from 9 million in 1940 to almost 15 million in 1945, a growth more rapid than at any time in American history. Management generally acquiesced in this union activity: with great profits to be made and a war to be won, it did not seem wise to goad militant workers into strikes.

Despite these gains, workers remained uneasy. John L. Lewis and other leaders led dramatic walkouts for better pay during the war. Work stoppages, though usually short-lived, increased from 2,968 in 1942 to 4,956 in 1944. In 1945, 4,750 stoppages affected 12 percent of the labor force and involved 3.4 million workers. And 1946, when wartime frustrations exploded, witnessed a record 4,985 stoppages involving 4.6 million laborers. Unionists, having begun to taste power and increased income, were insisting upon more in the future.

A similar revolution in expectations affected blacks, who made unprecedented gains during the war. Some of these advances were essentially symbolic—in 1943 the first black joined the American Bar Association; in 1944 the first black was admitted to a presidential press conference. Other changes were vitally important. The number of blacks who secured jobs in the federal government increased from 50,000 in 1939 to 200,000 six years later, and the appeal of jobs in northern and western cities pulled more than a million blacks out of the South.

This mass migration, one of the greatest in American history, persisted in the postwar period, dramatically changing the demographic, economic, and political world of black America. As late as 1940, 6.6 million of the nation's 12.8 million blacks lived in rural areas, the vast majority in the South (which was still the home for three-fourths of the black population). There, the color line remained rigid indeed. Jim Crow laws continued to enforce strict separation of the races—in waiting rooms, movie theaters, restaurants, restrooms, even drinking fountains. Schools, of course, were segregated. Poll taxes, all-white primaries, and other discriminatory methods effectively disfranchised all but a handful of determined black southerners. And widely understood social conventions reinforced blacks' low standing. Whites

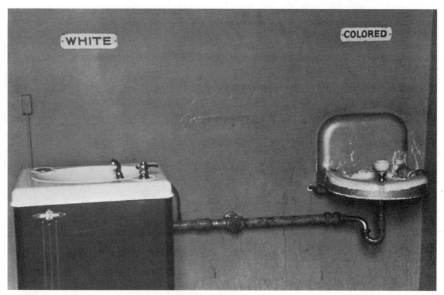

Jim Crow laws enforced strict separation of the races.

did not shake hands with blacks, or tip their hats. They did not dream of letting a black person into their homes through the front door. They regularly called blacks—no matter their ages—by their first names, or they addressed them as "boy," or "girl," or "aunty." Blacks, of course, were expected to address whites formally.

Southern life was harsh on blacks in countless other ways. Blacks went without decent medical care and rarely if ever entered a hospital. Their mortality rate was twice that of whites; their average life span was twelve years less. They were poorly educated. Of those over twenty-five years of age in 1940, only one in 100 was a college graduate; one in ten had no schooling at all. There was scarcely a black middle class in the South. Alabama, for instance, had four black lawyers (compared to 1,600 white lawyers); Mississippi had six (compared to 1,200). Blacks suffered all sorts of physical intimidation, abuse, and violence and were without legal recourse. "A white man," one scholar observed, "can steal from or maltreat a Negro in almost any way without fear of reprisal, because the Negro cannot claim the protection of the police or courts." Indeed, blacks played no role in southern law enforcement. In 1940 there were no black policemen in Mississippi, South Carolina, Alabama, Louisiana, Georgia, Arkansas, and Virginia. When arrested, blacks could expect physical beatings, harsh sentences, and draconian prison conditions.

The wartime and postwar migrations to the North and to cities (where 14 million of America's 20 million blacks lived by 1960) meant great changes in their lives. While they faced discrimination in the North—notably in employment and housing—they usually managed to find better-paid work than on the farms of the South, and they were free of southern-style racism. Though confined to ghettos, they inched ahead economically and began to develop a substantial middle class. Their very concentration (in Washington, Detroit, Newark, and other cities they

First Person

While the March on Washington Movement may find it advisable to form a citizens committee of friendly white citizens to give moral support . . . it does not imply that these white citizens . . . should be taken into the March on Washington Movement as members. The essential value of an all-Negro movement such as the March on Washington is that it helps to create faith by Negroes in Negroes. It develops a sense of self-reliance with Negroes depending on Negroes in vital matters. It helps to break down the slave psychology and inferiority-complex in Negroes which comes and is nourished with Negroes relying on white people for direction and support. This inevitably happens in mixed organizations that are supposed to be in the interest of the Negro.

A. Philip Randolph promotes black power, 1942.

comprised a majority or near majority of the population by 1960) gave them the chance for political power. As early as 1944, their votes were important in securing Roosevelt's fourth term. This geographical concentration—along with developments in mass communications—also facilitated community organization. In all these ways the war, by unleashing the migrations, had a deep and lasting impact on the status of blacks and on race relations in the United States.

As in the years between 1914 and 1919, this combination of migration and improved prosperity created mounting militancy among black leaders. The Congress of Racial Equality, an interracial organization devoted to pacifism as well as to civil rights, was founded in 1942. The NAACP, the largest of the interracial organizations, increased its membership during the war from 50,000 to 500,000. Most alarming of all to whites was the potential political power demonstrated by A. Philip Randolph, the porters' union leader who threatened to call a mass march on Washington in 1941 unless Roosevelt acted to prevent racial discrimination in federally subsidized employment. After much procrastination (for Roosevelt still hesitated to offend southern Democrats), the President relented far enough to issue an executive order setting up a Fair Employment Practices Commission. Easily his most significant contribution to racial justice, it stemmed entirely from black pressure. The lesson was not lost on later leaders of the black cause.

These advances merely reminded blacks how far America had to go. The poorly financed, understaffed FEPC was able to resolve only one-third of the 8,000 complaints it had time to hear. Of its forty-five compliance orders, thirty-five were ignored. Despite a Supreme Court ruling gainst white primaries, most blacks in the South continued to be disfranchised—through poll taxes, literacy tests, and other ruses. The armed forces, which were under federal control, flagrantly discriminated against blacks. The marines and army air corps simply excluded them, the navy gave them menial tasks, and the army segregated them under white officers. "Leadership," Secretary of War Stimson explained, "is not imbedded in the negro race yet and to try to make commissioned officers to lead men into battle—colored men—is only to work a disaster to both." It was not until 1944 that the navy integrated the crews of a few of its ships or that the army sent blacks into combat. By then the top brass was worrying about black unrest in the services. "My God! My God!" General Marshall exclaimed, "I don't know what to do about this race question in the army. Frankly, it is the worst thing we have to deal with. . . . We are getting a situation on our hands that may explode right in our faces."

As Marshall prophesied, the humiliations suffered by blacks (in and out of the army) created many conflicts during the war years. In 1943 blacks in Harlem rioted against discrimination. A race riot in Detroit the same year killed 34 and injured more than 700. The antiwhite Black Muslims began to make modest gains among the dispossessed. CORE leaders experimented with sit-ins (only in the North) and other forms of direct action. And countless blacks expressed themselves bitterly against a society that fought fascism abroad while ignoring injustice at home. One told Gunnar Myrdal, the Swedish social scientist investigating race relations, "just carve on my tombstone, here lies a black man killed fighting a yellow man for the protection of a white man." A "Draftee's Prayer" in a black newspaper added,

> Dear Lord, today
> I go to war:
> To fight, to die,
> Tell me what for?
> Dear Lord, I'll fight,
> I do not fear
> Germans or Japs;
> My fears are here.
> America!

Attitudes such as these captured one essential aspect of life on the home front. So long as the enemy fought on the field, a common goal of victory secured domestic peace most of the time. But it was a restless, increasingly factious peace. Blacks, like blue-collar workers, farmers, businessmen, veterans, and others, had sensed the chance for a better life, and they pressed urgently to enjoy it as the war came to a close. Better organized than earlier, they sought to advance their own interests with the same grim single-mindedness that they showed in battle. This militancy amid plenty, this revolution of expectations, this scramble not only for security but for slices of an ever-larger pie—all these were among the major social developments of the "Great Leap" of World War II.

Suggestions for Reading
Key books covering American politics and diplomacy in World War II are James M. Burns, *Roosevelt: Soldier of Freedom** (1970); and A. Russell Buchanan, *The United States and World War II,** 2 vols, (1964). See also John Snell, *Illusion and Necessity: The Diplomacy of World War II* (1963); and the revisionist account by Stephen Ambrose, *The Rise to Globalism: American Foreign Policy Since 1938** (1985). See also Gar Alperovitz, *Atomic Diplomacy: Hiroshima and Potsdam* (rev. ed., 1985), for another important critical study.

*Available in a paperback edition.

Other relevant books are Raymond O'Connor, *Diplomacy for Victory: FDR and Unconditional Surrender** (1971); Diane Shaver Clemens, *Yalta* (1970); and Robert Divine, *Second Chance: The Triumph of Internationalism During World War II* (1967). Important books on military policy include Kent Roberts Greenfield, *American Strategy in World War II: A Reconsideration** (1967); Stephen Ambrose, *The Supreme Commander* (1970), on Eisenhower; and Louis Morton, *Strategy and Command* (1962). For science policy consult Richard Rhodes, *The Making of the Atomic Bomb* (1986); Robert Jungk, *Brighter Than a Thousand Suns: A Personal History of the Atomic Scientists* (1958); and Martin Sherwin, *A World Destroyed: The Atomic Bomb and the Grand Alliance* (1975).

Sources dealing with Asia include John Dower, *War Without Mercy: Race and Power in the Pacific War* (1986); Ronald Spector, *Eagle Against the Sun: The American War with Japan* (1985); Akira Iriye, *Power and Culture: The Japanese-American War, 1941–1945* (1981); and Robert Butow, *Japan's Decision to Surrender* (1954).

For books on the early years of Cold War tensions see John Gaddis, *The United States and the Origins of the Cold War, 1941–1946** (1972); and George Herring, *Aid to Russia, 1941–1946* (1973).

The starting points for life in the United States during the war are Richard Polenberg, *War and Society: The United States, 1941–1945** (1972); and John M. Blum, *V Was for Victory* (1976). Other surveys are Richard Lingeman, *Don't You Know There's a War On?* (1970); Geoffrey Perrett, *Days of Sadness, Days of Triumph* (1973); Michael Adams, *The Best War Ever: America and World War II* (1994); and John Jeffries, *Wartime America: The World War II Home Front* (1996). For economic policy consult Eliot Janeway, *Struggle for Survival* (1951); John M. Blum, *From the Moregenthau Diaries: Years of War, 1941–1945* (1967); and Bruce Catton, *War Lords of Washington* (1948). See also Davis Ross, *Preparing for Ulysses* (1969), which deals with manpower and military policies; Walter Wilcox, *The Farmer in the Second World War* (1947); Nelson Lichtenstein, *Labor's War at Home: CIO in World War II* (1982); Joel Seidman, *American Labor from Defense to Reconversion* (1953); Vicki L. Ruiz, *Cannery Women, Cannery Lives: Mexican Women, Unionization, and the California Food Processing Industry, 1938–1950* (1987); and Mario García, *Mexican-Americans: Leadership, Ideology, and Identity, 1938–1960* (1987). Useful biographies of labor leaders include Saul Alinsky, *John L. Lewis* (1949); and Matthew Josephson, *Sidney Hillman* (1952). William Chafe's book on American women, cited in the bibliography for Chapter 6, is indispensable. See also Allan Winkler, *The Politics of Propaganda: The Office of War Information 1942–45* (1979); Leila Rupp, *Mobilizing Women for War* (1978); Maureen Hovey, *Creating Rosie the Riveter* (1984); George Flynn, *The Mess in Washington: Manpower Mobilization in World War II* (1979); and Ruth Milkman, *Gender at Work* (1987), on job discrimination.

The experiences of blacks during the war are detailed in Nicholas Lemann, *The Promised Land: The Great Migration and How It Changed America* (1991); Neil Wynn, *The Afro-American and the Second World War* (1975); Richard Dalfilume, *Desegregation of the Armed Forces, 1939–1953* (1969); August Meier and Elliott Rudwick, *CORE . . . 1942–1968* (1973); Robert Shogan and Thomas Craig, *The Detroit Race Riot* (1964); and Gunnar Myrdal, *An American Dilemma** (1944, rev.

ed. 1962), a classic sociological account. The fate of Japanese-Americans is well told in Jacobus ten Broek, et al., *Prejudice, War, and the Constitution* (1945); Roger Daniels, *Concentration Camps** (1971); Peter Irons, *Justice at War* (1983), which focuses on legal aspects; and Thomas James, *Exile Within: The Schooling of Japanese-Americans, 1942–1945* (1987). For the rise of gay culture see John D'Emilio, *Sexual Politics, Sexual Communities: The Making of a Homosexual Minority in the United States, 1940–1970* (1983). Lawrence S. Wittner, *Rebels Against War: The American Peace Movement, 1941–1960* (1969) covers its subject sympathetically. For constitutional developments see Edward S. Corwin, *Total War and the Constitution** (1947); Francis Biddle, *In Brief Authority* (1962), by Roosevelt's wartime attorney general; and J. Woodford Howard, *Mr. Justice Murphy* (1968).

Among the many books on America and the wartime plight of European Jews, see David Wyman, *The Abandonment of the Jews* (1984); Walter Lacquer, *The Terrible Secret: Suppression of the Truth about Hitler's "Final Solution"* (1980); and Arthur Morse, *While Six Million Died* (1968).

The "new look" policy

2

Acrimony at Home and Abroad, 1945-1952

When Roosevelt died in April 1945, liberals were distraught. TVA director David Lilienthal shuddered to think of "that Throttlebottom Truman. The country and the world doesn't deserve to be left this way." Remembering Truman's rise in the corrupt politics of Kansas City, the journalist Max Lerner asked, "Will a man who has been associated with the Pendergast machine be able to keep the panting politicians and bosses out of the gravy?"

Millions of Americans appeared to share this anxiety. After all, Roosevelt had been president for as long as many people could remember. Yet now, with the Germans still fighting, with Japan to be invaded, and with postwar problems yet to be tackled, the country seemed saddled with an uninspiring border state senator whom the party had plucked from relative obscurity. Truman himself seemed frightened about the responsibilities ahead. "Boys," he told reporters, "if you ever pray, pray for me now. I don't know whether you fellows ever had a load of hay fall on you, but when they told me yesterday what had happened, I felt like the moon, the stars, and all the planets had fallen on me."

Actually, people worried too much; the American political system was stable enough to withstand sudden shocks to the presidency. While Truman tried to master his office, delegates in San Francisco completed the task of devising a United Nations charter, which the Senate adopted by a vote of eighty-nine to two in July. In Europe, Allied forces overwhelmed the Germans, who surrendered on May 8. And in Asia, Americans pressed forward into Iwo Jima and Okinawa. The country's awesome military-industrial machine surged ahead, largely unaffected by the change of personalities in the White House.

Truman, moreover, showed himself capable of acting decisively. His most far-reaching decision in these early months was to authorize the dropping of atomic bombs on Hiroshima (August 6) and Nagasaki (August 9). Later, critics argued persuasively that in reaching this decision he did not ask advice on *whether* the bomb should be used but on *how*, and that he listened only to scientists and government officials who could have been expected to favor its use in war. In the process

First Person

If you judge from the articles and editorials which have been written in the past twenty years, and all the prayers which have been prayed, and all the mourning and preaching that has been going on, you would judge that we crossed some kind of moral boundary with the use of these weapons. The assumption seems to be that it is much more wicked to kill people with a nuclear bomb, than to kill people by busting their heads with rocks.

General Curtis Le May, a staunch advocate of nuclear weaponry, ridicules the "moralists" who complained about Hiroshima and Nagasaki.

he ignored the pleas of scientists who urged him to warn the Japanese or to demonstrate the bomb in an uninhabited area. Instead, Truman merely told the Japanese on July 26 to surrender unconditionally or face "prompt and utter destruction." Because this was what they had already been receiving from fire raids, it was not surprising that they kept on with the war.

The use of the atomic bombs may have been unnecessary. By July 1945 the Japanese knew they were doomed, and their moderates were exploring avenues to peace. If Truman had told them that they could retain their emperor, they might have agreed to surrender, particularly after the Soviet Union (honoring its pledge at Yalta) joined the war against them on August 8. At least, he could have awaited the impact of the Soviet declaration, and of further firebombings, which many later observers felt would have won the war without an American invasion. He definitely should have paused after incinerating close to 100,000 people in Hiroshima, instead of authorizing the air force to go ahead on its own and kill 40,000 to 75,000 more at Nagasaki. Truman's actions showed that he was more decisive — more impetuous, even — than reflective.

Truman strongly defended his decision. Warning the Japanese or demonstrating the bomb seemed risky. The Japanese, he reasoned, would ignore the warning and

Hiroshima after the atomic blast

First Person

Seven weeks later I returned to Alamogordo after I had watched the same model of the A-bomb devastate the city of Nagasaki. On that return visit I saw for the first time what the bomb had done to the desert. Over a radius of four hundred yards the ground has been depressed to a depth ranging from ten feet at the periphery to twenty-five feet in the center. All life within a mile, vegetable as well as animal, had been destroyed. There was not a rattlesnake left in the region, nor a blade of desert grass. The sand in the depression had been fused into a glasslike substance the color of jade, all of it radioactive. Eight hundred yards away a steel rigging tower weighing thirty-two tons had been turned into a twisted mass of wreckage. The one-hundred-foot-high steel tower at the top of which the bomb was exploded was completely vaporized. A herd of antelope that had been grazing several miles away had vanished. It was believed they had started on a mad dash for the wilds of Mexico. A number of cows at a similar distance developed gray spots from deposits of radioactive dust. These radioactive cows and their progeny became the nearest equivalent to "sacred cows" in the United States, being carefully studied for the effects of radiation.

William Laurence, a leading American reporter, recalls the power of the first atomic bomb, detonated in Alamogordo, New Mexico, in July 1945.

concentrate their remaining defenses against air attacks. Japan might even succeed in shooting down the plane carrying the bomb. Moreover, there was the chance that a bomb dropped in a demonstration might not work. How foolish the United States (and Truman) would look if that happened, especially as there were only two bombs ready for use in early August! For Truman, therefore, the decision involved little soul-searching. The United States had spent six years and billions of dollars developing the weapon, and once it had been successfully tested, he thought, it was silly not to use it.

Later, some critics contended that Truman authorized use of the bombs to demonstrate America's power to the Soviet Union and to end the war before the Russians could join it. Such concerns did influence men like James Byrnes, who became secretary of state in 1945. They also moved General Leslie Groves, head of bomb development, who recalled, "Russia was our enemy . . . and the project was conducted on that basis." But Truman appears to have focused mainly on Japan, not on the Soviet Union. Like Roosevelt, he was more preoccupied with short-run military concerns than with postwar diplomacy. At the time, the Japanese seemed prepared to fight to their last man, and in Okinawa they lost 110,000 men in eighty-three days, while killing 12,500 Americans, or 150 per day. (Later, in Vietnam, it was a bad *week* when 200 Americans died.) It was primarily to stop such losses as these, and to prevent the still more unthinkable bloodletting anticipated in an invasion of the home islands, that Truman did what he did.

At the time, Americans had no chance to debate the alternatives and no idea of Truman's options. But they did know that the bombs had worked and that Japan had finally surrendered. So they reacted not with horror at what had been done but with profound relief that the war was over. In this way Truman's popularity was further enhanced, his judgment seemingly vindicated. For the time being, there appeared little question of Truman's capacity to rule.

Domestic Controversies

1945–46

With characteristic briskness, Truman wasted little time after Japan's surrender before turning to problems at home, and on September 6, four days after V-J Day, he asked Congress to enact a "second Bill of Rights" for the American people. Among these rights, Truman declared, were "useful and remunerative" jobs for all, government assistance to farmers, protection for small businessmen against monopoly, decent housing for every family, "adequate medical care," "protection from the economic fears of old age, sickness, and unemployment," and the "right to a good education." These rights, he said, echoing Roosevelt, "spell security."

Truman's requests, to be known as the Fair Deal, aimed at consolidating the partial welfare state built during the Roosevelt years. Indeed, in calling for such measures as national health insurance he went beyond the New Deal. Inevitably his requests provoked controversy. To secure them from a conservative Congress, the new president was to need all the skill he could muster.

As the struggle developed, it was clear that Truman possessed some of the qualities necessary to win. One of these was his awareness that the president must lead. As he liked to say, "The buck stops here." Another was his initially friendly relations with congressmen of both parties. A senator for ten years, he had pleased New Dealers by supporting most of Roosevelt's policies, while his impartial chairmanship of a wartime committee investigating defense contracting ingratiated him with moderates and conservatives.

Truman made gestures to improve congressional-executive relations, which had deteriorated badly during the war. To placate the GOP, he named Senator Harold Burton, an Ohio Republican, to the first vacancy in the Supreme Court. He resurrected Herbert Hoover by appointing him to head a commission studying government reorganization. His appointment of Byrnes, a former congressman and senator from South Carolina, as secretary of state and of Fred Vinson, a popular Democratic congressman from Kentucky, as secretary of the treasury (and in 1946 as chief justice) were especially well received on the Hill. More than FDR, Truman appeared to appreciate congressional advice and counsel.

But Truman also left himself open to criticism. In making lesser appointments he showed a tendency to favor old friends from his days in the National Guard (he had been a captain in World War I) and in Missouri politics, where he had belonged to the malodorous Pendergast machine of Kansas City. To observers used to the intellectuals and brain trusters who had flourished under Roosevelt these appointees seemed an undistinguished lot. "The composite impression," the journalist I. F. Stone wrote, "was of big-bellied, good-natured guys who knew a lot of dirty jokes, spent as little time in their offices as possible, saw Washington as a chance to make 'useful' contacts, and were anxious to get what they could for themselves out of the experience. . . . The Truman era was the era of the moocher. The place was full of Wimpys who could be had for a hamburger."

The liberal admirers of FDR were especially offended by some of Truman's conservative appointees to important positions. These included John Snyder, a Missouri banker who held several major jobs before becoming secretary of the treasury in 1946, and Tom Clark, a conservative Texan who became attorney general and then a Supreme Court justice. By the end of 1946 almost all the important New Dealers whom Truman had inherited had resigned or been fired. Many of Roosevelt's advisers, he told a friend, were "crackpots and the lunatic fringe." He added, "I don't want any experiments; the American people have been through a lot of experiments, and they want a rest." Harry Dexter White, assistant secretary of the treasury under FDR and Truman, explained that when Roosevelt was alive, "we'd go over to the White House for a conference on some particular policy, lose the argument, and yet walk out of the door somehow thrilled and inspired to go on and do the job the way the Big Boss had ordered." Now, he added, "You go in to see Mr. Truman. He's very nice to you. He lets you do what you want to, and yet you leave feeling somehow dispirited and flat."

Truman also failed to maintain order within his administration during his first two years in office. Perhaps no one could have done so very well, for the transition from war to peace inevitably caused confusion. But Truman, still feeling his way, frequently seemed ill-informed, and he was often less decisive than he seemed. Harold Smith, Truman's budget director, expressed the dismay of many government officials. "I don't know what goes on around here," he confided to his diary in February 1946, "and that is a rather dangerous situation for all of us to be in. . . . The top people in government are solving problems in a vacuum, and the vacuum is chiefly in their heads."

Moreover, Truman's approach to Congress lacked finesse. Instead of working purposefully for one or two goals at a time, he outlined grandiose programs and left Congress to its devices. "What the country needed in every field," he said, "was up to me to say . . . and if Congress wouldn't respond, well, I'd done all I could in a straight-forward way." A progressive columnist for the *New Republic* later saw a disturbing pattern: "Truman would ask Congress for about 120 percent more than he expected. Congress, with a great show of indignation, would slash it to 75 percent. Truman would smile his little-man smile and bounce back with something else. It's a funny way to run a country."

Piecing these criticisms of Truman together made a most unflattering portrait. The new president, it appeared, was a poor judge of people, an anti-intellectual, a sloppy administrator, a rhetorical liberal, a heavy-handed manager of Congress. Possibly, he felt unprepared and insecure in the White House and overcompensated by sounding tough and decisive. In any event, he possessed little of the deftness and charisma that had characterized Roosevelt at his best.

In retrospect it is equally clear that Truman (like most contemporary politicians) did not address himself carefully to some domestic problems. Though he carried liberalism slightly beyond the bread-and-butter issues of the Roosevelt era—as in his support of civil rights—he was insensitive to the prevalence of poverty and the continuing maldistribution of income. Instead, he concentrated on meeting the presumed threat from the Soviets. To a degree, of course, any president in the late 1940s would have had to do the same. With Truman, however, the focus on foreign affairs meant that many domestic problems received low priority.

But most of the progressives who blamed Truman for the nation's troubles had to concede that he faced formidable obstacles. By 1945 the Democratic party was almost as sharply divided between its northern-urban and southern-western-rural wings as it had been in the 1920s. Though outnumbered, the rural wing, which opposed the urban liberalism of the New Deal, coalesced successfully with Republicans to dominate both houses of Congress. GOP House leader Joseph Martin and Charles Halleck, his right-hand man from Indiana, worked closely with southern conservatives like Howard Smith of Virginia, a rural reactionary who was a power on the House Rules Committee. The Senate was dominated by southern conservative Democrats, among them Harry Byrd of Virginia and Richard Russell of Georgia, and by Republican leaders like Robert Taft of Ohio.

A still greater barrier to domestic reform was the national mood. Having sacrificed during four years of war (and ten years of depression), Americans looked forward to enjoying the good life. They chafed at shortages, and they yearned for material goods. In doing so they helped build up enormous demand for a host of products that had barely existed, if at all, in 1940: television, heat-and-serve dinners, automatic transmissions, tubeless tires, air conditioning, hi-fis, filter cigarettes, dishwashers, freezers, tape recorders, and fiberglass. Americans began to fly in four-engine planes, to drive on superhighways, to live in ranch-style homes, to shop in supermarkets. With such a comfortable world within grasp it was easy, as it had been in the 1920s, for Americans to concentrate on their own private concerns.

This mood, however, was different from the "normalcy" of the 1920s, when people praised the virtues of rugged individualism. By 1945 the modest welfare state of FDR had come to stay, and highly organized special-interest groups fought single-mindedly to broaden their share in it. Veterans demanded benefits, farmers higher returns, unions better wages and working conditions, consumers more goods and lower prices. Where Harding and Coolidge could win acclaim by leaving

---

America's Mood:
The Public's View
of the Most Important Problem
Facing the Country,
According to Gallup Poll Results,
1949–52

1949	High cost of living
1950	War and the threat of war
1951	War and foreign policy
1952	Korean War

SOURCE: Adapted from *U.S. Foreign Policy: Context, Conduct, Content* by Marian Irish and Elke Frank. © 1975 by Harcourt Brace. Reproduced by permission of the publisher.

people alone, Truman (and his successors) had to act to sustain these groups in a standard of living that no society in world history had ever enjoyed before. He was confronted with one of the most powerful forces of the postwar era: the revolution in expectations.

Like Roosevelt, Truman had to rely on an often nonideological electorate. As studies of voters were beginning to show, most Americans did not act as "liberals" or as "conservatives." Rather, they voted as their parents or their peers did. Millions (some 40 percent of the eligible electorate) failed to vote at all even in presidential elections. It was therefore difficult for Truman (and for reformers in the next fifteen years) to mobilize a mass following or a Democratic party that would consciously demand enactment of a "liberal" program. Instead, he confronted interest groups and constituency-oriented congressmen and senators, few of whom felt much pressure from home for progressive legislation.

THE ISSUES

These obstacles, with Truman's own limitations, combined to defeat all of the Fair Deal goals in 1945–46. Congress brought an end to the wartime Fair Employment Practices Commission and filibustered to death efforts to create a new one. It failed to pass measures against poll taxes. It ignored or defeated bills for public housing and federal aid to education. Though it approved the Employment Act of 1946 (which established a Council of Economic Advisers and proclaimed the government's responsibility to step in against economic declines), it rejected amendments to commit the government to using Keynesian fiscal policies.

President Truman with three leading politicians from Texas: Senator Lyndon B. Johnson, former Vice-President John Nance Garner, and Congressman Sam Rayburn

The most pressing issues of Truman's first two years barely touched on his Fair Deal proposals. Rather, they concerned the economic consequences of the war. In trying to deal with them Truman received little but blows for his pains.

The pressures for a return to civilian life were overwhelming by mid-1945. Business interests demanded lower taxes, immediate demobilization, and the end of lend-lease and other measures assisting foreign competitors in international markets. Soldiers insisted on being allowed to come home, and office-holders were swamped with postcards from Asia labeled, "No boats, no votes." Under such pressure the politicians of both parties gave way. In November 1945 Congress approved a $6 billion tax cut, even though it would obviously contribute to inflation. The administration quickly disposed of most of its war plants, usually by turning them over to private interests on very generous terms. It let business move ahead quickly into civilian production. Given no choice by Congress, it cut lend-lease shipments. And it brought the boys home. The armed forces, 12 million strong in 1945, had only 3 million by mid-1946 and but 1.6 million by mid-1947.

This rapid demobilization was popular enough at first. But by the end of 1945 its costs were already becoming apparent. The return of so many soldiers to the domestic scene created great competition for jobs and enormous demand for housing. One veteran complained, "Six months ago I was piloting a B-29 against the Japs. Now I am trying to build a home in my home town. The first fight was easier. . . . " Though the economy opened up quickly enough to provide most veterans with jobs, the housing market, depressed since 1928, fell far short of demands.

Truman tried to alleviate the housing shortage: Through existing agencies such as the Federal Housing Agency he (and his successors) helped millions of Americans get government-insured mortgages at moderate rates of interest. He also called for more generous appropriations for public housing, but even the backing of Robert Taft failed to stop a predominantly rural coalition from blocking the proposal until 1949. Meanwhile, Truman made matters worse by authorizing the removal of federal controls on building materials. This action, one of many that attempted to placate private interests, undermined central direction of housing policy. It also meant that materials flowed into the areas that would bring builders immediate profit. These areas, as often in the construction business, were commercial, not residential or industrial.

The housing crisis, though serious, seemed almost trivial compared to the problem of inflation. To a large degree this too was inevitable after the war, because demand for consumer goods had been pent up since 1941, during which time Americans had saved unprecedented sums. The baby boom and the return of soldiers made this demand still more formidable. During the year and a half following the end of the war in September 1945, the consumer price index jumped almost 25 percent. This was a rate of increase greater than at any time since World War I. It seemed destined to wipe out all the hard-earned economic gains of war.

Truman, of course, could hardly bring prices down. That happened on a broad front only when supply caught up with demand—in 1948. Moreover, he was again stymied by the conservative coalition in Congress, which did away with firm price controls. Prices therefore rose almost uncontrollably during the summer of 1946. By November 1946 Truman removed the few controls that remained.

Truman's handling of inflation nonetheless made this difficult situation worse. Instead of demanding strong controls from the start, he belatedly stepped in to veto a bill establishing weak controls. His actions angered not only conservatives but also some of his own party leaders, who had advised him to accept the bill as the best to be had under the circumstances. "The government's stability policy," a top adviser complained, "is not what you have stated it to be, but is instead one of improvising on a day-to-day, case-by-case method, as one crisis leads to another—in short . . . there is really no policy at all."

In dealing with labor-management controversies Truman faced perhaps the profoundest domestic problems of the era. It was his political misfortune to confront an acrimonious situation in which unions tried to make up for wartime restraint by demanding sizable wage increases. Management refused, and millions of American workers went out on strike in late 1945 and early 1946. Both sides then turned to Truman, who had the power (stemming from the war) to authorize price increases. After a show of firmness, Truman gave way under business pressure by permitting price hikes of approximately 19 percent. Management then granted workers pay increases of 18 to 19 percent. Truman's actions settled some of the strikes, but only by encouraging the first of many postwar rounds of inflationary wage-price agreements between powerful interest groups. Consumers paid the bill in higher prices.

John L. Lewis then led the soft-coal miners out on strike on April 1, 1946. American industry, very dependent on coal, seemed threatened by what promised to be a long and divisive confrontation. At the same time railway engineers and trainmen also served notice of their intention to strike. Furious, Truman went before a joint session of Congress to demand emergency powers. As he was reading his message, he was handed a note advising him that the railway men had come to terms. But he went on with his address, which called on Congress to give him power to order federal troops into strike-bound industries, and even to draft strikers into the armed services.

It was a sign of the hysteria of the times that the House quickly approved this violation of labor's civil liberties. The Senate, however, ultimately listened to calmer men like Taft, the supposed enemy of organized labor, and rejected Truman's appeal. The episode showed how hard it was for Truman (and later presidents) to impose their will on organized labor. It revealed that he could be hot-tempered to the extent of endangering the liberties of working people. Few of his actions were more ill-considered or counterproductive.

Truman's frustrations in dealing with labor-management relations also revealed the political power that the labor movement had developed as a pressure group during the war. In some states, such as Michigan, industrial workers in the CIO virtually controlled the Democratic party. Elsewhere, labor's power was nowhere nearly so powerful as anguished conservatives contended (only a third of nonagricultural workers belonged to unions), but it was potentially formidable. The CIO's Political Action Committee served as an important source of funds and votes for prolabor candidates. The postwar era, some contemporaries thought, offered the chance for a fundamental political and social realignment, with political leftists and laborers uniting with increasingly militant civil rights activists to forge a social-democratic movement in the United States. In any event, the unions seemed strong; the sociologist C. Wright Mills called them the "new men of power."

But Mills accurately noted another characteristic of the postwar labor movement: it had lost much of the old militancy of the 1930s. In the late 1940s a few union leaders (many of them communists) tried to sustain the drive for social justice that had marked the sit-down strikers. An increasing majority of union members, however, preferred to steer clear of radical associations. Earning three or four times as much in real dollars as in the 1930s, often with wives bringing in added income, they were eager to enjoy the good life. In 1948 the pollster Samuel Lubell interviewed a class-conscious local of the United Automobile Workers that he had visited eleven years before, and he found that most of the members owned their own homes. These workers were consumers first—"haves," not "have-nots." They had cars, savings, many new household appliances. Like many similarly placed blue-collar workers, they lent their support to union leaders such as Philip Murray and Walter Reuther, who purged the CIO of communist members by 1949. This bitter internal struggle, which raged within the union movement for much of the 1940s, revealed the divisions within organized labor.

The new men of power, indeed, proved themselves willing to compromise in order to secure what their members seemed to want: better pay and benefits. Few union leaders—Reuther was an exception—paid much attention to the claims of blacks, who were discriminated against by unions as well as by employers, or to the millions of women who continued to work at lower wages than did men with comparable skills. In focusing on bread-and-butter issues, the unions soft-pedaled their once bitter demands for greater control over the processes of production. The "speedup" of assembly lines persisted. Other unions negotiated contracts that traded away the right to strike for big wage increases (which employers then passed on to consumers). By the late 1940s many of the once-militant unions had become

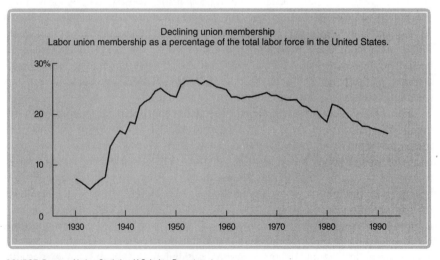

Declining union membership
Labor union membership as a percentage of the total labor force in the United States.

SOURCE: Bureau of Labor Statistics, U.S. Labor Department

Labor union membership, 1930–1990

large, sometimes sluggish bureaucracies without close contact with the rank and file. Though liberal on political issues, the unions were in many other important ways similar to other large pressure groups.

The fact remained, however, that as pressure groups the unions alarmed many contemporaries, who blamed Truman for labor-management problems. These problems, along with struggles over reconversion and price controls, badly damaged Truman's standing with the voters by late 1946. Gleeful opponents circulated cruel jokes about the President's blundering. One conjectured how Roosevelt would have handled matters by asking, "I wonder what Truman would do if he were alive." Republicans proclaimed that "to err is Truman" and repeated, "Had Enough?" In November, with meat shortages provoking fury among consumers, they succeeded in winning control over Congress for the first time since 1930. With liberals in disarray and with the conservative coalition riding high, Truman seemed doomed to electoral extinction in 1948.

THE EIGHTIETH CONGRESS

During the 1948 campaign Truman sounded one theme almost endlessly: the Republican Eightieth Congress of 1947–48 had been "good-for-nothing." Like most politicians at election time, he distorted the past, for the Congress had actually compiled a significant list of foreign policy legislation, including military assistance to Greece and Turkey, the Marshall Plan of foreign aid to Europe, and the National Security Act, which attempted to reduce interservice rivalries by setting up the Joint Chiefs of Staff and the Defense Department. The law also established the National Security Council and the Central Intelligence Agency. These agencies vastly increased the role of the military and intelligence services in subsequent decision making.

In giving the impression that Congress was totally obstructive, Truman also distorted the truth. What he should have said was that the majority of congressmen opposed labor union power, deficit spending, high taxes, and wage and price controls—that is, progressive fiscal policy and state regulation of private enterprise. Otherwise, they were often conciliatory. In the 1940s and 1950s most of them supported, though often belatedly, increases in social security and the minimum wage. Taft, the conservative leader, supported federal aid to education and public housing, both of which passed the Republican Senate in 1948, only to fail in the House. Not just a brave and lonely Harry S Truman but also conservatives and moderates helped sustain the partial welfare state of the New Deal in the 1940s: it offered too much to too many groups to be abolished.

Truman also conveniently overlooked his own equivocations. After doing little for civil rights in the first two years of his presidency, he used the election campaign to outline (but not to work hard for) a broad program that he knew Congress would never pass. He demanded national health insurance, about which he had said little during Democratic control of Congress in 1946. To appear forceful concerning inflation, he called for presidential power to control prices— authority he did not really want and knew he could not get. Overreacting to fears about communist subversion, he established loyalty boards, which had the power to ignore civil liberties of governmental employees. It was not surprising that many people thought that Truman cared less about broadening human rights than about getting himself reelected in 1948.

Still, Truman was correct in claiming that the Eightieth Congress was both conservative and partisan. Among its new members—the "class of '46"—were opportunists like Joseph McCarthy of Wisconsin (who replaced Robert La Follette, Jr.), and conservatives like John Bricker of Ohio and William Knowland of California. Led by Taft, one of the hardest-working, best-prepared Senate leaders of the postwar era, they were formidable foes to the administration.

In this frame of mind they joined with conservative Democrats to defeat the entire Fair Deal program. The Eightieth Congress rejected public housing, federal aid to education, and Truman's appeal for universal military training. It refused to relax immigration quotas or to aid displaced persons. Though it did not challenge well-established interest groups such as farmers and veterans or dismantle the social welfare programs of the New Deal, it complained loudly (and most unfairly) about Truman's "lavish" spending. To ensure that there would be no more three- or four-term presidents (like Roosevelt), it set in motion a constitutional amendment, ratified in 1951, that limited presidents to two terms.

Congress reserved its heaviest ammunition for tax and labor policies. Twice in 1947 it passed tax cuts, only to watch Truman veto them with the claim that they favored the wealthy and imperiled the budget. In the election year of 1948, however, enough of Truman's supporters deserted him to override a third presidential veto. In the area of labor law Congress approved, again over Truman's veto, the

Churchill, Truman, and Stalin at Potsdam, Germany, July 1945

Taft-Hartley Act of 1947. The measure enumerated unfair labor practices, outlawed the closed shop, required union officers to sign noncommunist oaths to secure access to the NLRB, and authorized the president to impose eighty-day "cooling off" periods before workers could start strikes threatening national health or safety. Furious, the unions called the act a "slave-labor law."

Neither the tax cut nor the Taft-Hartley law was as retrogressive as Truman and his supporters claimed. The tax cut, which administration economists had thought would be inflationary, helped sustain purchasing power during a recession in 1949, while the labor law proved a workable, if clumsy, measure that Truman himself employed in attempts to head off strikes in key industries. For all their complaints, unions were able to live with Taft-Hartley for decades thereafter.

But the struggles of the Eightieth Congress, especially over Taft-Hartley, did make a difference in American politics. In 1945–46 Truman had often seemed aimless and complacent. In battling against Taft-Hartley and the tax bills, his combative, partisan spirit arose. Progressives, though remaining suspicious of his motives, cheered him on. "Let's come right out and say it," one exulted. "We thought Truman's labor veto message thrilling." If it did nothing else, the strife of the Eightieth Congress enabled Truman to strike a pose—for that in part is what it was—for the "people" against the "interests." This fighting image, which gained him the support of many New Dealers, was valuable in an election year.

Cold War, 1946–48

The closing months of 1945 brought no respite from the tension that had been gathering between the United States and the Soviet Union. For the next three years—indeed for the next two decades—the Cold War, as it became known by 1947, was the paramount issue not only of international relations but of domestic politics.

Of the many forces that helped to foment tensions, the most important was Stalin's determination to safeguard Russian interests. By the end of 1945 it was clear that he had no intention of relinquishing his hold on eastern Europe. At the same time he systematically stripped East German industrial potential and shipped thousands of German citizens—Nazis, Stalin claimed—to forced-labor camps. He pressured Turkey for control of the straits leading from the Black Sea to the Mediterranean, and Iran for oil rights in Azerbaijan. In February 1946 he alarmed American observers by proclaiming that communism and capitalism were incompatible. Eric Sevareid, a progressive journalist, concluded that the speech made it "clear as daylight that the comintern, formalized or not, [was] back in effective operation. If you can brush aside Stalin's speech . . . you are a braver man than I."

These events led Western leaders to stiffen their response to Stalin. In a timely cable sent two weeks after Stalin's speech, George Kennan, a top American diplomat in Moscow, argued that Stalin was "only the last of that long succession of cruel and wasteful Russian rulers who have relentlessly forced their country on to ever new heights of military power. . . ." Churchill, out of power but widely admired in America, spoke two weeks later in Missouri of an "iron curtain" descending around eastern Europe. The Soviets, he declared, sought the "indefinite expansion of their power and doctrines." An approving Truman sat on the platform as Churchill delivered this speech. The President, convinced that he had to talk and act tough, also took decisive steps. By dispatching an American battleship to the eastern Mediterranean, he warned against further Russian pressure on Turkey, and by sending stiff notes protesting against Soviet behavior in Iran, he helped stave off Russian encroachment. The American people obviously supported a get-tough policy: 71 percent said they disapproved of Russia's international conduct, and 60 percent thought America "too soft" in dealing with Moscow.

American leaders reflected this hardening of opinion in 1946. In September, Secretary of State Byrnes proclaimed that the United States would henceforth forget about trying to secure Russian cooperation in the occupation of Germany. America would unilaterally strengthen its own zone. The Soviet Union, with good reason to fear a revitalized Germany, was understandably alarmed. Within a year and a half of the end of the European war, Germany, once the scourge of the Atlantic world, was becoming a front line of Western defense, while Russia, one of the Big Three, became the enemy.

In the same month Truman fell into an impasse that resulted in the firing of Secretary of Commerce Henry Wallace. While Byrnes was negotiating with the Soviets in Paris. Wallace gave a speech that said the Russians were trying to "socialize their sphere of interest just as we try to democratize our sphere of interest. . . . Only mutual trust would allow the United States and Russia to live together peacefully, and such trust could not be created by an unfriendly attitude and policy." Truman had looked at the speech beforehand, but too perfunctorily to realize how sharply it contradicted his own anti-Soviet position. Senator Arthur Vandenberg, with Byrnes in Paris, cabled "We Republicans can cooperate with only one secretary of state at a time." Having maneuvered himself clumsily into a corner, Truman thereupon fired Wallace. In so doing he cut an important spokesman for left-wing American opinion on foreign policy.

Truman proved especially unbudging on the crucial question of atomic energy. Moderates such as former Secretary of War Stimson had been arguing that Russia would soon be able to develop the bomb on its own and that America ought to earn Soviet good will by sharing scientific secrets. Having done so, the United States and the Soviet Union could develop plans for international supervision and inspection. "The chief lesson I have learned in a long life," Stimson said, "is the only way you can make a man trustworthy is to trust him; and the surest way you can make a man untrustworthy is to distrust him and to show your distrust."

Even during the war, however, America had withheld atomic secrets not only from Russia but from England—in part to secure industrial advantages in the postwar world. Truman, who reflected this attitude, ignored Stimson and listened instead to anticommunist advisers like financier Bernard Baruch and future Secretary of State Dean Acheson. They called for international inspection and for the gradual sharing of scientific information (which could not be kept secret anyway). But they opposed letting the Soviet Union in on American technical expertise. Russia, in short, was to be subjected to prying into her military installations while the United States retained a monopoly of bomb manufacture. Stalin, demanding

Legend:
- Areas annexed by USSR
- NATO Allies of U.S., 1955
- Allies of USSR, 1955
- Independent communist states
- Countries not allied with U.S. or USSR

Division of Europe, 1945–55

that America begin by destroying its stockpile, rejected the American proposal, and by the end of 1946 chances for international control of atomic weapons had disappeared.

A series of crises in the next year and a half intensified the Cold War. Indigenous guerrillas in Greece, some of them communists, threatened British influence in the eastern Mediterranean, and communist parties capitalizing on severe economic discontent seemed about to gain offices in France and Italy. Informed by England that it could no longer support the Greek government, Truman seized the opportunity to toughen American policy, and he called in March 1947 for $400 million in military aid to Greece and Turkey. This Truman Doctrine stated that "it must be the policy of the United States to support free peoples who are resisting subjugation by armed minorities or by outside pressures. . . . we must assist free peoples to work out their own destinies in their own way." He then defended the breathtaking scope of this doctrine by doing what Vandenberg recommended— "scaring hell out of the country." In May the same Republican Congress that was blocking Truman's domestic program granted his request.

A month later George Marshall, who had replaced Byrnes as secretary of state in January, called for massive aid to Europe. Seeking to deflect criticisms that America focused on providing military assistance to shore up nations against communism, Marshall explained that his aid program was "directed not against any country or doctrine but against hunger, poverty, desperation, and chaos." But the President admitted that the Truman Doctrine and the Marshall Plan (both of which bypassed the United Nations) were "two halves of the same walnut." Marshall himself observed that American economic assistance was aimed at permitting the "emergence of political and social conditions in which free institutions can exist." He also made European cooperation (and sharing of information about resources) a condition of getting aid—a requirement that the Soviets used as an excuse to refuse

	FOREIGN TRADE (in millions of current dollars)				INTERNATIONAL INVESTMENTS (in billions of current dollars)		
	EXPORT		IMPORT		U.S. INVESTMENTS ABROAD	FOREIGN INVESTMENTS IN U.S.	NET INVESTMENT POSITION (+ OR –)
	AMOUNT	% OF GNP	AMOUNT	% OF GNP	BALANCE (+ OR –)		
1925	5,272	5.4	4,419	4.6	+ 852	10.9[a]	3.9[a]	+ 7.0
1930	4,013	4.2	3,500	3.4	+ 514	17.2	8.4	+ 8.8
1935	2,304	3.1	4,143	5.7[b]	−1,839	13.5	6.4	+ 7.1
1940	4,030	4.0	7,433	7.4[b]	−3,403	12.3	13.5	− 1.2
1945	10,097	4.9	4,280	1.9	+5,816	16.8	17.6	− 0.8
1950	10,816	3.6	9,125	3.1	+1,691	32.8	19.5	+13.3
1955	15,563	3.9	11,562	2.9	+4,001	44.9	29.6	+15.3

American Enterprise Abroad, 1925–55

SOURCE: Adapted from *Historical Statistics of the United States* (Washington, DC., 1975), pp. 537, 542, 564.

[a]Data for 1924   [b]Percentages recomputed from Census data

the aid and to force its satellites to refuse also. And Kennan, whose memoranda had influenced Marshall's thinking, published an article in July (written in January) that urged America to embark on "long-term, patient but firm and vigilant containment of Russia." The Marshall Plan, like the Truman Doctrine, embraced this doctrine of containment.

Congress moved slowly in considering Marshall's request, but the Soviets played into the administration's hands by controlling Czechoslovakia in early 1948. In June they reacted to Western plans to create a more autonomous Federal Republic of Germany by blockading West Berlin. Truman responded with an airlift to relieve West Berlin. Congress then acquiesced by approving a peacetime draft—which lasted until 1973—and by passing the first of many authorizations for foreign aid.

These grants, so sharp a contrast to America's stinginess after World War I, helped restore European economic health. They showed how far the Cold War had dragged the country from isolation. But they were not solely altruistic. On the contrary, recipients of aid (which totaled some $100 billion in the next quarter century) were often required to buy American goods in return. For Truman and his successors, preserving "free" institutions among other things meant assisting American "free" enterprise. It also meant circling the Soviet Union with military force to ensure that such "freedoms" would thrive.

THE SOURCES OF AMERICAN ANTICOMMUNISM

To a degree, Russian-American rivalry was inevitable. As Alexis de Tocqueville had pointed out more than a century earlier, Russia and the United States were becoming the "two great nations in the world. . . . [E]ach seems marked out by the will of heaven to sway the destinies of half the globe." By 1945, with power vacuums in Europe and Asia, de Tocqueville's prophecy came true, for the two superpowers found themselves head-to-head for the first time in history. Conflict between such different societies was to be expected.

As Wallace pointed out at the time, however, America's attitude toward the Soviet Union after 1945 was unusually truculent, especially in contrast to its patience with Hitler from 1933 to 1940. Though dictatorial, suspicious, often ruthless, Stalin was not bent on world conquest, or even (as French and Italian communists discovered to their dismay) on controlling western Europe. Despite Truman's assertions, the USSR did little to assist communists in Greece. Rather, Stalin seems—Soviet secrecy makes his ambitions unclear—to have sought traditional Russian goals: expanded influence in Iran to the south, in Manchuria to the east, in Turkey in the southwest. Above all, he hoped to preserve Russian power in eastern Europe as protection against a rearmed Germany. In this sense Wallace was probably correct in stating that Russia wished to protect and communize its sphere of influence in much the same way that the United States wished to maintain its interests in Latin America and western Europe.

Why then did America act with such a show of energy and determination against the Soviet Union? The answer lay not only in Russian behavior, but also in domestic tensions and pressures within the United States.

Some of these stemmed from America's historical experience as the world's leading democratic nation. Until 1917, when Lenin led the Bolshevik revolution,

Americans had confidently cherished their experience; it was their "manifest destiny" to spread democratic institutions to the world. However, the rise of communism in Russia was a frightening specter—so much so that America refused even to recognize the new regime until 1933. Like fascism, communism threatened democratic government and individual freedom. It also struck at private property. It possessed a prophetic strain in its ideology—worldwide proletarian revolution—which lent credence to the American notion that communism and aggression were much the same. Americans. once so sure of their revolutionary appeal, now felt insecure and defensive, for they had to contend not only with Russian power but with a rival ideology of enormous appeal. Insecure nations, as both the Soviet Union and the United States revealed, often act impatiently and provocatively.

Americans especially feared communism's threat to capitalism. Already, the Soviets had cut off the markets (such as they were) of eastern Europe. What would happen if communism crept into Asia, Latin America, or—as seemed possible in 1947—into Greece and western Europe? The answer, Truman's advisers thought, was that the world of capitalist enterprise would suffer. A communistic world might therefore undermine America's dearly loved standard of living. This is not to say that economic motives dominated Truman's policies. They did not. But it was true that Truman, his advisers, corporate leaders, labor unions, and Americans generally sought the widest possible "Open Door" for American enterprise abroad. After all, capitalism and democratic government had expanded almost as one; the decline of one threatened the future of the other.

The presumed threat from the Soviet Union also aroused what Kennan later called the "American urge to the universalization or generalization of decision." By this he meant that the United states had frequently talked in sweeping, moralistic terms. Cherished principles—of constitutional government, individual liberty, and capitalistic free enterprise—were universally good. It followed that the United States must spread the blessings of capitalism and democracy around the world. This "globalism" was at the root of Truman's doctrine supporting all "free peoples." By late 1948 it virtually silenced contemporaries who sought a more sophisticated response to international problems.

As in the past, the "lessons" of history affected policy. In the 1930s, Truman now thought, appeasement had encouraged aggressors to provoke a war. There must be no more "Munichs." Moreover, World War II had disposed people to think in all-or-nothing terms. Coexistence, to use a term that hard-liners hated, had been impossible with Hitler; Stalin, too, had to be battled at every turn. Some Americans even considered a "preventive war" with the Soviet Union. Though responsible leaders never endorsed such a plan, their rhetoric grew almost as apocalyptic by the mid-1950s.

Domestic politics in America added to these pressures for firmness. Many of the most outraged anticommunists, including Polish-Americans, were Democrats from whom Truman sought support. So were many Catholics, who loathed the atheistic anticlericalism of Bolshevism. Moreover, isolationism virtually vanished, a casualty of war. Republicans like Vandenberg wondered if America could be isolated in the age of air power. Others feared to sound like appeasers. And conservatives were quick to oppose left-wing ideologies whether at home or abroad. The defection of such groups from the isolationist cause meant that Truman was safer politically when he struck back at the Soviet Union than he was when he turned the other cheek.

But Truman was no simple prisoner of public opinion. On the contrary, he had displayed his feelings toward Stalin as early as July 1941, when he said, "If we see that Germany is winning we ought to help Russia, and if Russia is winning we ought to help Germany." In office only a few weeks in 1945, he took such a firm line that Foreign Minister Molotov complained that he had never been spoken to so harshly in all his life. "Carry out your agreements," Truman snapped undiplomatically, "and you won't get talked to like that." Once America became the sole possessor of the A-bomb, he felt safer than ever in adopting an unbending line. Thereafter Truman made little effort to carry on Roosevelt's more cooperative policy with the Soviets.

These preconceived notions helped Truman to talk tough without qualms. They made him unreceptive to Soviet requests for economic aid. They induced him to overlook the fact that the bomb was not a credible deterrent in case of military clashes in western Europe. As the historian John Gaddis put it, the bomb represented the Impotence of Omnipotence. Truman's anticommunism also led him deliberately to exaggerate the Soviet threat. This was the approach that he used in 1947 in getting Congress to approve the Truman Doctrine. Far from trying to change the contours of public opinion, Truman exploited the prevailing anticommunist fears of most Americans. In so doing he helped escalate the Cold War.

Truman could have employed subtler ways of serving his ends. Indeed, the containment policy of the world's only nuclear power made Stalin even more suspicious than he already was. If Truman had really hoped to defuse the Cold War (and after 1946 there is no evidence that he did), he might have spent less time in futile talk about getting Russians out of eastern Europe. He might have recognized the foolishness of trying to keep knowledge of atomic energy from Russian scientists. He might have conceded the truth of the argument that the Truman Doctrine shored up undemocratic regimes in Greece and Turkey.

Truman's combativeness provoked relatively little domestic opposition at the time. Instead, he and other cold warriors struck most Americans as patriots against a worldwide communist conspiracy. Blunt, moralistic, and anticommmunist, Truman probably reflected the sentiments of most of his countrymen. As the election campaign approached, his determined foreign policy was an asset, not a liability.

Truman's Second Term

TRUMAN IN 1948

In early 1948 many liberal Democrats rebelled at the thought of renominating Truman for the presidency. Franklin D. Roosevelt, Jr., Hubert H. Humphrey, the young, progressive mayor of Minneapolis, and others backed General Eisenhower. The *New Republic* editorialized, "As a candidate for President Harry Truman should quit." "If Truman is nominated," the columnists Joseph and Stewart Alsop wrote, "he will be forced to wage the loneliest campaign in history."

Dixiecrat Strom Thurmond

After the conventions Truman's chances seemed little better. Though he secured the Democratic nomination (Eisenhower refused to be considered), a few left-wing leaders gave their support to Henry Wallace, who broke away to form the Progressive party. Their defection appeared likely to hurt Truman in key urban areas. And Republicans, rejecting Taft, named what appeared to be a strong ticket composed of the popular vote-getting governors Thomas Dewey of New York and Earl Warren of California. The derisive slogan "We're Just Mild About Harry" appeared an accurate description of Truman's appeal to voters.

Truman also had to contend with a party split over the ever more contentious issue of civil rights for blacks. By 1948, blacks were demanding a host of changes, including the end of job discrimination and of the Jim Crow laws segregating public accommodations. Led by lawyers like Thurgood Marshall (later the first black Supreme Court justice), they were then mounting legal challenges in the lower courts to school segregation and other forms of discrimination. Enlisting the aid of white liberals, they insisted on a strong Democratic civil rights platform in 1948. Party leaders were aware of the voting potential of blacks in key northern states and grudgingly acceded. Their action prompted many southern Democrats to bolt the convention. These formed their own States Rights Democratic (Dixiecrat) party and named Governor J. Strom Thurmond of South Carolina as their presidential candidate. The split over civil rights revealed the sharp divisions that rent the national Democratic party and exposed the growing groundswell for racial justice.

First Person

No presidential candidate in the future will be so inept that four of his major speeches can be boiled down to these historic four sentences. Agriculture is important. Our rivers are full of fish. You cannot have freedom without liberty. The future lies ahead. (We might add a fifth . . . The [T]VA is a fine thing and we must make certain that nothing like it ever happens again.)

The Louisville *Courier Journal* (November 1948) ridicules Dewey's passive campaign.

Until election day the public opinion polls showed Dewey with a strong lead. But it turned out they were wrong. The Dixiecrats failed to gain much support outside the Deep South. Indeed, their very presence in the campaign forced blacks and other civil rights advocates to recognize Truman's efforts, however limited, on their behalf. In November Thurmond won only four states, while Truman ran up large margins in black wards in the North.

Wallace's campaign disintegrated just as rapidly. Some observers, including many who backed his policies, found him vague and mystical. Others worried that he had become a tool of the communists and that many top Progressives were party members or fellow travelers. Labor leader Walter Reuther, a committed reformer, spoke for many anticommunist liberals in concluding that "Henry is a lost soul. . . . Communists perform the most complete valet service in the world. They write your speeches, they do your thinking for you, they provide you with applause, and they inflate your ego." Wallace's often muddled but apparently pro-Soviet sympathies at the height of the Cold War left most liberals with no one to turn to save Truman.

Dewey, too, failed to excite the voters. A trim and fastidious man, he struck one critic as a "certified public accountant in search of the Holy Grail." Others found him cold, curt, and aloof—it was said that "you have to know him really well to dislike him." Certain of victory, Dewey ran a bland campaign aimed at offending the smallest possible number of people. In the process he was vague and unclear on the issues, and he ignited little grass-roots enthusiasm. Fewer Republicans came to the polls in 1948 than in either 1940 or 1944.

Finally, Truman himself proved a feisty, opportunistic campaigner. At the convention he electrified the faithful by calling the "do-nothing" Eightieth Congress back into special session to act on Fair Deal legislation. He kept up the offensive. Republicans, he charged, were "just a bunch of old mossbacks . . . gluttons of privilege . . . all set to do a hatchet job on the New Deal." He then set off on a series of whistle-stop railroad tours, always on the attack. This partisan strategy developed by his aide, Clark Clifford, was contrived, but it had the virtue of placing the GOP on the defensive. It exploited Democratic ties with labor and the "have-not" coalition that had four times elected Roosevelt.

For all these reasons Truman surprised almost everyone by winning in November, with 24.1 million votes to Dewey's 22 million. Thurmond got less than 1.2 million, and Wallace only 1,157,000 and no electoral votes. The remarkably low turnout, more than a million less than in 1940, suggested that voters did not find

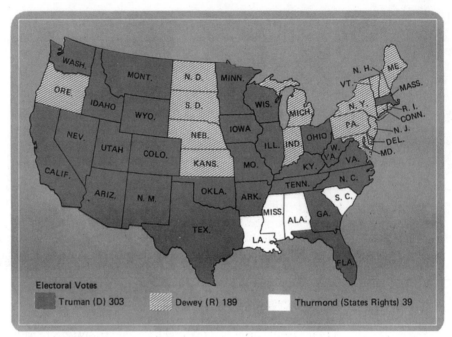

Election, 1948

either Truman or Dewey particularly attractive. Truman, in fact, failed to get 50 percent of the vote. But it also showed that the Democratic voting coalition forged during the depression remained effective and that the reforms of the New Deal were safe from attack. These were impressive reminders of the chronic weakness of the GOP and of the stability of American politics.

PROBLEMS, HOME AND ABROAD, 1949

President in his own right, Truman in January 1949 called on Congress to enact a broad-ranging program. It included health insurance, repeal of Taft-Hartley, extension of social security, increases in the minimum wage, civil rights legislation, federal aid to education, and larger appropriations for public housing. In foreign policy he broached the idea of supplying underdeveloped nations with technical assistance. Point Four, as it was called, revealed that the administration was beginning to worry about communism not only in western Europe but throughout the uncommitted world.

During the next two years Truman secured a few of these goals. Some of them, such as progress toward desegregation of the armed forces, came by executive order. Truman also strengthened the Civil Rights Division of the Department of Justice. Other reforms actually broke through the bottleneck on Capitol Hill. Congress passed a housing act including funds for public housing. It increased the minimum wage from forty cents to seventy-five cents, extended rent controls through 1950, and approved a displaced persons act admitting some 400,000 refugees to the United States. It raised social security benefits and broadened the program to cover

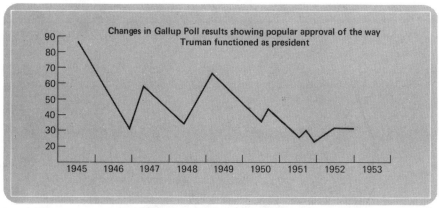

Changes in Gallup Poll results showing popular approval of the way Truman functioned as president

SOURCE: Adapted from p. 104 of *U.S. Foreign Policy: Context, Conduct, Content* by Marian Irish and Elke Frank. © 1975 by Harcourt Brace. Reproduced by permission of the publisher.

10 million new Americans. These were the most liberal measures passed by Congress since 1935.

But the conservative coalition in Congress still held its own. This was a disparate group composed of most southern Democrats, representatives of many rural and small-town areas, and all but a handful of the Republicans. It was never monolithic, and it sometimes broke ranks. But it consistently fought Truman's requests for civil rights legislation, national health insurance, and federal aid to education. It proved slow in providing funds for Point Four. It showed itself willing to revise Taft-Hartley, but when Truman insisted on repeal, Congress balked, and the act remained as it was. After 1949 it proved very stingy in appropriating funds for the public housing program, which never even approached the expectations of reformers. It also rejected an administration proposal to reform the farm subsidy programs inaugurated by the New Deal.

In the area of foreign policy Truman secured a major goal when Congress approved American participation in the North Atlantic Treaty Organization, a mutual defense pact that bound twelve signatories to fight against aggression. It was the first time in United States history that Congress had ratified a peacetime military alliance with European nations. Later in 1949 Congress added teeth to the pact by authorizing money for military aid to member nations. Because Stalin had no plans to attack western Europe, the NATO pact was of questionable military value. The military assistance plan propelled America further into the business of supplying arms to other nations. At the time, however, both NATO and military aid were described as essential to sustain the morale of western Europe. They proved highly popular measures during the struggle to win the Cold War.

Events in Asia all but obscured Truman's policies in Europe. Since 1945, when American marines had helped Chiang Kaishek strengthen his claims on North China, Truman had pursued Roosevelt's illusory hope for a peaceful, noncommunist China. But Chiang's corruption, and his failure to fight hard against the Japanese during the war, had already damaged his claim to rule, and Communist forces under Mao Zedong pressed forward. In 1946 Truman dispatched General George C. Marshall to China in an attempt to bring American influence to bear on the

Mao Zedong, 1937

situation. Marshall, like other emissaries before him, sought to reconcile Chiang and Mao. When the two sides agreed to a truce, it seemed that his patient efforts had succeeded. But by late 1946 the truce had broken down. Mao's forces pushed on, and Marshall returned home to become secretary of state.

Truman then requested a report from General Albert Wedemeyer, America's chief military emissary in China. Wedemeyer's advice, to escalate aid to Chiang and to send 10,000 American military "advisers" to China, received a cool reception from Marshall and others in the State Department, and Truman not only rejected Wedemeyer's report but kept it from Congress. Within a year and a half, in 1949, Chiang's forces collapsed, and in December he fled to Formosa (Taiwan). China, a land of more than 500 million people, was now a communist country.

Truman responded calmly to the "fall of China." His secretary of state after 1948, the tough, aristocratic Dean Acheson, spoke for the administration in defending America's policy since 1945. Sending in "advisers," he pointed out, would have led only to unnecessary loss of American life. Defeating Mao would have required a major land war on the Asian continent, a war that the United States had neither the men nor the will to fight, especially at a time when Stalin seemed to pose a threat in Europe. Chiang's own maladministration, not American neglect, had led to the communist victory. "Nothing this country did or could have done within the reasonable limits of its capabilities," Acheson argued, "would have changed the result; nothing that was left undone by this country has contributed to it."

The Truman-Acheson argument was irrefutable. Few Americans before 1949 had demanded any sizable commitment to Chiang, and the administration, which was focusing its attention in Europe, would have had serious trouble trying to mobilize support for massive aid in China as well. Moreover, almost no one at the time expected economic or military aid to do much good. Even Wedemeyer had conceded that Chiang was losing because of corruption and "lack of spirit, primarily lack of spirit. It was not lack of equipment. In my judgment they could have defended the Yangtze if they had had the will to do it." In opting for limited aid to Chiag between 1945 and 1949 the Truman administration followed Roosevelt in backing the wrong horse. But it had sense enough not to waste more money than it did (perhaps $2 billion by 1949), and to keep American men out of what would have been a bloodbath.

The fall of so much territory to communism was nonetheless difficult for many Americans to accept. The United States, the history books said, had never lost a war. It had beaten both the Germans and the Japanese. It had sole possession of the bomb. Why then had it "lost" China? Sensible observers replied that China was an ancient civilization that had never been America's to lose. They explained that Mao had triumphed on his own, with little aid indeed from Stalin. But many people refused to listen to reason. Deluded by the illusion of American omnipotence, they continued to ask where and how Truman had gone wrong.

Some of Truman's critics concluded that he had merely made mistakes. Others were "Asia-firsters" or members of the so-called China lobby. Many of these people, especially partisan Republicans, became unusually harsh. Truman, they charged, had been duped by procommunist sympathizers in the State Department. Moreover, the Russians exploded their own atomic bomb in September 1949: had procommunist scientists working for America turned over secrets to Stalin? By 1950, Truman had to confront a resurgence of popular, often irrational, fears about the spread of communism at home.

McCARTHYISM

Senator Joseph McCarthy of Wisconsin, the demagogue who capitalized on these fears, began his Red-hunting campaign in February 1950 by claiming in a speech in Wheeling to hold in his hand the names of 207 (or 57—accounts differ) communists in government. Though few people paid him much notice at first, he repeated, expanded, and varied his charges in succeeding speeches, and by March he was front-page news across the country. At last, it seemed to Truman's critics, a responsible person had evidence not only of procommunist sympathy in high places but of disloyalty and treason.

Before McCarthy and fellow Red-haters overreached themselves in late 1954 they broadened their cause into a powerful witch hunt that swept into many corners of American life. McCarthyism damaged morale in the State Department, cowed the Department of the Army, and exposed America's often hysterical anticommunism to the scorn of civilized people throughout the world.

McCarthyite fears of communism cut deeply into the fabric of American government. The Supreme Court in 1951 upheld the Smith Act of 1940, which had made it a crime even to advocate revolution. Its decision, in *Dennis* v. *U.S.,* resulted in the conviction and imprisonment of eleven top Communists and encouraged the Justice Department to proceed with further prosecutions. Ordinarily thoughtful conservatives, such as Taft, jumped on the anti-Red bandwagon as a means of courting votes and of avenging the bitterly disappointing Republican defeat in the election of 1948. McCarthy, he said, was a "fighting Marine who risked his life to

(margin handwritten notes:) CNP – Chuang   Communist –Mao *

preserve the liberties of the United States." If accusations proved unfounded, Taft advised, McCarthy should keep trying. Liberal politicians joined conservatives to approve the Internal Security Act of 1950. It required Communists to register with the attorney general, and it set up a Subversives Activities Board to review the loyalty of government employees. In vetoing it Truman correctly contended that the act was obscure, unfair, and unworkable. But 1950 was an election year, and practically no one dared to oppose the anticommunist onslaught. A Democratic Congress quickly passed the act over Truman's veto.

Heartened by such responses, Red-baiters became extreme in 1951–52. McCarthy charged that the Democratic party was "the property of men and women . . . who have bent to the whispered pleas from the lips of traitors . . . who wear the political label stitched with the idiocy of a Truman, [and] rotted by the deceit of a Dean Acheson." Marshall, he added, was "a man steeped in falsehood . . . who has resorted to the lie whenever it suits his convenience . . . [and who was part of a] conspiracy so immense and an infamy so black as to dwarf any previous venture in the history of man." Not to be outdone, Senator William Jenner of Indiana concluded that America was "in the hands of a secret inner coterie which is directed by agents of the Soviet Union. . . . Our only choice is to impeach President Truman and find out who is the secret inner government."

These statements were fueled by frustrations stemming from military stalemate in Korea and from Truman's refusal to divulge information concerning activities in the executive branch: without these broadening frustrations McCarthy and his allies might have gained no converts. Still, the statements were undocumented. The Red-baiters produced no evidence to support their accusations, and they never exposed a communist in government. Indeed, McCarthy himself made little effort to follow up his scattershot accusations. On the contrary, he remained a profane, sometimes half-sober rebel whose crusade against communism was aimed at securing the recognition he would need for his reelection campaign in 1952, and for higher political ambitions to follow. "That's it," he told friends who suggested anticommunism as an issue. "The government is full of communists. We can hammer away at them."

McCarthy's charges were as unnecessary as they were irresponsible, for Communists in America were weaker in 1950 than at any time since the 1920s.

First Person

What the phenomenon of McCarthyism did . . . was to implant in my consciousness a lasting doubt as to the adequacy of our political system. . . . A political system and a public opinion, it seemed to me, that could be so easily disoriented by this sort of challenge in one epoch would be no less vulnerable to similar ones in another. I could never recapture, after these experiences of the late 1940s and early 1950s, quite the same faith in the American system of government and in traditional American outlooks that I had had, despite all the discouragements of official life, before that time.

One veteran diplomat (George Kennan) recalls the devastating impact of McCarthyism on American life.

Anticommunist labor leaders had deprived them of positions of strength that they had enjoyed in the CIO. The government, especially after Truman created loyalty boards in 1947, had launched systematic (and often unconstitutional) loyalty checks on federal employees. Russian moves such as the coup in Czechoslovakia and the blockade of West Berlin had driven all but the avid Stalinists out of the party. By the time McCarthy started his crusade, the Communist party had already fallen into the decline that cut its membership from a high of around 80,000 in 1945 to less than 3,000 in the late 1950s. Many of these were FBI agents.

Because McCarthy himself was so crude and reckless, and because communism at home was dwindling, it was hard for contemporary defenders of civil liberties to explain his appeal. In retrospect, however, it is clear that several forces combined to make him the dangerous demagogue that he was.

Among these was McCarthy himself. His very irresponsibility made him a frightening foe, for he thought nothing of charging his critics with communist sympathies. Politicians, therefore, were careful not to antagonize him. McCarthy was also a master at using the press, which treated his sensational charges as page-one news. Shrewdly, he called press conferences early in the morning to tell reporters that earthshaking disclosures were soon to be announced. Alerted, the afternoon papers printed banner headlines, "McCarthy New Revelations Expected Soon." Newsmen for morning papers then besieged him for the latest developments, and McCarthy obliged by leading them to believe a key witness was about to be found. Hence the morning headlines, "Delay in McCarthy Revelations: Mystery Witness Sought." Tactics such as these brought McCarthy maximum publicity.

McCarthy was also fortunate in his timing. Before he seized on the communist issue to advance his political fortunes, other Red-baiters, notably the reckless House Un-American Activities Committee (HUAC), had set the stage for a crusade against alleged domestic subversion. McCarthy was an opportunistic Johnny-come-lately to the Red scare of the late 1940s. Just as he inaugurated his campaign, Alger Hiss, a former State Department official accused of espionage, was convicted of perjury—after two widely publicized trials. His conviction, which followed on a congressional investigation spearheaded by Representative Richard Nixon of California, appeared to prove that communists infested the government. McCarthy was further helped by the revelation in 1950 that Klaus Fuchs, a British physicist, had passed American atomic secrets to the Soviets. Legal proceedings stemming from the Fuchs case culminated three years later in the conviction and execution for espionage of Julius and Ethel Rosenberg, American communists allegedly involved in the atomic plot. Actually, these cases did not prove much. If Hiss was a communist agent—which he steadfastly denied—he appears to have given the Russians nothing of value. Fuchs helped the Russians along on research that they were mastering on their own. The Rosenbergs, whose guilt was still being hotly debated many years later, were in no way associated with the government. Still, Hiss was a convicted liar, and the Fuchs case was proof of the need for security. McCarthy, many Americans told themselves, might be a little rough in his methods, but his goals were noble. If permitted to continue, he would uncover the "traitors" in government.

Powerful interest groups further assisted McCarthy's campaigns. Among these were defense contractors and the military forces that had suffered from demobilization. Not all these groups thought well of McCarthy's methods—indeed, he later infuriated the army brass by accusing it of harboring communists. But campaigns against communism obviously assisted demands for defense spending. With such potent forces supporting McCarthy's goals, or at least acquiescing in them, he had advantages lesser demagogues would have lacked.

McCarthyism also seemed to offer simple answers to the complex questions of the Cold War. China went communist, he explained, because State Department "traitors" willed it so. Russia developed the A-bomb because people like Fuchs told them how to do it. McCarthy's road to salvation seemed quick and easy; it exercised an appeal that more complex, more accurate explanations were slow to provide.

His conspiracy theory appealed in particular to superpatriotic Americans who responded warmly to attacks on intellectuals, left-wing sympathizers, New Dealers, and well-educated, upper-class easterners like Acheson. "I watch his smart-aleck manner and his British clothes and that New Dealism," Senator Hugh Butler of Nebraska exclaimed of Acheson, " . . . and I want to shout, Get out. Get out. You stand for everything that has been wrong with the United States for years." Butler, a Republican, had partisan reasons for welcoming assaults on the "striped-pants boys" in the State Department. But like many Americans he suspected the worst of the so-called Eastern Establishment. In this way McCarthy had the best of two worlds: by hammering at communism he could appeal to conservatives, and by slashing at intellectuals and the Eastern Establishment he could win the approval of ordinary people.

Others who reacted positively to McCarthy included a number of ethnic Americans, especially blue-collar Catholics. By 1950 most of these people were second- or third-generation Americans. Many had fought in World War II. As ethnics and Catholics they frequently suffered discrimination, and they were rarely accepted as "100 percent Americans." McCarthy, himself a Catholic, seemed one of them. By supporting his movement, ethnics could prove their patriotism, indeed their super-patriotism. Catholics could demonstrate their support of a movement directed against atheistic communism. For these reasons McCarthyism was relatively strong in many heavily Catholic urban areas and in Catholic states like Massachusetts, where some politicians shared his concerns. "McCarthy," said John F. Kennedy, "may have something."

Not all political figures acted as cautiously as Kennedy. Some, especially those who represented rural, Protestant states, felt freer to speak out in defense of civil liberties. But most office holders, including many liberals, were almost as anticommunist as McCarthy himself. They might deplore his methods, but they were committed to a hard-line Cold War policy. This is not to suggest, as some historians have, that Truman's exaggerations about Soviet designs made McCarthyism inevitable. But it is to say that the Cold War waged by the administration after 1945 helped develop the atmosphere of fear in which McCarthy thrived. To this extent McCarthyism was a broad-based (though unorganized) phenomenon, promoted by the rhetoric of liberal as well as conservative politicians.

In this sense McCarthyism was but the latest of many eruptions of intolerance in American history. Federalists had tried to silence their "radical" Jeffersonian foes by introducing the Alien and Sedition acts of 1798. Know-Nothings, nativist politicians of the 1850s, had developed considerable support in their campaign against

Catholics and foreigners. Waves of prejudice against aliens had swept the country in tense periods since the 1870s. The Red scare of 1919, the sharpest explosion of all, had broken out against foreigners as well as leftists. By the early 1950s the "hyphenated-Americans" no longer seemed much of a threat. But the communists did. It was easy to make them a scapegoat for the nation's problems.

McCarthyism was above all the product of partisan politics at midcentury. For years American politicians had courted favor by preaching against the evils of communism. Some, such as Nixon, had built political careers by doing it. Like McCarthy, these people wanted desperately to run the Democrats out of the White House, and anticommunism, by 1950, seemed the most effective issue to employ to that end. Thus it was that when McCarthy ran again in 1952 he scored best in areas that had traditionally been Republican. The connection between McCarthyism and Republicanism was vitally important in giving purpose and direction to the anti-communist crusade.

To counter such implacable opposition, Truman might have been well advised to take it seriously. This probably would have involved giving a bipartisan congressional committee access to classified executive documents concerning alleged security risks. Without publicizing information about individuals, the committee might have established the facts concerning McCarthy's charges. Deprived of the claim that Truman was hiding pertinent data, McCarthy would have had to quiet down or to watch his accusations be torn to shreds.

Truman, however, hardly considered such a strategy. McCarthy, of course, would have insisted on being named to such a committee. If Democrats in Congress had refused to grant his demand, McCarthy would have shouted that he had been excluded. If they had agreed to it, they chanced having McCarthy give classified (and probably misleading) evidence to the press. Either way, the administration—to say nothing of the alleged security risks—might suffer.

Accordingly, Truman resorted to the doctrine of executive privilege: McCarthy would get no documents from him. He stepped up his campaign to rid the government of alleged security risks. Henceforth employees had to furnish proof, beyond a "reasonable doubt," of their loyalty. He encouraged Democrats in Congress to pursue their own counterinvestigation of McCarthy's charges. But these approaches merely suggested that Truman had something to hide. And in November 1950, Senator Millard Tydings of Maryland, the conservative Democrat who had chaired the investigation, went down in defeat before a Red-baiter who came close to outdoing McCarthy himself. Thereafter few Democrats wanted to sling stones at the Goliath of American politics. From February 1950 until the end of his tenure in the White House, President Truman had to endure his Wisconsin tormenter.

THE TRAVAIL OF KOREA

On June 25, 1950, communist forces from North Korea poured across the thirty-eighth parallel and attacked the pro-Western government of South Korea. Acting quickly, Truman authorized American forces under General Douglas MacArthur to go to South Korea's aid. At first it seemed as if MacArthur's troops might be destroyed. But the Americans and South Koreans held on until September, when MacArthur engineered a brilliant amphibious counterattack north of the enemy's lines. His forces then drove across the thirty-eighth parallel and smashed northward until they came within reach of the North Korean border with China.

If MacArthur's counteroffensive had stopped near the parallel, or if it had moved less precipitously toward China, the war might have ended there and then, a glorious triumph for Truman and for the anticommunist cause. As it was, the Chinese threw masses of men into battle, and American soldiers fell back into South Korea. General Matthew Ridgway, who replaced MacArthur in April 1951, restored order, but the conflict dragged on until a truce was arranged in July 1953. It divided the country along lines similar to those in force before the 1950 invasion and sustained in power Syngman Rhee, the anticommunist ruler of South Korea. For the West, therefore, the war had succeeded in preventing communist gains; Truman's intervention had not been wasted. It also resulted in a huge escalation of defense spending from approximately $14 billion in 1949 to $44 billion in 1953. This figure, some 60 percent of the federal budget, sparked a boom in the economy lasting until 1954. But the conflict left 34,000 Americans dead in battle and 103,000 wounded. It wholly diverted attention—and funds—from domestic reforms. It greatly strengthened the role of the military and of defense contractors in American society. And because Truman refused to escalate the war still faster, he played readily into the hands of McCarthyites, who demanded total victory. The war slowly but steadily destroyed the administration's standing with the electorate.

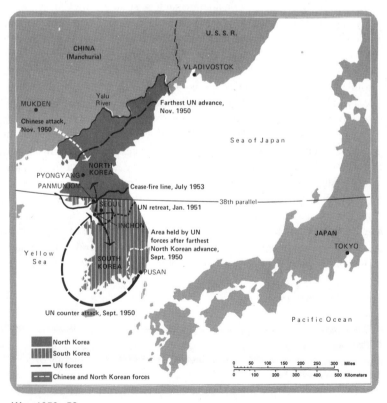

Korean War, 1950–53

Such a protracted war naturally prompted sharp debate over the wisdom of Truman's actions. Some critics complained that American policies had helped provoke the war in the first place. Others questioned his decisions to involve the United States in the fighting and then to press on over the thirty-eighth parallel. Many others denounced him for refusing to broaden the war once the Chinese had jumped into it.

The complaint that America helped to provoke the war was favored by right-wing critics at the time. Truman, they argued, had practically invited a North Korean invasion by removing American occupation troops from South Korea in 1949 and by leaving Rhee's government almost defenseless against the well-drilled forces of the North. Dean Acheson, they emphasized, had outlined an American "defense perimeter" in Asia that appeared to exclude Korea. With such a "soft spot" exposed, the communists, supplied by the Soviet Union, naturally pounced on it in June 1950.

Later left-wing critics, revisionists who renewed the debate over Korean policy, in the 1960s, challenged Truman's policies from a different perspective. Rhee, they argued, was a dictatorial nationalist who had regularly vowed his intention to reunite Korea, by force of arms if necessary. His very presence antagonized the North. When he lost support in the May 1950 elections, revisionists suggested, he determined to provoke border incidents to reestablish his image and perhaps to force the United States to defend his regime. Other revisionists went still further in chastising the Truman administration. Pointing to a position paper of the National Security Council (NSC-68), they showed that Truman's leading defense planners had agreed early in 1950 to seek enormous increases in American military might. How better to get the money out of Congress than by tempting or provoking the North Koreans to attack?

Because the relevant documents are unavailable to historians, it is impossible to know why North Korea attacked in June 1950. It is therefore hazardous to evaluate the critiques of Truman. But some facts seem clear. Obviously, the United States was unwise in leaving Rhee's forces so weak and in implying that South Korea lay outside America's primary lines of defense. Conceivably, Truman could have assisted moderate factions to take over in South Korea. Such a policy—military preparedness allied to political and diplomatic moderation—might have preserved peace on the peninsula.

Still, Truman and Acheson had sound reasons for their prewar policies. The President's military advisers, including General MacArthur, had regularly called for the removal of American troops from South Korea, a place they considered costly to defend and of little strategic value. The military also needed all the strength it could find to bolster NATO. Moreover, arming Rhee properly seemed impossible—Congress would not have supplied the funds—and unwise, for Rhee might then have staged his own attack on the North. And though Truman might have worked to dispose of Rhee, whose power was slipping in early 1950, North Korea acted first. For better or worse, America and Syngman Rhee were thrust together against a common foe.

The revisionist case distorts two other essential points. First, for whatever reasons, it was not South Korea but North Korea that mounted the attack, which was too well planned and coordinated to pass as a mere border incident. Second, though many American military leaders wanted to increase defense spending, there is no evidence to suggest that they yearned for a war in Korea, which they continued to dismiss as of little importance. Indeed, such a war would drain Western defenses in Europe, which was Washington's major concern. The Korean War was a conflict that few people in America had expected and that fewer still were very happy to be involved in.

Truman's decision to resist the North Korean invasion prompted other criticisms. If Korea was hard to protect and of little military value, why bother to defend it? Key senators like Taft demanded to know why Truman did not consult Congress or ask for a formal declaration of war. Instead, Truman merely secured United Nations sanction for common "police action" against the aggressor. (This was possible because the Soviet Union, angry that the UN refused to admit the communist regime in China, was boycotting the Security Council at the time.) Later, when the war deteriorated into an apparently endless stalemate, Truman's failure to consult Congress cost him dearly. Still later it offered a precedent for Presidents Kennedy and Johnson to send American troops to Vietnam without congressional sanction.

Truman easily brushed aside such complaints. The North Korean invasion, he declared, was part of a communist design to test America's will in the Cold War. The United States must fight to show that it would hold the line, that it would not repeat the disastrous appeasement policy of the 1930s. There must be no more Munichs. He added that he had to act quickly. If America waited for Congress to debate the issue, the North Koreans would overrun the peninsula.

Truman's arguments were a little self-serving, for no one could prove that either China or the Soviet Union had masterminded the invasion. And while it was true that Truman had to act quickly, he could still have requested congressional approval at any time in the early weeks of the war. But the speed of the invasion made his arguments so hard to refute that even critics like Taft grudgingly supported American intervention. In responding as he did Truman acted decisively, even courageously. Years later it is possible to fault his disregard of Congress, but harder to question the wisdom of the basic decision itself.

Truman's most controversial decision was authorizing MacArthur to push on toward the Yalu River, North Korea's northern border with China. His action seemed sensible at the time, for MacArthur had the enemy on the run. It reflected the almost unanimous counsel of his top military and diplomatic advisers and of Allied leaders. The Chinese, Truman was reassured, were too tired to get involved in Korea. Moreover, Asian peoples were no match for America's technological superiority. "We are no longer fearful of their [Chinese] intervention," MacArthur told Truman at a special meeting on Wake Island in October. "The Chinese have 300,000 men in Manchuria. . . . Only 50,000 to 60,000 could be gotten across the Yalu River. They have no air force. Now that we have bases for our air force in Korea, if the Chinese tried to get down to Pyongyang [the North Korean capital near the thirty-eighth parallel] there would be the greatest slaughter."

The astonishingly successful intervention of the Chinese in November 1950, of course, quickly proved the tragic foolishness of such advice. Truman's advisers, including not only MacArthur but also the Central Intelligence Agency, deserved criticism for predicting that the Chinese would stay out. But Truman himself might

First Person

Now I give the people in Peiping credit for being intelligent enough to see what is happening to them. Why they should want to further their own dismemberment and destruction by getting at cross purposes with all the free nations of the world who are inherently their friends and have always been friends of the Chinese against the imperialism coming down from the Soviet Union I cannot see.

Dean Acheson suggests (September 1950) that China will not intervene in Korea. He used "Peiping" in place of "Peking," a more common usage at the time. It is now known in the West as Beijing.

have paused before accepting such counsel, for the Chinese had implied through diplomatic channels that they would attack UN forces who pushed north of the thirty-eighth parallel. In ignoring such a possibility Truman and his advisers displayed exaggerated faith in Western technology and contempt for Oriental military potential. As George Kennan pointed out at the time, Truman and his aides were also bemused by the insidious belief, another product of the modern age, that total victory is the purpose of war. In urging MacArthur to drive toward the Yalu, Truman went rashly beyond containment to seek what later became known as a policy of liberation.

The conflict with China accelerated the war's most dramatic clash of wills—between Truman and MacArthur. As the Chinese advanced, the general became progressively more restive and querulous. Truman, he complained, should escalate the war. The administration must blockade mainland China, "unleash" Chiang Kaishek for raids in North Korea or South China, and authorize air-sea attacks on enemy "sanctuaries" in Manchuria. Without such steps, MacArthur insisted, America could never win the war.

Truman, however, shrank from embarking on such a course. He recognized that any attempt to blockade China's long coastline would tie up a substantial part of America's navy, which was needed elsewhere. A blockade might also lead to confrontation with other nations, including the Soviet Union. In any event, a blockade could do nothing to stop the flow of supplies that came overland from the Soviet Union.

With similar prudence, Truman rejected the idea of helping Chiang raid China. Contrary to MacArthur's assumption, such attacks would not have prompted native uprisings against the communist regime—Chiang remained too unpopular. Rather, Nationalist incursions, to be at all effective, would have required an enormous American commitment. The United States might have become involved in a renewal of the Chinese civil war, an eventuality that MacArthur himself shied away from.

Truman was equally wise to refrain from bombing Chinese bases in Manchuria. Strategic bombing during World War II had suggested that such attacks rarely worked wonders. They would have done nothing to stop China's major asset, masses of foot soldiers who needed only the most meager rations to keep pressing toward the south. Employing bombers would also have frightened America's Western allies, who needed no reminding that Russian territory touched the Yalu. As General Omar Bradley, the army chief of staff, put it, such escalation would have involved the nation in "the wrong war, at the wrong place, at the wrong time, and with the wrong enemy."

MacArthur, however, was an imperious egotist who could barely conceal his contempt for Truman. Having served in the Pacific for much of his life, he failed to comprehend the administration's primary concern for Europe. He had equally little understanding of the sensitivities of the Western allies, whom he considered unreliable. He was a passionate globalist who believed that the United States, all by itself, should protect the world against the tide of Marxism. "I believe we should defend every place from communism," he declared. "I believe we are able to. . . . I don't admit that we can't hold communism wherever it shows its head." For all these reasons he was among the most sincere of Asia-firsters. "It seems strangely difficult for some to realize," he wrote House Minority Leader Martin in April 1951, "that here in Asia is where the Communist conspirators have elected to make their play for global conquest . . . that here we fight Europe's war with arms while the diplomats there still fight it with words; that if we lose the war to communism in Asia the fall of Europe is inevitable; win it and Europe would probably avoid war

General Douglas MacArthur in Korea, 1950

and yet preserve freedom." With characteristic flourish, MacArthur closed his letter by proclaiming, "There is no substitute for victory."

As MacArthur had intended, Martin made the letter public. A classic confrontation then ensued between civilian and military authority. Truman had already tired of MacArthur's insubordination. He had also doubted MacArthur's handling of the war. Now MacArthur had gone the limit, ignoring presidential orders to keep quiet and challenging the very essence of administration policy. Certain of the course he had to follow, Truman nonetheless requested the advice of his chiefs of staff, who agreed that MacArthur had to go. The President then relieved him from command. If he hoped to preserve civilian rule, he could hardly have done otherwise.

The news of MacArthur's dismissal prompted critics to heap abuse on Truman's head. The GOP National Committee proclaimed that the President had perpetuated a "super Munich." McCarthy grumbled, "The son of a bitch ought to be impeached." MacArthur then began a triumphal return to the United States, where throngs of people crowded to sing his praises. To an emotional session of Congress he pulled out all the stops: "I still remember the refrain of one of the most popular barracks ballads of that day which proclaimed most proudly that 'Old soldiers never die; they just fade away.' And like the old soldier of that ballad, I now close my military career and just fade away—an old soldier who tried to do his duty as God gave him the light to see that duty. Good-bye."

Truman wisely did not attempt to match such theatrics. But he did work to strengthen America's military posture in Asia and elsewhere. In 1951 America signed separate bilateral defense pacts with Japan and with the Philippines. It agreed to the so-called ANZUS treaty, a mutual defense pact involving Australia and New Zealand. In part to secure French agreement to the inclusion of West Germany in NATO, it stepped up aid to French forces in Indochina. By 1954 the aid had totaled $1.2 billion in a losing cause.

Truman also called upon loyalists in Congress to expose MacArthur's bombast. Led by Senator Richard Russell, they brought out the fact that all three chiefs of staff had rejected MacArthur's argument. By the summer of 1951 Truman's patience began to bring modest results, and MacArthur disappeared to the back pages. But MacArthur's dismissal had served as a public acknowledgment that total victory was impossible, that "limited war" would continue to be the policy of the administration. And limited war, as one writer put it, was like a slight case of pregnancy. In their heads Americans might understand the necessity for restraint; in their hearts they wanted to win, as their country always had. Or they wanted to get out. Unless the administration could find an honorable way to end the fighting, it would suffer dearly at the polls in 1952.

Reversal in 1952

Early in 1952 Truman announced he would retire at the end of his term. He had little choice, for almost no one in his party wanted him to run again. Since 1950 he had suffered not only at the hands of McCarthyites and MacArthurites but also from corruption among some of his own friends and aides. Only 23 percent of the American people, a record low, signified their approval of his administration in late 1951.

With Truman out of the way, the Democrats turned to Governor Adlai Stevenson of Illinois. Though a relative newcomer to electoral politics, Stevenson had already captured the affection of many reporters and intellectuals, who admired his intelligence, eloquence, and patrician cultivation. Urban bosses liked his stand on labor and welfare issues and noted his apparent strength at the polls in Illinois. Witty and articulate, Stevenson could be expected to carry on the New Deal–Fair Deal tradition and to defend Truman's internationalist policies. Though Stevenson was perhaps too intellectual for mass taste, he seemed a fresh contrast to the tired regulars who had surrounded Truman. To the columnist Marcus Childs, the governor was "Lincolnian"; to David Lilienthal he was a tower of "wisdom and wit and strength"; to Max Lerner, a liberal writer, he was the "first figure of major stature to have emerged since Roosevelt."

Republicans, meanwhile, took no chances. Rejecting Taft, the controversial favorite of the Right, they selected General Eisenhower as their nominee. "Ike" was genial, nonpartisan, and widely admired as a war hero; he was expected to offend no one. As Truman's appointee to develop a NATO army, he was clearly a "Europe-firster," whom no one could accuse of being an isolationist or a McCarthyite. Only the nomination of Richard Nixon as Eisenhower's running mate—creating a ticket that one critic likened to an alliance between Ulysses S. Grant and Dick Tracy—suggested that the GOP might pursue an abrasively partisan line in the campaign.

As the campaign developed, Eisenhower edged closer to his party's right wing. At the so-called Surrender on Morningside Heights in New York City, he met Taft, who had been nursing his grievances in silence, and agreed to support a conservative domestic policy if elected. He endorsed (with some qualifications) the party's platform calling for the "liberation" of countries under communist control. With other partisan orators he stressed the anti-Truman slogan of K_1C_2— Korea, Communism, and Corruption. Nixon denounced Stevenson as "Adlai the appeaser," who "carries a Ph.D. from Dean Acheson's cowardly college of communist containment." Leaving nothing to chance, Eisenhower tried to secure McCarthyite

First Person

It would very very fine if one could command new and amusing language— witticisms to bring you a chuckle. Frankly, I have no intention of trying to do so. The subjects of which we are speaking these days, my friends, are not those that seem to me to be amusing. . . . Is it amusing that we have stumbled into a war in Korea; that we have already lost in casualties 117,000 of our Americans killed and wounded; is it amusing that the war seems to be no nearer to a real solution than ever; that we have no real plan for stopping it? Is it funny when evidence was discovered that there are Communists in government . . . ?

Eisenhower, stepping up his crusade against communism and the war in Korea, slashes at Stevenson's attempts at humor.

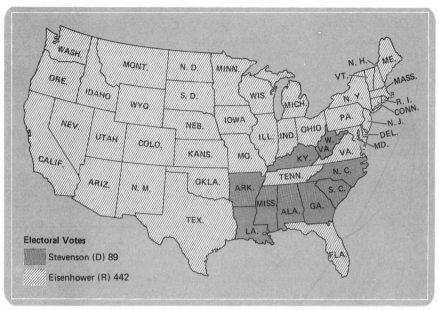

Election, 1952

support by deleting a paragraph from a Wisconsin speech praising his old boss, General Marshall. He closed the campaign by promising to go to Korea if elected. Ike, it appeared, would get the country out of the "mess" that Truman had caused in Asia.

Stevenson countered Eisenhower's attacks with wit and energy. But as a Democrat he was inevitably associated with Truman's policies. No one, therefore, was surprised when he was overwhelmed in November. Though he received 27.3 million votes, 3.2 million more than Truman in 1948, he still trailed Eisenhower, who attracted a record 33.9 million voters, 12 million more than Dewey's total four years earlier. Breaking deeply into the Democratic coalition. Eisenhower swept all the big urban states and carried four states in the ordinarily Democratic South. Republicans even won majorities in both houses of Congress, for the second time since 1930. The result not only ended twenty years of Democratic dominance; it appeared to be a virtual revolution overthrowing the electoral universe that Al Smith and Franklin D. Roosevelt had forged in the previous generation.

Democratic gains in congressional elections throughout the 1950s revealed that no such revolution had taken place. Republicans, weakened in the depression years, remained the minority party. But the election of 1952 suggested the enormously important effect that an attractive candidate could have, and the degree to which voters were prepared to split their tickets. It also showed that the South, which had begun to rebel against Truman in 1948, was heading toward the Republican column in national elections. Above all, the election of 1952 left little doubt that voters wanted a change in the White House. Like Hoover in 1933, Johnson in 1969, and Nixon in 1974, Truman left office under clouds of disapproval.

Such a verdict, if that is what it was, was unfair, for Roosevelt's "Throttlebottom" had proved a competent if uninspiring leader. Though partisan in dealing with Congress, he had managed to preserve the partial welfare state of the New Deal. Though inflexible and unsophisticated in diplomacy, he had occasionally proved enlightened, as in his support of foreign aid for Europe, and sometimes decisive, as in his intervention in Korea. When he left office in early 1953, it remained to be seen whether the GOP—out of the White House for twenty years—could do much better.

Suggestions for Reading

Among the many accounts of foreign policy in the Truman years are Daniel Yergin, *Shattered Peace: The Origins of the Cold War and the National Security State* (1977); Herbert Feis, *From Trust to Terror: The Onset of the Cold War, 1945–1950* (1970); Gregg Herken, *The Winning Weapon* (1980), on the A-bomb; John Gaddis, *Strategies of Containment* (1982); Melvyn Leffler, *A Preponderance of Power: National Security, the Truman Administration, and the Cold War* (1992); and the critical book by Walter La Feber, *America, Russia, and the Cold War, 1945–1971** (1972). See also the books by Gaddis, Ambrose, and Alperovitz mentioned at the end of chapter 1. Revisionist accounts include Thomas Paterson, *Soviet-American Confrontation* (1974); and Lloyd Gardner, *Architects of Illusion* (1970). An important memoir is George Kennan, *Memoirs, 1925–1950** (1967). Gaddis Smith, *Dean Acheson** (1972) is a useful biography. For an examination of the early Cold War in light of recently opened archives, see Gaddis, *We Now Know: Rethinking Cold War History* (1997).

Books on more specialized topics include Tang Tsou, *America's Failure in China, 1941–1949** (1963); E. J. Kahn, *The China Hands* (1975); and William Stueck, *The Road to Confrontation: American Policy Toward China and Korea, 1947–1950* (1981). For the Korean War, consult Rosemary Foot, *The Wrong War* (1985); Ronald Caridi, *The Korean War and American Politics* (1968); William Stueck, *The Korean War: An International History* (1995); and William Manchester, *American Caesar* (1978), on MacArthur.

The most balanced books on the Truman administration are Robert Donovan, *Conflict and Crisis* (1977) and *Tumultuous Years* (1983); Michael Lacey, ed; *The Truman Presidency* (1989), a fine collection of essays; and Alonzo Hamby, *Beyond the New Deal: Harry S. Truman and American Liberalism* (1973). Hamby, *Man of the People: A Life of Harry S. Truman* (1995) and David McCullough, *Truman* (1992) are well-written biographies of President Truman. Bert Cochran, *Harry S. Truman and the Crisis Presidency* (1973) is critical. Barton Bernstein and Allen Matusow, eds., *Politics and Policies of the Truman Administration** (1970), is revisionist. Richard Kirkendall, ed., *The Truman Period as a Research Field: A Reappraisal* (1974), offers conflicting interpretations. For political trends see V. O. Key, Jr., *Southern Politics* (1949); and the book by Samuel Lubell cited at the end of chapter 6. For the 1948 campaign consult Norman Markowitz, *The Rise and Fall of the People's Century* (1973); and Irwin Ross, *The Loneliest Campaign** (1968). James T. Patterson, *Mr. Republican: A Biography of Robert A. Taft** (1972) is a biography.

*Available in a paperback edition.

Books dealing with aspects of domestic policy are Edmund Flash, Jr., *Economic Advice and Presidential Leadership* (1965), on the Council of Economic Advisers; R. Alton Lee, *Truman and Taft-Hartley* (1967); Allen Matusow, *Farm Policies and Politics of the Truman Administration* (1967); Richard O. Davies, *Housing Reform During the Truman Administration** (1966); Leonard Dinnerstein, *America and the Survivors of the Holocaust* (1982); and A. E. Holmans, *United States Fiscal Policy, 1945–1959* (1961). For labor, see Bert Cochran, *Labor and Communism: The Conflict that Shaped American Unions* (1977); Maeva Marcus, *Truman and the Steel Seizure* (1976), David Brody, *Workers in Industrial America* (1980); Nelson Lichtenstein, *The Most Dangerous Man in Detroit: Walter Reuther and the Fate of American Labor* (1995); and Robert Zieger, *The CIO, 1935–1955* (1995). For civil rights see William Berman, *The Politics of Civil Rights in the Truman Administration* (1970); Donald McCoy and Richard Ruetten, *Quest and Response* (1973); Richard Kluger, *Simple Justice: The History of Brown v. Board of Education and Black America's Struggle for Equality* (1975); Daryl Michael Scott, *Contempt and Pity: Social Policy and the Image of the Damaged Black Psyche, 1880–1996* (1997); and Jules Tygiel, *Baseball's Great Experiment* (1983), on Jackie Robinson and big league baseball.

The subject of anticommunism has attracted numerous writers. Among the important books are David Shannon, *The Decline of American Communism* (1959); Earl Latham, *The Communist Conspiracy in Washington** (1966); Alan Harper, *The Politics of Loyalty, 1946–1952* (1969); David Oshinsky, *A Conspiracy So Immense* (1983), a biography of McCarthy; and Robert Griffith, *The Politics of Fear** (1970), which focuses on partisanship and the Senate. Other major studies are Stanley Kutler, *The American Inquisition* (1982), on the court and civil liberties; Athan Theoharis and John Stuart Cox, *The Boss: J. Edgar Hoover and the Great American Inquisition* (1988); Stephen Whitfield, *The Culture of the Cold War* (1991). Lary May, ed., *Recasting America: Culture and Politics in the Age of the Cold War* (1989); Ellen Schrecker, *No Ivory Tower: McCarthyism and the Universities* (1986); Richard Fried, *Nightmare in Red: The McCarthy Era in Perspective* (1990); and Mary Sperling McAuliffe, *Crisis on the Left: Cold War Politics and American Liberals, 1947–1954* (1978). Studies that criticize the Truman administration include Athan Theoharis, *Seeds of Repression: Harry S. Truman and the Origins of McCarthyism* (1971); and Richard Freeland, *The Truman Administration and the Origins of McCarthyism* (1972). Daniel Bell, ed., *The Radical Right** (1963) focuses on the social origins of anticommunism.

Broad studies on the postwar era include William Chafe's excellent *The Unfinished Journey: America Since World War II* (1991); Steven Gillon, *Politics and Vision: The ADA and American Liberalism, 1947–1984* (1987); Robert Bremner and Gary Reichard, ed., *Reshaping America: Society and Institutions, 1945–1960* (1981); James T. Patterson, *Grand Expectations: The United States, 1945–1974* (1997); Paul Boyer, *By the Bomb's Early Light* (1985), on the bomb in American culture, 1945–1950; Alonzo Hamby, *Liberalism and Its Challengers: FDR to Reagan* (1985); William Leuchtenburg, *In the Shadow of FDR* (1983), a history of FDR's legacy into the Reagan years; and Daniel Yergin, *The Prize* (1991), a sweeping history of the role of oil in the modern world.

The Maritime Administration: Grain to Europe, troops to Korea

3

The Middle-Class World of the 1950s

"We've grown unbelievably prosperous and we maunder along in a stupor of fat," the historian Eric Goldman wrote in 1960. "We live in a heavy, humorless, sanctimonious, stultifying atmosphere, singularly lacking in the self-mockery that is criticism. Probably the climate of the late 1950s was the dullest and dreariest in all our history." The journalist William Shannon agreed. The decade, he wrote, was one of "flabbiness and self-satisfaction and gross materialism. . . . The loudest sound in the land has been the oink and grunt of private hoggishness. . . . It has been the age of the slob."

Many other contemporary writers echoed Goldman and Shannon. The decade of the 1950s, these critics recognized, was a period of considerable prosperity. This prosperity was cause, of course, for great personal satisfaction among millions of Americans. But the critics were ambivalent at best. The period, they complained, was like the 1920s: materialistic, self-satisfied, conformist, politically conservative, and apathetic.

The Case Against the '50s

Primary targets of such criticism were the suburban middle classes, which expanded dramatically in the postwar years. In 1940, 74.4 million of America's 132 million people (56 percent) had lived in cities, then defined by the census as places with 2,500 or more people. By 1950, the Census Bureau recognized that this arbitrary definition excluded millions who lived in suburbs; so it broadened its definition of urbanized areas to include "densely settled urban fringes . . . around cities of 50,000 inhabitants or more." By this definition the number of urbanites rose to 96.5 million in 1950, 124.7 million in 1960, and 149.3 million in 1970— 73.5 percent of America's rapidly expanding population of 203 million. Meanwhile

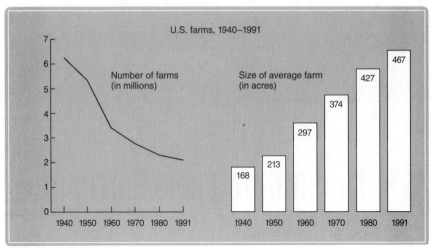

SOURCE: U.S. Department of Agriculture
U.S. farms, 1940–1991

the number classified as "rural farm" dropped precipitously, from 30 million in 1940 to 23 million in 1950 to only 13.4 million in 1960.

These figures did not mean that central cities were growing. Quite the contrary, many of America's largest cities lost people between 1950 and 1960. These one-time city people, plus millions more from the countryside, were flocking to the "settled urban fringes," which—thanks to the ubiquitous automobile—grew three times as rapidly as the overall population. By 1960 a "megalopolis" stretched much of the way between Boston and Washington. Suburban areas around newer cities of the "Sun Belt"—Los Angeles, Dallas, Houston, Phoenix, San Diego—expanded fantastically. By 1970 some 80 million Americans lived in "suburbs." This was approximately 15 million more than lived in central cities, and more than the nation's entire population in 1900.

Naturally, the motives that inspired so many migrants varied widely. Millions fled the urban cores to escape countermigrations of blacks: in the 1950s alone America's twelve largest cities lost 2 million whites while gaining 1.8 million non-whites. Millions more sought to better their social and economic status, to improve educational opportunities for their children, and to secure space and privacy. Some of these migrants were wealthy business and professional people who lived in style many miles from downtown sections. Others were blue-collar workers of limited means—people who borrowed heavily to buy tiny houses or to rent flats in hastily constructed apartment buildings. Such suburban areas, sometimes heavily industrial, offered few of the amenities ordinarily associated with life outside the central city. The variety of suburbs, and of the motivations of the people who caused them to grow, almost defy description.

Generally, however, it is fair to identify millions of the suburbanites as belonging occupationally to the middle classes, which grew rapidly during the, postwar era of bureaucratization, specialization, and technological change. As the number of farmers declined, and that of manual workers increased only slightly, the number of Americans classified as white-collar workers rose rapidly throughout the decades

Suburban mothers and their children add to the local color in one of Levittown's modern shopping centers.

since 1940. By the mid-1950s such people outnumbered blue-collar laborers for the first time in American history. By 1970 they were close to 40 million strong, compared to 28.5 million blue-collar workers, 11 million service workers, and 3 million farm workers. Having escaped blue-collar status, many of these white-collar families sought the space, the privacy, and the life-styles of the older middle classes. In this way suburbanization and the process of becoming middle-class tended to develop together, and to establish themselves as significant demographic movements of the 1950s.

Most of the people who moved to suburbs, studies suggested, were happy in their new surroundings. Their housing was not only newer but often roomier. They were moving up in the world. They were living near people like themselves. But many contemporary critics refused to see the good side of suburbanization. Places like Levittown, Pennsylvania, one of many mass-produced communities catering to lower- and middle-income groups, seemed to them boring, monotonous, and intolerant. So did more costly but aesthetically dull developments plastered on the once rural landscape. John Keats, author of the antisuburban book *The Crack in the Picture Window* (1961), dismissed them as "developments conceived in error, nurtured by greed, corroding everything they touch." To him as to other observers it seemed almost criminal that once picturesque countrysides should be bulldozed for houses and apartments, each with a TV antenna scarring a treeless sky. It seemed that a conspiracy of mercenary builders and ignorant architects was fastening a noose of vulgarity around the nation's cities.

Critics worried also about the human values nurtured by such humdrum surroundings. The "heroes" of Keats's book were John and Mary Drone—bored, purposeless materialists, Richard and Katherine Gordon, authors of *The Split-Level Trap* (1961), thought that the monotony of suburban existence promoted mental

---

First Person

Little boxes on the hillside
Little boxes made of ticky-tacky
Little boxes on the hillside.
Little boxes all the same.
There's a green one and a pink one
And a blue one and a yellow one
And they're all made out of ticky-tacky
And they all look the same.

The folk singer Malvina Reynolds describes American postwar life.

---

anguish and "Disturbia." And William H. Whyte, Jr.'s, widely discussed *Organiza-tion Man* (1956) bemoaned the fate that met the middle-class suburbanites of Park Forest, Illinois. Though Whyte considered Park Forest a pleasant, friendly place where newcomers were made to feel at home, he concluded that it was hell for people who valued privacy and nonconformity. The middle classes, Whyte implied, were facing a vast suburban sprawl (what others called "slurbs") of mediocrity and conformity.

The sociologist David Riesman made many of the same points in his book *The Lonely Crowd* (1950), which described the growth of conformist pressures not only in suburbia but in all areas of middle-class life. To Riesman, America had moved from an "inner-directed" culture in which people (through parental guidance) developed individualized goals, to an "other-directed" society molded by peer-group pressures. Such a society, Riesman realized, could be more stable and even more tolerant than one composed of self-made men. But it helped create unventure-some little people like the boy who was asked, "Would you like to be able to fly?" and who answered, "I would like to be able to fly if everybody else did."

To writers like Dwight Macdonald the alleged deadness of contemporary life was especially clear in the arts. Unlike Great Britain or other Western societies,

---

First Person

Whereas the inner-directed middle-class boy often had to learn after twenty to adjust, to surrender his adolescent dreams and accept a burgher's modest lot, the other-directed boy never had such dreams. In a profound sense he never experiences adolescence, moving as he does uninterruptedly with the peer-group, from the nursery years on. He learns to conform to the group al-most as soon as he learns anything. He does not face, at adolescence, the need to choose between his family's world and that of his own generation or between his dreams and a world he never made.

David Riesman laments the passing of "inner direction."

Macdonald thought, America could not sustain a High Culture. Instead, it had purely commercial television and radio, comic books and cartoon strips that sold by the millions, and "masscult," a parody of High Culture that featured sentimental painters like Norman Rockwell and pseudotheologians like Norman Vincent Peale. Worse, America was becoming swamped by "midcult," which Macdonald thought "watered down and vulgarized" the standards of High Culture. Examples of midcult were Hemingway's *Old Man and the Sea* (1952) and selections by such purveyors of "culture" as the Book-of-the-Month Club. Macdonald, an intellectual snob, thought that America was a nation of cultural philistines.

Many of these critics focused on what they saw as the self-indulgence, purposelessness, and lack of discipline in American society during the 1950s. The United States, wrote the novelist John Updike, "is like an unloved child smothered in candy. God doesn't love us any more. He loves Russia. He loves Uganda. We're fat and full of pimples and always yearning for more candy. We've fallen from grace." The economist John Kenneth Galbraith, in his book *The Affluent Society* (1958), showed that Americans spent billions on consumer goods—TV sets, home freezers, household gadgets, and above all, automobiles—while scrimping on necessary public services. Conservatives worried that the consumer society of the 1950s was inducing national flabbiness. "If you ask me," George Kennan wrote,

> whether a country that is in the state this country is in today: with no highly devel-oped sense of national purpose, with the overwhelming accent of life on personal comfort and amusement, with a dearth of public services and a surfeit of privately sold gadgetry . . . if you ask me whether such a country has, over the long run, a

First Person

> *I drive my car to supermarket,*
>   *The way I take is superhigh,*
> *A superlot is where I park it,*
>   *And Super Suds are what I buy.*
>
> *Supersalesmen sell me tonic—*
>   *Super-Tone O, for relief.*
> *The planes I ride are supersonic.*
>   *In trains I like the Super Chief.*
>
> *Supercilious men and women*
>   *Call me superficial—me.*
> *Who so superbly learned to swim in*
>   *Supercolossality.*
>
> *Superphosphate-fed foods feed me;*
>   *Superservice keeps me new.*
> *Who would dare to supersede me,*
>   *Super-super-superwho?*

The writer John Updike echoes complaints about American materialism, 1954.

good chance of competing with a purposeful, serious, and disciplined society such as that of the Soviet Union, I must say that the answer is "No."

Other critics, including the distinguished sociologist Pitirim Sorokin, worried that Americans, lacking a sense of purpose, were wallowing in sex. He concluded: "Unless we develop an inner immunity against these libidinal forces, we are bound to be conquered by the continuous army of omnipresent sex stimuli." Sorokin's worries were exaggerated. Though Alfred Kinsey, an Indiana University researcher, published tomes (*Sexual Behavior in the Human Male* [1948] and *Sexual Behavior in the Human Female* [1953]) showing that large numbers of young people were indulging in premarital sex, he scarcely supported the notion that sexual immorality was sweeping the nation. His researches suggested that American sexual behavior had been changing since the 1910s and 1920s, not only in the supposedly degenerate postwar years. The very alarm displayed at the publication of Kinsey's "statistical filth" underlined the continued power of conventional ideas concerning sex in the American consciousness.

Many of the broadsides against philistinism were equally ahistorical. Scores of previous observers had lambasted America's material greed and cultural crudity. Like Macdonald, they tended to be elitists who refused to accept the simple fact that people in most societies prefer personal comfort to High Culture. As one sensible writer pointed out, "The critic waves the prophet's long and accusing finger and warns: 'You may *think* you're happy, you smug and prosperous striver, but I tell you that the anxieties of status mobility are too much; they impoverish you psychologically, they alienate you from your family'; and so on. And the suburbanite looks at his new house, his new car, his new freezer, his lawn and patio, and to be sure, his good credit, and scratches his head, bewildered." Postwar Americans were not more materialistic than earlier generations—just incomparably richer. They were able to buy and to enjoy things that their parents could only dream about.

As careful critics recognized, it was also simplistic to paste labels—such as conformist or materialistic—on a society as diverse as the United States. What might apply to the corporate middle class (or some part of it) did not necessarily

First Person

. . . youngsters, instead of being sheltered and disciplined as they once were, are now exposed to the seamy side of sex in its rawest forms before they have the faintest concept of its total meaning in life. We have only to look about us to realize that, as a nation, we are preoccupied—almost obsessed—with the superficial aspects of sex, with sex as a form of amusement. This is not true sex, with the corollaries of love, marriage and childbearing. It is an almost hysterical bandying about of sex symbols, coming close to fetish worship. (Consider the present over-emphasis of the breast, the stressing of erotic qualities in perfume.)

Dr. Goodrich C. Schauffler, a gynecologist, joins others in the 1950s in bewailing the triumph of sex.

describe farmers, blacks, ethnics, blue-collar people, or many others in the enormously varied middle classes. What may have been true of some suburbanites was not in the least true of others—who resembled each other (if at all) primarily in their dependence on the automobile and their geographical mobility. It was equally hazardous to contend that "other-directedness" was new or on the upswing. Indeed, peer-group pressures in nineteenth-century American towns may have been more formidable than in the ever-changing suburbs of the 1950s. Those who perceived only conformity also overlooked the continuing stress on personal achievement and—especially in the prosperous postwar years—the yearning for self-growth. The very attention accorded such books as *Organization Man* suggested that many Americans, including the middle classes who were supposedly so mindless, were as anxious as their ancestors had been to surmount the homogenizing pressures of life.

A similar yearning for self-expression prompted some of the major trends in art forms during the decade. Poets and dramatists reacted against the social realism of the 1930s and insisted on writing for themselves, not for causes. "A successful poem," the writer Leslie Fiedler explained, "is a complete and final act; if it leads outward to other action, it is just so far a failure." The director Alan Schneider later added, "We all have got to stop looking at all our plays as though they were socialist realism. . . . We can no longer go back to the well-made play because we haven't got a well-made world."

Reflecting similar ideas, young painters like Jackson Pollock developed a wholly nonrepresentational style variously called Abstract Expressionism and Action Painting. They argued that a work of art must embody the spontaneous, individual emotions of the creator. Art was a process of expression, not a static final product. Pollock, indeed, came to stand on his canvasses, flinging paint on them with apparently reckless abandon. "What was to go on the canvas," the critic Harold Rosenberg explained approvingly, "was not a picture but an event. . . . It is the artist's existence . . . he is living on the canvas. . . . What gives the canvas meaning is . . . the way the artist organized his emotional and intellectual energy as if he were in a living situation."

This desire to be one's self, to overcome organizational constraints, helped to explain the critical acclaim bestowed in the 1950s on novelists otherwise as diverse

First Person

The quest, I am beginning to think, whether it be for money, for notoriety, reputation, increase of pride, whether it leads us to thievery, slaughter, sacrifice, the quest is one and the same. All the striving is for one end. I do not entirely understand this impulse. But it seems to me that its final end is the desire for pure freedom. We are all drawn toward the same craters of the spirit—to know what we are and what we are for, to know our purpose, to seek grace. And, if the quest is the same, the differences in our personal histories, which hitherto meant so much to us, become of minor importance.

Saul Bellow's character Joseph in *Dangling Man* (1946) expresses a feeling later echoed by many of the most memorable characters in postwar American fiction.

Jack Kerouac

as J. D. Salinger, Saul Bellow, and John Updike. In *Catcher in the Rye* (1951) Salinger's "hero" is Holden Caulfield, a supersensitive adolescent bent on preserving innocence against "perverts" and "phonies" who wanted him to conform. Most of Bellow's protagonists, in books such as *Dangling Man* (1946), *Adventures of Augie March* (1949), and *Herzog* (1961), are bemused men who revolt against what Augie called the "shame of purposelessness." Like Huckleberry Finn (who also had "adventures"), they tried to be true to themselves. Updike's Rabbit Angstrom in *Rabbit Run* (1961) is a similarly confused young man who looks desperately—and unsuccessfully—for ways to bring back the excitement and meaning of his high school days. Characters like these were fearful, confused, buffeted about—sometimes victims of larger forces. But they did not surrender. Some were existentialist antiheroes who at least survived.

These thrusts against conformity led in the late 1950s to a vogue among more radical students for books like C. Wright Mills's *Power Elite* (1956), Jack Kerouac's *On the Road* (1957), and Paul Goodman's *Growing Up Absurd* (1960). The three men held differing social philosophies: Mills was a Marxist sociologist; Kerouac, a "beat" novelist who celebrated free-wheeling nonconformity; Goodman, a philosophical anarchist who combined Veblen's passion for productive labor, Freud's stress on the need for physical love, and the urban planner Ebenezer Howard's vision of decentralized communities and garden cities. Yet all three men agreed that America—in Goodman's words a "rat race," in Mills's a "great salesroom, an enormous file, an incorporated brain, a new universe of management and manipulation"—stifled creative talent. For them, as for many less radical

---

First Person

. . . we get a clear but exaggerated picture of our American society. It has: slums of engineering—boondoggling production—chaotic congestion—tribes of middlemen—basic city functions squeezed out—garden cities for children—indifferent workmen—underprivileged on a dole—empty "belonging" without nature or culture—front politicians—no patriotism—an empty nationalism bound for a cataclysmically disastrous finish—wise opinion swamped—enterprise sabotaged by monopoly—prejudice rising—religion otiose—the popular culture debased—science specialized—science secret—the average man inept—youth idle and truant—youth sexually suffenng and sexually obsessed—youth without goals—poor schools.

Paul Goodman, in *Growing up Absurd* (1960) expresses a radically unhappy view of American society.

---

thinkers, large-scale organization was the enemy. Their appeal to young nonconformists suggested that the 1950s were less serene and complacent than they sometimes appeared.

CAUSES FOR ALARM

Still, there was no denying that some aspects of American life in the 1950s supported the critics of conformity and materialism. One of these was the growth of the huge, bureaucratic corporation. As Adolf Berle and Gardiner Means had pointed out in the early 1930s—and as James Burnham had stressed in his *Managerial Revolution* (1939)—"faceless" bureaucrats were dominating the ever-growing corporations. These early writers had worried more about the power of such organizations than about the psyches of their employees. But by the 1950s it was clear that many corporations (to say nothing of government, the biggest bureaucracy of all) stressed "teamwork" and frowned on mavericks. Some, such as IBM, even outlined acceptable standards of dress and decorum. Alarmed, Mills perceived the coming of a "white collar" society in which people would be "estranged from community . . . in a context of distrust and manipulation, alienated from work and, in the personality market, from self, expropriated of individual rationality, and politically apathetic." Mills exaggerated the capacity of organizations to transform people's minds. But he was perceptive in pointing to the growth of propagandists for "togetherness" and the "need to belong."

The call for togetherness also helped sustain a cult of domesticity in the 1950s. More than ever before—or so it seemed—Americans yearned to enmesh themselves in the "tender trap" of marriage, parenthood, and the nuclear family. During the late 1940s and early 1950s people continued to marry young and to have children quickly. As a result the baby boom, which demographers had expected would decrease shortly after World War II, continued until 1964. The nation's population increased from 151 million to 180 million people between 1950 and 1960. This was the largest growth in any decade of American history (before or since). The rate of

First Person

These schools were not only to teach general management, but—most important—they were to give our managers a feeling for IBM's outlooks and beliefs. After a time we found that the schools tended to put too much emphasis on management, not enough on beliefs. This, we felt, was putting the cart before the horse. We felt that it was vital that our managers be well grounded in our beliefs. Otherwise, we might begin to get management views at odds with the company's outlook. If this were to happen, it might possibly slow down our growth and change our basic approach to the management of our company.

The head of IBM defends his company's schools of indoctrination.

increase (19 percent) was the greatest since 1910, when heavy immigration had helped to swell the pace of growth.

Few people during the 1950s expressed much alarm about the ecological results of such expansion. The baby boom, they said, helped to sustain prosperity, especially in the construction industry, which was kept busy building approximately 1 million new homes per year throughout the 1950s. By 1960 more Americans owned their homes (with mortgages) than rented, for the first time in the twentieth century. The majority of such homes had the creature comforts that the media promoted as necessary for the joys of domesticity and parenthood.

 The presumed blessings of domesticity helped to weaken feminism in the 1950s. Feminists, the Women's Bureau of the federal government had announced a few years earlier, were a "small but militant group of leisure class women [giving vent] to their resentment at not having been born men." Adlai Stevenson added, "The assignment for you, as women and mothers, you can do in the living room with a baby in your lap or in the kitchen with a can opener in your hand. . . . There is much you can do about our crisis in the humble role of housewife. I could wish you no better vocation than that." Dr. Benjamin Spock, whose *Baby and Child Care* (1946) was a huge seller in the 1950s and 1960s, urged the government to pay mothers so they would not leave the home for employment.

Defenders of domesticity overlooked continuing growth in female employment, a profound demographic development that helped sustain the movement for women's liberation a decade later. But movies and magazines undercut feminism. Hollywood glorified sweet types like Doris Day and Debbie Reynolds or sex objects like Marilyn Monroe. Fashion designers popularized spike-heeled shoes, crinolines, and the "baby doll" look. The "ladies" magazines extolled the satisfactions of motherhood and home management. In many ways, the culture outlined—and women appeared to accept—primarily private and domestic roles for women in the 1950s.

There was cause also to worry about the impact of the mass media, particularly television, which one critic labeled the "cheekiest, vulgarest, most disgraceful form of entertainment since bear-baiting, dog-fighting, and the seasonal Czarist Russian

For many women in the 1950s, the domestic role of motherhood was said to be the ideal.

pogrom." Like others, he lamented the omnipresence of violence, the virtual absence of serious drama, above all the pandering to the commercial nature of the medium. Like the mass-circulation magazines and newspapers, TV constantly flashed expensive luxury goods before the consumer. No one, of course, could prove that TV or the other media actually caused people to buy certain goods, much less to become conformists. Indeed, it was possible that the bombardment of varied images undercut provincialism and broadened the vision of millions. But by 1960 it was also clear that TV, by invading practically every American home for several hours a day, was projecting a peculiarly consumerist and middle-class world. It was also ignoring (or stereotyping) the millions who belonged to minority groups.

Another sign of blandness in the 1950s was what some contemporaries labeled the "new piety." By 1960 this was reflected in a rise in the percentage of Americans (63 percent) who identified with a religious denomination. (Only 48 percent had so identified in 1940.) Lesser manifestations of this trend abounded: a new stamp issue proclaimed "In God We Trust"; "under God" was added to the pledge of allegiance; the Eisenhower administration regularly opened cabinet meetings with a prayer. Subway posters proclaimed. "Go to church. You'll feel better. Bring your troubles to church and leave them there." Capitalizing on this search for faith, the evangelist Billy Graham efficiently used modern techniques of merchandizing and salesmanship in speaking to millions during the postwar era, while Bishop Fulton J. Sheen and the Reverend Norman Vincent Peale reached out to the middle classes over the radio and in magazine columns. "Flush out all depressing, negative, and tired thoughts," Peale told his readers- in *Look* magazine. "Start thinking faith, enthusiasm, and joy."

This kind of exhortation was nothing new in the American experience, where faith in faith had long enjoyed support. Peale's "power of positive thinking" was a religious version of the quest for individualism. Nor was the search for faith strictly confined to the middle classes: the rapid growth of evangelical and fundamentalist churches during the postwar era suggested that millions of Americans, including many migratory blacks and poor whites, earnestly sought spiritual comfort amid the forces of urbanization and technological change. But the theologian Will Herberg was correct in stressing, in *Protestant Catholic Jew* (1956), that for many Americans religion had lost its theological meaning. Instead, the churches supported a "civic religion," which sustained the status quo and the "American Way of Life." Far from promoting a deeply religious Great Awakening, the search for piety often revealed a quest for social status and identity.

Like the churches, schools reflected this concern for helping people find their place in mass society. A focus on "life adjustment" challenged many earlier pedagogical theories, including the stress on the Three R's, Dewey's idea that schools could promote social reform, or the progressive hope that teachers might stimulate the latent creativity of children. Instead, schools offered subjects like "How can I look my best?" "How can I get along better with others?" and "How can hobbies contribute to my social growth?" The historian Richard Hofstadter complained that one New York community required a course in "Home and Family Living" for all children in grades seven through ten. The course featured such topics as "developing school spirit," "clicking with the crowd," and "what can be done about acne?" Other reformers worried that college youth in the 1950s had become the "Silent Generation," interested in football, fraternities, and, upon graduation, in well-paid security with General Motors, Wall Street, and Madison Avenue. Campus radicalism was so hard to detect that Kenneth Keniston, an acute observer of American youth, complained as late as 1962, "I see little likelihood of American students ever playing a radical role, much less a revolutionary one, in our society."

Hofstadter and others exaggerated the staying power of "life adjustment" in the curriculum. Indeed, exponents of rigorous academic training (who complained that students weren't "learning" anything) successfully counterattacked in the late 1950s, especially after the Soviet Union beat the United States in the race to outer space. Diatribes against campus complacency were also shortsighted, for American university students had historically shown little sustained interest in social reform. Thousands of college students in the 1950s indeed came from upwardly mobile families, and many of them were second- or third-generation Americans; higher education, they believed, was a ticket to a better life, not a place for social activism. Finally, it is clear that some critics of American education placed too much faith in the potential of schools to transcend environmental forces. Schools, after all, are rarely much different from society at large. But that was partly Hofstadter's point: schools, like churches, like corporations, seemed bent on preserving the existing order.

This focus on sustaining social stability found approving interpreters among America's leading intellectuals of the 1950s. These included the historian Daniel Boorstin and the sociologist Daniel Bell. Both welcomed what they considered the consensus of American society. In *The Genius of American Politics* (1953) Boorstin described the national experience as one in which compromise and practicality overcame ideologies and class conflicts. Bell, a prolific writer, gathered many of his essays into a volume entitled *The End of Ideology* (1960). America, he said, was a flexible, pluralistic nation in which many groups vied for position. It was a much more humane society than the Soviet Union, which vividly exposed the dangers of absolutist ideology. These defenders of "consensus" underrated the degree of ethnic, racial, and class conflict in the American past, and they falsely assumed that ideology—or at least activism—was dead. "It's like an old man proclaiming the end of sex," one youthful rebel later sneered. "Because he doesn't feel it anymore, he thinks it has disappeared."

Bell was right, however, in arguing that leftist thinkers made little headway in the 1950s. Thanks to the Cold War, and especially to Korea, the Communist and Socialist parties virtually disappeared. The Progressive party lost what little hope it had had for survival as a political force when Henry Wallace deserted it to back the Korean War. Liberal groups such as the Americans for Democratic Action continued to press for progressive domestic reforms, but they remained on the defensive against McCarthyites who branded intellectuals as "parlor pinks" or communists. Protecting itself, the ADA insisted loudly that it, too, hated the Reds. The weakness of the Left in the 1950s revealed the pervasive impact of the Cold War, the intimidating force of McCarthyism, and the dominance of "middle American" values.

AFFLUENCE

The primary support for such attitudes was the unparalleled affluence of the decade. In constant 1958 dollars the GNP had already jumped from $227 billion in 1940 to $355 billion in 1950. During the 1950s it leaped again, to $488 billion in 1960. In per capita terms this meant an increase from $1,720 in 1940 to $2,699 in 1960. (The figure was $3,555 in 1970.) It was reflected in striking advances in life expectancy, education levels, and disposable income. In the 1950s, consumer credit rose from $8.4 billion to $45 billion. Workers, who had labored an average of forty-five hours a week in the 1920s, were on the job less than forty hours by 1960. Most received annual vacations of at least two weeks. The simplest way to describe the affluence of the 1950s is to note that the average American had twice as much real income to spend (and more time to spend it in) in the mid-1950s as in the boom times of the late 1920s.

Many forces produced this growth. Among them was the willingness of the private sector to risk funds for investment. Between 1946 and 1958, when a slump hit the economy, Americans pumped an average of $10 billion per year into new plant and equipment. Another was technological change. Labor-saving devices wiped out many jobs, especially in agriculture and in such industries as textiles, where the labor force declined by more than 30 percent between 1945 and 1960. Indeed, technological unemployment disproportionally hit poor farmers, miners, and blue-collar industrial workers in the urban Northeast and Midwest. There, large regions comprising millions of people became "depressed areas." But technological advances also created jobs, especially for white-collar "service" workers. Such areas as electronics and plastics expanded phenomenally during the years between 1945 and 1960.

Economic Growth, 1950–60, Compared to Selected Years
before and after this Period

| | NATIONAL PRODUCT AND INCOME (in billions of current dollars) | | |
	GNP	PERCENT CHANGE FROM GNP OF PRECEDING YEAR (+ OR –)	DISPOSABLE PERSONAL INCOME
1929	103.1	+ 6.2	83.3
1933	55.6	− 4.2	45.5
1940	99.7	+10.2	75.7
1944	210.1	+ 9.7	146.3
1946	208.5	− 1.6	160.0
1950	284.8	+11.0	206.9
1951	328.4	+15.3	226.6
1952	345.5	+ 5.2	238.3
1953	364.6	+ 5.5	252.6
1954	364.8	+ 0.1	257.4
1955	398.0	+ 9.1	275.3
1956	419.2	+ 5.3	293.2
1957	441.1	+ 5.2	308.5
1958	447.3	+ 1.4	318.8
1959	483.7	+ 8.2	337.3
1960	503.7	+ 4.1	350.0
1970	977.1	+ 5.0	691.7
1973	1,294.9	+11.8	903.7
1978	2,107.6	+11.7	1,452

SOURCE: Adapted from Council of Economic Advisers, "Annual Report, January 1975" in *Economic Report of the President* (Washington, D.C., 1975), pp. 249, 267, 269.

The public sector played an indispensable role in promoting this prosperity. Much of the economic growth of the period stemmed from governmental expenditures for World War II and Korea. Military spending, which approached $40 billion per year in the peacetime years of the 1950s, accounted for approximately 60 percent of federal budgets and 10 percent of the GNP. Overall public expenditures — federal, state, and local — had amounted to only 10 percent of the GNP in 1929; by the mid-1950s they accounted for more than 25 percent. Governments directly employed more than 8 million people by 1957, double the number in 1940. Government work, overwhelmingly white-collar, was the fastest-growing area of the economy.

Books like Galbraith's *The Affluent Society* accurately exposed many limits to this affluence: depressed areas, slums, inadequate health care, decaying urban schools, racial injustice. The distribution of income remained inequitable; in 1955 the poorest fifth of American families earned 4.8 percent of the national income, while the top fifth earned 41.8 percent. Also, the rate of economic growth slowed down considerably late in the decade. In 1960, nearly 40 million Americans lived below a "poverty line" of $3,000 for a family of four. This was 22 percent of the population. Galbraith's *The Affluent Society* also stressed the power of consumerism. Americans, he observed, were caught in an often frantic effort to accumulate as many consumer goods—especially automobiles—as they could. This quest imposed great pressures on working families. Millions of such families ran up large debts and had to work extremely hard to maintain the ever more expensive life-styles promoted by the mass media. To a considerable extent, consumerism also obscured the needs of less fortunate Americans for tax-supported public services, most of which increased only slightly during the 1950s. Busy trying to amass personal possessions, many middle-class people tended to ignore the poor.

In pointing out these flaws, however, critics like Galbraith and others left the false impression that Americans in the 1950s were more than usually materialistic and self-centered. Historically, that is very questionable. Indeed, the truly astonishing economic growth of the 1950s (and later of the 1960s) promoted not only materialism but also a better quality of life; not only conformity (perhaps) but also the exposure to education, travel, and mass communications which widened people's range of interests; not only superficial religiosity but also (perhaps) greater tolerance of minority creeds and colors; not only mass suburbanization but also upward social and economic mobility bettering the lives of some blacks and many thousands of second- and third-generation ethnics. By 1960 the United States, the richest nation in the world, was incomparably wealthier than it ever had been. In such a new world it was hardly surprising—or necessarily unfortunate—that the quest for material comfort and personal pleasure seemed important in the culture.

THE FRUSTRATIONS OF THE RIGHT

Those who hoped for social reform found this complacency ominous indeed. As progressives were forced to recognize, people were tired of partisan controversy over domestic policies. They wanted to be left alone to enjoy their material rewards. Though Americans voted Democratic in congressional elections (even in 1956), they did not coalesce to demand progressive legislation. Like the 1920s, the decade was the despair of reformers.

In such an atmosphere McCarthyism continued to thrive. Because the GOP controlled the Congress in 1953, McCarthy became chairman of his own investigating committee, which he used to step up his accusations of communist subversion in government. His top aide, Roy Cohn, and Cohn's friend, G. David Schine, undertook a reckless and widely publicized tour of American embassies in Europe, where they searched for leftist books in government libraries and made a laughingstock of the State Department. A few books were actually burned. McCarthy cowed the new administration into permitting security checks on high-ranking employees, some of whom were forced to resign not because they were disloyal but because they were what the government now vaguely termed "security risks." Among these was J. Robert Oppenheimer, "father of the atomic bomb," whose security clearance was taken away in December 1953, on the grounds that he opposed development of the H-bomb and had associated with left-wingers in the 1930s. A newsman who returned to Washington after an extended absence in 1954 was appalled. "I let myself into the State Department," he wrote, "and there encountered a few 'Acheson holdovers' cowering in their corners. They were aged and their voices were low. But oddly enough, some of the new Republican appointees whom I met seemed to have muffled voices too. . . . it was like Vienna all over again, where we had learned to beware of eavesdroppers."

McCarthy then turned his guns on the army, which had refused to give preferential treatment to Schine, a draftee. When the army proved slow to cooperate, McCarthy exploded. "You are a disgrace to the uniform," he told Brigadier General Ralph Zwicker. "You're shielding communist conspirators. You're not fit to be an officer. You're ignorant." Attacks such as these made the hearings, which were televised in the spring of 1954, the most compelling entertainment of the year.

In making such accusations, McCarthy overreached himself. Seeing McCarthy on TV, many Americans began to realize how crude he was. Conservative supporters of the military establishment stiffened. As his appeal ebbed, the Senate roused itself against his insults. (He had described Senator Robert Hendrickson of New Jersey as a "living miracle in that he is without question the only man who has lived so long with neither brains nor guts.") In December 1954 the Senate at last voted, sixty-seven to twenty-two, to "condemn" McCarthy for bringing the Congress into disrepute. Senate Republicans split evenly on the question, with all Democrats present voting to condemn. McCarthy remained in the Senate, but he was burned out, a casualty of his exaggerations, his alcoholic tendency, and his tiresome repetitions. Three years later, at the age of forty-eight, he died.

The McCarthy–Army hearings. Senator Joe McCarthy presents "facts" to the obvious disbelief of special counsel for the Army Joseph Welch, on the left.

McCarthy's downfall, however, did not deter the extreme right wing, which became ever more shrill by the early 1960s. It included members of such superpatriotic groups as the John Birch Society and the Christian Anti-Communist Crusade. Robert Welch, founder of the John Birch Society, insisted that the Soviets were proceeding against America "on the soundest of strategy. It calls for paralyzing their enemy and their enemy's will to resist by internal subversion before ever striking a blow." Eisenhower, Welch concluded, was a "dedicated, conscious agent of the communist conspiracy."

This "Radical Right," as it was called, was much too extreme to be taken seriously by the voters. Unlike McCarthyism, which had some grass-roots support, it appealed primarily to superpatriots and reactionaries who had been ranting against "big government" since 1933. Still, by 1961, a Gallup poll reported that the goals of the John Birch Society were approved by 7 million Americans. The far Right's hostility to Big Government also had the backing of aggressive conservatives in Congress.

By mid-decade many of these men were focusing their attacks on the Supreme Court, which they said was "coddling" communists and other undesirables, including blacks. Led by Chief Justice Earl Warren, whom Eisenhower appointed to the court in 1953, the judges revealed their liberal orientation in 1954 by ruling unanimously (in *Brown* v. *Board of Education*) against public school segregation. The decision capped years of litigation by black families in several states—families that suffered abuse and economic hardship during their ordeals in the courts. "Separate educational facilities," the Court said in reversing precedents dating from *Plessy* v. *Ferguson* (1896), "are inherently unequal . . . segregation is a denial of the equal protection of the laws." The Court in 1955 then called for public school desegregation with "all deliberate speed." Outraged, Senator James Eastland of Mississippi denounced the Court's "monstrous crime. . . . These antagonistic decisions are . . . bent upon the destruction of the American form of government and the mongrelization of the white race." Nineteen southern senators and seventy-seven representatives signed a manifesto in 1956 that bound them to "use all lawful means to bring about a reversal of this decision which is contrary to the Court and to prevent the use of force in its implementation." Among southern senators only Lyndon Johnson of Texas and Estes Kefauver and Albert Gore of Tennessee refused to sign.

Having infuriated the South, the Court then aroused zealous anticommunists and advocates of "law and order." In *Service* v. *Dulles* (1957) it reinstated John Service, a State Department expert on China who had been dismissed in 1951 after six loyalty clearances. The decision forced the administration to clarify its procedures concerning so-called security risks in government. In *Mallory* v. *U.S.* (1957), it ruled that an accused rapist had been illegally charged because he had been held too long before being brought before a magistrate. Alleged criminals, the Court ruled, must be arraigned "without unnecessary delay." And in *Yates* v. *U.S.* (1956) the Court reversed the conviction of fourteen Communists jailed under the Smith Act of 1940. Mere advocacy of revolution, the Court stated, did not constitute grounds for convictions. The government must prove that defendants had "organized" revolution and that they had succeeded. The ruling caused the government to drop plans for further prosecutions of Communists.

These decisions began a judicial trend, much accelerated in the 1960s, toward stronger guarantees for accused criminals and subversives. They showed that the

Court had moved beyond the paralyzing anticommunism of the McCarthy era. The Bill of Rights, it seemed, meant what it said. But the decisions also prompted right-wingers to finance "Impeach Earl Warren" billboards along the nation's highways. Edward Corwin, professor of constitutional law at Princeton, wrote the *New York Times* to complain that the Court had gone on a "virtual binge" and "should have its aforesaid nose tweaked." Most alarming to liberal friends of the Court, a bipartisan congressional coalition almost put through legislation in 1958 that would have stripped the Court of its appellate jurisdiction in cases dealing with loyalty pro-grams, contempt of Congress, state sedition statutes, regulations of employment and oaths of allegiance in schools, and admission to state law practice. Only careful maneuvering by Majority Leader Lyndon Johnson managed the forty-nine to forty-one vote that prevented the bill from passing the Senate.

A handful of liberal Democratic senators struggled against these right-wing pressures of the 1950s. They included Hubert Humphrey of Minnesota, a crusader for civil rights; Estes Kefauver of Tennessee, who battled for curbs on monopoly and false advertising; and Paul Douglas of Illinois, an innovative reformer who de-veloped in the 1950s much of the economic legislation of Kennedy's New Frontier and Johnson's Great Society. Still influential in the national party, liberals nomi-nated a ticket composed of Stevenson and Kefauver in 1956. (Senator John F. Kennedy, less experienced and less liberal than Kefauver, sought the vice-presi-dency and failed.) The prominence of such men suggested that liberalism was not dead in the 1950s.

But it remained on the defensive. In 1956 Democrats feared to mention national health insurance in their platform. Stevenson, attempting to placate the South, exclaimed during his campaign that the federal government must not send in money or troops to enforce desegregation. "I think that would be a great mistake," he said. "That is exactly what brought on the Civil War. It can't be done by troops, or bayonets. We must proceed gradually, not upsetting habits or traditions that are older than the Republic."

Stevenson lost more heavily to Eisenhower in 1956 than he had in 1952. But if he had won, he would have had no chance of putting a liberal program through Congress. There the power lay, as it had since the Democrats won majorities in 1954, with moderates led by Johnson in the Senate and by his Texas friend, Sam Rayburn, speaker of the House. Both men were cool to liberals like Humphrey and Douglas. Even in 1959, when a band of young liberals entered Congress, and in 1961, when President Kennedy launched his New Frontier, these moderates remained in control. This "Four-Party Government," as political scientist James MacGregor Burns described the coexistence of the more conservative congressional wings of both parties with their more liberal national wings, remained a basic real-ity of American politics in the 1950s.

President Eisenhower

Dwight D. Eisenhower, who presided over these developments, was the nation's most admired war hero in 1945. Decent and accommodating, he had seemed a nonauthoritarian officer as well as a just and likable man. Truman had told him at Potsdam, "General, there is nothing that you may want that I won't try to help you get. That definitely and specifically includes the presidency in 1948."

By that time, of course, Truman had changed his mind. But many politicians of both parties yearned to nominate their hero, both then and in 1952. Like the American people, they were taken by his presence, his air of command, by what the reporter Robert Donovan called his "leaping and effortless smile." People responded also to his moderation, his balanced judgment, and his apparent aloofness from the intrigue of politics. The new president, it appeared, was heaven-sent to deliver the nation from the acrimony of the early 1950s. Like a benign father bringing peace to a quarrelsome tribe, Eisenhower seemed untouchable at the polls.

Even liberals were prepared to accept him at first. Though to the right of Stevenson, he seemed to provide a sharp contrast to the conservatives in his party who had supported Taft. This image was more appearance than reality, for the new president considered Taft socialistic on such issues as public housing and aid to education. Nevertheless, Eisenhower was apparently willing to maintain the government's active role in the economy. "Never again," he said during the campaign, "shall we allow a depression in the United States." As soon as we "foresee the signs of any recession and depression . . . the full power of private industry, of municipal government, of state government, of the Federal Government will be mobilized to see that that does not happen." This "Modern Republicanism," as his liberal supporters in the eastern wing of the party liked to call it, suggested that the GOP had left Hooverism far behind.

In the late 1960s and 1970s historians of his administration began to appreciate still another of Eisenhower's virtues. This was his shrewdness. Far from having been a placid father figure (a "counterrevolutionist entirely surrounded by men who know how to profit from it," the journalist Elmer Davis had complained in the 1950s), he seemed in retrospect to have been in purposeful control of his administration at all times. Even his convoluted syntax, which had been laughable at the time, seemed part of a deliberate plan. "Don't worry, Jim," he allegedly told his press secretary James Hagerty, who was nervous about an imminent session with

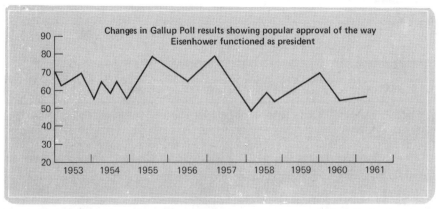

SOURCE: Adapted from *U.S. Foreign Policy: Context, Conduct, Content* by Marian Irish and Elke Frank. © 1975 by Harcourt Brace. Reproduced by permission of the publisher.

reporters. "If that question comes up, I'll just confuse them." As the liberal writer Murray Kempton put it (with some exaggeration) in 1967, Ike "was the great tortoise upon whose back the world sat for eight years. We laughed at him; we talked wistfully about moving; and all the while we never even knew the cunning beneath the shell."

Writers like Kempton, however, could not ignore qualities that prevented Eisenhower from making maximum use of his personal popularity. Among these was a passivity and lack of sophistication that astonished veteran observers in Washington. The best way to prevent selfishness in labor unions or management, he told the cabinet at one point, was to appeal to their sense of fair play. The way to deal with McCarthy was to ignore him. "I will not get into the gutter with that guy," he remarked, as if keeping himself pure would cleanse the country. Eisenhower also told political aides that he would not descend into making "idiotic promises or hints about elect-me-and-I-will-cut-your-taxes-by-such-and-such-a-date! If it takes that kind of foolishness to get elected, then let them find someone else for the job." In fact, Eisenhower was neither so unsophisticated nor so nonpartisan as he sounded. Even his handling of McCarthy—as he may have suspected—had the virtue of letting his adversary find the rope to hang himself. However, his passive approach to important questions was hardly inspiring or purposeful leadership.

This approach rested on his view that the presidency must not become too expansive. "I am not one of those desk-pounding types," he explained, "that likes to stick out his jaw and look like he is bossing the show. I don't think it is the function of a President of the United States to punish anybody for voting as he likes." He told his cabinet appointees, "You have full authority. I expect you to stand on your own two feet. Whatever you decide goes. The White House will stay out of your hair." Because big government, like large corporations, had to rely on bureaucrats and managers, his approach had the virtue of freeing him from details. But the deliberate dispersal of power led also to inertia and procrastination. Eisenhower, in I. F. Stone's words, would be a "president in absentia, with a sort of political vacuum in the White House which other men will struggle among themselves to fill."

Eisenhower's administration reflected his instinctive distaste for involving himself in the legislative process. He rarely applied pressure, and he often sounded ignorant even of important matters. After a Senate committee unanimously reported

First Person

I haven't checked these figures, but eighty-seven years ago, I think it was, a number of individuals organized a governmental setup here in this county, I believe it covered eastern areas, with this idea that they were following up based on a sort of national independence arrangement and the program that every individual is just as good as every other individual.

Liberals frequently parodied Eisenhower's inelegant syntax. This parody imagines him delivering Lincoln's Gettysburg Address.

out to the floor a significant education bill in 1954, he blurted to newsmen, "I do not know the details of that particular legislation. . . . I'd suggest you go to [HEW] Secretary [Oveta Culp] Hobby to find out where we stand." At a press conference following introduction of his Justice Department's civil rights bill in 1957 he told reporters, "I was reading part of that bill this morning, and I—there were certain phrases I didn't completely understand. . . . I would want to talk to the attorney general." No President since Coolidge had been more poorly informed about what was happening on the Hill.

His practice of paying little attention to details let aides like Sherman Adams, his chief assistant, and top cabinet officials handle many important decisions. Adams, a former governor of New Hampshire, was abrupt, flinty, as cold to self-important officials as New Hampshire granite in winter. Until 1959, when ruffled politicians drove him from power by showing that he had used his influence for personal gain, he made more enemies for Eisenhower than friends. On presidential orders, he kept many important questions from receiving top-level discussion and debate. If the "buck" stopped in the Oval Office under Truman, it often floundered in the anterooms from 1953 to 1959.

Other important decisions were left in the hands of conservative businessmen more notable for their wealth than for their political experience. Democrats, indeed, wisecracked that Eisenhower's first cabinet consisted of eight millionaires and a plumber (union leader Martin Durkin, who lasted less than a year as secretary of labor). Newsman James Reston added that "there is scarcely a member of the cabinet who can make a moving extemporaneous speech. It is humorless, obvious, unintellectual (almost anti-intellectual), and lacking in the one thing it has talked so much about—a crusading spirit."

Chief among these men, especially during the first term, were Secretary of Agriculture Ezra Taft Benson, Treasury boss George Humphrey, and Charles E. Wilson, who assumed command of the Defense Department. Benson, who served for the entire eight years of Eisenhower's presidency, was a devout Mormon who opened cabinet meetings with a prayer. He was an equally devout economic reactionary who vowed to get the government out of the business of supporting farm prices. In so doing, he hoped that marginal farmers would quit the land, overproduction would cease to be a problem, and federal aid would be unnecessary. This approach infuriated all farmers, marginal or otherwise, who demanded government assistance to 90 percent parity or more. The aroused farm bloc in Congress coalesced to defeat most of his efforts. For all Benson's persistence, overproduction escalated during the decade, and prices sagged. To keep pace, federal spending for agriculture rose from $1 billion in 1952 to $5.1 billion in 1961. Benson, like his predecessors, failed to change the course of American farm policy.

George Humphrey was an old-fashioned fiscal conservative who considered it his job to reduce spending. "We have to cut one-third out of the budget," he said in 1953, "and you can't do that just by eliminating waste. This means, wherever necessary, using a meat axe." In 1957, when Eisenhower announced a mildly expansionary budget for the coming year, Humphrey bluntly called for restraint, saying that without it "we're gonna have a depression which will curl your hair." This contradiction created total confusion over the administration's economic program until 1958.

Wilson was equally eager to cut back governmental expenditures. During the congressional elections of 1954 he went to Detroit, where thousands of unemployed were clamoring for aid, to celebrate individual initiative. "I've got a lot of sympathy for people where a sudden change catches them," he said, "but I've always liked bird dogs better than kennel-fed dogs myself. You know, one who'll get out and hunt for food rather than sit on his fanny and yell." As this remark suggests, Wilson had an affinity for impolitic statements. One, in 1953, expressed his economic philosophy: "What was good for our country was good for General Motors, and vice versa." Another avowed his belief in nuclear weaponry, chiefly because it cost less than large standing armies. "We cannot afford to fight limited wars," he said. "We can only afford to fight a big war, and if there is a war, that is the kind it will be." Appalled by such remarks, James Reston suggested that Wilson had invented the automatic transmission so he would have one foot free to put in his mouth.

Men like Wilson and Humphrey were not out of place in Eisenhower's administration. On the contrary, they reflected the President's fiscal conservatism. Ike once told the cabinet, Sherman Adams reported later, that "if he was able to do nothing as President except balance the budget he would feel that his time in the White House had been well spent." During his eight years as president, federal spending rose by only $8 billion, or 11 percent, while the population as a whole increased by approximately 18 percent. Reluctance to pursue an expansionary fiscal policy cost him dearly by the late 1950s, when his attempts to limit spending helped to promote the deepest recession since the 1930s. Unemployment, which had remained at approximately 4 percent in the peacetime years of 1955 to 1957, suddenly jumped to 6.8 percent in 1958, a figure that involved close to 5 million people. The economy continued to flounder until 1961, so badly that it caused large drops in tax revenue—which in turn created huge budget deficits. Not surprisingly, Democrats insisted that only they could "get the country moving again." Economic recession did more than anything else to harm the GOP in the election of 1960.

Random quotations from Eisenhower during the decade suggest his conservative views on other issues. On welfare: "If all Americans want is security, they can go to prison." On national health insurance: "I have been against compulsory insurance as a very definite step toward socialized medicine. I don't believe in it, and I want none of it myself." On the appointment of Warren as chief justice: "Biggest damn fool mistake I ever made." On the TVA (privately): "I'd like to sell the whole thing, but I suppose we can't go that far." On the *Brown* v. *Board of Education* ruling (publicly): "I think it makes no difference whether or not I endorse it. What I say is—the Constitution is as the Supreme Court interprets it; and I must conform to that and do my very best to see that it is carried out in this country," and (privately): "I personally think the decision was wrong."

Occasionally, of course, Eisenhower proved flexible enough to accommodate pressure groups. Reactionaries like Barry Goldwater, in fact, grumbled that he was promoting a "Dime Store New Deal." Eisenhower assented to modest increases in Social Security and in the minimum wage, and to small appropriations for public housing. In 1958 he approved the National Defense Education Act, which Congress hurried through in response to Russia's successful satellite, the Sputnik. The NDEA program provided federal aid for science and language training. In 1960 Eisenhower signed the Kerr-Mills Bill, which offered federal matching money to states that enacted their own health insurance plans for the elderly poor. And in perhaps the most important measure of his administration he signed a multibillion-dollar federal highway construction act in 1956. The measure passed because it satisfied all the important interest groups: state highway officials, who sought federal money; trade unions, who needed jobs for their members; farmers, who wanted better roads to market their goods; and city officials, who yearned for faster links with other urban centers. Unlike social welfare legislation, it commanded bipartisan majorities, for everyone thought well of the automobile. It passed Congress with ease.

The Civil Rights Movement

The quest for civil rights accelerated in the 1950s and became the most revealing test not only of Eisenhower's philosophy but also of white America in general. After the Court's rulings in 1954–55 reformers thought optimistically that a new era of race relations was at hand. But Jim Crow statutes continued to enforce racial discrimination in southern housing, transport, and public accommodations. Overtly racist organizations—Citizens Councils, White Americans, Incorporated, the Society for the Preservation of White Integrity—sprang up throughout the South. Moreover, the Court's school decisions did nothing to change the pattern of race relations in the North. There, blacks continued to face systematic job discrimination. There, too, discrimination in housing, along with racially determined school districting, had long resulted in de facto school segregation. Blacks especially resented their exclusion from white residential areas, many of which were developing modern schools to cope with the population explosion. Levittown, Pennsylvania, one of developer William Levitt's mass-produced, lower-middle-class housing projects, had 60,000 residents in 1957, not one of whom was black. That was because Levitt, fearful of "white flight" if blacks were permitted to move in, had steadfastly refused to open the development to Negroes. When a black family bought a home that year from a white owner there, sullen mobs of local residents milled about the house. A rock shattered the home's picture window. Cars, bedecked with Confederate flags, tore by noisily in the night. After two months of this kind of intimidation, the governor made it clear that he would tolerate no more such harassment, and the trouble stopped. But it was not until three years later, after blacks brought suit charging that discrimination in the sale of homes purchased with federally assisted mortgages was unconstitutional, that Levitt himself finally began selling homes directly to blacks.

Meanwhile, "massive resistance" in the South proved especially effective in stalling all efforts to end Jim Crow laws and school segregation. To subvert the Court, southern leaders employed countersuits, economic pressures, physical intimidation, and violence to stop black children from entering their white schools. Whites also resorted to a variety of legal ruses to evade the Court's rulings. One was to establish state-supported "private" schools—of course, for whites only. Another was "pupil placement" laws. These authorized local school boards to assign students to schools on the basis of their ability to adjust to new

First Person

I am convinced that the Supreme Court decision set back progress in the South at least 15 years. . . . It's all very well to talk about school integration—if you remember that you may also be talking about social disintegration. Feelings are deep on this, especially where children are involved. . . . You take the attitude of a fellow like Jimmy Byrnes. We used to be pretty good friends, and now I've not heard from him in the last eighteen months—all because of bitterness on this thing. . . . We can't demand perfection in these moral things. All we can do is keep working toward a goal and keep it high. And the fellow who tries to tell me that you can do these things by force is just plain NUTS.

Eisenhower expresses himself on the issues of school desegregation and civil rights.

surroundings, their "mental energy," or their "morals, conduct, health, and personal standards." Some of these measures even secured later legal sanction. In 1958, in *Shuttlesworth* v. *Birmingham Board of Education*, the Court upheld Alabama's pupil placement law. This ruling, permitting the white South to subvert the court's direction that desegregation take place with "all deliberate speed," enraged civil rights militants.

The modern civil rights movement, which reflected the anger and impatience of blacks at these evasions, surfaced on a broad scale in Montgomery, Alabama, in December 1955. There a black woman named Rosa Parks, tired of Jim Crow laws on the city's buses, refused to surrender her seat to a white man and was fined for breaking the law. Local black leaders responded by developing a boycott of the buses. Led by a charismatic young minister, the Reverend Martin Luther King, Jr., the city's 50,000 blacks carried out the boycott for almost a year. In doing so, they practiced nonviolent protest. The city's whites, by contrast, responded by denouncing King as a dangerous radical (he was not: he did not demand that blacks sit where they pleased, only that seating be done on a first-come, first-served basis, with blacks filling in seats from back to front and whites from front to back). Extremists went further, bombing black homes and churches.

Beset, King's followers seemed destined for defeat, especially after the courts upheld a suit brought by whites against black car pools. But King and his followers held firm, and the Supreme Court ruled in November 1956 that Alabama's laws requiring segregation on buses were unconstitutional. Shortly thereafter, following more violence by whites, the buses were finally integrated. The bus boycott marked the first large-scale, well-publicized, and successful use of direct-action tactics on behalf of civil rights in the South.

The boycott also marked the rise to national prominence of King, who thereafter spread the gospel of nonviolent protest. In the next thirteen years, King's eloquence, faith, and commitment to nonviolence provided inspirational leadership for blacks and for ever-increasing numbers of whites. Many of these people maintained ties with older, established organizations such as the NAACP and the National Urban League. But they also grew increasingly impatient with strictly

Montgomery bus boycott, 1955

legal assaults on discrimination, and they came to distrust governmental figures—judges, congressmen, politicians generally. For them, direct-action tactics such as King's were much more attractive means of protest. Their courageous activities, indeed, became the driving force behind the civil rights movement. They were necessary to prod an often reluctant and slow-moving government into trying to better race relations in America.

The President was not wholly blind to these developments. In a series of executive actions he moved to improve conditions in the District of Columbia and in military camps. In 1957, when Governor Orval Faubus of Arkansas directly defied federal authority, thereby encouraging hostile mobs to bar nine blacks from entering a previously all-white school in Little Rock, Eisenhower ultimately sent in troops to sustain token desegregation. He signed civil rights acts in 1957 and 1960, the first passed since Reconstruction. These laws established a federal commission on civil rights. They also gave the government added powers to promote equal voting rights in the South. Most important, Eisenhower's attorney general, Herbert Brownell, recommended competent, indeed courageous, men to federal judgeships in the South. In the next few years these men did much to strike down legal precedents promoting racial segregation in the South.

But Eisenhower honestly believed that changing popular attitudes must underlie government efforts to alleviate racial tensions. When it came to changing racial views, he said, "we cannot do it by cold lawmaking, but must make these changes by appealing to reason, by prayer, and by constantly working at it through our own efforts." Accordingly, he proposed no governmental attacks on racial injustice in the North and said nothing against southern violence, including the lynching of Emmett Till, a young black boy brutally murdered in Mississippi. Eisenhower's refusal to applaud the Court's decisions also encouraged the southern resistance. Indeed, Faubus acted defiantly because he assumed that the White House would do nothing to stop him. In 1958 and 1959 the governor closed Little Rock's high school altogether rather than submit again to the law of the land. As reformers had warned, the Deep South easily circumvented the civil rights acts of 1957 and 1960, which Eisenhower did nothing to promote. In his attitude toward civil rights the President revealed that he, like many contemporaries, failed to perceive the revolution in expectations that had been growing among blacks since World War II.

Popular complacency, to say nothing of the barriers posed by the Right and by Congress, would have prevented even the most charismatic of leaders from accomplishing very much during the 1950s. Therefore, Eisenhower was not alone responsible for the decade's conservative legislative record. Moreover, he proved responsible in his use of presidential power. No postwar president was as respectful of the constitutional prerogatives of Congress. Particularly in his second term, however, he failed to respond to economic stagnation, to urban blight, and especially to the movement for racial justice. Within a few years that movement escalated into militant protest that forced the hands of Eisenhower's successors.

The Cold War Continues, 1953–61

Containment, the Republican platform announced in 1952, was "negative, futile, and immoral." It abandoned "countless human beings to a despotism and Godless terrorism." The United States, the party implied, must take steps to "liberate" these downtrodden masses from their oppressors.

The atmosphere in Moscow was hardly more promising for détente. When George Kennan arrived in May 1952 to take up his duties as ambassador, he found Soviet personnel at the embassy too terrified even to help him with his bags, much less talk with him. He discovered that five guards had been assigned to follow him, that he was prevented from talking privately with people, and that his residence was electronically bugged. When he complained of such treatment, and compared Stalin's regime with Hitler's, he was declared *persona non grata* by the Soviet government. Not until the spring of 1953, when Charles ("Chip") Bohlen was finally confirmed as the new ambassador, did America get around to replacing him.

During Eisenhower's years in the White House several developments promised to soften this frigid state of affairs. Most important of these was the death of Stalin in March 1953 and his replacement by new figures, including Nikita Khrushchev, who became the major power in Russia by 1956. A gradual relaxation of tensions followed, leading to a treaty in 1955 that made Austria a neutral, independent state. Another key development was the Korean armistice in July 1953. Most important, though little realized at the time, China, Japan, and western Europe were developing into powers in their own right. By the 1960s the bipolar confrontation between Russia and America was giving way to a multiplication of power blocs.

Both nations acted sporadically to take advantage of these forces for coexistence. In 1953 Eisenhower startled hard-liners by calling for disarmament, and in 1955 he appealed for a condition of "open skies" over Russia and the United States,

America's Mood:
The Public's View
of the Most Important Problem
Facing the Country,
According to Gallup Poll Results,
1953–60

1953	Korean War
1954	Threat of war
1955	Working out a peace
1956	Threat of war
1957	Keeping out of war
1958	Economic conditions
1959	Keeping peace
1960	Relations with Russia

SOURCE: Adapted from *U.S. Foreign Policy: Context, Conduct, Content* by Marian Irish and Elke Frank. © 1975 by Harcourt Brace. Reproduced by permission of the publisher.

a proposal aimed at promoting meaningful arms control. In 1955 Russia attended a summit conference at Geneva—the first between Soviet and American heads of state since the meeting at Potsdam ten years earlier. Though the conference settled nothing, it showed that the Russians were willing to mingle with American diplomats. In 1956, when Khrushchev denounced Stalin as a "distrustful man, sickly and suspicious," and recounted his "crimes" and "tortures" while head of state, it seemed that the Soviet Union was taking a more conciliatory course.

Despite this potential for mutual understanding, relations between Russia and the United States remained cold throughout the 1950s. The Soviet suppression of the Hungarian revolution in 1956, its threats to isolate West Berlin, and finally its apparent support of revolutionary activity in Cuba and other parts of Latin America, all antagonized the Western powers. America's containment policy, which encircled Russia with naval power and military bases and which included the use of high-level reconnaisance planes to spy on Soviet territory, kept the Russians uneasy and resentful. Persistent American talk about liberating eastern Europe was more provocative still. As both sides developed hydrogen bombs and intercontinental ballistic missiles, the tension mounted.

Assigning blame for these tensions to individuals is neither easy nor especially helpful. Eisenhower and Khrushchev led societies whose fundamental differences prompted widespread feelings of insecurity and mutual distrust. Neither man enjoyed the freedom of action to end the Cold War. Indeed, as McCarthy's influence suggested, domestic obstacles to changing American attitudes remained strong. The military, defense contractors, and the leading labor unions continued to promote a tough line. Influential politicians, including Republican Senate Leader William Knowland, constantly demanded that the administration act more firmly than it did. By contrast, advocates of détente were weak and scattered, and disarmament groups such as the Committee for a Sane Nuclear Policy (SANE) seemed almost subversive. In foreign affairs, as in domestic policy, Eisenhower operated under popular, institutional, and political constraints.

In contending with these forces, however, Eisenhower named as his secretary of state John Foster Dulles, one of America's most outspoken anticommunists. The nephew of Robert Lansing, Wilson's secretary of state, and the grandson of John Foster, secretary of state under Benjamin Harrison, Dulles had been intimately involved in the making of foreign policy since 1907, when as a Princeton undergraduate he served as secretary to the Hague Peace Conference.

If Eisenhower seriously hoped for détente, he would have done well to choose someone else. For it was Dulles who drafted the "liberation" plank for the party in 1952. A stern Presbyterian, Dulles loathed "atheistic communism," and he took a moralistic approach to foreign policy. A skilled lawyer, he handled negotiations like a prosecutor in a criminal trial, not like a diplomat hoping for compromise. His rigid, humorless approach made him the butt of wits, who dubbed him "Dull, Duller, Dulles." It earned him the cordial dislike not only of the Soviets but also of many French and British statesmen of the period. He was hardly the man to promote international good will.

Dulles was acutely aware of the fate that had befallen Acheson, his predecessor, at the hands of men like McCarthy. He resolved therefore to give the Right no cause for suspicion. This meant actively supporting security investigators, who terminated the appointments of some 5,000 State Department employees by August 1953, and demoting officials who might appear to be at all "soft" on communism. Among those who were not reassigned, and who therefore retired early, was Kennan, America's foremost expert on the Soviet Union. Sherman Adams, who tried to be objective, later conceded that Dulles' "point of view was often negative" and that he had induced a "strong aversion among foreign service career men to anything imaginative and original."

With Eisenhower's support, Dulles also acted to commit the new administration to hard-line policies. In January 1953 Eisenhower inserted a section in his state of the union message calling in effect for the "unleashing" of Chiang Kaishek. It appeared to be aimed at promoting the "liberation" of mainland China from communism. In March Dulles made no effort to work for détente following the death of Stalin. At the same time he let the Chinese Communists know, again with Eisenhower's blessing, that the United States might use nuclear weapons in Korea if they did not soon agree to an armistice. When the armistice was signed in July, it appeared that his nuclear blackmail (perhaps assisted by a more moderate Soviet line following the death of Stalin) had helped to end the war.

By 1954, when he enjoyed Eisenhower's full confidence, it was clear that Dulles planned to rely on two related policies to sustain his anticommunist world view. One, which he spelled out in April, was already implicit in Secretary of Defense Wilson's policy of the "new book" — heavy dependence on nuclear weapons and strategic bombing. A potential aggressor, Dulles explained, "should know in advance that he can and will be made to suffer for his aggression more than he can possibly gain by it. This calls for a system in which local defensive strength is reinforced by more mobile deterrent power. . . . [T]he main reliance must be on the power of the free community to retaliate with great force by mobile means at places of its own choice." In simpler language this policy of "massive retaliation" meant "more bang for the buck," an approach that Russia emulated in policies dubbed "more rubble for the ruble."

The related policy, which critics labeled "brinkmanship," was part of the Eisenhower-Dulles approach from the time it was first used against the Chinese concerning Korea. Its central assumption was that unfriendly nations understood nothing but force, especially nuclear force. Therefore, the United States must be prepared to threaten war. "The ability to get to the verge without getting into the war," Dulles wrote, "is the necessary art. If you cannot master it, you inevitably get into war."

In applying these doctrines Dulles and Eisenhower paid particular attention to Asia. It was there that Republican stalwarts like Senator Knowland demanded firmness. It was there, too, that threats seemed worth making, for Asian communists lacked the nuclear might of the Soviet Union. The first test was in Indochina, where rebels were gaining in their long war against French colonialism. Responding to French pleas, the Truman administration had already pumped millions of dollars into the area. But the forces of Ho Chi Minh, a Communist who led a broad-based nationalist coalition, trapped the French at Dien Bien Phu in May 1954 and threatened to drive them out of the country.

Many high-ranking members of the Eisenhower administration joined Dulles in recommending the use of American naval and air power—perhaps including atomic weapons—to assist the French. These included Admiral Arthur Radford, chairman of the joint chiefs of staff, and Vice-President Nixon. Eisenhower, too, believed that the loss of Indochina to communism would be contagious. "You have a row of dominos set up," he observed, "and you knock over the first one, and what will happen to the last one is the certainty that it will go over very quickly. So you have a beginning of a disintegration that would have the most profound influences." Before pursuing this "domino theory," however, Eisenhower insisted that Dulles consult congressional leaders and the Allies. As Eisenhower perhaps anticipated, they rejected the idea of using American force against a popular revolutionary movement on the other side of the globe. Bowing to the inevitable after the ensuing fall of Dien Bien Phu, the United States accepted (but refused to sign) an accord worked out at Geneva. It created the countries of Laos, Cambodia, and Vietnam, the last to be divided temporarily at the seventeenth parallel pending elections in 1956 that were to determine the government of a unified nation.

To counter this loss to the West, Eisenhower embarked on what later critics termed "pactomania": formation of the South East Asia Treaty Organization later in 1954. Its signatories, the United States, Great Britain, France, Australia, New Zealand, the Philippines, Pakistan, and Thailand, contracted to consult in the event of a communist attack on one of them. A separate protocol covered Laos, Cambodia, and Vietnam. SEATO, however, did not include such important Asian nations as India, Indonesia, and Burma; it set up no military force like that which was being developed under NATO; and it required the members only to consult not to fight. It became little more than a convenient excuse for American participation in Asian affairs.

The next test of administration policy in Asia involved China, where the Nationalists, who had fled to the island of Formosa, and the mainland Communists had been threatening each other since 1950. The administration continued the futile policy of nonrecognition of Mao Zedong's regime. In 1954 Dulles also negotiated a treaty that committed the United States to defend Formosa and the neighboring Pescadore Islands against attack from the mainland. The Communists responded by lobbing shells at Quemoy and Matsu, two Nationalist-held islands close to the mainland. Eisenhower then asked Congress for blanket authority to use force in the area as he, the commander-in-chief, saw fit. This was a shrewd maneuver, for it left him armed in advance—as Truman never had been in Korea—with congressional sanction. Nine years later President Johnson was to employ a similar tactic following alleged attacks on American ships in the Tonkin Gulf. As the more avid Asia-firsters complained, however, Eisenhower's action stopped short of "unleashing" Chiang Kaishek or of adopting massive retaliation against the communists. Mao's forces bombed the islands sporadically throughout the 1950s and took the Tachens, a small group of islands north of Quemoy and Matsu, without any countermove from the United States. As in Indochina, Eisenhower stopped short of getting America's militarly involved.

The failure to dislodge Mao in China revealed the inapplicability of the "liberation" policy. Liberation proved equally futile in eastern Europe, where the Soviets tightened their control throughout the 1950s. When Poland and East Germany rebelled against Russian rule, America did nothing. In 1956, when Russian tanks quashed a revolution in Hungary, the Eisenhower administration again stood by helplessly. Liberation, like massive retaliation, was useful rhetoric for domestic political consumption. But it was too extreme to receive widespread endorsement either at home or among America's allies. And in the absence of large ground forces, which Eisenhower was cutting back, it was incredible to the communists.

Moving into Hungary would have been particularly difficult, for two days before Soviet tanks rolled into Budapest, the Western allies broke openly over policy in Egypt. In 1954, General Gamal Abdel Nasser, the nationalistic strongman who had taken over in Egypt, induced Great Britain, which controlled the Suez Canal, to remove its troops from the area by 1956. Nasser then turned to the United States, Britain, and the World Bank for a loan to build the High Aswan Dam to harness the Nile River. At first Dulles encouraged the project, which appeared settled at the end of 1955.

Nasser, however, made threatening statements to Israel, which had been a source of great irritation to the Arab world since its creation in 1948. In May 1956 Nasser recognized Communist China. He also negotiated an arms deal with Czechoslovakia, one result of which was to permit the arrival in Egypt of hundreds of Soviet technicians. To Dulles, the prospect of communist infiltration was disturbing enough, but Nasser also mortgaged Egypt's cotton crop—the nation's primary source of revenue—to pay for the arms. How, Americans asked, was Egypt to repay the loan for Aswan? Southern senators in particular complained that the United States was promoting foreign competition against American cotton. Their complaints revealed the thrust of economic considerations in postwar foreign policy. All these developments caused the United States to procrastinate in authorizing the loan. Egypt, impatient, then let it be known it would turn to the Soviet Union. This threat, however, prompted an immediate counteraction from Washington, which announced that the loan was off.

America's decision outraged Nasser, who immediately nationalized the Suez Canal and closed it to Israeli shipping. Tolls, Egypt said, would help pay for the dam. The Soviet Union then came through with the aid that Dulles had refused. Two months later, after communications between Dulles and the Western allies had all but broken down, Israeli troops stormed into the Sinai Peninsula. Britain and France, in what was obviously a well-planned move, assisted Israel.

When Russia stood behind Egypt, it looked as if World War III was on the horizon. Eisenhower, however, determined not to aid the Western allies, and America sponsored a United Nations resolution condemning Israel, Britain, and France, and proposing that UN forces be dispatched to stabilize the situation. Without American backing, the invaders had no choice but to pull out.

Eisenhower's action revealed his essential good judgment concerning military affairs. Fighting a war, even a limited one, to promote Western colonialism in Egypt would have been unwise. Indeed, he showed considerable even-handedness in dealing with the complex hatreds and rivalries of the region. But the confrontation exposed embarrassing rifts in the Western alliance, rifts that Dulles' sometimes cavalier diplomacy had helped to deepen. In the Arab world it enormously expanded the popularity of Nasser, who resented his treatment at the hands of the West. At least briefly, it enabled Russia to claim that it had come to the aid of anticolonialism in the Middle East.

The Suez crisis also exposed the Eisenhower administration's difficulties in dealing with the powerful nationalistic forces then animating the Third World. To Dulles, as to most Americans at the time, nations like Egypt were important only in terms of the Cold War. "Neutralism," he said, "was immoral." America's task was to prop up pro-Western regimes, whether dictatorial or not—not to work for social reforms. Governments that turned to the Left, as Egypt's did under Nasser, must somehow be restrained. Reflecting this view, the Eisenhower administration employed the CIA in covert operations. When Mohammed Mossadegh, prime minister of Iran, nationalized foreign oil holdings, the United States organized a coup in 1953 and returned the pro-Western shah, Mohammed Reza Pahlavi, to power. In 1954 the CIA airlifted arms and supported rebel troops who overthrew the elected regime of Jacobo Arbenz Guzmán of Guatemala. Arbenz, a leftist, had aroused the wrath of conservatives by expropriating (and offering compensation for) the uncultivated land holdings of the United Fruit Company, a major force in Central America. The overthrow of Arbenz brought a more compliant government to power, and United Fruit regained its land.

In the Middle East the Eisenhower administration attempted to preserve its influence by proclaiming the so-called Eisenhower Doctrine, approved by Congress in 1957. This promised military aid to friendly governments, thus helping to promote arms sales in that already explosive region. It also authorized Eisenhower to dispatch troops to counter communist advances. Using this authority, the President helped preserve anticommunist factions in Jordan in April 1957. In the summer of 1958 he went still further, by sending marines into Lebanon to preserve a right-wing government that was unconstitutionally clinging to power. These actions temporarily sustained Western influence in the area. They did nothing to come to terms with the forces of nationalism and reform in the Middle East.

President Eisenhower and Soviet Premier Khrushchev enjoying a light moment during Khrushchev's visit in 1959. Those sharing the joke are, from left to right: Vice-President Richard M. Nixon, UN Ambassador Henry Cabot Lodge, Jr., Eisenhower, Secretary of State Christian Herter, and Khrushchev.

Eisenhower's administration also encountered sharp anti-American feelings in Latin America. Vice-President Nixon, visiting Venezuela in 1958, was stoned as his car drove through the streets of Caracas. Cuba's Fidel Castro, relying heavily on anti-American feelings, overthrew the dictatorial regime of Fulgencio Batista in 1959. "Revolution," the president's brother Milton Eisenhower concluded in 1960, "is inevitable in Latin America. The people are angry. They are shackled to the past with bonds of ignorance, injustice, and poverty. And they no longer accept as universal or inevitable the oppressive prevailing order. . . ."

These events in Latin America symbolized the Eisenhower administration's troubled life in foreign affairs during the second term. In 1957 the Soviets electrified the world by being the first to fire a satellite into space. Americans, once, secure and arrogant in their presumed scientific superiority, reacted with surprise and shock. In 1958 Dulles grew ill (he died of cancer in 1959), and Eisenhower assumed more direct control of policy, working harder than before for détente; in 1959 Khrushchev even paid a celebrated visit to the United States, and another summit conference was scheduled for Paris in May 1960. On the eve of the conference, however, the Soviets shot down an American U-2 reconnaisance plane that had been photographing Russian installations. In this atmosphere the summit conference broke up on the very first day, and the Soviets withdrew an invitation for Eisenhower to visit Moscow later in the year. For the remainder of Eisenhower's presidency Soviet-American relations were more frigid than ever.

A summary judgment of the Eisenhower administration's foreign policy must begin by reiterating the constraints under which he had to operate: strong

pro

anticommunism among the public, economic pressures against détente, the power of the military-industrial complex, and, not the least important, Russian provocations such as the suppression of the Hungarian revolt. Moreover, Eisenhower himself ordinarily showed balanced judgment—in Vietnam, over Quemoy and Matsu, over Suez. He secured peace in Korea, and he kept the country from war for the next seven and a half years. Rhetoric aside, he continued, rather than reversed, the major policies of the Truman administration. As revisionists have rightly observed, he seems among the least bellicose of America's postwar presidents.

con

But questions remain. What if he had consistently pursued détente in the aftermath of Stalin's death? Suppose he had never named Dulles secretary of state, or, having named him, had taken command himself, as he began to do in 1958? And suppose further that he had appreciated the strivings of the Third World? If he had done these things, he might at least have succeeded in better educating the citizenry about the dangers of rocket-rattling in the nuclear age.

The End of the Eisenhower Order

John F. Kennedy's victory over Richard Nixon in the presidential election of 1960 appeared a striking repudiation of the past. After all, Kennedy was only forty-three when he took office—the first president to be born in the twentieth century, and the second youngest (next to TR) in American history. He was the first Roman Catholic

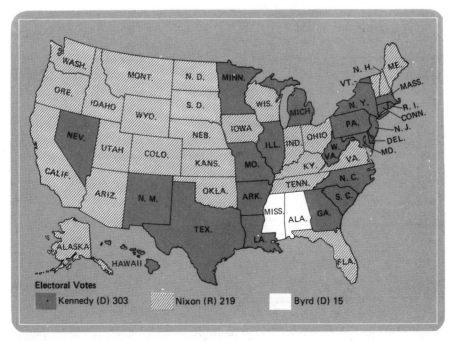

Election, 1960

First Person

In the councils of Government, we must guard against the acquisition of unwarranted influence, whether sought or unsought, by the military-industrial complex. The potential for the disastrous rise of misplaced power exists and will persist.

We must never let the weight of this combination endanger our liberties or democratic processes. We should take nothing for granted. Only an alert and knowledgeable citizenry can compel the proper meshing of the huge industrial and military machinery of defense with our peaceful methods and goals, so that security and liberty may prosper together.

Eisenhower warns against the military-industrial complex, 1961.

to be elected President: Americans, it seemed, had progressed far since repudiating Smith in 1928. Most important, he imparted an air of vigor and purpose to the country. By struggling for progressive domestic policies, he pledged to get the country moving again. He was to help the nation cross a "New Frontier."

People who expected wonders from the new President, however, would have done well to observe several aspects of the campaign. Kennedy was not the liberals' favorite—that had been either Humphrey or Stevenson, who still commanded widespread support in a third bid for the nomination. In selecting Lyndon Johnson as his running mate, Kennedy merely underlined the political caution he had displayed in four years as a representative and eight years as an uninfluential senator from Massachusetts. "I'm not a liberal at all," he told an interviewer. "I never joined the ADA [Americans for Democratic Action] or the American Veterans Committee. I'm not comfortable with those people." Reassuring conservatives, he added, "I believe in the balanced budget," except in a "*grave* national emergency or *serious* recession." Eleanor Roosevelt, speaking for many liberals who distrusted Kennedy, explained, "I would hesitate to place the difficult decisions that the next President will have to make with someone who understands what courage is and admires it, but has not quite the independence to have it."

People like Eleanor Roosevelt were especially critical of some of Kennedy's statements. In 1949 he had charged that Truman had "lost" China. "Those responsible for the tragedy of China must be searched out and spotlighted," he proclaimed. "What our young men had saved, our diplomats and presidents had frittered away." Pursuing an anticommunist line during the campaign in 1960, he berated the Eisenhower administration for its "softness" regarding Quemoy and Matsu and appealed to Cold War passions. "The enemy," he told an audience in Salt Lake City, "is the communist system itself—implacable, insatiable, unceasing in its drive for world domination. For this is not a struggle for the supremacy of arms alone—it is also a struggle for supremacy between two conflicting ideologies: Freedom under God versus ruthless, godless tyranny."

During his unprecedented television debates with Nixon—debates that probably enhanced his appeal with millions of voters who did not know him as well as Nixon—Kennedy also adopted a bellicose stance regarding Cuba's

Fidel Castro, who was pursuing an anti-American line. When Eisenhower clamped an embargo on Cuba. Kennedy complained that it was "too little too late" and that it followed an "incredible history of blunder, inaction, retreat, and failure." The United States, he proclaimed, must "strengthen the non-Batista exiles in the United States and in Cuba itself." This was a demagogic statement, for he knew that anti-Castro military forces were even then being secretly trained by the Eisenhower administration. In making it he exposed the passion for winning that critics perceived in the Kennedys. He showed that Cold War rhetoric was not the preserve of Nixon alone.

The results of the election failed also to produce much of a mandate for anyone. Kennedy did poorly in Protestant sections, where the political scientist V. O. Key detected "massive shifts" away from the Democratic ticket. Overall, his Catholicism hurt him more than it helped. Kennedy's total vote of 34.2 million exceeded Nixon's by only 118,000. Without very narrow victories in crucial states such as Pennsylvania, Missouri, and Illinois (where vote frauds in Democratic Cook County may have made the difference), Kennedy would have lost the election. And his new Congress, while nominally Democratic, had twenty additional Republicans in the House to bolster the conservative coalition.

It is hazardous to speculate on the major reasons for Kennedy's victory. Among them, however, was probably Nixon himself, who proved an energetic but unattractive candidate. Kennedy benefited also from Eisenhower's foreign policy setbacks, especially the U-2 affair. His constant focus on the nation's economic stagnation probably helped him most of all. He scored well—like many northern Democrats since the 1930s—in the populous black, ethnic, and industrial wards of urban America. He carried twenty-seven of the nation's forty-one largest cities, including all the biggest ones, where he rolled up a plurality of 2.7 million votes. This continuity in voting patterns reveals that Eisenhower's triumphs in 1952 and 1956 had been aberrations attributable to his unique personal appeal, and that Kennedy won because normally Democratic America reverted to form.

For these reasons the election suggested important continuities with the past. The nation remained essentially Democratic, as it had since Franklin D. Roosevelt perfected the art of blaming Hoover for the world's problems. It remained divided, though less so than earlier, along religious lines. It responded, or so it seemed, as strongly as ever to appeals for fiscal conservatism, and to candidates of the political center. And it listened as attentively as before to inflammatory Cold War rhetoric. For all the talk about a New Frontier, it was fair to say in 1960, as it had been in 1952, that America, affluent and middle-class, still yearned as much for stability and consensus as for dramatic change.

Suggestions for Reading

A well-written survey of aspects of American life since 1945 is William Leuchtenburg. *A Troubled Feast** (1973). See also Marty Jezer, *The Dark Ages: Life in the U.S., 1945–1960* (1982); and a somewhat opposing view of the 1950s by William O'Neill, *American High* (1986). J. Ronald Oakley, *God's Country: America in the Fifties* (1986), is excellent. Books on the economy include John Brooks, *The Great Leap** (1966); Michael Harrington, *The Other America** (1962), a vivid account of

*Available in a paperback edition.

poverty: James Patterson, *America's Struggle Against Poverty, 1900–1985* (1986); and David Potter, *People of Plenty** (1954), a wide-ranging book concerning the effect of abundance on the American character. Two books by John Kenneth Galbraith offer challenging accounts of American economic life: *American Capitalism** (1952) and *The Affluent Society** (1958). Richard Polenberg's *One Nation Divisible: Class, Race, and Ethnicity in the United States Since 1938* (1980), is valuable, as is Richard Pells, *The Liberal Mind in the Conservative Age* (1986). See Godfrey Hodgson, *America in Our Time: From World War II to Nixon* (1976), a provocative interpretive account of the era.

Social trends are the subject of Elaine Tyler May, *Homeward Bound: American Families in the Cold War* (1988); Landon Jones, *Great Expectations: America and the Baby Boom Generation* (1980); Robert Wood, *Suburbia** (1959); Kenneth Jackson, *The Crabgrass Frontier* (1985), a sweeping history of American suburbs; Scott Donaldson, *The Suburban Myth** (1969); and William Whyte, *Organization Man** (1956). Like Whyte and Porter, David Riesman, et al., discuss the American national character in the provocative *Lonely Crowd** (1950). Books dealing with aspects of thought and culture in the 1950s include Thomas Hine, *Populuxe* (1986), on design; Lary May, ed., *Recasting America: Culture and Politics in the Age of the Cold War* (1989), a collection of essays; George Lipsitz, *Class and Culture in Cold War America* (1982); James Baughman, *The Republic of Mass Culture: Journalism, Filmmaking, and Broadcasting Since 1941* (1992); Erik Barnouw, *Tube of Plenty: The Evolution of American Television* (1975); Lawrence Lipton, *The Holy Barbarians* (1959), on the "beats"; Sam Hunter and John Jacobus, *American Art of the Twentieth Century* (1974); and Richard Kostelanetz, ed., *The New American Arts* (1971). Barbara Ehrenreich, *Hearts of Men: American Dreams and the Flight from Commitment* (1983) is a spirited set of essays on cultural trends.

For religious trends see Will Herberg, *Protestant Catholic Jew** (1960), a challenging sociological analysis of modern American religion; Digby Baltzell, *The Protestant Establishment: Aristocracy and Caste in America** (1964); William McLoughlin, *Billy Graham* (1960); Richard Fox, *Reinhold Niebuhr* (1985); and David Harrell, *All Things Are Possible* (1975), on faith healers and evangelical religion. C. Wright Mills offers a sharp critique of American society in *White Collar** (1951); and *Power Elite** (1956). Conservative attacks on urban policies are Edward Banfield, *The Unheavenly City Revisited** (1974); and Martin Anderson, *The Federal Bulldozer* (1974). But see also Herbert Gans, *The Urban Villagers** (1962). For educational trends see Diane Ravitch, *Troubled Crusade* (1983) on education, 1945–80; Raymond Wolters, *The Burden of Brown: Thirty Years of School Desegregation* (1984); and David J. Armor, *Forced Justice: School Desegregation and the Law* (1995). For aspects of postwar science and medicine see Paul Starr, *The Social Transformation of American Medicine* (1982); John Burnham, *How Superstition Won and Science Lost: Popularizing Science and Health in the United States* (1987); and James Patterson, *The Dread Disease: Cancer and Modern American Culture* (1987).

Studies of politics in the 1950s include Stephen Ambrose, *Eisenhower* (2 vols., 1983–84); Charles Alexander, *Holding the Line: The Eisenhower Era, 1952–1961* (1975); Herbert Parmet, *Eisenhower and the American Crusades* (1972); James Patterson, *Mr. Republican: A Biography of Robert A. Taft* (1972); and James

Sundquist, *Politics and Policy: The Eisenhower, Kennedy, and Johnson Years** (1968). Fred Greenstein, *The Hidden Hand Presidency* (1982), attempts to refurbish Eisenhower's reputation. See also Robert Ferrell, ed., *Eisenhower Diaries* (1981). Books on political trends are Samuel Lubell, *The Revolt of the Moderates* (1956); Norman Nie, et al., *The Changing American Voter* (1979); and Edwin Diamond and Stephen Bates, *The Spot: The Rise of Political Advertising on Television* (1992).

For the civil rights revolution consult Harvard Sitkoff, *The Struggle for Black Equality, 1954–1992* (1993); Robert Weisbrot, *Freedom Bound: A History of America's Civil Rights Movement* (1990); Taylor Branch, *Parting the Waters: America in the King Years, 1954–1963* (1988); and Branch, *Pillar of Fire: America in the King Years, 1963–1965* (1998); Steven Lawson, *Black Ballots: Voting Rights in the South, 1944–1969* (1976); Charles Eagles, ed., *The Civil Rights Movement* (1986); Juan Williams, ed., *Eyes on the Prize: America's Civil Rights Years, 1954–1965* (1987); John Dittmer, *Local People: The Stuggle for Civil Rights in Mississippi* (1994); and J. Harvie Wilkinson, *From Brown to Bakke: The Supreme Court and School Integration, 1954–1978* (1980). Other relevant books on the court are Bernard Schwartz, *Super Chief* (1983), on Earl Warren; Morton Horwitz, *The Warren Court and the Pursuit of Justice* (1998); Kluger, cited in the bibliography for Chapter 11; G. Theodore Mitau, *Decade of Decision . . . 1954–1964* (1968); and Paul Murphy, *The Constitution in Crisis Times, 1918–1969* (1972). Books on Martin Luther King include David Lewis, *King* (1970); and David Garrow, *Bearing the Cross* (1986). Southern resistance is covered in Numan Bartley, *The Rise of Massive Resistance* (1966); and Neil McMillen, *Citizens' Council* (1971). See also Howard Zinn, *SNCC* (1964); Clayborne Carson, *In Struggle* (1981), on the SNCC; and William Chafe, *Civilities and Civil Rights* (1980), on race relations in Greensboro.

Useful books on foreign policy include Gregg Herken, *Counsels of War* (1985); Richard Immerman, *The CIA in Guatemala* (1982); Douglas Kinnard, *President Eisenhower and Strategy Management* (1977); Robert A. Divine, *Eisenhower and the Cold War* (1981); Stephen Rabe, *Eisenhower and Latin Amnerica* (1987); Justus Doenecke, *Not to the Swift: The Old lsolationists in the Cold War Era* (1979); Seyon Brown, *Faces of Power: Constancy and Change in U.S. Foreign Policy from Truman to Johnson** (1968); Townsend Hoopes, *The Devil and John Foster Dulles* (1973); and the books on the Cold War cited at the end of the previous chapters. See also David Wise and T. B. Ross, *The U-2 Affair* (1962); J. C. Campbell, *In Defense of the Middle East* (1960); and Henry Kissinger, *The Necessity for Choice** (1961), on military policies. Two books dealing with the CIA are L. B. Kirkpatrick, *The Real CIA* (1968); and the less flattering account by Davis Wise and T. B. Ross, *The Invisible Government** (1964).

Two books on the rise of the space program are Tom Wolfe, *The Right Stuff* (1979), a brilliantly written account; and Walter McDougall, *. . . The Heavens and the Earth* (1985), a broad historical treatment. Robert Divine, *Blowing in the Wind: The Nuclear Test Debate, 1954–1960* (1978) is a solid account of its subject.

John Kennedy and son, 1963

4

The 1960s: From Altruism to Disenchantment

Many idealists found the early 1960s the most exciting time in modern American history. Young civil rights activists were staging interracial sit-ins and freedom rides. The Reverend Martin Luther King, Jr., was dramatizing the crusade for racial justice. The folksinger Bob Dylan was composing memorable ballads for peace and justice. Chief Justice Earl Warren was leading the Supreme Court toward breakthrough decisions broadening the Bill of Rights. And John F. Kennedy, youthful, energetic, articulate, was in the White House. Despite his assassination in November 1963, many progressives kept the faith, and under Lyndon Johnson's leadership they enacted a remarkably wide-ranging body of reforms in 1964 and 1965. The 1960s, it seemed, were to witness the triumph of social justice in America.

The New Frontier

Kennedy's upbringing offered clues to anyone who wished to predict his behavior as president. His maternal grandfather had been a colorful mayor of Boston; his paternal grandfather, a politically active saloonkeeper. Both had been upwardly mobile Irish Catholics eager to gain acceptance in America. Kennedy's father, Joseph, made millions in a variety of speculative endeavors, contributed generously to the Democratic party, and was rewarded with the coveted ambassadorship to Great Britain. Fiercely competitive, Joseph instilled his own energy and ambition in his children. As president, Kennedy was to exalt activity and vigor almost as ends in themselves and to insist that the United States compete strenuously against its enemies. Though fatalistic in many ways—he thought of himself as an "idealist without illusions"—he clothed his doubts in an altruistic rhetoric that captured the mood of the time. "Ask not what your country can do for you," he proclaimed. "Ask what you can do for your country."

a- unselfishly concerned

In seeking to implement his goals Kennedy deliberately rejected Eisenhower's low-key approach. He revealed—at least in his rhetoric—that he planned to use all the tools at his command and that opponents could expect retaliation from the White House. Kennedy replaced Eisenhower's businessmen with a corps of academicians, intellectuals, and dynamic younger executives, and he rejected the staff system. "Whereas Eisenhower wanted decisions brought to him for approval," one political scientist has written admiringly, "Kennedy wanted problems brought to him for decision."

Such an administrative style had obvious pitfalls. The reporter Joseph Kraft thought that Kennedy, like Truman, was rather too fond of action for action's sake. The President's "bang-bang" style, he complained, "favors people who know exactly what they want to do. It is tough on people who have dim misgivings—even if those misgivings happen to be very important." But most observers praised the new president's methods. Under Eisenhower, I. F. Stone wrote, "Teamwork was conducted much in the manner of a football game—frequent huddles, great attention to coordinating everybody, and interminable periods spent catching breath between plays." Kennedy's approach, by contrast, resembled basketball. "Everybody is on the move all the time. . . . The President may throw the ball in any direction, and he expects it to be kept bouncing."

Reporters responded especially favorably to Kennedy's sense of humor. Told of Vatican unhappiness with his politics, the President quipped, "Now I understand why Henry the Eighth set up his own church." When people grumbled that his brother Robert was too young to be attorney general, he joked that Bobby might as well get some experience before practicing law. Reporters also welcomed his mental quickness and his accessibility, and people who saw him on television were immediately struck by his poise and good looks. In the TV age of the 1960s, when style and image frequently counted for as much as substance, Kennedy enjoyed great advantages.

These assets appeared to help in his dealings with a still-conservative Congress. In early 1961 his followers in the House succeeded, by the narrow margin of 217 to 212, in liberalizing the obstructive Rules Committee. Later, Congress increased the federal minimum wage, set aside funds for manpower training and area redevelopment, and passed a trade expansion act that promised to lower tariffs throughout the industrialized noncommunist world. Before his death the House approved a multibillion-dollar tax cut, which the Senate passed early in 1964. This was a Keynesian measure that deliberately risked short-term budgetary deficits in the hope of promoting purchasing power. Kennedy's conversion in 1962 to the "New Economics" was the most striking manifestation of his gradual receptiveness to unorthodox ideas.

Kennedy also kept his promise to pull the country out of its economic slump. Increases in defense spending pumped new billions into the economy. So did his program to place a man on the moon: by 1969, when Neil Armstrong got there, the government had spent some $25 billion on space exploration. In part because of these expenditures, an upswing in the economy developed in 1961 and lasted until the early 1970s—the longest uninterrupted period of growth in modern American history. During this time the number of Americans living below the poverty line dropped from 40 million to around 25 million people. Though these unprecedented advances did not change the maldistribution of income, they were widely hailed. By developing faith in the government's ability to promote socioeconomic change, these impressive gains smoothed the way for Johnson's Great Society programs in 1964–65.

Though most liberals favored the tax cut, they observed that it was part of a generally cautious economic policy. During his tenure Kennedy made no serious effort to plug notoriously large loopholes in the tax laws. He worked harder for increases in defense spending than for social welfare. He encouraged Congress to enact tax breaks for big business. Even the tax cut, John Kenneth Galbraith grumbled, was "reactionary Keynesianism" that helped people spend more on unnecessary gadgetry. "I am not sure what the advantage is," he said, "in having a few more dollars to spend if the air is too dirty to breathe, the water too polluted to drink, the commuters are losing out on the struggle to get in and out of the cities, the streets are filthy, and the schools so bad that the young, perhaps wisely, stay away, and hoodlums roll citizens for some of the dollars that they save in taxes."

By late 1963 reformers were recognizing the limitations of other New Frontier laws. Efforts for tariff reduction, for instance, foundered amid disagreements among the Western allies. The manpower training program could barely keep pace with technological change, and it had no effect on hard-core poverty—a problem neglected until the end of Kennedy's presidency. Area redevelopment encountered opposition from business interests, which protested the granting of aid to potential competitors, and from labor leaders, who complained when federal money went to nonunion employers. In 1963, only two years after passage of the act, these pressure groups succeeded in killing a proposed increase in funds for the program.

Congress prevented many other measures from passing at all. These included medicare, federal aid to education, funds for mass transit, and creation of the Department of Urban Affairs. Some people thought that the lawmakers might be

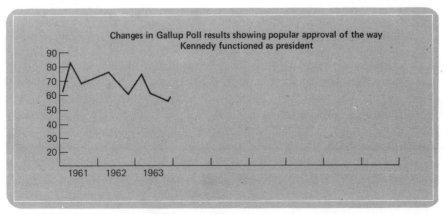

SOURCE: Adapted from p. 104 of *U.S. Foreign Poilcy: Context, Conduct, Content* by Marian Irish and Elke Frank. © 1975 by Harcourt Brace. Reproduced by permission of the publisher.

Kennedy's popularity reached a peak in mid-1961, when 83 percent of respondents approved of his presidency. He reached a low of 57 percent shortly before his assassination in 1963.

more responsive in 1964, an election year. But at the time of Kennedy's death the legislative logjam seemed as imposing as in the 1950s. The *New York Times* commented: "Rarely has there been such a pervasive attitude of discouragement around Capitol Hill and such a feeling of helplessness to deal with it. This has been one of the least productive sessions of Congress within the memory of most of its members."

Those who blamed Kennedy for this unproductive record were a little unfair. Like Truman before him, he lacked three advantages necessary for success on Capitol Hill: reliable progressive majorities, the support of pressure groups, and a popular mandate as expressed at the polls. Congressmen, accordingly, paid more attention to well-organized constituents than to presidential persuasion. "You can twist a fellow's arm once or even twice," a Kennedy aide explained. "But the next time he sees you coming he starts to run."

Kennedy's efforts on behalf of a bill for aid to education revealed the power of these forces. As Kennedy well knew, opponents included many Republicans and southern Democrats. Some of them objected to spending large sums of money for social programs; others feared that government aid would lead to federal dictation of curricula. In packing the House Rules Committee in early 1961, the President weakened these conservatives at their main bastion of defense. He also dissuaded Representative Adam Clayton Powell, a Harlem congressman, from attaching his antisegregation amendment to the bill. A similar provision, which denied aid to segregated schools, had forced almost all southerners, liberal or conservative, into opposing aid to education in the 1950s.

With these obstacles surmounted, Kennedy ran into yet another pressure group: the Catholic Church. As a Catholic, he felt he had to deny aid to parochial and private schools. Otherwise, angry Protestants would have accused him of religious favoritism. This decision, however, led prominent Catholic churchmen to oppose the bill. After much maneuvering, the measure sank under such pressure. Only later, in the more ecumenical spirit of the mid-1960s—and under a Protestant president who favored aid to parochial schools—did the bill command sufficient support to pass.

Kennedy's relations with influential spokesmen for big business provided another example of the way in which pressure groups could stymie presidential power. The President took office hoping to conciliate corporate leaders. "I'm not against business," he said. "I want to help them if I can." To prove his point, he named Douglas Dillon, a prominent banker who had been undersecretary of state in the Eisenhower administration, as secretary of the treasury, and Robert McNamara, head of the Ford Motor Company, as secretary of defense. But many business leaders remained uneasy, and when prices dipped on the stock market, they were quick to blame the White House. Annoyed, Kennedy commented, "I understand every day why Roosevelt, who started out such a mild fellow, ended up so ferociously antibusiness. It's hard as hell to be friendly with people who keep trying to cut your legs off."

His struggle with steel executives in 1962 merely intensified this hostility. This controversy began when Roger Blough, head of U.S. Steel, raised prices in defiance of an understanding previously reached with the White House. Other large steel companies followed Blough's example. Angry, Kennedy bared the weapons of the

"Kennedy bending steel," referring to his struggle with U.S. Steel in 1962.

modern presidency. Antimonopolists in Congress, led by Kefauver, threatened an investigation. The Federal Trade Commission announced it would look into price agreements among large producers. McNamara implied that the Defense Department might deny contracts to corporations that refused to cooperate with Washington. The FBI appeared to be using its formidable powers to gather information against Blough's allies. Kennedy himself made it clear that he would have to review his policies favoring generous tax allowances to business. He observed, "My father always told me that all businessmen were sons of bitches, but I never believed it 'til now." Shortly after this display of strength Blough backed down slightly.

Kennedy's actions, while well orchestrated, were not by themselves so potent as they appeared. Blough's retreat stemmed less from fear of the administration (though that mattered) than from the decision of Inland Steel, a dangerous competitor, to keep its prices at existing levels and therefore to bid for a larger share of the market. Inland's action—in part the result of Kennedy's responses—showed that some competitive pressures existed even in an industry as oligopolistic as steel. But Inland's role also revealed that Big Government and the presidency needed outside help to get their way. In this regard the confrontation offered a clear example of the institutional obstacles facing elected officials.

As if these obstacles were not burden enough, Kennedy had personal liabilities that hurt his chances on the Hill. Some congressmen remembered him as a former colleague who had spent as much time socializing and promoting his personal ambition as he had fulfilling the duties of committee work. For these reasons he had never been an "insider" in Congress. Others sensed correctly that he was much more interested in foreign affairs than in domestic policy and that he found many congressmen long-winded and boring. As James Reston pointed out, Kennedy disliked "blarneying with pompous congressmen and simply would not take the time to do it." Still others were put off by the elitist tone of his administration. "All that Mozart string music and ballet dancing down there," one congressman remarked, "and all that fox hunting and London clothes. He's too elegant for me." This populistic reaction to Kennedy's style showed that hostility to the Eastern Establishment—an ill-defined entity—remained a force in American politics. It suggested further that the very traits assisting the president in his dealings with the media and with eastern urban elites could become liabilities in managing Congress.

Kennedy also showed rather less forcefulness than he had led some progressives to expect. Always a pragmatic politician, he shied away from promoting controversial programs. "There is no sense in raising hell and then not being successful," he said. This caution led him to rely on congressional magnates like Speaker of the House Sam Rayburn or Senators Richard Russell of Georgia and Everett Dirksen of Illinois, the GOP leader. By avoiding confrontations, he hoped to win the massive victory in 1964 that might give him the mandate he needed.

The Revolution in Civil Rights

Progressives found Kennedy particularly cautious in the area of civil rights, where dramatic and far-reaching events were already outdistancing the politicians. In February 1960 black students in Greensboro, North Carolina, had kicked off a new, more militant phase of the civil rights movement by sitting down at a segregated lunch counter and refusing to move until served. After an hour the management closed the counter, and the students left. Their forthright action, reminiscent of the sit-ins conducted by blue-collar workers in the 1930s, quickly attracted the attention of other southern blacks and of liberal whites. Within weeks, members of the three large militant civil rights groups—King's Southern Christian Leadership Conference, the rapidly growing Congress of Racial Equality (CORE), and the newly formed Student Nonviolent Coordinating Committee (SNCC)—were conducting similar sit-ins throughout the South. More militant than the older, established organizations such as the NAACP and the Urban League, these impatient groups rejuvenated the movement for civil rights.

This militancy intensified and spread during the years of Kennedy's presidency. As early as May 1961 CORE activists began staging integrated "freedom rides"

America's Mood:
The Public's View of the Most Important
Problem Facing the Country,
According to Gallup Poll Results,
1961–63

1961	Prices and inflation
1962	War, peace, and international tensions
1963	Racial problems

SOURCE: Adapted from *U.S. Foreign Policy: Context, Conduct, Content* by Marian Irish and Elke Frank. © 1975 by Harcourt Brace. Reproduced by permission of the publisher.

into the South in order to desegregate transportation facilities. Angry mobs stoned their buses, set them afire, and beat the demonstrators. Southern authorities arrested the freedom riders, while federal authorities, fearful of further mob action, acquiesced. Though the freedom rides, like the sit-ins, largely failed to achieve the immediate goal of striking down Jim Crow, they exposed again the extremism of southern whites and steeled the resolve of the civil rights crusaders.

Of the many protests and demonstrations that broke out in the South during the next two years, two were especially dramatic. The first involved the effort in 1962 of James Meredith, a black man, to enroll as a student at the University of Mississippi. Meredith was challenged by Governor Ross Barnett and by angry crowds of

Water hoses against nonviolence: Civil rights protesters in Birmingham, Alabama, 1963

whites, who went on a rampage of protest in September. In a night of violence on the campus, two people were killed and 375 injured, including 166 federal marshals belatedly sent in to prevent trouble. Barnett's demagogic stand, like that of Alabama governor George Wallace, revealed the presumed political advantages to be reaped by overtly racist white politicians in the South.

The other demonstration, in Birmingham in April 1963, was a milestone in the history of the American civil rights movement. The protest was carefully planned by King and other leaders. Civil rights workers trained volunteers in the techniques of nonviolence and schooled them (through staged "sociodramas") to endure verbal abuse and beatings. The protesters then engaged in weeks of peaceable marches, sit-ins, and pray-ins. When arrests thinned their ranks, schoolchildren filled their places. If southern whites had employed restraint, they might have outlasted the demonstrators. But local authorities led by Eugene ("Bull") Connor lost their patience, repelling the nonviolent activists with cattle prods, high-pressure water hoses, and dogs. The ferocity of Connor's countermeasures, shown to nationwide television audiences, unleashed a wave of revulsion throughout the country and immeasurably aided King's cause. Shortly afterward, white authorities in Birmingham agreed to desegregate stores and to upgrade some black workers.

Many forces combined to unleash this activist phase of the movement. Basic to the activism was the impatience of southern blacks, whose expectations had escalated following the Brown decisions in the 1950s, and whose rage was intense. Angry and idealistic, they were impatient with what they considered the calculations of the politicians and the legalism of groups such as the NAACP. Led skillfully by King and others, they received much support from the churches, from the federal courts, and from increasing numbers of whites, many of whom were moved by religious commitments. The protesters benefited—especially at Birmingham—from TV. "Before television," an NBC official exclaimed, "the American public had no idea of the abuses blacks suffered in the South. We showed them what was happening: the brutality, the police dogs, the miserable conditions. . . . We made it impossible for Congress not to act." This statement, while exaggerated, was accurate in pointing to the need of King and his allies to secure the backing of white liberals in the North.

Overtaken by these events, Kennedy seemed vaguely sympathetic with the movement. During the 1960 campaign he had insisted that a presidential "stroke of the pen" could wipe out racial discrimination in federally supported housing. He had helped get Martin Luther King, Jr., out of jail in Georgia—an act that solidified his vote among blacks in the North. Once in office, he appointed blacks to important offices—such as Robert Weaver as head of the Housing and Home Finance Agency, and Thurgood Marshall, a top NAACP lawyer, to a judgeship on the United States Circuit Court. When confronted by recalcitrant governors like Barnett and Wallace, he reluctantly used federal authority. The Justice Department, under his brother Robert, successfully attacked segregation in southern airports, and it brought more suits in support of voting rights than the Eisenhower regime had done since passage of the Civil Rights Act of 1957.

But the Kennedys remained too cautious to suit the activists. Forgetting the rhetoric of the 1960 campaign, the President waited until after the midterm elections of 1962—by which time hundreds of pens had been sent to him through the mail—to issue his order against discrimination in housing. The order, carefully limited and gently applied, had little impact. Bowing to men like James Eastland of Mississippi, chairman of the Senate Judiciary Committee, he appointed several segregationists to southern judgeships. And he disappointed activists by refusing to introduce a civil rights bill. "When I feel that there is a necessity for a congressional action, with a chance of getting that congressional action," he said in early 1961, "then I will recommend it to the Congress." For the next two years he adhered to this opportunistic course.

Con

By mid-1963 the actions of men like Bull Connor forced Kennedy to take a stronger stand. He did so for several reasons. One was revulsion: during the trouble at Birmingham he remarked that a photograph of a German shepherd leaping at a black woman made him "sick." He also had practical reasons for acting. The trouble, he recognized, harmed America's image abroad. It threatened to move beyond his control, perhaps into wholesale racial violence throughout the country. When Alabama authorities in June 1963 refused to register two black students who sought to enter the university, he decided he had to act. In a nationwide TV address, he called for a federal civil rights law to attack racial injustice. Congress, he implored, must see to it that "race has no place in American life or law."

As Kennedy had foreseen, however, Congress was in no hurry to respond. Indeed, southern senators clearly planned an all-out filibuster against the bill. Restless blacks then determined to "march on Washington." Worried about violence, Kennedy tried to discourage the demonstrators from marching; failing in that effort, he labored hard behind the scenes to minimize the role of the most

Martin Luther King, Jr., tells the throngs attending the 1963 march on Washington, "I have a dream. . . ."

militant members of the march. In that quest he was largely successful, and the 200,000 who assembled remained true to the cause of nonviolence. The highlight of the event was the impassioned, memorable speech by King pressing the goal of racial integration, and focusing on his "dream" of the future. "I still have a dream" he exclaimed. "It is a dream chiefly rooted in the American dream." He anticipated that "one day on the red hills of Georgia, the sons of former slaves and the sons of former slave owners will be able to sit together at the table of brotherhood."

Even in these last months of his life, however, Kennedy failed to grasp the intensity behind the drive for racial justice. His proposed civil rights bill was moderate. It limited the Justice Department's injunctive powers against racial discrimination to the areas of schools. Its public accommodations section affected only those enterprises having a "substantial" impact on interstate commerce. Recognizing these loopholes, progressives in the House toughened the bill by authorizing the attorney general to intervene in any civil rights suit initiated by private parties. It was this tougher bill, not Kennedy's milder version, that the House passed in January 1964, two months after the assassination in Dallas.

Both then and later, many observers criticized Kennedy for his caution concerning civil rights (and other domestic reforms). To a degree, these critics underestimated the formidable political obstacles facing him, especially in Congress before mid-1963. As late as March of that year—before the demonstrations in Birmingham—almost all people agreed that Congress would have hotly resisted any civil rights proposal. In moving cautiously Kennedy probably was in tune with majority opinion. Moreover, he proved flexible enough to change in 1963. At that time he not only pushed for civil rights legislation but also set his staff to work on proposals that ultimately—in the hands of President Johnson— emerged as a "war against poverty." He could justifiably argue that his rhetoric for a New Frontier helped develop popular support for domestic reforms that were passed later.

Of course, he never got the chance to prove what he might have done later. Moreover, it was not surprising that activists grew impatient. Kennedy, they said, was not so much altruistic as manipulative. He displayed more style than substance, more profile than courage. His rhetoric, other critics added, aroused exaggerated hopes and ultimately weakened the credibility of government. Though these criticisms were harsh, they revealed the disenchantment of many people late in 1963. Kennedy, James Reston concluded, had "touched the intellect of the country but not the heart."

New Frontiers Abroad

Perhaps no twentieth-century president was readier than Kennedy to engage the nation in world affairs. "Let every nation know," he proclaimed, ". . . that we shall pay any price, bear any burden, . . . support any friend, oppose any foe to assure the survival . . . of liberty." Confident about his expertise in the realm of foreign policy, he accelerated the centralization of policy making in the White House, where McGeorge Bundy, a former Harvard dean, expanded the role of national security adviser. Kennedy's secretary of state, Dean Rusk, was expected to have a lesser part. Bundy and Rusk, like Kennedy himself, tended to approach the world in the dualistic terms of the Cold War. "Our first great obstacle," Kennedy said, "is still our relations with the Soviet Union and China. We must never be lulled into believing that either power has yielded its ambitions for world domination."

Kennedy's globalism, his anticommunism, and his self-assured activism led him into one of the greatest blunders in the history of American foreign relations: the attempt in April 1961 to overthrow Fidel Castro in Cuba. The reasons for this decision seemed compelling enough beforehand. By 1961 Castro was welcoming Soviet aid and influence. Eisenhower's administration had been training anti-Castro exiles in Guatemala—clearly, Kennedy felt, the military training should be made use of. The Central Intelligence Agency under Allen Dulles (John Foster's brother) warned that it was "now or never" in the struggle against Castro's growing power in Latin America. Dulles outlined a plan calling for American logistical support of an invasion by the exiles. Anti-Castro guerillas in Cuba, the CIA thought, would rise in support of the invasion and topple the regime. When the Joint Chiefs of Staff supported the CIA's argument, the administration had every reason to anticipate success.

A few people expressed doubts about the wisdom of the plan. Among them were Senator J. William Fulbright, head of the Senate Foreign Relations Committee, and Marine Commandant David Shoup. Castro, Fulbright said, was a thorn in the flesh but not a dagger in the heart. Shoup was more dramatic. He prepared an overlay map of Cuba and laid it on one of the United States. It showed that Cuba stretched some 800 miles, from New York to Chicago; clearly, it could not be conquered quickly. Shoup then placed a second overlay on the others. It was of a tiny island. What is that? he was asked. "That, gentlemen," he replied, "represents the island of Tarawa [where Shoup had won a Medal of Honor in World War II] and it took us . . . 18,000 marines to take it." The military lesson could not have been more obvious.

Kennedy's top people, however, were activists by temperament. Placing great faith in America's superior technological capacity, they assumed that a preinvasion air strike would wipe out Castro's defenses and assure the success of the landing. They also thought that an invasion would unleash popular discontent with the government. These characteristically American attitudes—exaggerated faith in technology, blindness to nationalism in the Third World—left Fulbright and Shoup without significant support. With little hesitation, the National Security Council approved the plan on April 4.

The invasion—at the Bay of Pigs on April 17—was an unrelieved disaster. The open movement beforehand of exiles both in Guatemala and in Florida made it easy for Castro to anticipate the attack. Moreover, the air strike failed to destroy Castro's air force. With only six operational fighters he was able to knock out five of twelve planeloads of paratroopers, to strafe ground troops, and to disable a munitions ship loaded with exile soldiers. A few top officials then tried to persuade Kennedy to authorize the use of American planes as air cover. Kennedy refused, for he knew it was too late to salvage success. Castro then mopped up the remaining invaders.

The New Frontiersmen showed a less bellicose side on other foreign questions in 1961 and 1962. The Kennedy administration promoted an Alliance for Progress in the Western Hemisphere. The Alliance promised to outlay some $20 billion by 1970 in American aid for social and economic programs. Other priorities, among them the war in Vietnam, later prevented the program from amounting to much. But Kennedy's apparent hostility to right-wing elites in Latin America suggested that he sympathized with progressive forces. His support of the Peace Corps, which promoted educational, technological, and social change in the area (and in underdeveloped regions throughout the world), further enhanced his reputation in Latin America. By 1964 America's relations south of the border were a little warmer than they had been in 1960.

Elsewhere in the Third World, Kennedy showed more restraint than he had in Cuba. In Laos, where communists, moderates, and right-wing forces struggled for control, he resisted the temptation to involve American manpower and supported instead a neutral coalition. After extended talks in Geneva, Averell Harriman, America's chief negotiator, worked out such an arrangement in 1962. The Pathet Lao, the native communist forces supported by Russia and North Vietnam, soon resumed the fighting, and Laos remained a war-torn land. But Kennedy had at least avoided direct American participation. His toleration of neutralism in the Third World, while inconsistently expressed, contrasted sharply with Dulles' hostility in the 1950s.

Kennedy also exhibited toughness with Khrushchev, who treated his young American adversary contemptuously at a brief meeting in Vienna in June 1961. America, the Soviet leader warned at the time, must agree to a German peace treaty by December. Otherwise, Russia would sign a separate agreement permitting East Germany to control access routes into West Berlin. Kennedy responded by reaffirming America's commitment to Berlin, by mobilizing reserve units, and by using the confrontation to get higher defense appropriations from Congress. Russia

The Kennedys and the Khrushchevs in Vienna

reacted by raising barriers (soon to become the Berlin Wall) preventing the flow of East German refugees to the West. Suddenly, American and Russian tanks faced each other at the line between the zones. Fighting, perhaps leading to nuclear war, appeared at hand. But the military forces avoided incidents, Khrushchev let his deadline pass without further action, and tensions gradually subsided. Kennedy's management of the confrontation showed that he was ready to employ brinkmanship to secure his ends.

The young President's handling of the Cuban missile crisis in 1962 revealed even more clearly his tendency to toughness and brinkmanship. The crisis began in October when U-2 planes discovered that the Soviets were emplacing offensive missiles on Cuban soil. Many angry American officials counseled for an air strike to prevent completion of the missile sites, and for a time it appeared that the President would authorize it. After tense discussions, however, this option was postponed. Instead, the administration proclaimed a "quarantine," or blockade, of the island. For two days Russian ships headed for the blockade, and the United States stood "eyeball to eyeball" with the Soviet Union. It was the most frightening confrontation of the Cold War. Khrushchev, however, proved wise enough to avoid naval engagements thousands of miles from Russian territory. He ordered the ships to turn about and promised to remove the missiles if the United States ended the blockade and renounced any intention of invading Cuba. The next day he changed his mind and sent a much more hostile message. Kennedy, however, shrewdly pretended that the second cable had never arrived. America acceded to Khrushchev's initial deal, and the crisis was over.

The President's defenders have emphasized his restraint during this confrontation. Kennedy, they point out, resisted pleas for an immediate air strike, then had the cunning to ignore the second Soviet note. Moreover, the President's admirers add, he showed wisdom as well as restraint. Permitting the installation of offensive missiles in Cuba, they insist, would have altered the balance of power by giving the enemy greater "first strike" potential. They argue also that JFK had to prove his toughness to Khrushchev, who had (presumably) found him indecisive at Vienna and during the Bay of Pigs fiasco. Kennedy, they conclude, had to act firmly or risk more provocative Soviet behavior concerning Berlin and western Europe.

These arguments are difficult to disprove—for Khrushchev's behavior seemed both antagonistic and erratic. But it is questionable whether his brinkmanship was necessary. Though Khrushchev acted provocatively, his policy in Cuba would have made little difference in the existing military situation: offensive missiles were already well emplaced on Soviet soil. Indeed, in one sense Khrushchev was merely emulating the United States, which had missiles pointing at the Soviet Union from nearby Turkey.

Recognizing this parallel, Adlai Stevenson, who was Kennedy's ambassador at the UN, had recommended tentatively during the crisis that America avoid confrontation by suggesting an exchange. Russia would pull its missiles out of Cuba, and the United States would dismantle its bases in Turkey. Because the Turkish installations were not needed—Kennedy had previously ordered them removed, only to be disobeyed by the Pentagon—Stevenson's idea seemed a more measured response than a blockade. In any event, as Stevenson and others pointed out at the time, there was little to lose by trying to negotiate first. If Russia proved obdurate, there was still time for sterner stuff. But though the Russians were led to believe that the Turkish bases would be dismantled once the crisis was over, the administration's main—and public—response was the blockade. People like Stevenson, White House aides implied, lacked backbone.

Ironically the missile crisis had the unanticipated effect of sobering both sides in the Cold War. Shaken, both Kennedy and Khrushchev paid more attention to nuclear disarmament, and in the summer of 1963 Averell Harriman succeeded in negotiating a Russian-American ban on nuclear testing on land, on the seas, and in the atmosphere. The measure did not permit on-site inspection, nor did it prohibit underground testing, which continued. Would-be nuclear powers like France and China refused to ratify it. But Kennedy properly called it "an important first step toward peace, a step toward reason, a step away from war." At the time of his assassination in Dallas, a few months later, Russian-American relations were more relaxed than they had been since the end of World War II. For this improvement Kennedy's administration could take some of the credit. George Kennan was one of many who praised him accordingly. "I am full of admiration, both as an historian and as a person with diplomatic experience," he wrote before Kennedy's death, "for the manner in which you have addressed yourself to the problems of foreign policy. . . . I don't think we have seen a better standard of statesmanship in the present century."

Kennan did not comment on the legacy of Kennedy's administration in two other key areas of foreign policy: defense planning and Vietnam. In the former Kennedy was both opportunistic and demagogic. He came to office having argued on insufficient evidence that America was on the short end of a "missile gap." By February 1961 he knew otherwise. The United States, in fact, had an edge over the Soviets. Yet he acted immediately to improve America's airlift capacity, to speed up Polaris submarine development, and to "accelerate our entire missile program." Using the Berlin stalemate as an excuse, he asked for and received $6 billion in additional defense appropriations in the next six months alone. Russia's response, naturally enough, was to accelerate the production of its own weaponry.

Throughout his administration Kennedy stressed the necessity of balanced defenses—which meant readying America for guerilla warfare as well as nuclear conflict. It was with such wars in mind that he created, over Pentagon protests, the Green Berets, and that he flew to Fort Bragg to pick their special equipment. Given these actions, it was ironic that his admirers praised Secretary of Defense McNamara for restoring civilian control over military policy. McNamara's feat could make a difference only if the "civilians" approached the Cold War differently from the "military." Under Kennedy they ordinarily did not. Far from curbing the potential of the military-industrial complex, the Kennedy administration left it better equipped to fight on land, at sea, or in the air—anywhere, it seemed, in the world.

That "anywhere" was Vietnam. Since the Geneva accord of 1954, which had promised elections in 1956 to determine the political nature of a unified country, conditions there had steadily deteriorated. The Eisenhower administration, recognizing that Ho Chi Minh would win such elections, conspired with South Vietnam

First Person

Vietnam represents the cornerstone of the Free World in Southeast Asia, the keystone to the arch, the finger in the dike. Burma, Thailand, India, Japan, the Philippines and, obviously, Laos and Cambodia are among those whose security would be threatened if the red tide of Communism overflowed into Vietnam. . . . Moreover, the independence of Free Vietnam is crucial to the free world in fields other than the military. Her economy is essential to the economy of all the Southeast Asia; and her political liberty is an inspiration to those seeking to obtain or maintain their liberty in all parts of Asia—and indeed the world. The fundamental tenets of this nation's foreign policy, in short, depend in considerable measure upon a strong and free Vietnamese nation.

Kennedy on Vietnam, 1956.

to see to it that they were never held. Instead, America spent some $2 billion by 1960 to support South Vietnam's Ngo Dinh Diem, a vehemently anticommunist Catholic nationalist. But Diem failed to win popular acceptance, and by 1957 his opponents in the south, derisively labeled the Vietcong (Vietnamese Communists), were starting to rebel. When Kennedy took office, civil war was raging. The Diem regime, though dictatorial and repressive, could not control roads more than 100 yards from urban centers—and these only at night.

Kennedy was perceptive enough to recognize the excesses of Diem's regime, especially its repressive treatment of Buddhists. In September 1963 he stated, "I don't think that unless a great effort is made to win popular support that the war can be won out there. In the final analysis it is their war. They are the ones who have to win it or lose it." When Diem proved increasingly uncooperative, Kennedy cut back economic aid. A month later, in November, a military coup overthrew and killed Diem. Though Kennedy had not foreseen Diem's assassination, he knew in advance of the coup and made no attempt to prevent it. By letting the coup take place, the President showed that he did not want to associate America with ineffective repressive regimes.

But Kennedy's growing disillusion with Diem never meant support for Ho Chi Minh. On the contrary, JFK strongly opposed the rebels. "The Free World," he said, "must increasingly protect against and oppose communist subversive aggression as practiced today most acutely in Southeast Asia." His vice-president, Lyndon Johnson, had underscored America's commitment by going to Vietnam and publicly hailing Diem as the Winston Churchill of Southeast Asia. General Maxwell Taylor, a forceful advocate of larger American ground forces, and Walt W. Rostow, a top presidential adviser, had insisted that Kennedy must step up aid to the Diem regime. By early 1963 McNamara and others were reporting confidently about favorable "kill ratios" and "actual body counts." By November America had some 17,000 military "advisers" in Vietnam, some of whom were engaging in combat and getting killed. This was more than eight times the number that had been stationed there at the end of Eisenhower's administration.

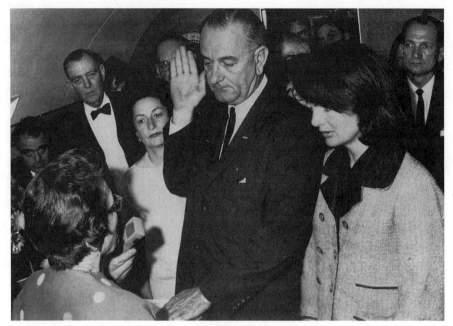

Vice President Lyndon B. Johnson, flanked by his wife Lady Bird and Jacqueline Kennedy, is sworn in as president on the day that JFK was assassinated.

This escalation was not necessarily a prelude to an inevitable American involvement. Kennedy did not want to engage in a ground war in Southeast Asia. Had he lived, he might have acted with restraint. But the fact remains that Kennedy's stand on Vietnam, like his defense policy, was disingenuous. Far from crossing "new frontiers" in foreign policy, he traveled over much old terrain. When he was shot to death in Dallas on November 22, 1963, the stage was well set for Cold Warriors to escalate the war.

The Johnson Years, 1963–68

Few presidents have received as much abuse as Lyndon Johnson, Kennedy's successor. By the late 1960s stories circulated about his towering ego, his crudity, his cruelty to members of his staff. The historian Eric Goldman, who served briefly as a consultant to the White House, repeated an alleged exchange between Johnson and an aide. Upset by criticism, the President supposedly asked, "Why don't people like me?" The friend replied: "Because, Mr. President, you are not a very likable man."

Liberals especially distrusted Johnson. From 1949, when he entered the Senate, through the 1950s, when he worked with conservatives of the Eisenhower administration, they had found him uncooperative. They observed his assiduous protection of oil and gas interests, his coolness to civil rights, and his close relations with hus-

First Person

I dreamed about 1960 myself the other night, and I told Stuart Symington [Democratic Senator from Missouri] and Lyndon Johnson about it in the cloakroom yesterday. I told them about how the Lord came into my bedroom, anointed my head and said, "John Kennedy, I hereby appoint you President of the U.S." Stuart Symington said, "That's strange, Jack, because I too had a similar dream last night in which the Lord anointed me and declared me, Stuart Symington, President of the United States and of Outer Space." Lyndon Johnson then said, "That's very interesting, gentlemen, because I too had a similar dream last night and I don't remember anointing either one of you."

Kennedy jokes about Johnson's egotism prior to the 1960 campaign.

tlers like Bobby Baker, a top aide during his Senate years. In his fondness for wheeling and dealing, for long pointed collars and shiny suits, and his backroom stories, Johnson seemed like a riverboat gambler, albeit with the drawl and the swagger of a Texas tycoon.

These unflattering portrayals overlooked other sides of Johnson. Though he alienated liberals, it was not because he was instinctively conservative but because he had to satisfy his Texas constituency. Indeed, he had begun his political career in the 1930s as an ardent New Dealer. Roosevelt himself had regarded him as future presidential material. Thereafter Johnson became an extraordinarily effective Senate majority leader from 1954 to 1960. As he grew more secure in his political base, he tentatively accepted many liberal programs, including the civil rights bill of 1957 — which could not have become law without his patient negotiations on Capitol Hill.

Johnson's detractors also tended to ignore traits that made him one of the most dynamic chief executives in American history. One of these was his unflagging energy in working with Congress. Unlike Kennedy and Eisenhower, who disliked the hard negotiating involved in securing legislation, he undertook it himself. By 1968 this passion to be at the center of the action had worn him out. It deprived him of the assistance of men of ideas, who found him increasingly domineering. But it enabled him to know exactly how congressmen stood on issues and to move quickly in rewarding his friends and punishing his foes. No president since Roosevelt, his idol, had shown such careful attention to the details of legislation.

LBJ often resorted to what was known as the "Johnson Treatment," described by one senator as a "great overpowering thunderstorm that consumed you as it closed in on you." Johnson, the columnists Rowland Evans and Robert Novak explained, bore in on people he wishes to convince, "his face a scant millimeter from his target, his eyes widening and narrowing, his eyebrows rising and falling. From his pockets poured clippings, memos, statistics, mimicry, humor, and the genius of analogy [which] made the Treatment an almost hypnotic experience and rendered the target stunned and helpless."

President Johnson gives Harold Wilson, Prime Minister of Great Britain, the "Treatment."

In applying such methods Johnson had advantages denied Kennedy. Among these were friendships with powerful figures on the Hill. Senators like Richard Russell of Georgia and Harry Byrd of Virginia had had little reason to help Kennedy; with Johnson, a crony of many years' standing, it was harder to be obstructive. Another advantage was his southern background, which made his support of civil rights all the more impressive. His Protestantism gave him an edge that Kennedy had lacked in handling the explosive question of aid to parochial schools. Above all, Johnson came to office at a time when Americans were shocked by Kennedy's assassination. As in 1933, they were yearning for purposeful leadership.

Johnson used these advantages brilliantly in late 1963 and 1964. On November 27, five days after the assassination, he made Kennedy's program his own by appearing before Congress and reminding it of the unfinished New Frontier, especially in the realm of civil rights. "No memorial oration or eulogy," he said, "could more eloquently honor President Kennedy's memory than the earliest possible passage of the civil rights bill for which he fought so long. . . . I urge you again, as I did in 1957 and again in 1960, to enact a civil rights law so that we can move forward to eliminate from this nation every trace of discrimination and oppression that is based upon race or color."

In 1964, Johnson persisted in similar appeals to carry out Kennedy's program—with breathtaking results. Congress approved the $13.5 billion tax cut Kennedy had called for in June 1963. It passed a controversial bill authorizing federal funds for mass transit. It quickly enacted an $800 million "war against poverty" program. And it passed the first effective civil rights bill since Reconstruction. The Civil Rights Act of 1964 created a Fair Employment Practices Committee, banned discrimination in public accommodations, gave the attorney general injunctive powers in cases involving school segregation as well as voting rights, and authorized the government to withhold funds from public authorities practicing racial discrimination.

Given the national mood, these measures might have passed in any event. Still, Johnson made a difference. The poverty program, though originally conceived in the closing weeks of the Kennedy administration, owed its shape and scope to LBJ's efforts. The tax cut escaped the Senate Finance Committee only after he shrewdly promised Senator Byrd, the committee chairman, that he would cut federal spending. The bill then passed the Senate, seventy-seven to twenty-one, with the consensus that he demanded. Johnson was most effective of all in shepherding the civil rights bill. Instead of settling for half a loaf, he encouraged House liberals to tack on tougher amendments to Kennedy's original bill. As moderates had warned, his action provoked a Senate filibuster. But Johnson held firm, and fence-sitting senators soon began to feel the pressure from home. After fifty-seven days the Senate invoked cloture for the first time in the history of civil rights legislation.

As if to ensure Johnson's continued success, the Republicans then nominated Senator Barry Goldwater of Arizona to oppose him in November. Right-wingers hailed the choice, for Goldwater was an avowed reactionary who opposed civil rights legislation and progressive federal taxation and who called for bombing in Vietnam. At the GOP convention he antagonized moderates in his own party by courting support from the right-wing John Birch Society. "Extremism in defense of liberty is no vice," he proclaimed. His partisans proclaimed, "In Your Heart You Know He's Right," but opponents countered with "In Your Guts You Know He's Nuts."

In fact, Goldwater's nomination suggested a trend of the future: the rise of conservative ideology in American politics. The successes of other right-wing politicians of the late 1960s and 1970s—Governor George Wallace of Alabama, Governor Ronald Reagan of California—revealed that many Americans were dissatisfied not only with liberalism but with the center as well. In 1964, however, Goldwater's ideology seemed particularly extreme. No major-party candidate for the presidency had ever seemed farther from the mainstream of American political thought.

Johnson took full advantage of Goldwater's exposed position on the issues. The GOP stance on Vietnam, LBJ implied, was irresponsible. "We are not going South and we are not going North," he said on September 28. "We are going to continue to try to save their own freedom with their own men, with our leadership and our officer direction." On October 21 he added (in the same vein as FDR in 1940), "We are not going to send American boys nine or ten thousand miles away from home to do what Asian boys ought to be doing for themselves." On domestic questions he emphasized his liberal sympathies by naming Hubert Humphrey as his running mate, and he appealed to the center by reminding people of Goldwater's extremism. "Right here is the reason I'm going to win this thing so big," he told a friend. "You ask a voter who classifies himself as a liberal what he thinks I am and he says 'a liberal.' You ask a voter who calls himself a conservative what I am and he says 'a conservative.' You ask a voter who calls himself a middle-roader, and that is what he calls me. They all think I'm on their side."

First Person

A supreme congressional politician, President Johnson was an incompetent and ineffective national politician. This should not have been too surprising. After all, he had had experience in only two national campaigns: one when he was the vice-presidential candidate; the other when he was running for President against a man Noam Chomsky [a radical antiwar intellectual] could have beaten. In his political instincts he was more a South American caudillo than a North American leader. . . . The President as a man impressed increasing numbers of Americans as high-handed, devious and disingenuous, the embodiment of a political system that wilfully deceived the people and denied them a voice in vital decisions.

Arthur Schlesinger, Jr., a liberal historian and Kennedy partisan, offers a widely held view of Johnson, 1969.

To no one's surprise Johnson won overwhelmingly, by 43.1 million to 27.1 million. Goldwater carried only Arizona and five southern states. The GOP, once moribund in Dixie, now seemed wrecked everywhere else. Democrats also secured huge majorities of 68 to 32 in the Senate and 295 to 140 in the House. The enormous shifts in voting since 1960 showed that the electorate was becoming unpredictable and unstable in presidential elections.

Exhilarated, LBJ interpreted the election as a mandate for further domestic reform. "Hurry, boys, hurry," he told his aides. "Get that legislation up to the Hill

The Voting Rights Act: Percentage of Adult White and Black Registrations in the South, 1964 and 1969

	1964		1969	
	WHITE	BLACK	WHITE	BLACK
Alabama	69.2	19.3	94.6	61.3
Arkansas	65.6	40.4	81.6	77.9
Florida	74.8	51.2	94.2	67.0
Georgia	62.6	27.4	88.5	60.4
Louisiana	80.5	31.6	87.1	60.8
Mississippi	69.9	6.7	89.8	66.5
North Carolina	96.8	46.8	78.4	53.7
South Carolina	75.7	37.3	71.5	54.6
Tennessee	72.9	69.5	92.0	92.1
Texas			61.8	73.1
Virginia	61.1	38.3	78.7	59.8
Total	73.4	35.5	83.5	64.8

SOURCE: U.S. Department of Commerce, *Statistical Abstract of the United states, 1970* (Washington, D.C., 1970), p. 369; and Steven Lawson, *Black Ballots, 1944–1969* (New York: Columbia University Press, 1976) p. 331.

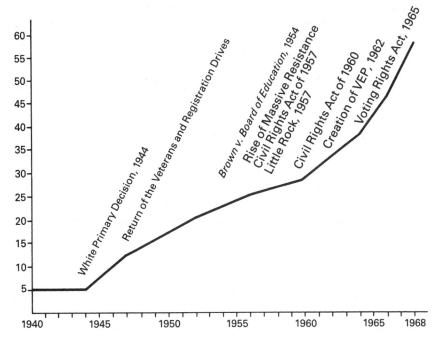

SOURCE: Steven Lawson, *Black Ballots, 1944–1969* (New York, Columbia University Press, 1976), p. 341.

Percentage of voting-age southern blacks registered, 1940–68

and out." Driven at a furious pace, the Democratic Congress responded with the most far-reaching legislation since 1935. Chief among its accomplishments were medicare and aid to elementary and secondary education. Medicare, funded by an increase in Social Security taxes, provided for health care to the aged. A corollary program, Medicaid, offered state and federally financed care to poor people who qualified for public assistance. The education act set aside an initial appropriation of $1 billion. Much supplemented in succeeding years, it gave the federal government an unprecedented role in educational policy.

Hardly pausing for breath, Congress approved many other reforms in 1965. It appropriated generously for manpower training, authorized $900 million to improve conditions in Appalachia, passed a housing act that included provisions for rent supplements, set aside $1.6 billion more for the war against poverty, and established the Economic Development Act for depressed areas with the potential for growth. It created the Department of Housing and Urban Development and the National Endowment for the Arts and the Humanities, authorized an additional $2.4 billion for education, including colleges and universities, and approved a new immigration law ending discriminatory quotas based on pseudoscientific theories of race and ethnicity.

When police in Selma, Alabama, roughed up blacks seeking to register to vote, new outrage exploded among civil rights advocates. Prodded by Johnson, Congress approved the Civil Rights Act of 1965. This far-reaching piece of legislation authorized federal examiners to register voters, and it banned literacy tests. Along with passage of the Twenty-fourth Amendment (1964), which outlawed the poll tax in federal elections, it enabled thousands of formerly disfranchised people to register, to vote, and later to elect black officials in record numbers throughout the South. It was a fitting capstone to a congressional session of unparalleled productivity, and it made Johnson—once the whipping boy of liberals—the most successful champion of progressivism since FDR.

DISILLUSIONMENT WITH LIBERALISM

That very year, however, the euphoria began to disappear. Altruism turned to frustration, then to disenchantment. By 1966 Americans were tiring of listening to the "best and brightest"—the journalist David Halberstam's apt phrase describing the liberals, intellectuals and "experts" who had ruled since 1961. Explaining this rapid change in mood tells much about the strengths and limitations of modern liberalism, about the stubbornness of the nation's problems, about the relative weakness of governmental institutions, and—in the last analysis—about the power of traditional attitudes.

This change of mood quickly affected Capitol Hill. Between 1966 and 1968 liberal lawmakers increased the minimum wage, created a Department of Transportation, and established a Model Cities program. In 1968 they approved another civil rights act—against discrimination in housing. But by then Congress was already cautious in authorizing funds for rent supplements, housing, and the war against poverty. For the next two decades congressional advocates of liberal reform remained as stymied as they had been from 1937 to 1963.

Johnson's programs, by falling far short of expectations, were partly to blame for these developments. Funds for Appalachia, many people observed, went primarily for short-run projects and to road-building, which gave out-of-state profiteers access to valuable raw materials. Aid to education failed to provide money for teachers' salaries or for renovation of urban schools, which continued to deteriorate. The quality of public education seemed to decline, not to improve. Medicare, too, left reformers dissatisfied: it proved to be very expensive, assisted only the elderly, was financed by regressive Social Security taxes, and failed to bring about reforms in the medical establishment.

Liberals complained, too, about federal welfare policies. Many government programs, such as aid to the blind, to the disabled, and to dependent children, continued to require state contributions—stipulations that resulted in wide variations and (especially in the poorer southern states) in wholly inadequate standards. Welfare recipients had to meet strict residency requirements (declared unconstitutional in 1969) and unnecessarily demeaning tests. These provisions required an ever-increasing bureaucracy of social workers. Though dedicated and humane, these workers offended militants who demanded an end to "snooping" and to governmental "paternalism" in general. Social workers, one young slum dweller protested, "are rat fink types. They act like they think we're not human. They think they've got all there is, and all they do is convert us to think and do what they think and do."

Easily the most controversial of the Great Society programs was the much ballyhooed "war on poverty," which Johnson hailed as a "milestone in our 180-year search for a better life for our people." This broad-ranging program operated under a newly created Office of Economic Opportunity (OEO), which received close to $10 billion in federal money between 1965 and 1970. Among its programs were loans for farmers and rural co-ops, aid to migrant workers, and adult education. More significant were VISTA (Volunteers in Service to America), which was a "domestic Peace Corps" of young people who lived with and provided services to the poor; the Job Corps, residential centers offering counseling and job training for unskilled young people; and the Neighborhood Youth Corps, a program providing work and on-the-job training for students and dropouts. Most important of all were the community action agencies under the Community Action Program (CAP). These agencies, of which there were 1,000 by the end of the decade, sought to develop neighborhood solutions to the problems of poverty. Some focused on educational programs such as Head Start for preschool children and Follow-Through for elementary school students. Others concentrated on developing legal services for the poor. Still others worked hard to develop family planning services or to provide day-care centers for children. All the community action agencies were supposed to avoid "paternalism" by giving poor people "maximum feasible participation" in planning.

By the late 1960s, it appeared that the war on poverty was facing severe problems. Of all its efforts, only the Neighborhood Youth Corps and work experience programs were actually providing jobs to help the employable poor. Indeed, the war in Vietnam, by heating up the economy, did much more than did the OEO to create jobs. The "unemployable" poor—the aged, crippled, and, above all, nonsupported mothers and their dependent children—had to turn to the nation's creaking welfare "system." By 1969 the plight of such people (the number of mothers and dependent children on relief had risen from 3.5 million to 8 million since 1961) was so desperate that the Nixon administration proposed (unsuccessfully) a program of assistance payments setting a floor below which family incomes would not be permitted to fall.

Many of the limitations of the war on poverty (and other programs) stemmed from lack of funds. Average expenditures per year by the OEO were approximately $1.7 billion. Even when added to the $1 billion per year for poor school districts under the education act of 1965, this was a piddling sum that could not begin to take care of the 25 to 35 million Americans who were classified as poor in the middle and late 1960s.

Even with proper funding, the war on poverty would have had political problems. The community action programs were a case in point. Though most of them were well run, a few fell into the hands of the wrong kinds of entrepreneurial leaders: in Syracuse, an extreme example, $7 million of the $8 million expended by mid-1967 went for salaries and administration—and only $1 million to the poor. Leaders in a few communities soon adopted the fashionable revolutionary rhetoric and the racial separatism of the late 1960s (see Chapter 5). These leaders, though not numerous, alarmed local politicians, who moved quickly to prevent federal money from flowing toward rivals for power. In 1967 the politicians succeeded in getting Congress to require state approval of community action initiatives. Thus expired—in two years—the much-acclaimed stress on local administration and on "maximum feasible participation" of the poor.

The CAPs suffered also from misconceptions. One of these was the assumption that poverty could be fought on a neighborhood basis. This view, useful in promoting participation by the poor, underestimated the mobility in and out of the slums. It also tended to ignore the larger structural problems—low wages, under-employment, racial discrimination—that lay at the root of much poverty in America. The warriors against poverty also assumed—again with little evidence to guide them—that poor people could organize themselves. This was not always the case; in many areas, the poor were too weak, exploited, or ignorant to unite. Elsewhere, racial and ethnic groups confronted one another. In retrospect, it is probably fair to say that the poor would have benefited more from WPA-like public employment programs or from legislation guaranteeing a minimum annual income for all. Such

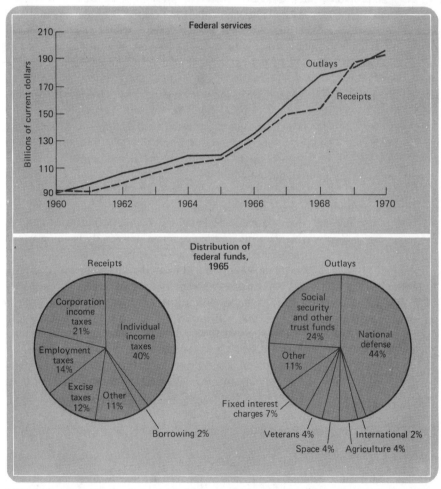

SOURCE: U.S. Bureau of Census, *Statistical Abstract of the United States: 1974*, 95th ed. (Washington, D.C., 1974), p. 220; distribution of funds projected by *Statistical Abstract of the United States: 1964*, p. 387.

Growth of federal services, 1960–70, and percentage distribution of federal funds by function, 1965

programs would have done more to give poor people pride, economic security, and the ability to think of the future.

Some of these misconceptions stemmed from Johnson's passion for rapid accomplishment. He simply did not give Congress time to contemplate its actions. As the sociologist Nathan Glazer observed later, the war on poverty was enacted with "nothing like the powerful political pressure and long-sustained intellectual support that produced the great welfare measures of the New Deal." Other critics complained that Johnson, like most New Deal liberals, relied too heavily on the presumed benefits of federal spending. Throw money at problems, he seemed to say, and they will go away. The journalist David Broder observed, "His primary purpose was to provide all the tangible benefits that Federal initiative could devise and Federal money could buy. There was no pause to consider how each of the new Federal programs meshed with all the others, or whether the function was one the national government could most appropriately undertake." To Broder and others Johnson's programs merely encouraged pressure groups to demand ever greater sums from Uncle Sam.

To the extent that these critics perceived Johnson as a lavish spender they were unfair. As the war on poverty revealed, the money expended on domestic programs between 1965 and 1968 was modest. Progressives demanded much more to attack social problems. Critics were closer to the mark, however, in suggesting that spending on welfare services—as opposed to providing public employment or a guaranteed minimum income—was no panacea. In this sense Johnson was indeed something of a paternalist—a policitican trying to develop middle-class behavior and values in poor people while at the same time doing little to give them jobs and money.

Johnson's greatest problem—and Kennedy's before him—was in promising so much. Kennedy had talked about getting the country moving again, about crossing new frontiers. Johnson went still further: there was to be a "war" on poverty, an end to racial injustice, a "Great Society." Such high-sounding rhetoric was inspiring, at least for a while. But it helped to arouse unrealistic expectations, radical protest, middle-class backlash, and political conservatism. It led others, including many young radicals, to blame Johnson for "running out of ideas" and to attack liberals in general. "Liberalism," one militant said, "drifts in smug self-satisfaction, preening itself with its pragmatic and value-free cleverness in social problem solving. . . . The time for radicalism has struck."

Most of these criticisms were unfair. LBJ was much more than a simple opportunist. The civil rights acts of 1964 and 1965 were among the most far-reaching pieces of legislation passed in American history. In criticizing such reforms many radicals could do little more than demand more of the same; other radicals called for changes that were simply unrealizable within the framework of American values and institutions.

Still, by the late 1960s the disillusion with Johnsonism was not wholly groundless. LBJ's Vietnam policy (see Chapter 5) was an unmitigated disaster that drained support—and funds—from domestic programs and divided the country. Moreover, like his idol FDR, Johnson stopped short of fundamental social change. He made no effort to reform the tax laws, to redistribute income, or to attack monopoly. He was slow to perceive the flaws in welfare and urban programs.

Accordingly, many thoughtful observers began to question the state's ability to solve social problems. "There is mounting evidence," the writer Peter Drucker said, "that government is big rather than strong; that it is fat and flabby rather than powerful; that it costs a great deal and does not achieve much. . . . The citizen less and less believes in government and is increasingly disenchanted with it." James Sundquist, a liberal political scientist, added in 1968: "There are many signs that the capacity of the United States to make policies and establish programs in the domestic field has outrun its capacity, or its determination, to finance and administer them." Amid doubts such as these about the welfare state, it is not surprising that reformers were forced onto the defensive after 1965.

APPARENTLY INTRACTABLE PROBLEMS

Poverty in the Cities   Johnson's critics also underestimated the size of the problems to be confronted. These, by the mid-1960s, revealed a socially divided nation. Poverty, as books like Michael Harrington's *The Other America* (1962) revealed, affected as much as one-fifth of America's population, or nearly 40 million people, in 1960. Moreover, racial tensions pervaded American life. The rapid migrations to the North of southern blacks posed especially large problems in the cities. Between 1950 and 1970 the black population in metropolitan areas increased by 7 million. Yet these cities offered fewer blue-collar jobs than had been available in earlier years. Thus the densely crowded cores of cities teemed with unemployed minorities. In New York, where the numbers were especially large, the welfare load increased from 530,000 in 1965 to 1.2 million in 1972, or one-sixth of the city's population. New York's ghettos, like those in other cities, also suffered from high rates of drug abuse, infant mortality, and family breakup. To outsiders, the ghettos also seemed to be hotbeds of crime.

White alarmists failed to put these problems in a broad perspective. Cities often offered wider economic opportunities than did farming regions or small towns, which languished in the postwar era. Compared to the black rural areas in the South, poverty-stricken Puerto Rico, or rural Mexico, America's cities seemed heaven-sent. But Americans were correct in recoiling in fear from the spread of hard drugs on the streets and in recognizing that many ghetto areas were highly dangerous. Fearful whites anxiously fled such areas—in a "white flight" that accelerated the growth of nearby suburbs. Confronted with such widespread hostility to cities—and to the blacks with which they were intimately identified—Johnson and urban reformers had difficulty finding support.

Those who continued to press for urban programs in the late 1960s were divided about what to do. Some, like Lewis Mumford, complained of the density and ugliness of American cities; others, such as Jane Jacobs, author of *The Death and Life of Great American Cities* (1963), thought that heterogeneous, closely settled neighborhoods such as Greenwich Village in New York were the ultimate in civilized living. Some reformers continued to press for public housing, but others complained that slums were a reflection, not a cause, of racial prejudice and lack of economic opportunities. Others despaired. "Once upon a time," one reformer mused sadly, "we thought that if we could only get our problem families out of those dreadful slums, then papa would stop taking dope, mama would stop chasing around, and junior would stop carrying a knife. Well, we've got them in a nice new apartment with modern kitchens and a recreation center. And they're the same bunch of bastards they always were."

Advocates of racial justice were equally divided by the end of the decade. Most reformers continued to favor desegregation in housing, schools, and employment. Destroy the legal basis for discrimination, they said, and tensions would abate. Some liberals, however, developed doubts about cherished beliefs. In 1965, Daniel Moynihan authored a study for the government, *The Negro Family*. It stressed the social disorganization of black families. Despite increases in black income, he argued, illegitimacy afflicted a larger percentage of nonwhite families than in the 1950s. Many activists challenged these findings, which they said resurrected old stereotypes about fun-lovin', indolent "darkies" who drifted from woman to woman. Find economic opportunities for black men, they argued, and families would stabilize. To others, however, reports such as Moynihan's were unhappy reminders that class and cultural forces as well as "white racism" would continue to plague attempts to promote racial harmony.

The Great Society reformers also had the formidable task of trying to maintain harmony within the West's most polyglot society. According to the 1960 census, America had more than 19 million nonwhites (a term that included Orientals and Native Americans as well as blacks), 9.3 million foreign-born whites, and 23.8 million people of mixed or foreign-born parents. The white ethnics, including masses of Mexicans who crossed the border as illegal aliens, comprised nearly 20 percent of the nation's population of 183 million in 1960. Many faced sharp hostility from older-stock Americans. Shut off from the mainstream, many of these ethnic Americans responded by guarding their cultural identities or by demanding redress. Obviously, the melting pot had failed to boil away America's religious, cultural, and ethnic divisions. So long as these existed, it remained difficult to mobilize a reform coalition based on class lines.

Economic interest groups further divided potential coalitions for reform. Unions, businessmen, farmers, and professional groups competed against self-conscious blacks and ethnics for governmental favor. Almost all had pipelines to Congress or to the bewildering large federal bureaucracy that had "modernized" the American political system since the 1930s. Neither Johnson nor other postwar American presidents really had the power to control these groups or the bureaucrats who assisted them. Indeed, it was to fight back against these forces that Kennedy and Johnson dramatically increased the White House staff and that Nixon, even more anxious for control, resorted to a range of illegal intelligence-gathering activities.

Large corporations were by far the most powerful of these groups. By mid-decade one-half of the productive assets of American manufacturing was controlled by 150 corporations; two-thirds was held by 500. General Motors, America's largest corporation, made $2 billion in profits after taxes in 1965, a sum greater than the revenue for forty-eight of the fifty states. Its sales exceeded the gross national product of all but nine nations in the world. Other big companies spread into far corners of the world during the 1960s. By 1970 American firms sold some $200 billion worth of goods abroad, three-fourths of which were made in

First Person

By all but the pathologically romantic, it is now recognized that this is not the age of the small man. But there is still a lingering presumption among economists that his retreat is not before the efficiency of the great corporation, or even its technological proficiency, but before its monopoly power. . . . This, by the uncouth, would be called drivel. Size is the general servant of technology, not the special servant of profits. The small firm cannot be restored by breaking the power of the larger ones. It would require, rather, the rejection of the technology which since earliest consciousness we are taught to applaud. It would require that we have simple products made from readily available materials by unspecialized labor. . . . If the market thus reigned, there would be, and could be, no planning. No elaborate organization would be required. The small firm would then, at last, do very well. All that is necessary is to undo nearly everything that, at whatever violence to meaning, has been called progress in the last half century. There must be no thought of supersonic travel, or exploring the moon, and there will not be many automobiles. . . .

John Kenneth Galbraith analyzes the "technostructure," 1968.

American-owned overseas plants. United States private investment abroad (including portfolio investment in overseas securities) grew from $19 billion in 1950 to $49 billion in 1960, and to $101 billion in 1968. International Telephone and Telegraph, among the largest of these "multinational" corporations, had operations in ninety countries, 400,000 employees, and a president who earned $812,000 a year in salary. Like other such corporations, it possessed considerable potential influence over American foreign policies.

Corporate influence at home was still more obvious. The large firms not only employed millions of Americans but also served as important social and welfare institutions. Their investments in pension funds, which increased from $4 billion in 1940 to $100 billion in 1965, deeply affected the stock market and the level of general economic activity. The large corporations also continued to depend on, and to influence, government defense spending. Frequently unrestrained by competition, they remained free to increase prices, thus promoting inflation even in times of recession. As John Kenneth Galbraith argued in 1968, large corporations formed a potent "technostructure" that made many of the nation's most fundamental decisions concerning production, wages, and technological change. J. P. Morgan would have been gratified.

If Johnson had been disposed to challenge the corporations—which he was not—he would have been unable to rely on their historic adversaries, the labor unions. Though union membership increased slightly in absolute numbers during the postwar years, the labor movement was hurt by the migration of many industries to the South, which was traditionally antiunion, and by the rapid expansion of the middle class, which took the place of growth in blue-collar employment. Between 1955 and 1968 the percentage of unionized people in nonagricultural employment declined from 33 to 28 percent. Some of the stronger unions, such as the Teamsters (which had almost 2 million members by 1970), were plagued by corruption. The writer Norman Mailer concluded that such unions "sat closer to the Mafia than to Marx." Though Mailer exaggerated (as usual), he—and other critics—were right in noting the continuing decline of labor militancy, which had been a cutting edge for social change in the 1930s.

The relative complacency of unions did not mean that industrial workers enjoyed lives of comfort, or even that they felt secure. On the contrary, they were among the first to be laid off during hard times. Their work on the assembly line seemed ever more tedious and alienating as definitions of the "good life" focused on the desirability of creative labor. Still, strong unions enjoyed economic "clout" undreamed of in the 1920s. Like many other interest groups, they used it to advance their own goals, not to promote the social welfare of the less fortunate. The proliferation of such well-organized groups in America tended to fragment the political parties, to embattle the Congress, and to stymie efforts after 1965 to heal the nation's racial, ethnic, and urban divisions.

THE WARREN COURT: A CENTER OF CONTROVERSY

Reformers took some comfort from the most activist Supreme Court in American history. Liberal justices like Earl Warren, Hugo Black, William O. Douglas, and

The Warren Court: (From left) John M. Harlan, Abe Fortas, Hugo L. Black, Potter Stewart, Chief Justice Earl Warren, Byron R. White, William O. Douglas, Thurgood Marshall, and William J. Brennan, Jr.

William J. Brennan, Jr., validated the sit-ins of the early 1960s and the civil rights acts of 1964 and 1965. In *Engel* v. *Vitale* (1962) and subsequent decisions they ruled against required prayers and Bible reading in public schools. In a series of cases starting with *Baker* v. *Carr* (1962) the Court struck at legislative malapportionment on both the state and national levels. Population, it declared, should ordinarily be the basis for representation. The Court then acted to broaden the rights of accused criminals. In *Gideon* v. *Wainwright* (1963) it declared that indigents charged with felonies in state courts had the right to free counsel; in *Escobedo* v. *Illinois* (1964) it stated that police must permit alleged offenders to consult lawyers during interrogation; and in *Miranda* v. *Arizona* (1966) it required police to warn suspects that any statement they made could be used against them and that they had the right to remain silent and to get free counsel. The Court ruled against state laws banning the use of contraceptive devices, and against laws censoring allegedly pornographic material. All these cases marked significant departures from past judicial decisions.

These decisions infuriated conservatives. White supremacists reacted as angrily as they had to *Brown* v. *Board of Education* in the 1950s. Traditionalists predicted (with some truth) that the apportionment decisions would involve the courts in what Justice Felix Frankfurter, a dissenter, called the "political thicket" of legislative districting. Catholics, fundamentalists, and others heatedly denounced the decisions concerning contraception. Bible reading in the schools, and censorship. Advocates of "law and order" complained that the Court was "coddling" criminals and hampering effective police work. In 1968 they passed the Crime Control and Safe Streets Act, which sanctioned so-called voluntary confessions in federal courts even if suspects were not informed of their rights. The act also authorized police to hold suspects for up to six hours before arraigning them and to use wiretapping for a variety of purposes.

Most of the complaints were considerably exaggerated. Far from opposing religion, the Court permitted states to supply free textbooks to parochial schools. Church property remained exempt from taxation. Decisions concerning criminals merely gave indigents in state courts the rights that they already possessed in federal courts and that wealthier law-breakers such as the Mafiosi had long enjoyed. The apportionment rulings were unprecedented—Warren himself regarded them as

Economic Growth, 1961–70, Compared to Selected Years before and after This Period

	NATIONAL PRODUCT AND INCOME (in billions of current dollars)		PER CAPITA DISPOSABLE INCOME (in current dollars)
	GNP	PERCENT CHANGE FROM GNP OF PRECEDING YEAR (+ OR −)	
1940	99.7	+10.2	573
1945	211.9	+ 0.9	1,074
1949	256.5	− 0.4	1,264
1961	520.1	+ 3.2	1,984
1962	560.3	+ 7.7	2,065
1963	590.5	+ 5.4	2,138
1964	632.4	+ 7.1	2,283
1965	684.9	+ 8.3	2,436
1966	749.9	+ 9.5	2,604
1967	793.9	+ 5.9	2,749
1968	864.2	+ 8.9	2,945
1969	930.3	+ 7.6	3,130
1970	977.1	+ 5.0	3,376
1980	2,732	+ 9.8	9,916
1985	3,998	+ 6.2	11,817

SOURCE: Adapted from *Economic Report of the President,* (Washington, D.C.,1975), p. 249, 267, 269; and *Statistical Abstract of the United States: 1987* (Washington, D.C., 1986), pp. 416–19.

the most significant judgments of his tenure. But by the 1960s they seemed long overdue. By then only the Court could have broken the political logjams that had permitted gross overrepresentation for rural areas. Warren also exaggerated the impact of these decisions, which most often enhanced the political power of growing suburban areas. They did relatively little to aid the poor or minority groups. The nation's most deliberately malapportioned institution, the United States Senate, remained constitutionally sacrosanct.

What mattered, however, was what people thought the Court was doing. With crime disturbing America's cities it was convenient to blame the Court's decisions concerning police behavior. As blacks became more "uppity," segregationists were quick to chastise the judges, especially for decisions striking down laws against intermarriage and against sexual relations between blacks and whites. By 1966 a Harris poll discovered that 65 percent of Americans opposed the tribunal's actions concerning criminals. They feared not only crime but the different life-styles of some blacks and long-haired whites. The liberal decisions of the Warren court provided a convenient scapegoat for these cultural concerns.

These criticisms were the more forceful because the Court was an appointive institution whose jurisdiction over sociopolitical issues was unclear. Indeed, many thoughtful Americans shared Justice Frankfurter's complaint that the Court was concerning itself too much with socioeconomic matters. Problems such as malapportionment, he insisted, were for popularly elected presidents and legislators to cure. To such critics, democratic institutions—Congress, the presidency, the states—ought to deal with these social problems. The courts, they insisted, ought to mind their own business.

Affluence—Bane of Social Reform?

Affluence also accounted for some of the disenchantment of the late 1960s. For a time the unprecedented economic growth of the period assisted the activists. The New Economic Policy, reformers were able to maintain, proved that purposeful government did make a difference. Moreover, prosperity freed thousands of Americans, especially college students, from preoccupation with earning their daily bread. The impulse for reform in the early 1960s, like that in the progressive era (but unlike that of the New Deal) coincided with a decided upswing in the business cycle and with the movement of thousands of people into the middle classes.

But affluence was a mixed blessing, for it prompted great expectations. Poor people, blacks, ethnics, though better off than ever before, knew from TV and other modern communications how much they were missing. Indeed, the gap between black and white income was widening, not narrowing. Lower-income groups, feeling a sense of relative deprivation, grew restless and demanding.

Rising affluence also had an ambivalent impact on the spirit of reform among the politically influential middle and upper middle classes. On the one hand, they sensed that the country could afford more generous welfare policies. Poverty, indeed, was "un-American." On the other hand, the pervasive appeal of consumer goods was seductive. Gains in real income meant the chance to buy big cars and stereo sets, to travel, or simply to buy a home and settle down. Privatism often conflicted with support for social change.

This is another way of saying that American attitudes toward the needy had really changed rather little since the 1930s. Although people continued to believe that the state ought to help those who could not help themselves, they also retained much of their historic distrust of Big Government. They favored laws to enhance better equality of opportunity—a cherished American value—but often balked at programs promoting equality of social condition. When the have-nots attempted to secure social as well as legal equality, a "silent majority" opposed them. This instinctive retreat from social reform complicated the problems Johnson faced in trying to attack racism, poverty, and injustice.

For all these reasons Johnson had to strike quickly. If he had waited for lengthy studies or debate, he would have missed the first chance in thirty years to get significant social legislation on the statute books. His dilemma suggests the plausibility of a cyclical model of social reform. This posits that bursts of social legislation, long blocked by Congress, by unstable parties, by state and local governments, by the affluence and complacency of the politically influential middle classes, by historic fears of Big Government, occasionally cascade over the barriers, only to be followed by troughs of conservatism. This theory is not helpful in predicting when or why such bursts occur, but it helps explain why they dissipate so quickly. It suggests that Johnson, for all his limitations, deserves credit for exploiting the mood of altruism while it lasted.

Suggestions for Reading

William Leuchtenburg's *A Troubled Feast** (1973) is a readable account of domestic developments in the United States during the 1960s and early 1970s. Other helpful books are John M. Blum, *Years of Discord: American Politics and Society, 1961–1974* (1991), and Godfrey Hodgson, *America in Our Time* (1976). James Sundquist's *Politics and Policy** (1968) is the most thorough account of policy making; Richard Polenberg's *One Nation Divisible* (1980) is a fine study of social trends. Allen Matusow, *The Unraveling of America* (1984) is a well-researched and critical account of the 1960s. Todd Gitlin, *The Sixties* (1987) is a provocative account by a 1960s radical.

Other books on politics include Arthur Schlesinger, Jr., *A Thousand Days** (1965), and Theodore Sorenson, *Kennedy* (1965). Both are pro-Kennedy accounts written by insiders. James M. Burns, *John Kennedy** (1960), is a remarkably objective campaign biography. The same author's *Deadlock of Democracy** (1963) is an engaging interpretation of executive-congressional relations and presidential leadership from the late eighteenth century on. David Burner and Thomas West, *The Torch Is Passed: The Kennedy Brothers and American Liberalism* (1984), is useful, as is Burner's brief *John F. Kennedy* (1988), Herbert Parmet, *Jack: The*

*Available in a paperback edition.

Struggle of John F. Kennedy (1980) and *JFK: The Presidency of John F. Kennedy* (1983) are scholarly accounts. Garry Wills, *The Kennedy Imprisonment* (1982) is highly critical of JFK and his family. Books on electoral trends include Theodore White, *Making of a President, 1960** (1961), and *Making of a President, 1964* (1965); and Norman Nie et al., *The Changing American Voter* (1979). Other books dealing with aspects of the Kennedy administration are Lawrence Fuchs, *John Kennedy and American Catholicism* (1967); Grant McConnell, *Steel and the Presidency—1962** (1963); Seymour Harris, *Economics of the Kennedy Years** (1964); Carl M. Brauer, *John F. Kennedy and the Second Reconstruction* (1977); and Hugh Davis Graham, *The Civil Rights Era: Origins and Development of National Policy, 1960–1972* (1990).

Lyndon Johnson's memoirs, *Vantage Point** (1971), are a self-serving account of his presidency. Robert Dallek, *Lone Star Rising: Lyndon Johnson and His Times, 1908–1960* (1991) and *Flawed Giant: Lyndon Johnson, 1960–1973* (1998) are well done. A brief study is Paul Conkin, *Big Daddy from the Pedernales* (1986). Devastatingly critical is Robert Caro, *The Years of Lyndon Johnson: The Path to Power* (1982) and *Means of Ascent* (1989), which deal with Johnson's life to 1949. See also Jeff Shesol, *Mutual Contempt: Lyndon Johnson, Robert Kennedy, and the Feud That Defined a Decade* (1997). A psychologically oriented study is Doris Kearns, *Lyndon Johnson and the American Dream* (1976). For welfare policies see Patterson, *America's Struggle against Poverty* (1986); and Frances Fox Piven and Richard Cloward, *Regulating the Poor: The Functions of Poor Relief** (1972). A highly critical study of liberal welfare policies is Charles Murray, *Losing Ground: American Social Policy, 1950–1980* (1984). Jane Jacobs, *Death and Life of Great American Cities** (1961), is a provocative discussion of cities and urban policy. Thomas Sugrue, *The Origins of the Urban Crisis: Race and Inequality in Postwar Detroit* (1996), is an effective case study with broader applications, while Daniel Moynihan and Nathan Glazer, *Beyond the Melting Pot** (1963), reveals the ethnic dimensions of life in New York City. Mark Gelfand's *A Nation of Cities: The Federal Government and Urban America, 1933–1965* (1975), is authoritative.

Books on foreign policy in the 1960s include Michael Beschloss, *The Crisis Years: Kennedy and Khrushchev, 1960–1963* (1991); Warren I. Cohen, *Dean Rusk* (1980); Peter Wyden, *The Bay of Pigs* (1979); and Richard Walton, *Cold War and Counterrevolution** (1972), which is critical of Kennedy. David Halberstam, *The Best and the Brightest* (1972), is a sustained critique of liberal foreign policy under Kennedy and Johnson. For the missile crisis see Robert Kennedy, *13 Days* (1969); Elie Abel, *Missile Crisis** (1966); and especially Graham Allison, *Essence of Decision** (1971).

For Vietnam in the 1950s and early 1960s consult George Herring, *America's Longest War* (1986); Stanley Karnow, *Vietnam* (1983), a large study; Frances FitzGerald, *The Fire in the Lake* (1972), on cultural conflict; Guenter Lewy, *America in Vietnam* (1978), a defense of U.S. policies; Arnold Isaacs, *Without Honor: Defeat in Vietnam and Cambodia* (1983); William Shawcross, *Morality, Reason, and Power: Cambodia, Holocaust, and Modern Conscience* (1984); Gloria Emerson, *Winners and Losers* (1976), on domestic consequences; Lawrence Baskir and William Strauss, *Chance and Circumstance* (1978), a provocative analysis of the draft during the war; D. Michael Shafer, ed., *The Legacy: The Vietnam War in the American Imagination* (1990); and Wallace Perry, *Bloods: An Oral History of the War by Black Veterans* (1984). See also George M. Kahin and J. W. Lewis, *The United States and Vietnam** (1967); Bernard Fall, *The Two Vietnams** (2d rev, ed. 1967); and Neil Sheehan et al., *The Pentagon Papers** (1971). See also Richard Barnet and Ronald Müller, *Global Reach: The Power of the Multinational Corporations* (1974).

Black power

5

Turmoil, 1965–1968

On March 31, 1968, a deeply lined, worn-looking Lyndon Johnson appeared on television to announce his retirement from the presidency at the close of his tenure in January 1969. He said, "I shall not seek, and I will not accept, the nomination of my party for another term as president."

Though his announcement came as a surprise, it was greeted with relief by millions of Americans. By that time Gallup polls were reporting that only 36 percent of the people approved of his conduct of the presidency. Militants were so angry and threatening that Johnson hardly dared appear in public. Like Hoover before him, he had fallen victim to his own stubbornness and to unusually chaotic and turbulent times.

Among the many manifestations of this discord, which rent the country after 1965, three were outstanding. The first, the breakdown of the interracial civil rights movement, was followed by explosive social unrest, including race riots in the cities. The second, escalation of fighting in Vietnam, led to massive antiwar activity. The third, the rise of radical protest movements and of the "counterculture," was in part the consequence of the other two and in part the cause of further divisions in society. Together these three forces produced domestic turmoil unprecedented in twentieth-century American history.

From Interracialism to Black Power

Since 1960, when the sit-ins first attracted national attention, the civil rights movement had been the vanguard of domestic reform. In providing a cause worthy of sacrifice it sustained the idealism that assists broader movements for change. The activists who gave up their work or their studies and who risked their lives to participate in the sit-ins, freedom rides, and demonstrations between 1960 and 1963 forged, in interracial organizations such as SNCC, an inspiring "beloved community."

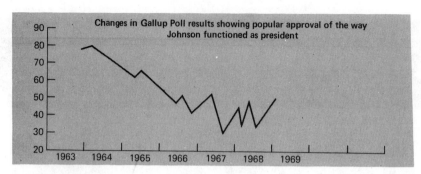

SOURCE: Adapted from *U.S. Foreign Policy: Context, Conduct, Content* by Marian Irish and Elke Frank. © 1975 by Harcourt Brace Jovanovich. Reproduced by permission of the publisher.

Johnson reached the peak of his popularity shortly after he assumed the presidency in 1964, when 80 percent of respondents approved of the way he conducted his office. He reached a low in mid-1967, when only 32 percent approved of his presidency.

As early as 1963, however, internal divisions were beginning to split the interracial coalition. By 1966 this disintegration produced widespread disillusion.

One source of discord was the militants' ever-intensifying awareness of the limits of legal action in combating racial discrimination in the South. More black children attended segregated schools in the Deep South in 1964 than in 1954, the year of the supposedly epochal *Brown* decision. Until 1964 Jim Crow laws flourished throughout the region. Despite legal guarantees, blacks (and many poor whites) still were denied the vote. Though the civil rights acts of 1964 and 1965 eventually rectified some of these abuses, they came too late to pacify activists.

Militants in the North grew equally angry by 1965. Whites, they complained, discriminated against blacks in the crucially important areas of education and housing, where de facto segregation was the rule. Urban renewal, activists added, usually meant "Negro removal." James Baldwin commented bitterly that housing projects "are hated almost as much as policemen, and that is saying a great deal. And they are hated for the same reason: both reveal, unbearably, the real attitude of the white world, no matter how many liberal speeches are made." Like many others, Baldwin recognized that the civil rights acts did almost nothing to assist social welfare or racial justice in the North, where more than half of America's blacks lived by 1970.

Even before 1965 growing discontent among Negro slum dwellers led to an increase in the strength of the Black Muslims. Led by their Messenger, Elijah Muhammed, the Muslims combined faith in Islam with vehement separatism, anti-Semitism, and black racism. Like Marcus Garvey (and Booker T. Washington), they called for black self-help. But they had no use for accommodation. Whites, they said, were agents of the devil; blacks must consider them enemies and refuse to mingle with or intermarry with them. Integrationists such as Martin Luther King, Jr., Elijah Muhammed argued, were tools of white society.

This black racism did not become a mass movement: perhaps no more than 20,000 people belonged to the Muslims during the mid-1960s. But it appealed to some people to whom the interracial organizations seemed tame. It enlisted Cassius Clay (later Muhammed Ali), the heavyweight boxing champion of the world. It pro-

First Person

When I am dead—I say it that way because from the things I know, I do not expect to live long enough to read this book in its finished form—I want you to just watch and see if I'm not right in what I say: that the white man, in his press, is going to identify me with "hate."

He will make use of me dead, as he has made use of me alive, as a convenient symbol of "hatred"—and that will help him to escape facing the truth that all I have been doing is holding up a mirror to reflect, to show, the history of unspeakable crimes that his race has committed against my race.

You watch, I will be labeled as, at best, an "irresponsible" black man. I have always felt about this accusation that the black "leader" whom white men consider to be "responsible" is invariably the black "leader" who never gets any results. You only get action as a black man if you are regarded by the white man as "irresponsible." In fact, this much I had learned when I was just a little boy. And since I have been some kind of a "leader" of black people here in the racist society of America, I have been more reassured each time the white man resisted me, or attacked me harder—because each time made me more certain that I was on the right track in the American black man's best interests. The racist white man's opposition automatically made me know that I did offer the black man something worthwhile.

Yes, I have cherished my "demagogue" role. I know that societies often have killed the people who have helped to change those societies. And if I can die having brought any light, having exposed any meaningful truth that will help to destroy the racist cancer that is malignant in the body of America—then, all of the credit is due to Allah. Only the mistakes have been mine.

The conclusion to *The Autobiography of Malcolm X* (1965).

moted the rise of Malcolm X, a charismatic leader who broke with Elijah Muhammed in 1963 to form the Organization for Afro-American Unity before he was assassinated by black gunmen in February 1965. At that point he had renounced his black racism and begun to encourage interracial cooperation such as he thought existed under Islam. Though he had not been able to put his ideas into practice when he died, he had attracted a growing following. His death made him something of a martyr. His appeal, like that of the Muslims, exposed the bitterness affecting many blacks even at the peak of interracial cooperation in the early 1960s.

By 1964 racial tensions began to divide civil rights workers in the South. Idealistic activists endured great discomfort and real danger in trying to register blacks to vote. Others, staffing a growing network of "freedom schools" for blacks in rural Mississippi, also encountered white violence. Two white activists, Andrew Goodman and Michael Schwerner, were killed along with James Chaney, a black, in Mississippi in 1964. But some northern white girls were shocked by what they perceived as the sexual aggressiveness of their black co-workers. Others—relatively affluent, upwardly mobile college students—were staggered by what they thought to be the ignorance and laziness of blacks in the rural South. "I really don't understand how they [blacks] can sit on the porch from six in the morning until nine in the evening without crossing their legs," one white wrote. Another added, "[Negroes] speak our same language but they look at things differently. Religion,

Sex. It's sort of a different culture." Still other whites, accustomed to assuming positions of leadership in biracial movements, grew resentful as blacks sought to direct their own revolution.

Blacks easily detected these white attitudes. White activists, they countered, returned to exclusive northern suburbs when the registration drives were over, leaving blacks to face angry segregationists in the South. Blacks complained also about the mass media, which exalted the idealism—and sometimes exaggerated the contributions—of the whites while taking the blacks for granted. Some black militants developed misconceptions of their own about sex. "I think all those white girls down here sat up North dreaming about being raped by some big black Negro," a southern black said, "and came down here to see what it was like." The problem of leadership was especially divisive. Only black people, the militants argued, could understand the black experience. Whites, in any event, had no business trying to tell blacks what to do.

Militant young blacks came especially to distrust "paternalistic" white liberals as much as segregationists. President Kennedy, they believed, coopted the movement by preventing militants from taking a prominent role in the march on Washington in 1963. Black activists from Mississippi complained bitterly in 1964 when liberals unseated their Freedom Democratic party delegation at the 1964 Democratic Convention. For many, indeed, the fate of the FDP, which had selected its delegation only after heroic drives for voter registration, was a final bitter pill. Integration and nonviolence, these blacks were coming to believe, were goals for "Uncle Toms." "Do I really want to be integrated into a burning house?" Baldwin asked. Whites, he added, would give in only under the threat of force—"the fire next time."

Baldwin was prophetic. One consequence of this bitterness was racial violence in northern cities. This began on a relatively small scale in Harlem and in Rochester in 1964. In August 1965, five days after Johnson signed the civil rights law, black rioting broke out anew in the Watts district of Los Angeles. It caused the deaths of thirty-five people and property damage estimated at more than $30 million. In 1966 minor disturbances occurred in Chicago and other places, and in 1967 the greatest explosions of all took place in Newark, where 26 died and more than 1,000 were injured, and in Detroit, the worst conflagration since the Chicago race riot of 1919. At Detroit 43 died and 2,000 were hurt. Much of the city's black belt was burned or destroyed. In 1967 alone 83 people were killed in 164 disorders (eight of them major), causing more than $100 million in property damage.

First Person

Certain fundamental matters are clear. Of these, the most fundamental is the racial attitude and behavior of white Americans toward black Americans. Race prejudice has shaped our history decisively in the past; it now threatens to do so again. White racism is essentially responsible for the explosive mixture which has been accumulating in our cities since the end of World War II.

President Johnson's commission on the urban riots concludes its account of the causes of urban disorder in the 1960s.

Some observers thought that envy of white prosperity and consumer culture motivated the rioters. "The rebellion," one rioter conceded, ". . . was all caused by the commercials. I mean you saw all those things you'd never be able to get. . . . Men's clothing, furniture, appliances, color TV. All that crummy TV glamour just hanging out there." These observers pointed out that black rioters in the 1960s, unlike those of 1919, did not physically assault white people; they retaliated instead against businesses in ghetto areas. The rioters, indeed, were generally careful not to harm people and usually confined their destructive behavior to white-owned buildings in their own communities.

Other people blamed the disturbances on destitute migrants—"riffraff" cast adrift in strange cities. Or they said that some of the rioters were engaged in fun and games, like students tearing up Fort Lauderdale during spring vacation. Firm police action, it was believed, would restore order. Still others suggested that class conflict lay at the root of the trouble. Many of the troublemakers, they argued, were poor blacks, sometimes joined by poor whites.

Most of these explanations contained a little truth, for motives varied. But one major cause of the rioting was what the blacks called "police brutality." Many of the riots were sparked by reports of harsh police behavior toward blacks in the ghettos. The study commissions also noted that the rioters included few "riffraff"— these were too disorganized and marginal to play much of a part. Rather, the majority of rioters were upwardly mobile blacks who felt most deeply what President Johnson's commission called "white racism." Though these blacks had gained economically, they sensed that they had far to go to close the widening gap that separated them from the white middle classes, and that whites would never let them move out of the ghetto. Thus it was that some of the worst riots, as in Watts and Detroit, occurred where blacks were relatively well off and relatively well treated— where expectations had been whetted the most.

White and Nonwhite Family Income, 1950–70
(Percent distribution of families, by race of head of family)

WHITE FAMILIES	UNDER $2,000	$2,000–$5,999	$6,000–$9,999	OVER $10,000
		(In current dollars)		
1950	22.2	62.6	11.6	3.5
1955	15.3	54.1	23.8	6.8
1960	11.0	41.3	32.5	15.3
1965	7.7	30.1	35.3	27.1
1970	3.8	18.7	25.9	51.6
NONWHITE FAMILIES				
1950	53.4	43.2	3.2	0.3
1955	39.7	51.7	7.9	0.6
1960	31.7	47.9	15.4	4.9
1965	20.7	49.7	20.5	9.0
1970	11.1	35.0	25.6	28.2

SOURCE: Adapted from *Statistical Abstract of the United States,* 1974 (Washington, D.C., 1973), p. 382.

Another cause—and consequence—of the riots was the developing cry for "black power." This phrase, which frightened whites throughout the late 1960s, first gained currency in June 1966, when James Meredith was shot and wounded while making a demonstration walk from Memphis, Tennessee, to Jackson, Mississippi. King and others then moved in to complete the march. But Stokely Carmichael, the head of SNCC, rejected King's faith in white liberals and in nonviolence. "We have got to get us some black power," he said. "We have to organize ourselves to speak for each other. That's black power. We have to move to control the economics and politics of our community."

To some extent, the development of black power organizations after 1965 merely exposed openly what had existed for some time: divisions among black leaders in the movement. Many blacks, while recognizing the indispensable contributions of Martin Luther King, Jr., resented the way in which he seemed to receive the credit (from white-dominated media) for the movement's successes. Local leaders of black communities in southern towns were especially bitter when King and other spokesmen for the interracial organizations "took over" the organizing drives, only to leave town when the publicity subsided. Still other advocates of black power, including some young activists from the North, did not share the religious style or the evangelical manner of leaders like King—"de Lawd," they sneered. In these ways, the quest for black power reflected formerly obscured divisions—by age, by region, by social class—within the heterogeneous American black community itself.

The major force behind the drive for black power, however, was the rage that men like Carmichael felt against white attempts to dominate the movement. Some black power spokesmen, indeed, made Carmichael sound like a moderate. H. Rap Brown, who took over as head of SNCC in 1967, explained that "John Brown was the only white man I could respect and he is dead. The Black Movement has no use for white liberals. We need revolutionaries. Revolutions need revolutionaries." Julius Lester, an SNCC field secretary, published a book entitled *Look Out Whitey! Black Power's Gon' Get Your Mama!* "Now it is over," he said, "the days of singing freedom songs and the days of combatting bullets and billy clubs with love. We Shall Overcome (and we have overcome our blindness) sounds old, outdated, and can enter the pantheon of the greats along with the IWW songs and the union songs. As one SNCC veteran put it after the Mississippi march, 'Man, the people are too busy getting ready to fight to bother with singing any more.'" Huey Newton, a leader of the Black Panthers, founded in 1966, added that blacks must arm themselves in defense against the police and the military. "We make the statement," he said, "quoting from Chairman Mao, that Political Power comes through the Barrel of a Gun."

In the cultural realm "black power" did much to develop pride among black people. Carmichael said, "The only thing we own in this country is the color of our skins. . . . We have to stop being ashamed of being black. A broad nose, a thick lip, and nappy hair is us, and we are going to call that beautiful whether they like it or not." This "Black is Beautiful" theme (which Langston Hughes and others had promoted forty years earlier) cut down the sale of bleaches, hair straighteners, and other cosmetics that blacks had bought for decades in attempts to hide their racial characteristics. It affected advertising, films, art, and poetry. It led to courses in black history, to renewed appreciation for African culture, and to growing

First Person

The media claims that I teach hate. Hate, like love, is a feeling. How can you teach a feeling? If Black people hate white people it's not because of me, it's because of what white people do to Black people. If hate can be taught, ain't no better teacher than white people themselves. I hate oppression. I am anti anybody who is anti-Black. Now if that includes most white people in America, it ain't my fault. That's just the way the bones break. I don't care whether or not white people hate me. It's not essential that a man love you to live. But "the man" has to respect you.

H. Rap Brown of SNCC offers his view of race relations.

confidence among black people generally. As James Brown's popular song proclaimed "Say It Loud—I'm Black and I'm Proud."

By using the rhetoric of violence, however, spokesmen like H. Rap Brown cut deep divisions into the civil rights movement. Roy Wilkins of the NAACP, whose legal defense fund had been indispensable to civil rights activists—and who was far from being an "Uncle Tom"—said that such rhetoric was the "father of hatred and the mother of violence." A. Philip Randolph, who had threatened an all-black march on Washington in 1941, considered the new version of black power a "menace to peace and prosperity." King complained that "returning violence for violence multiplies violence, adding deeper darkness to a night already devoid of stars. Darkness cannot drive out darkness; only light can do that."

These nonviolent leaders stressed that blacks, working with white allies, could attain power through economic organization and voter solidarity. They insisted that Carmichael, Brown, and other extremists represented only a very small minority of blacks. The moderates in the movement made other telling points. First, they said, many of the advocates of black power were ideologically empty-headed and romantic. Others, they said, spouted violent rhetoric that intensified white "blacklash." Above all, the moderates said, separatism was unrealistic. Blacks, comprising 11 percent of the population, needed white help if they were to succeed. And blacks could be destroyed if they forsook nonviolence. Hatred and violence, King said, "intensify the fears of the white majority, and leave them less ashamed of their prejudices against Negroes."

King, however, could not wish away either the urban riots or the extremist rhetoric of the militant minority, both of which antagonized whites. As early as June 1966, 85 percent of whites thought blacks were too demanding, compared to only 34 percent in 1964. House Republican leader Gerald Ford asked, "How long are we going to abdicate law and order—the backbone of our civilization—in favor of a soft social theory that the man who heaves a brick through your window or tosses a fire bomb into your car is simply the misunderstood and underprivileged product of a broken home?" Johnson himself grew peevish, especially when Rap Brown branded him a "white honky cracker." After appointing a commission to study the riots, he rejected its call in 1968 for far-reaching federal reforms. "They always print that we don't do enough," he snapped. "They don't print what we do."

Reactions like these did not mean that a white backlash was overrunning the country or that the civil rights movement had failed. Polls in the more peaceful years after the riots revealed that most Americans approved of the gains that had been made. The civil rights laws remained on the books, blacks registered and voted in unprecedented numbers, and schools and universities were desegregated, especially in the Deep South. By 1970 southern blacks enjoyed as much legal protection as blacks in the North, where de facto segregation had long prevailed. But black spokesmen began pressing for more social and economic equality, including the end of discrimination in housing, and busing to achieve racial balance in the schools. At this point many whites balked, and the struggle for racial justice entered a period of stalemate. The drive that had characterized the civil rights movement in the early 1960s seemed eons past by 1970.

Vietnam, 1964–68

Three days after Kennedy's assassination President Johnson conferred with Henry Cabot Lodge, Jr., America's ambassador to South Vietnam. Lodge confirmed what people already sensed: the assassination of Diem earlier in the month had increased political instability in South Vietnam, while doing nothing to facilitate the military struggle. Another president, recognizing that South Vietnam was engaged in a civil war, might have refrained from increasing America's commitment of 17,000 men. But not Johnson, who persisted in blaming North Vietnam and China for the fighting in the south. Johnson told Lodge, "I am not going to be the president who saw Vietnam go the way China went."

In 1964 Johnson did his best to conceal this determined attitude from the electorate. Troop levels were increased, but only to 21,000. During the election campaign he ridiculed the notion that he might escalate the number of American soldiers in Vietnam. After the Vietcong attacked American facilities at Bien Hoa in October, he declared, "We are not going to drop bombs."

Even before the 1964 election, however, signs appeared of deceptions that lay ahead. Early in August Johnson announced that North Vietnamese torpedo boats had attacked American destroyers in the Tonkin Gulf thirty miles off North Vietnam. He suppressed the truth: that the American warships had been assisting South Vietnamese commando raids; that the destroyers had been in combat zones close to shore; and that the alleged assaults, on dark nights in rough seas, may have been imagined by nervous American officers. The supposed attacks, in any event, caused no damage. Feigning outrage, Johnson ordered American planes to smash North Vietnamese torpedo bases and oil installations—targets picked carefully two months earlier. He also asked Congress to authorize him to take "all necessary measures to repel any armed attack against the forces of the United States and to prevent further aggression." An alarmed (and uninformed) Congress acceded, unanimously in the House and eighty-eight to two in the Senate. Like Truman after the North Korean invasion, Johnson never troubled to ask for a declaration of war. The Tonkin Gulf resolution gave him latitude to increase the American presence there over the next four years.

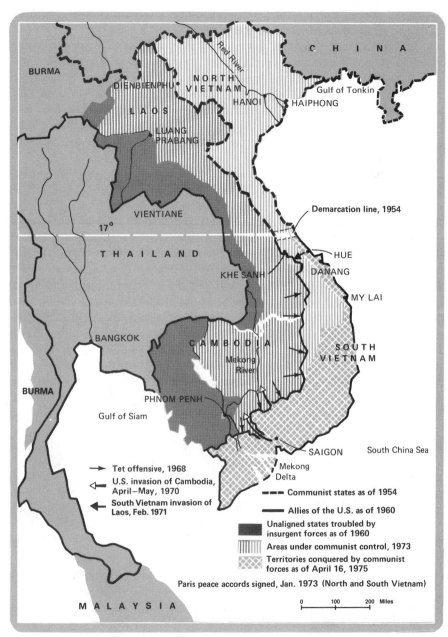

BURMA

DIENBIENPHU NORTH
LAOS VIETNAM
LUANG HANOI HAIPHONG
PRABANG Gulf of Tonkin

Red River

C H I N A

VIENTIANE

Demarcation line, 1954

17°

T H A I L A N D
HUE
KHE SANH DANANG
MY LAI

BANGKOK
C A M B O D I A SOUTH
VIETNAM
Mekong
River

BURMA

PHNOM PENH

Gulf of Siam
SAIGON South China Sea
Mekong
Delta

→ Tet offensive, 1968
◁ U.S. invasion of Cambodia,
April–May, 1970
◀ South Vietnam invasion of
Laos, Feb. 1971

= = = Communist states as of 1954
—— Allies of the U.S. as of 1960
Unaligned states troubled by
insurgent forces as of 1960
Areas under communist control, 1973
Territories conquered by communist
forces as of April 16, 1975
Paris peace accords signed, Jan. 1973 (North and South Vietnam)

M A L A Y S I A
0   100   200 Miles

Vietnam War and fall of Indochina, 1954–75

The escalation itself occurred early in 1965 after Vietcong rebels killed seven Americans and wounded 109 at Pleiku. Within twelve hours of getting the news, American planes retaliated by dropping bombs in the North. Three days later Johnson authorized regular bombing, again on targets chosen in 1964. In April, after Vietcong attacks had almost succeeded in blowing up the American embassy in

Saigon, he stepped up the dispatch of ground troops. By early 1966 the United States had nearly 200,000 soldiers in South Vietnam.

When critics complained of American escalation, Johnson reminded them of his efforts for peace. In April 1965 he promised both sides long-term economic aid. On December 24, 1965, he called a bombing halt, which lasted until January 31, 1966. He named Averell Harriman an ambassador-at-large and sent him on well-publicized missions in search of peace. In October 1966 Johnson went to Manila to pledge that the United States would pull out of Vietnam within six months of the end of the shooting. Later in the year secret negotiations to end the war started in Poland.

It is unlikely that Johnson really expected these overtures to succeed. Instead, he remained fixed in his central goal: to keep South Vietnam within the noncommunist orbit. Because its pro-American puppet governments had little popular support, this policy required further escalation, which destroyed chances for accommodation. By mid-1966 America had 265,000 troops in South Vietnam; by the end of 1967 it had more than 500,000. The war cost an estimated $100 billion per year by 1968—the amount spent yearly on *all* federal expenditures as recently as 1964. Bernard Fall, the best-informed writer on Vietnam at the time, estimated that it cost the United States between $300,000 and $500,000 per enemy death as of early 1966.

Johnson relied heavily on massive bombing of North Vietnam. The attacks sought to destroy military installations, oil reserves, and railway lines and to slow down the flow of supplies from the north to the Vietcong. The raids, however, were probably counterproductive. North Vietnam, which had given little aid to the Vietcong before 1965, responded to the attacks by stepping up its delivery of goods.

Children fleeing from napalm attack, South Vietnam, 1972

The raids also smashed urban areas and killed countless North Vietnamese civilians. Frequently American bombers used napalm, an incendiary substance that set human flesh aflame.

In the south, American military action was equally devastating. "Pacification" programs to secure the countryside entailed burning of villages, forcible uprooting of civilians, and desecration of ancestral burial grounds. "Search and destroy" missions killed thousands of villagers. Overwhelming American firepower defoliated forests, destroyed rice crops, and shattered the economy. Some American troops perpetrated atrocities, such as the one in the village of My Lai in 1968, which resulted in the killing of 347 civilian men, women, and children. During Johnson's presidency the war caused the deaths of some 28,000 Americans, perhaps 100,000 South Vietnamese, and untold numbers of Vietcong rebels. Civilian deaths approached a million.

Long before Johnson left office, opponents of the war inveighed against these policies. Like progressive isolationists in 1917 and 1940, they complained that the war was undermining support for reform at home. More generally, they protested the immorality of bombing civilians, the abuse of presidential power, and the impact of the war on America's relations with the rest of the world. Critics such as Walter Lippmann and the political scientist Hans Morgenthau pointed out that the United States had no economic or strategic interests in Vietnam worth such a commitment.

Johnson remained deaf to such arguments. He brusquely dismissed dissidents within his administration. "Kennedy," one observer explained, "didn't mind

U.S. Military Forces in Vietnam, and Casualties, 1957–85
(All U.S. forces withdrawn by January 27, 1973)

	MILITARY FORCES	KILLED IN BATTLE[a]	WOUNDED IN BATTLE[b]
1957–64	23,300[c]	269	1,600
1965	184,300	1,427	6,100
1966	385,300	5,036	30,100
1967	485,600	9,461	62,100
1968	536,100	14,617	92,800
1969	475,200	9,416	70,200
1970	234,600	4,230	30,600
1971	156,800	1,373	9,000
1972	24,200	360	1,200
1973–85	0	1139	50
TOTAL			
1957–85	x	47,328[d]	303,600

SOURCE: Adapted from *Statistical Abstract of the United States, 1987* (Washington, D C., 1986).

x Not applicable [a]Includes servicemen who died of wounds, or while missing or captured [b]Includes wounded not requiring hospital care [c]For 1964 only [d]Excludes 10,449 servicemen who died in accidents or from disease

disagreement. It didn't bother him. But disagreement really bothers this president. He is going to do what you dislike anyway; so let's not upset him by having an argument in front of him." In such an atmosphere it was not surprising that few top-ranking officials dared dispute him, or that those who did, like McNamara in 1967–68, left office. As late as March 16, 1968, six weeks after the devastating Tet offensive by the Vietcong, which brought pleas for de-escalation from the new secretary of defense, Clark Clifford, Johnson held to his position. "Let's get one thing clear," he said. "I am not going to stop the bombing. I have heard every argument on the subject, and I am not interested in further discussion." Though he finally softened his stance two weeks later—announcing the end of bombing in the north (save near the demarcation line) and reporting that America was beginning peace talks in Paris—these were not major concessions to his advisors but minor changes in tactics. The rebels demanded that America withdraw, and the talks in Paris went nowhere.

Johnson's stubbornness derived from many misconceptions. Among them was his characteristically American view of communism as a united, worldwide conspiracy. This attitude led him to ignore opportunities for Soviet-American détente. In Latin America it caused him in 1965 to send marines to challenge left-wing forces in the Dominican Republic. In Southeast Asia it prompted him to ignore the simple fact that the conflict in South Vietnam was a civil war. Communist China, he said, was responsible for the "aggression" of Ho Chi Minh from the north. By focusing on China, Johnson vastly underestimated the tenacity of the South Vietnamese rebels. Theirs was a war of revolution, not only against puppets like Diem but against decades of Western imperialism. This revolutionary nationalism helped to explain why superior American firepower, to say nothing of 500,000 men, failed utterly to control the countryside.

Johnson also placed exaggerated faith in money and technology. When the North Vietnamese ignored his offer of economic aid in 1965, he was uncomprehending. "I don't understand it," he said. "George Meany [head of the AFL] would've grabbed at a deal like that." Encouraged by the overly optimistic statistics of Secretary of Defense McNamara, he persisted in believing that American air superiority would eventually destroy the enemy. But the bombing failed to stem the flow of supplies from the north. Vietnam, an agricultural country where supply routes wound through dense cover, was singularly ill-suited for strategic bombing.

Ironically, the appalling cost of these misconceptions prompted doubts in America about long-held liberal dogmas. Among these was the view that a strong presidency was a positive good. In domestic policy, this remained an article of liberal faith. In foreign affairs, however, it seemed that isolationists like Charles Beard and Robert Taft had been wise in demanding an important role for Congress. Growing distrust of the presidency added immeasurably to discord that tore the nation apart after 1965.

Another partial casualty of the war was globalism—the view that the United States must preserve "freedom" everywhere. To many Americans, the war in Vietnam ultimately proved that this was not possible. The United States was not omnipotent; it had to think about priorities. Most of those who turned against globalism were not isolationists—they supported the United Nations, NATO, and aid to Israel. But they demanded a reduced presence in Asia, and they looked for ways to defuse the Cold War. They pointed especially to the split between the Soviet Union and China. This break, already deep in the 1960s, led both communist nations to look for détente with the United States. Thanks in part to the rethinking of foreign policy engendered by Vietnam, even hard-liners like Richard Nixon were later induced to respond.

The Antiwar Movement

Second thoughts such as these hardly moved policy makers in the 1960s, and were therefore but small consolation to Americans who were suffering under the travails of the longest war in the nation's history. Besides devastating Vietnam, the war shattered the reform coalition in the United States and ultimately promoted the most alarming inflation since 1946. As much as any other development of the decade, the war eclipsed the idealism and hopefulness of the Kennedy era and precipitated the unrest that gripped the country between 1965 and 1968.

Prompting this unrest was an increasingly militant antiwar movement. By late 1965 students and faculty were already starting to hold "teach-ins" about the war, to stage mass demonstrations, to conduct "bleed-ins" seeking blood for the Vietcong, to burn their draft cards, and to chant, "Hey, hey, LBJ, how many kids did you kill today?" A stop-the-bombing march in Washington in November 1965 attracted 20,000 protesters, including Norman Thomas, the veteran socialist leader, James Farmer, the head of CORE, and Dr. Benjamin Spock.

Many developments helped to swell the antiwar movement after 1965, which soon included large numbers of returning veterans as well as students and others. One, of course, was the enormous American escalation, which became too obvious to hide by 1966. Another was the coverage—in news photographs and on television—of American patrols burning Vietnamese villages, of refugees fleeing the smoke of battle, of horribly burned and wounded women and children, of mutilated American soldiers. These scenes of bloodletting, plus the mounting casualty figures, made it increasingly difficult for Americans to believe the White House and the Pentagon. The "credibility gap" added desperation and fury to the protests.

America's Mood: The Public's View of the Most Important Problem Facing the Country, According to Gallup Poll Results, 1964–68	
1964	Integration
1965	Vietnam
1966	Vietnam
1967	Vietnam
1968	Vietnam

SOURCE: Adapted from *U.S. Foreign Policy: Context, Conduct, Content*, by Marian Irish and Elke Frank. © 1975 by Harcourt Brace. Reproduced by permission of the publisher.

Young people, especially college students, provided much of the energy behind the antiwar movement. Many of these activists were veterans of student efforts to alleviate poverty in the cities. Larger numbers had participated in the civil rights struggle, where they had learned the tactics of nonviolent mass protest. Most agreed with Martin Luther King, Jr., who proclaimed that the United States was "the greatest purveyor of violence in the world."

Other young people had more personal reasons for joining the struggle against war: they did not want to fight in Vietnam. As draft calls mounted (from 5,000 per month in 1965 to 50,000 per month in 1967), students—most of whom had previously secured exemptions—began to be inducted. Alarmed, they moved from quiet disagreement with the war to participation in teach-ins on campus to mass protests. Their parents often supported them. By 1967 the antiwar crusade had become a broad-based movement including pacifists, leftists, civil rights activists, draft-age students, war veterans, and substantial numbers of previously apolitical middle-class parents. By 1968, after the Tet offensive, these people were angry enough to demonstrate against the Pentagon, to challenge LBJ himself in the political arena, and to turn college campuses into cockpits of turmoil.

The Youth Rebellion

The growth of education in the postwar period was staggering. In 1940 the average level achieved by Americans was grade eight. At that time one out of six people of college age attended colleges or universities; one in twelve graduated. By the late 1960s the average grade level was twelve; 50 percent of college-age youth went on to college; and more than 20 percent graduated. Expansion of the nation's colleges and universities reflected major themes of twentieth-century American history: affluence, professionalization, and the rise of the middle class.

Until the early 1960s the campuses were peaceful, and students appeared to worry more about fraternities and football than about social issues. In the Kennedy years, however, many students became more politicized. Some joined New Leftist groups like the Students for a Democratic Society. Others led civil rights

---

Educational Trends, 1940–80: Percentage
of Americans over Age 25 Having Completed
High School or College

	HIGH SCHOOL ONLY	FOUR OR MORE YEARS OF COLLEGE
1940	24.5	4.6
1950	34.3	6.2
1960	41.1	7.7
1970	55.2	11.0
1980	66.3	16.3

SOURCE: Andrew Hacker, ed., *A Statistical Portrait of the American People (New York: Viking, 1983), p. 251.*

demonstrations, served in the Peace Corps, or volunteered in the war against poverty. These altruists were not a majority of students, let alone of young people generally: only 12 percent of students identified themselves as part of the "New Left" even at the peak of campus unrest in 1970. But the protesters attended some of the nation's largest and most prestigious universities. They were articulate. Their role in civil rights demonstrations at Birmingham and Selma suggested that they could make a difference in the world.

By the end of the decade, many of these campuses displayed the same turmoil that affected society at large. Beginning with a demonstration for free speech at Berkeley in 1964, youthful protest became steadily more radical. In 1968, agitators at Columbia seized the president's office and forced the university to shut down. Elsewhere, militants littered campus offices, stormed buildings, shouted down visiting speakers, staged strikes, and battled police ("pigs") called in to restore order. In all, 221 major demonstrations took place on the campuses between January and June 1968. Until 1971, America's universities periodically seemed to be centers of revolution.

Among the forces prompting such unrest were the social divisions outside the university. Like the radicals in the 1930s, activists protested against racism, concentration of wealth, and the "power elite." They also complained about bureaucratic government, "snooping" by federal agencies, the draft, and "globalism." Like radical students elsewhere—for unrest gripped universities throughout the world at the time—they tended to question all authority. Their enemies were not only the universities but racism, social inequality, the military-industrial complex, and—almost swallowing all other causes by 1970—the hated war in Vietnam.

Student unrest at Berkeley brought in troops in 1969.

Other students concentrated their assaults on the universities. Places like Berkeley, the new rebels complained, had become enormous bureaucratic institutions — "multiuniversities" that treated students like IBM cards. Urban universities like Harvard and Columbia, students protested, gobbled up surrounding areas once occupied by poor people. As the Vietnam War escalated, militants also protested against campus institutions such as ROTC. Others busied themselves exposing the connections between multiuniversities, defense contractors, and the CIA. For all these students, universities were visible and vulnerable manifestations of a repressive Establishment.

Idealistic students complained especially that universities were degree mills where young people did what they were told so that they could enter the Establishment at the age of twenty-two. Other critics, like Paul Goodman, went further and opposed compulsory education. "We have been swept on a flood-tide of public policy and popular sentiment," he argued, "into an expansion of schooling and an aggrandizement of school-people that is grossly wasteful of youth and effort and does positive damage to the young."

Though few people went so far as Goodman, many students lent their support to (or at least acquiesced in) the demands of antiestablishment minorities. Their ideology was drawn from a variety of sources. Unlike the radicals of the 1930s, many of whom were moved by Marx, the New Left of the 1960s (except for a handful who admired China's Mao or Cuba's Ché Guevara) eschewed programmatic approaches to revolution. Rather, they relied on demonstrations and other direct-action tactics. Inspired by the civil rights demonstrations, and then by the attention given to advocates of black power, they moved quickly into confrontation against the Vietnam War and the "power elite."

It later became almost fashionable among pundits to deride these militants. The campus unrest of the late 1960s, people began to argue, was orchestrated by a small minority, most of whom were sons and daughters of radicals in the 1930s. The militants, critics added, were affluent, self-indulgent hypocrites who were quick to join the Establishment after graduation; antiwar protesters wanted primarily to escape the draft. Conservatives also argued that transitory demographic imperatives prompted the campus unrest. High birth rates in the 1940s and early 1950s, they contended, combined with growth in higher education to create a uniquely large number of college students by the late 1960s. No such revolt of youth, these analysts concluded, was likely to recur.

Though there was some truth in these observations, conservatives ruefully admitted that the young people were persistent and that they scored a few victories. Students forced administrative and curricular changes in some universities. Off campus they were the backbone of the civil rights and antiwar movements. Many of the protesters made permanent commitments to social change by fighting environmental pollution, by enlisting in Common Cause, or by backing Ralph Nader and other foes of commercial and governmental exploitation. Many worked for antiwar political candidates in 1968 and 1972. The student movement, like the struggle for black power, was neither wholly negative nor wasted.

It was a fact, however, that many student victories were pyrrhic by 1968. Indeed, youthful excesses alarmed many reformers as well as conservatives. These reformers agreed that many American institutions needed changing. But they lamented what they considered the anti-intellectualism and fundamental disrespect for rational discourse that characterized some of the extremists. The reformers also resented the rhetoric of the young radicals. Slogans such as "Don't Trust Anyone Over Thirty," to say nothing of well-publicized campaigns like the "Filthy Speech" movement at Berkeley, were hardly calculated to appeal to the majority of Americans. Neither were insults to pro-war speakers, veterans, "pigs," and other symbols of authority. Excesses such as these created backlash, divided the movement, and probably sapped its effectiveness.

The Counterculture

Some young-people did not content themselves with unsettling the universities and damning the war. They embraced what became known in the late 1960s as the counterculture. The overlapping of the two movements, radical protest and rebellion against the life-styles and values of the 1950s, gave unprecedented visibility to the youth movement of the 1960s.

The surface manifestations of the counterculture in themselves alienated traditionalists. Increasing numbers of young men (and some adults) let their hair grow long, donned love beads, and dressed in faded jeans, work shirts, and sandals. Young women, sometimes doing without bras or shoes, also flouted conventional sexual and social mores. Many of these people used marijuana or other more dangerous drugs, and they lived as "hippies" in rural communes or in seedy urban areas like San Francisco's Haight-Ashbury district. The very sight of such apparently unkempt and amoral people was offensive to many Americans.

Traditionalists also grew alarmed at the taste in popular music shared by many young people in the late 1960s. Earlier in the decade idealistic youth had flocked to hear folk musicians like Bob Dylan, Malvina Reynolds, and Joan Baez sing lyrics of social protest. Baez asked (in complaining about radioactivity), "What Have They Done to the Rain?" Pete Seeger chimed in, "Where Have All the Flowers Gone?" Though lyrics such as these were socially conscious, they did not much worry most Americans. One radical complained that Baez talked only about "clouds, flowers, butterflies . . . and the like." Arlo Guthrie, a leading folksinger, conceded that "you don't accomplish very much singing protest songs to people who agree with you. Everybody just has a good time thinking they're right."

Within the next three years, however, social protest songs gave way to lyrics celebrating drugs. John Lennon, one of the Beatles, scored a hit with "Lucy in the Sky with Diamonds," and Dylan himself wrote "Mr. Tambourine Man." Both frankly embraced the use of drugs. Another singer explained, "You take the drugs, you turn up the music real loud, you dance around, you build up a fantasy." By the late 1960s the most popular entertainers included groups like the Doors and the Rolling Stones. Jim Morrison of the Doors relied primarily on sexuality for his effect and was twice arrested for indecent exposure. Mick Jagger, leader of the Rolling Stones, unleashed not only sexual instincts but also violence. In 1969 at Altamont in California he called on the Hell's Angels, a gang of motorcyclists, to keep order at one of the Stones' concerts. When the crowd grew unruly, the Angels stomped a black man to death on the stage.

The counterculture repudiated not only war but also traditional life-styles and values.

Advocates of the counterculture neither sought nor welcomed such violence. But they continued to defy convention. At the end of the decade masses of young people flocked happily to extravaganzas such as the "Woodstock" concert at Bethel, New York, in 1969. This attracted some 400,000 people. For three days the majority seemed content to lie about, to share marijuana, and even to fornicate in the open. "Everyone swam nude in the lake," a journalist wrote. "Balling was easier than getting breakfast, and the 'pigs' just smiled and passed out the oats."

There was more to the counterculture than lovebeads and rock concerts. True believers posed sharp challenges to existing values. For them there was a "generation gap." Like Dustin Hoffman, "hero" of the hit movie *The Graduate* (1969), they rejected what they considered the hypocrisy of people over thirty. Paul Simon's song *Sound of Silence* symbolized the gigantic gap that prevented understanding between young people and their parents. The "revolution," these youths believed, was cultural and generational. Young people must advance to new thresholds of freedom. To Charles Reich, whose *Greening of America* (1969) celebrated the new culture, this meant rejecting the materialism and competitiveness of previous epochs and creating a world of love, beauty, and peace. The counterculture, another writer suggested, meant a "vision of a new American identity — a collective identity that will be blacker, more feminine, more oriental, more emotional, more intuitive, more exuberant — and, just possibly, better than the old one."

Central to the ideas of these true believers was the conviction that older people were repressed. Adults, caught in what Paul Goodman called the "rat-race," were supposedly afraid to let themselves go. Herbert Marcuse, whose writings appealed to intellectuals on the Left, argued that affluence was abolishing poverty in society. Eros, the symbol of affluence and the end of scarcity, would ultimately conquer aggression. The avant-garde must transcend repression to live by an "aesthetic ethos." As the historian John P. Diggins pointed out, beliefs such as these aligned the counterculturists more closely with the "lyrical left" that had challenged middle-class values prior to World War I than with the "old" Marxist left of the 1930s. Like Randolph Bourne, many believed that "imagination is revolution." Some added that drags helped to explode repressions. The key was "not politics but psychedelics."

Surmounting repression meant rejecting taboos about sex. If Eros was to conquer, people must feel free to indulge in premarital sex, to reject life in the nuclear family, to practice homosexuality. It followed — to some — that censorship was wrong. By 1970 traditionalists were appalled at the spread of "X-rated" movies, of "gay liberation," and of "swingers" magazines featuring photos of naked people advertising their wares. One such magazine had a circulation of 50,000 by 1972. As never before, free-wheeling sexuality was becoming a virtue, and pornography a consumer durable.

If sex was one avenue to transcendence, rejection of science was another. Theodore Roszak, a leading proponent of the counterculture, argued that American society resembled a "world's fair in its final days, when things start to sag and disintegrate behind the futuristic façade." To overcome this technological debauch, people needed to reject scientism, computerism, reason generally. Roszak and others sought a more decentralized, less industrialized, less competitive cosmos. It was to discover such an Eden that the true believers moved to rural communes and scratched at the soil with hand-made tools.

In all these ways the foes of contemporary culture joined others in the 1960s who swelled the age-old chorus against materialism. "American civilization," Normal Mailer cried, "had moved from the existential sanction of the frontier to the abstract ubiquitous sanction of the dollar bill." Another writer added, "People no longer have opinions: they have refrigerators. . . . The only way to catch a spirit of the times is to write a handbook on home appliances." Like Andy Warhol, a "pop" artist who occupied himself painting such commercial symbols as Campbell's soup cans and Marilyn Monroe, these critics thought that consumerism was the essence of American culture.

To replace material values, Roszak and others called for a return to spiritualism. By this they did not mean orthodox religious faiths. Rather, like Henry Thoreau and the transcendentalists, they wanted human beings to achieve enlightenment through communion with nature. People, Roszak said, must develop a "new culture in which the nonintellective capacities of personality" will predominate. This faith in intuition underlay a growing attention in the 1960s to mysticism, astrology, and Oriental philosophy. Human beings, these people believed, must seek harmony with, not victory over, the natural world.

Love of nature assisted a broader movement for ecological balance, which gripped thousands of Americans who otherwise had little use for the counterculture. Among these were scientists who raised frightening visions. Barry Commoner, a Washington University biologist, argued that nuclear explosions, automobiles, detergents, and pesticides polluted the environment and increased the percentage of carbon dioxide in the atmosphere. Soon, he warned, temperatures would increase, the polar ice caps would melt, and water would inundate the seaports. Paul Ehrlich, author of *Population Bomb,* crusaded for birth control, the ultimate guarantee of environmental protection. Mothers' milk contained so much DDT, he said, that it would be banned if sold on the market. He added, "We must realize that unless we are extremely lucky everybody will disappear in a cloud of blue steam in twenty years."

Many scientists challenged such forecasts of doom. While conceding the dangers of population growth in underdeveloped nations, they observed that the American birth rate was declining in the 1960s to the lowest level, except for the 1930s, in American history. Others insisted that pesticides were necessary to grow food for the world's hungry masses and that nuclear power—widely used in Europe—was the wave of the future. Alarmists like Commoner, they thought, failed to grasp Theodore Roosevelt's central point—that resources must be used wisely for orderly growth.

Still, there was no denying one important theme of many of the ecologists: that modern American society was incredibly wasteful and destructive. Awareness of such demands on resources led many people to recycle glass and paper, to join consumer movements, and to push the Pill. Others challenged the desirability of growth itself. The counterculturists could hardly take full credit for awakening these activists to the nation's wastefulness—conservation, after all, was not new to the 1960s. But their passion for the harmonious life helped the movement for ecology to spread. It was their most lasting legacy.

By the end of the decade it became increasingly clear that sharp differences divided the youth movement. While many members of the counterculture held vaguely New Left views on social issues, they were essentially nonpolitical. Their primary grievance was with bourgeois life-styles, not with capitalism, or with political leadership. In response, New Leftists and black power advocates accused the "flower children" of trying to cop out of society, instead of fighting it. The crusade for sexual liberation, C. Wright Mills grumbled, was a "gonad theory of revolution." These differences, resembling nineteenth-century divisions between transcendentalists and abolitionists, split the young radicals in manifold ways and left them considerably less potent than alarmists perceived.

Extremists further damaged the image of the youthful counterculturists—just as they hurt the New Left. Among these were Jerry Rubin and Abbie Hoffman, self-styled leaders of the Yippies. They were long-haired, unkempt, savagely expressive. "When in doubt, BURN," Rubin counseled in 1967. "Fire is the revolutionary's god. . . . Burn the flag. Burn churches. Burn. Burn. Burn." People should "farm in the morning, make music in the afternoon, and fuck wherever and whenever they want to." Rubin and Hoffman were essentially antipolitical; they were indulging themselves, not organizing a revolution. Yet their rhetoric—overcovered by the media—disgusted many men and women of peace. It was easy for the public to lump together the hippies and the New Leftists and to perceive a united and outrageous movement against the established ways of life.

People like Rubin especially appalled some of America's older leftists, who complained that the counterculture was anti-intellectual, self-indulgent, and elitist. One critic observed that Rubin and others mistook "vividness, intensity, and urgency for cultural sensitivity and responsible morality." Paul Goodman, commenting on his experiences with members of the counterculture, said, "They did not believe there was such a thing as the simple truth. To be required to learn something was a trap by which the young were put down and coopted. Then I knew that I could not get through to them. I had imagined that the worldwide student protest had to do with changing political and moral institutions, to which I was sympathetic, but I now saw that we had to do with a religious crisis of the magnitude of the Reformation in the fifteen hundreds, when not only all institutions but all learning had been corrupted by the whore of Babylon."

Calm observers of the counterculture understood that figures like Rubin and Hoffman spoke for only a small minority of people. They recognized that the huge majority of Americans still cherished the work ethic, nuclear families, and curbs on pornography. They noted that the media, playing up the bizarre and colorful aspects of the hippie world, vastly exaggerated the numbers involved. Indeed, it became steadily more obvious that there was a larger cultural gap between the mass of blue-collar young people and the counterculturalists than there was between the generations.

In 1968, however, few people made clear distinctions such as these. They could not know that the youth movements would lose momentum by the early 1970s. With the media playing up extremists like Rubin and Hoffman, with long-haired demonstrators battling police outside the Pentagon, with campuses in turmoil, with hippies advocating free and open sex, with blacks tearing up the ghettos, it seemed that traditional values and institutions were endangered. By 1968 "backlash" among "middle Americans," a vague term embracing blue-collar workers, conservatives, and others who were angry and frightened by domestic turmoil, was growing throughout the country.

Gay Power, Brown Power, Red Power, Women's Power

The rise of protest movements and the counterculture alerted other aggrieved Americans to the potential of group solidarity. By the end of the decade these people, too, had become highly vocal and increasingly demanding. Homosexuals, for instance, angrily resisted the efforts of New York police to raid a gay bar, the Stonewall Inn, in 1969; the encounter is often cited as a turning point in the evolving organizational consciousness of gays and lesbians since the 1960s.

Others who developed a heightened sense of collective grievance were many ethnic leaders. Though the more acculturated groups—Irish-Americans,

Cesar Chavez, the man behind the movement for farm labor reform.

Italian-Americans—tended to work within the existing "system," others shared the rage that animated blacks. Leaders of the Puerto Ricans, who were treated as badly as blacks, staged strikes and demonstrations. Native Americans, hidden away on arid reservations, conducted sit-ins to demand revision of old "treaties" with the government. César Chavez, the charismatic leader of the National Farm Workers, championed the cause of "Chicanos" in California. With the aid of eastern sympathizers, who helped boycott nonunion produce, he secured modest concessions from landowners.

Chavez, an organizer in the old CIO tradition, did not endorse separatism. Other disgruntled leaders did. Some Native Americans raised the flag of "red power." Radical Chicanos called for "brown power," or *La Raza,* a culture divorced from white American society. Like the advocates of black power, they represented minorities within their movements. But their militance forced the moderates to take tougher stands, and their tactics of direct action created confrontations with civil authorities. Their rage exposed the continuing power of ethnocultural divisions in American society and of the obstacles that had prevented proscribed groups from developing more than the rudiments of a middle class.

"Power" ideologies also helped to promote a revival of organized feminism, which had been quiescent since the 1920s. As Betty Friedan pointed out in *The Feminine Mystique* (1963), an influential demand for equal rights, the intervening decades had actually witnessed setbacks for the feminist cause. Smaller percentages of women were in colleges in 1960 than in the 1920s. Women formed steadily lower percentages of the professionally employed (which included teachers) and of holders of M.A. and Ph.D. degrees. As late as the mid-1960s, 90 percent of school board members were men, although the school board was considered a woman's

Betty Friedan's *The Feminine Mystique* helped spur the resurgence of organized feminism in the 1960s.

"place." Studies revealed that poverty and unemployment among women, especially among black women, were widespread in the 1960s and that the gap separating men's and women's wages was widening. Friedan and others protested particularly against the plethora of state laws discriminating against women. These prohibited women from serving on juries, from making contracts, and even from holding property. And women who wanted to enter politics were regularly rebuffed. Shirley Chisholm, a black congresswoman from New York, recalled that her sex was a larger obstacle than her color. "I was constantly bombarded by both men and women," she said, "that I should return to teaching, a woman's vocation, and leave politics up to men."

Long-developing demographic and economic trends helped feminists like Friedan to be heard. Thanks in part to birth control pills, which permitted women to plan their lives with some assurance, and in part to the huge expansion of clerical opportunities, the growth in female employment accelerated. By 1965 more than 25 million women were regularly employed. Of married women with young children, almost 40 percent held jobs by 1968—a startling increase of nearly 15 percent since the mid-1950s. The majority of these women worked because they needed the money to support themselves or to help their families, not because they wished to liberate themselves from the home. But the existence of such an army of female wage-earners virtually assured a more decent reception to arguments for equal justice in work.

At this point the civil rights and peace movements offered models for "women's power." They helped train women in direct action tactics. They revealed also that many male activists were chauvinists who expected women to wash dishes and cook the meals while others "manned" the barricades. The position of women in the struggle for racial justice, Stokely Carmichael had sneered, should be prone. Friedan explained, "The absolute necessity for a civil rights movement for women had reached such a point of subterranean explosive urgency by 1966, that it took only a few of us to get together to ignite the spark—and it spread like a chain reaction." With others she helped form the National Organization for Women in 1966. Soon NOW and other more militant groups were employing the same aggressive tactics—sit-ins, demonstrations, protest meetings—that had inspired activists for other causes.

A variety of goals engaged the feminists. Some focused on changing what they considered the corrosive effect of sexism on the psychological health and morale of women. "Consciousness-raising" sessions proliferated to explore and attack the sources of male domination. Other feminists concentrated on promoting sexual freedom, including lesbianism. Many demanded an end to antiabortion statutes. They also criticized male gynecologists for recommending "unnatural" childbirth and surgeons for performing excessive operations for cancer of the breast and of the uterus. Women, they insisted, must be free to control their own bodies. Still others demanded changes in traditional family patterns that, they said, relegated women to subordinate domestic roles. Most of these causes were neither new nor necessarily "radical." To the extent that they challenged family patterns, however, they worried and offended many Americans.

Less alarming to traditionalists were the feminists who focused on the need for equal treatment—in hiring, in universities, on the job. These women, strong in

NOW, worked hard for an equal rights amendment to the Constitution, a dream of militant feminists since 1920. Like blacks and ethnics, the activists also crusaded for recognition of their past accomplishments, for courses in women's history, and for coeducation in sex-defined courses, such as woodworking for boys and home economics for girls. They made especially effective use of the prohibition of discrimination on grounds of sex in Title VII of the 1964 Civil Rights Act. This title had been added by segregationists who had hoped to weaken support for the entire bill. To their dismay, it later enabled women to employ the force of the government in the struggle against discrimination in federally assisted employment and education.

For a variety of reasons, many of these demands did not prove so frightening in the 1960s as the related movement for black power. Women, after all, were already working in large numbers: to cede them more equal rights was only reasonable. The growth in female white-collar employment may also have weakened traditional concepts of masculinity and blurred sex roles. Though men feared job competition, they were prepared at least to admit that not all women must languish at home. Most important, the movement for women's rights was nonviolent, and it was led by middle-class white people. For all its vehemence, it was not likely to overturn society.

By 1968 traditionalists could take further comfort in the fissures that divided the movement. From the beginning many black women devoted their energies to the cause of civil rights for blacks. Women's liberation, they insisted, was a diver- sion. Some working-class women objected that the Equal Rights Amendment, which proposed to wipe out sex-oriented laws, would deprive them of protective labor legislation. Such splits were hardly surprising, for women comprised 51 percent of the population. Nor were the disagreements entirely new—similar divisions had weakened the feminist cause since the nineteenth century. Still, they permitted opponents of "women's lib" to anticipate further disagreements in the 1970s.

But these cracks in the movement could not hide the fact that the new feminism was more widespread than campaigns earlier in the century. Even women who called themselves moderates were often aroused by demands for equal treatment before the law. And militant women, like blacks and other minorities, welcomed agitation and turmoil if they accelerated social change. For some traditionalists, therefore, the "new" women seemed threatening. To these and other conservatives, the future of the nation appeared to hinge on the forthcoming electoral campaign of 1968.

The Incredible Campaign of 1968

On January 3, 1968, Democratic Senator Eugene McCarthy of Minnesota surprised the pundits by announcing he would challenge President Johnson on an antiwar platform. In many ways he seemed ill-suited to such a formidable task. A devout Catholic who had seriously considered becoming a monk and an intellectual who numbered the poet Robert Lowell among his advisers, he was hardly a typical representative of American politics. But for many people his stand on the war and his courage in challenging an incumbent president were qualifications enough. And when the Vietcong damaged American installations (including the embassy at Saigon) during the daring Tet offensive beginning January 31, Johnson fell further on the defensive. The attack was mostly a failure in the field, but it revealed the hollowness of support for the South Vietnamese regime, as well as the bankruptcy of the administration's foreign policies. With thousands of student volunteers making campaign arrangements, McCarthy came close to beating Johnson in the New Hampshire primary on March 12. He seemed likely to win the next important confrontation, in Wisconsin on April 2. Johnson's awareness of McCarthy's popularity helped to precipitate his startling announcement on March 31 that he would not run for renomination.

Though McCarthy won with ease in Wisconsin, he immediately faced challenges within the Democratic party. Centrists in the Democratic coalition, including many labor leaders, leaned toward Vice-President Hubert H. Humphrey. Right-wingers flocked to Governor George Wallace of Alabama, who was anti-intellectual, openly racist, and hawkish on the war. No one doubted that Wallace commanded widespread support among segregationists in the South and among advocates of escalation. But he displayed much more than a sectional appeal. By denouncing the counterculture, the New Left, and the Eastern Establishment, he appealed to many "middle Americans," ethnics, and blue-collar workers. His impressive showings in northern primarie—34 percent in Wisconsin, 30 percent in Indiana, 43 percent in Maryland—suggested that backlash was widespread indeed.

As the campaign progressed, McCarthy demonstrated his lack of appeal to blacks. In the best of times the weakness would have been a liability for a prospective Democratic candidate. But after April 4 it became doubly serious. On that day James Earl Ray, a white former convict, shot and killed Martin Luther King on the balcony of a Memphis motel. Outraged blacks responded immediately by rampaging through ghettos in Chicago, Washington, and other American cities. McCarthy was naturally appalled by the assassination. But most blacks continued to regard him as the candidate of the white student elite—which in large part he was. Someone else would have to be found who could unite the black masses and antiwar activists and appeal to the center as well.

That someone seemed to be Robert Kennedy, who announced his candidacy after the New Hampshire primary. His belated entry earned him few plaudits for courage, and McCarthy supporters abused him for his opportunism. But Kennedy possessed useful assets. He was rich, intelligent, highly organized, and charismatic. More than all other candidates in 1968, he aroused widespread support among blacks, Chicanos, and many Catholics and blue-collar workers. By calling for de-escalation of the war he gradually cut into McCarthy's support among the white student Left. Though he lost to McCarthy in a primary in Oregon, he won impressively everywhere else. He peaked on June 4, when he won the biggest test of all in California.

Whether he could have gone on to win the nomination is hard to judge. Perhaps not, for the Johnson loyalists hated him. In any case, he never got the chance. On the night of the California primary, as he walked down a kitchen corridor in a Los Angeles hotel, he was shot and killed by Sirhan Sirhan, a crazed Jordanian immigrant. To millions of blacks and poor people his assassination, following so closely on the murder of King, was proof of the violence and divisions that rent American society.

Kennedy's death eliminated the last chance for the triumph of antiwar forces at the Democratic convention in Chicago. McCarthy stayed in to the end, but his defeat in California exposed his limitations as a vote getter. Bereaved Kennedy partisans tried to make a candidate of Senator George McGovern, an antiwar liberal from South Dakota. At that late date, however, McGovern elicited little enthusiasm. After *antiwar* bitter struggles over the platform and seating of delegates, the party regulars excluded most of the insurgents. They then chose Humphrey by a margin of more than two to one over McCarthy and McGovern and balanced the ticket by naming liberal-leaning Edmund Muskie, a senator from Maine, as the vice-presidential nominee.

These nominations seemed almost worthless as a result of tumult that convulsed Chicago. As the convention opened, left-wing protesters moved into the city. Most of them were nonviolent whites working for McCarthy. Some, however, were determined to provoke confrontations with Mayor Richard Daley, who had earned notoriety after King's assassination by ordering his police to "shoot to kill" arsonists and to "shoot to maim" looters. Daley erected chain-link fences and barbed wire to protect the convention site and surrounded it with police. Some of the activists responded by taunting and insulting the "pigs," who charged wildly into crowds, clubbing and gassing passersby as well as demonstrators. The "police riot," as the Walker Report later described it, shattered what hope had remained for rapprochement between the Democratic center and the youthful Left. For Humphrey, "beneficiary" of this police activity, the convention was a disaster.

Richard Nixon, the Republican nominee, seemed certain to profit from this Democratic disarray. His victory at the GOP convention was a triumph of ambition, persistence, and party loyalty. After losing to Kennedy in 1960, he had failed in a race for the governorship of California in 1962. Tired and petulant in defeat, he had told reporters, "You won't have Nixon to kick around any more, because, gentlemen, this is my last press conference." Rebounding, he became a conscientious party worker, supporting Goldwater in 1964 and traveling widely for GOP congressional candidates in 1966. His smooth performance during the preconvention campaign bested right-wingers who had supported California governor Ronald Reagan and liberals who had favored governors Nelson Rockefeller of New York and George Romney of Michigan. It also impressed a few who had disliked him in the past. "The Nixon of 1968," said Theodore White, chronicler of presidential elections, "was so different from the Nixon of 1960 that the whole personality required reexplanation. . . . There was . . . a total absence of bitterness, of the rancor and venom that had once colored his remarks."

As the campaign developed, Nixon failed to generate enthusiasm. Despite his appeals for "law and order," it was clear that George Wallace, running as the presidential candidate of the American Independence party, would capture much of the right-wing vote. Nixon also waffled on Vietnam. In 1966 he had proclaimed, "We believe this is a war that has to be fought to prevent World War III." By early 1968 he was saying that America must "end the war," but refusing to say how or when he would do it. And many people, remembering his partisan, Red-baiting past refused to believe there was a "new Nixon." As if these were not handicaps enough, he yoked himself to Governor Spiro Agnew of Maryland, his choice for vice-president.

Inexperienced and maladroit, Agnew repeatedly insulted ethnic groups. He was one of the most ill-qualified vice-presidential candidates in modern times.

Humphrey, meanwhile, labored earnestly to salvage what he could from the discord of the convention. Many union leaders, supporting the war and distrusting the GOP, gave him their backing. So did some black spokesmen, who recalled his enthusiasm for civil rights as far back as the 1948 convention. Humphrey built bridges with the antiwar supporters by edging away, though much too slowly for McCarthy, from Johnson's policies. And he benefited from the energetic campaigning of Muskie, a Catholic who appealed to many ethnic voters. On October 31, when Johnson announced that he was stopping all bombing in North Vietnam, it seemed that Humphrey might have a chance.

Johnson's move came too late. On election day Nixon and Agnew triumphed over the Democrats. Considering the woeful state of the GOP in 1964, their victory was impressive. It suggested that voters were becoming much less partisan, indeed, more independent, than they had been in the heyday of the Democratic coalition under Roosevelt.

The results, however, hardly gave Nixon much cause for rejoicing. In winning he received 31,770,222 votes, less than 1 percent more than Humphrey's 31,267,744. He took only 43 percent of the total vote, the smallest share for a victor since Wilson's in 1912. He also failed to dent large Democratic majorities in Congress. Analysts concluded that a higher turnout among blacks would have given Humphrey the margin for victory, and that the Democratic coalition, though slipping, had not disap-

Nixon and Agnew

peared. Voters, they added, had not been attracted to Nixon. As in so many presidential elections since World War II, they had rejected the party in power.

This negativism showed most clearly in the votes for Wallace and his warlike running mate, General Curtis LeMay. Although Wallace carried only five states (all in the Deep South), he won 9.9 million votes. This was 13.5 percent of the turnout, the highest for any third-party candidate since Robert La Follette in 1924, and the highest ever for a candidate on the Right. Wallace's supporters included large numbers of northerners as well as southerners, young people as well as old, blue-collar workers (who defied union spokesmen) as well as wealthy conservatives. His appeal proved that a significant cross section was disgusted with the major parties, with radical youth, with liberalism generally. It showed also that millions still wanted to win the war, even if it meant adopting LeMay's suggestion of bombing North Vietnam into the Stone Age. For people such as these Nixon's victory over Humphrey was small consolation.

The Left was especially discouraged by the campaign of 1968. Nixon had proclaimed the slogan of "Bring Us Together Again." But he had shown little discernible longing to include in his happy circle the antiwar activists, the blacks, or young people generally. He had denounced the liberal Supreme Court, talked threateningly (though vaguely) about restoring "law and order," and hinted (again vaguely) about cutting back Great Society programs. Given the frustration, indeed the fury, felt by many activists, his victory did not auger well for social peace in the years ahead.

The result of the election should presumably have comforted the center. To a degree it did. Moderates considered it cause for congratulation that the American

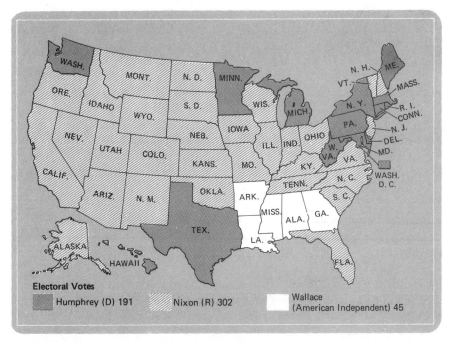

Electoral Votes

Humphrey (D) 191   Nixon (R) 302   Wallace (American Independent) 45

Election, 1968

people had gone peaceably to the polls and had authorized without protest a transfer of great political power from one party to the other. As so often in the American past, the two-party system had helped to undermine extremes. This stability was impressive amid such turbulent events.

But thoughtful analysts also asked: stability for what? In being forced to decide between two middle-of-the-road candidates (Wallace was never a plausible winner) the voters had not been given much of a choice. And in remaining so vague, Nixon had done little to enlighten them. Millions probably voted for him because they wanted respite from social experimentation. But did they want Nixon to dismantle the Great Society? Polls suggested not. Millions also supported him because they were tired of "Johnson's war." But did that mean they expected Nixon to stop the fighting or to escalate it? Here the polls were disturbing, for they showed that Americans were confused by the war. McCarthy's supporters, for instance, included many who wanted to end the conflict by moving in with the full force of American military power.

This confusion and ambiguity was the most unsettling feature of the campaign of 1968. Far from toning down the discord of the previous three years, it frustrated reactionaries as well as radicals and reduced even the center to apprehensiveness and uncertainty. As Americans were shortly to discover, the stability they had bought by letting Nixon "Bring Us Together Again" was to be short-lived indeed.

Suggestions for Reading

Useful starting points for understanding Johnson's foreign policy are Philip L. Geyelin, *Lyndon B. Johnson and the World* (1966); H. W. Brands, *The Wages of Globalism: Lyndon Johnson and the Limits of American Power* (1994); Larry Berman, *Lyndon Johnson's War: The Road to Stalemate in Vietnam* (1989); and Melvin Small, *Johnson, Nixon, and the Doves* (1987). For the intervention in the Dominican Republic see Theodore Draper, *Dominican Revolt** (1968); and Jerome Slater, *Intervention and Negotiation* (1970).

Books on domestic unrest include the Report of the National Advisory Commission on Civil Disorders* (1968); and the report of the Scranton Commission on Campus Violence* (1970). Hugh Davis Graham and Ted Gurr, *Violence in America** (1969), provides some historical background. See also Robert Fogelson, *Violence as Protest* (1971); and Robert Conot, *Rivers of Blood, Years of Darkness** (1968), which deals with the riot in Watts. Two eyewitness books by Norman Mailer are *Armies of the Night** (1968), on the demonstration at the Pentagon in 1968; and *Miami and the Siege of Chicago** (1968), on protest at the national conventions. Morris Dickstein, *Gates of Eden: American Culture in the 1960s* (1977), is a readable survey of its subject.

Among the many books on young people in the 1960s are Kenneth Keniston, *Young Radicals** (1968); Lewis Feuer, *The Conflict of Generations* (1969); and Seymour Lipset, *Rebellion in the University* (1972). Books read widely at the time are Theodore Roszak, *Making of a Counter Culture** (1969); and Charles Reich, *Greening of Amnerica** (1970). Paul Goodman, *Growing Up Absurd** (1960), is a lucid account of what alienated young people. Charles Silverman, *Crisis in the*

*Available in a paperback edition.

Classroom* (1970), and David Riesman and Christopher Jencks, *The Academic Revolution* (1969), cover their subjects thoroughly. A broad historical account is Helen Lefkowitz Horowitz, *Campus Life* (1987). Books dealing with left-wing ideology include Kirkpatrick Sale, *SDS* (1973); Peter Clecak, *Radical Paradoxes: Dilemmas of the American Left, 1945–1970* (1973); and Irwin Unger, *The Movement: A History of the American New Left, 1959–1972** (1974). See also James Miller, *"Democracy Is in the Streets"* (1987), on antiwar protests; and John Diggins, *The Rise and Fall of the American Left* (1991). Todd Gitlin, *The Whole World Is Watching* (1980), criticizes media coverage of the Left.

For the attitudes of militant blacks in the 1960s see James Baldwin, *The Fire Next Time** (1963); Malcom X, *Autobiography** (1965); Stokely Carmichael and Charles Hamilton, *Black Power** (1967); and Julius Lester, *Look Out Whitey!* (1968). Peter Coleman, *The Death and Life of Malcom X* (1973), is excellent. E. U. Essien-Udom, *Black Nationalism** (1962), describes the Black Muslims. See also David J. Garrow, *Protest at Selma: Martin Luther King, Jr. and The Voting Rights Act of 1965* (1978); and Steven Lawson, *In Pursuit of Power: Southern Blacks and Electoral Politics, 1965–1982* (1985). Surveys of other minorities include Matt Meier and Feliciano Rivera, *The Chicanos** (1972); Stan Steiner, *La Raza** (1970); and Oscar Lewis, *La Vida** (1966), on Puerto Ricans. Michael Novak, *Rise of the Unmeltable Ethnics* (1970), describes the failure of the melting pot.

Books that help in understanding the rise of feminism are Robert Lifton, ed., *The Woman in America* (1965); Lois Banner, *Women in Modern America** (1974); Cynthia Harrison, *On Account of Sex: The Politics of Women's Issues 1945–1968* (1987); and the book by William Chafe cited in Chapter 6. Important feminist statements are Betty Friedan, *The Feminine Mystique** (1963); and Germaine Greer, *The Female Eunuch** (1972). See also Judith Hole and Ellen Levine, *Rebirth of Feminism* (1971); Jo Freeman, *The Politics of Women's Liberation* (1975); Chafe, *Women and Equality* (1977); Joan Hoff-Wilson, ed., *Rites of Passage: The Past and Future of the ERA* (1986); Kristin Luker, *Abortion and the Politics of Motherhood* (1984); Andrea Dworkin, *Right-Wing Women* (1983); Lillian Faderman, *Odd Girls and Twilight Lovers: A History of Lesbian Life in 20th Century America* (1991); and Sara Evans, *Personal Politics: The Roots of Women's Liberation in the Civil Rights Movement and the New Left* (1979).

For politics, especially in 1968, consult the thorough account by Lewis Chester, et al., *An American Melodrama** (1970); and David Farber, *Chicago, 1968* (1987). Theodore White, *Making of a President, 1968** (1969), is useful. Marshall Frady, *Wallace** (1970), is entertaining and provocative. On Wallace's impact, see Dan Carter, *The Politics of Rage: George Wallace, the Origins of the New Conservatism, and the Transformation of American Politics* (1995). David Halberstam, *The Unfinished Odyssey of Robert Kennedy* (1968); and Jeremy Larner, *Nobody Knows: Reflections on the McCarthy Campaign of 1968* (1970), add insights. Richard Scammon and Ben Wattenberg, *The Real Majority* (1970), is a well-written, balanced account of electoral trends. Arthur M. Schlesinger, Jr., *Robert F. Kennedy and His Times* (1977), is a highly readable biography. See also Samuel Hays, *Beauty, Health, and Permanence: Environmental Politics in the United States, 1955–1985* (1987).

President Ronald Reagan

CHAPTER
6

Unsettling Times:
From Nixon to Reagan

In his first inaugural President Nixon repeated the "bring us together" note he had sounded during his campaign. "We are torn by division," he said. "To a crisis of the spirit, we need an answer of the spirit. And to find that answer, we need only look within ourselves. . . . We cannot learn from one another until we stop shouting at one another—until we speak quietly enough so that our words can be heard as well as our voices. For its part, government will listen."

Limited Advances, 1969–73

During the first few years of Nixon's tumultuous presidency, there were some signs that he was succeeding in promoting domestic harmony. Racial unrest seemed to subside. Contrary to expectations, the ghettos began to quiet in 1969, and they stayed relatively peaceful throughout the 1970s. Some people attributed the calm to prosecutions that had driven militants like Carmichael and Rap Brown into jail or exile. Others concluded that blacks had come to doubt the wisdom of destroying their own property. As one Watts leader put it, "The rioting phase, where we burn down businesses in our own areas, is over. The whole movement is in another direction— toward implementing black power and finding our own dignity as a people."

Blacks did not obtain much "power," but they did score some successes. Thanks to the Supreme Court, which ruled in 1969 (*Alexander* v. *Holmes*) that school desegregation must proceed "at once," the percentage of blacks in formerly all-black schools fell from 68 percent to 18 percent between 1968 and 1970. Statistics revealed that blacks, though still failing to capture a larger share of the national income, were developing a sizable middle class. The number who attended college rose between 1966 and 1970 by 85 percent—to 434,000. And blacks began to make use of the vote. By 1971 there were 13 black congressmen, 81 mayors, 198 state legislators, and 1,567 black local office holders. These advances were significant. Few people in 1960 could have predicted them. Nevertheless, discrimination still plagued the nation. The controversy over busing in the schools, perhaps the most acrimonious domestic issue of the early 1970s, showed that many white Americans still refused to accept residential integration or to go much beyond tokenism in the schools.

Feminists, too, made modest gains in the 1970s. Writers like Robin Morgan, author of *Sisterhood Is Powerful* (1970), and Germaine Greer, author of the *Female Eunuch* (1971), offered forceful briefs for women's liberation. In 1972 activists founded *Ms.,* the first feminist magazine to attract a sizable circulation. In the same year Congress approved legislation banning sex discrimination in colleges and universities receiving federal aid. In 1973 the Supreme Court (*Doe* v. *Bolton, Roe* v. *Wade*) ruled against state laws prohibiting abortions in the "first trimester," and both houses of Congress approved the Equal Rights Amendment, which feminists had been seeking for fifty years. A total of twenty-two states—of thirty-eight needed—ratified the amendment the same year.

Thereafter, feminism suffered reverses. Many black women continued to be cool to the movement. So did large numbers of married working women—who were too intent on keeping their jobs (or on earning enough money to return to the home) to spend time on campaigns for women's rights. NOW moderates complained that lesbians and sexual radicals exposed the movement to distortion and ridicule. Other articulate women led a countermovement. One of their most forceful leaders, Phyllis Schlafly, was a conservative whose idols were Thomas Edison, Elias Howe (inventor of the sewing machine), and Clarence Birdseye, all of whom had promoted comforts of domesticity. "A man's first significant purchase," she said, "is a diamond for his bride, and the largest financial investment of his life is a home for her to live in." Reflecting such attitudes, Nixon vetoed a bill in 1973 that would have provided funds for day-care centers. Meanwhile, Congress and many state legislatures banned federal Medicaid funding for abortions, thereby discriminating against the poor. And opponents campaigned against ratification of the ERA, which they said would destroy the "special place" of women in the home.

First Person

The women's movement promises to affect radically the life of virtually everyone in America. Only a small part of the population suffers because it is black, and most people have little contact with minorities. Women are 51 percent of the population, and chances are that every adult American either is one, is married to one, or has close social or business relations with many.

The feminist revolution will overturn the basic premises upon which these relations are built—stereotyped notions about the family and the roles of men and women, fallacies concerning masculinity and femininity, and the economic division of labor into paid work and homemaking.

If the 1960s belonged to the blacks, the next ten years are ours.

Lucy Komisar, an activist for women's liberation, explains her goals (1970).

Yet feminists, like blacks, could take some comfort in the progress they had made since the early 1960s. A majority of women told pollsters that they approved the general goals of the movement. Of all the protest movements that started in the 1960s—for peace, for black power, for brown power—the struggle for women's rights seemed most durable.

Other reformers took limited pleasure in accomplishments of the Democratic Congresses between 1969 and 1972. The legislators voted huge increases in Social Security benefits and extended the life of the 1965 Voting Rights Law. The Twenty-sixth Amendment to the Constitution, approved in 1971, extended voting rights to eighteen-year-olds. Though Congress fell far short of solving the nation's festering urban and racial problems, it did increase funding for some domestic purposes. In part because of a recession that descended on the economy in 1969, spending for food stamps—to go to 11 million poor people—rose from $250 million in 1969 to $2.2 billion in 1971. Nonmilitary federal expenditures as a percentage of the GNP almost doubled between 1969 and 1972. In historical perspective this was a dramatic rise in social welfare spending.

The lawmakers occasionally proved responsive to the pressures for environmental protection applied constantly by Ralph Nader and many others in the early 1970s. Among the several measures approved were the Water Quality Improvement Act, which attempted to control pollution caused by industry and power companies; the Clean Air Act, which called for changes in the manufacture of automobiles; and the Resource Recovery Act, which promoted recycling of solid wastes. Congress also refused funds for the Supersonic Transport (SST), a huge, noisy airplane that the administration had strongly favored. The Environmental Protection Agency, established in 1970, sued corporate or municipal leaders who violated federal standards. Despite these laws, many corporations found ways to evade or to postpone stringent regulation. Careless oil drilling and pumping continued to cause damage. Most alarming, Americans continued to squander resources at an alarming rate. But as the birthrate approached the point of zero population growth, advocates of ecological balance continued to hope that the nation could learn to exist without destroying its environment.

Nixon could claim little credit for these developments. Indeed, he was cool to legislation for social welfare or environmental protection. But many observers welcomed his apparent expertise in the realm of foreign affairs. Here he, like Kennedy, paid little attention to the State Department. Its secretary until late 1973, William Rogers, played an insignificant role in policy making. Nixon relied instead on Dr. Henry Kissinger, his national security adviser. Kissinger, a German immigrant who had become a professor of government at Harvard, was a skilled negotiator and an exponent of power politics. The way to avoid nuclear catastrophe, he believed, was to seek détente with the Soviet Union and China. These powers, with Japan and western Europe, could cooperate with the United States to prevent brush fires from escalating into World War III.

Kissinger's policies did not work wonders in 1969–71. In the Middle East they failed to end tensions heightened by Israel's stunning victory over Arab countries in the Six-Day War of 1967. Nixon and Kissinger also did not deserve much credit for the limited détente that did develop with Russia and China by 1972. Rather, these communist powers, at odds with each other, assumed considerable initiative for developing slightly better relations with the West. Still, the administration helped to defuse the Cold War and to moderate the militancy of postwar American foreign policy. Nixon, once the Cold Warrior extraordinaire, had revealed his capacity for change.

The President even seemed to make progress toward de-escalating the war in Vietnam. In 1969 he announced the Nixon Doctrine, which proclaimed that allies could expect American aid, but not troops, when confronted with internal revolt. He added that he would end the draft within two years. Encouraged by Secretary of Defense Melvin Laird, he propounded Vietnamization, as it became called. The United States, Nixon said, would build up the Vietnamese military so that it could stand on its own. To institute this policy, the President began withdrawing American troops. In 1968 there had been 543,000; by September 1972 there were 39,000. Though later developments revealed the serious limitations of Vietnamization, the troop withdrawals were a popular step toward disengagement.

The Persistence of Discord

From the beginning of Nixon's presidency, however, the discord of the Johnson years persisted. For the universities, in fact, the spring of 1969 was the most disruptive to date. Police moved in to restore order at Howard, the University of Massachusetts, Pennsylvania State, and San Fernando State. Conflicts between black and white students erupted in violence at the University of Wisconsin and City College of New York. Harvard students invaded University Hall, rifled files, and were thrown out by state police. And at Cornell armed blacks seized the student union, leading the university president to capitulate to their demands. The backlash that followed such demonstration—perpetrated by a small minority of students—was one of many forces that culminated in scanty funding for colleges and universities in the early 1970s.

Meanwhile, unrest among workers mounted. The 1970s were for public service employees what the 1930s had been for industrial workers. Teachers, nurses, police officers, garbage collectors, firefighters, and transit employees formed militant unions, picketed city hall, and staged walkouts that would have seemed revolutionary in Calvin Coolidge's day. A strike of postal workers tied up the nation's mails for a week and forced the National Guard to take charge in New York City. Despairingly, Congress established an independent postal service that was expected to soften discontent. Inflation stemming from a war-heated economy accounted for much of this conflict. So did new visions of the "good life" and meaningful work. White-collar and service workers in the 1970s, like so many Americans in the prosperous postwar years, were joining the revolution of rising expectations.

Continuing violence was particularly frightening. In early 1970 bombs tore up the Manhattan offices of IBM, General Telephone and Electronics Corporation, and Mobil Oil. Antiwar revolutionaries claimed credit for the explosions. Shortly thereafter two black militants, followers of Rap Brown, were killed when one of their homemade bombs went off prematurely. And in March 1970 three young radicals were blown to pieces in their "bomb factory" in Greenwich Village. Two other revolutionaries, cut and bleeding, fled from the scene.

These were but the most striking manifestations of apparent social upheaval in the years after 1968. In New York City bomb threats averaged 1,000 a month in 1969–70. Within fifteen months 368 bombs actually exploded. In 1970 the FBI reported 35,202 assults on policemen, four times the number in 1960. People were not even safe in the air: skyjacking diverted seventy-one planes in 1969 alone. The drug traffic seemed particularly frightening. When rock stars Jimi Hendrix and Janis Joplin died from overdoses, some of the worst fears seemed confirmed.

The most shocking violence of the early 1970s took place in prisons, many of which were breeding grounds for racial confrontations between convicts and authorities. One such outbreak occurred in August 1971 at San Quentin prison, where George Jackson, one of the three black "Soledad brothers" (actually not related), was caged for allegedly killing a white guard at Soledad prison a year earlier. Using a smuggled pistol, Jackson broke out of his cell and demanded the release of twenty-seven prisoners. He then murdered three white guards and two trusties before falling in a rain of shots himself. Militants, outraged by his death, dressed him in a Black Panther uniform and gave him a martyr's funeral.

Jackson's death helped to trigger the most bloody prison riot in American history. This occurred at Attica, New York, home of 2,254 convicts, 75 percent of whom were black or Puerto Rican. All the 383 guards were white, and racial incidents were common. In September 1971 angry blacks staged a rebellion that was quickly joined by more than 1,200 inmates. They grabbed 39 hostages, seriously hurt a guard, barricaded themselves in a cell block, and issued demands on the warden. When the prisoners threatened to cut the throats of their hostages, the authorities waited no longer. In the assault which followed, police gunfire killed 30 prisoners and 10 guards. To some observers, like *The New York Times's* Tom Wicker, the Attica riot displayed the callousness of officials like Governor Rockefeller, the violence of police, and the urgent need for prison reform. To many others it was "proof" of the savagery of the criminal population—especially of blacks—and of the need for "law and order."

NIXON AT BAY, 1969–71

Nixon, of course, was not to blame for such violence. But to many Americans—progressives, college activists, blacks—he was an unsympathetic figure. Between 1969 and mid-1971 they grew increasingly hostile to the President. They focused on four themes: his personal style, his domestic policies, his "southern strategy," and Vietnam.

Objections to Nixon's style ranged from the frivolous to the profound. Americans who had looked to the White House for cultural leadership disliked his patronage of pro football, middlebrow music, and Norman Vincent Peale. Others considered him banal, hypocritical, and sanctimonious. People wondered about his close friendships with C. G. ("Bebe") Rebozo, a wealthy real estate operator, and with Robert H. Abplanalp, a businessman, who helped Nixon finance the purchase of property worth $600,000 at Key Biscayne, Florida, and San Clemente, California. Nixon's taste for regal living, it was revealed later, cost the government $10 million in improvements and security measures. To his critics, "Tricky Dick" was becoming "King Richard."

Nixon's style was above all secretive and suspicious. Extremely sensitive to criticism, he avoided contacts with the press. Faced with important decisions, he frequently slipped off to the presidential retreat at Camp David, Maryland, or to one of his tightly guarded compounds in Florida and California. Even his cabinet found him remote and unsupportive. Two of the more popular among his appointees, Secretary of the Interior Walter Hickel and HEW Secretary Robert Finch, left or were fired by the end of 1970. Like reporters, they complained that Nixon surrounded himself with a much-expanded White House staff of ambitious, unscrupulous young lawyers, public relations men, and advertising executives. Nixon's closest domestic advisers, H. R. Haldeman and John D. Erlichman, had no experience in government. Tough, cold, and devoted to their boss, they excluded visitors, insulted important politicians, and narrowed the circle of decision making.

The President's economic policies aroused special concern. Some of his angriest critics, surprisingly enough, were conservatives. When Nixon proclaimed, in January 1971, "I am now a Keynesian," they were appalled. They were equally shocked to discover that the budget deficit for the 1970–71 fiscal year amounted to more than $23 billion, only $2 billion less than the record set during Johnson's last year in office. Nixon's toleration of unbalanced budgets provided added evidence of his flexibility (critics said of his lack of principle) and of the political clout enjoyed by pressure groups.

Conservatives had other complaints about Nixon's domestic policies. They resented Hickel's rigorous enforcement of the laws protecting the environment. They grumbled especially about the influence of Daniel Patrick Moynihan, a Harvard professor whom Nixon named to head the newly created Urban Affairs Council. Under Moynihan's persistent coaching Nixon endorsed the controversial Family Assistance Plan, which would have guaranteed an income of $1,600 a year (plus food stamps valued at $800 or more) to a family of four. The plan promised cash payments to the hitherto neglected working poor. Michael Harrington, a socialist, termed FAP "the most radical idea since the New Deal." But Democrats in Congress ultimately sidetracked the measure—in part because they demanded more generous benefits, in part because they disliked Nixon, in part because the President (to gain conservative support) appeared to threaten able-bodied heads of households with loss of benefits if they failed to register for job training or to accept work. Congress's rejection of the measure meant that America's porous welfare "system" staggered on.

Most criticism of the President's domestic policies came from liberals. They recognized that Nixon, like Kennedy, was primarily interested in foreign affairs. Indeed, Nixon once commented, "I've always thought this country could run itself domestically without a President." He added, "All you need is a competent cabinet to run the country at home." This attitude antagonized reformers, most of whom could not get past the "Berlin Wall" erected by Haldeman and Erlichman. Long before Congress counterattacked in 1973–74, many of its most influential members were barely on speaking terms with the White House.

The liberals were particularly critical of Nixon's handling of the economy, which grew ragged and unstable between 1969 and 1972. The administration's tight money policy, they claimed, harmed investment and impeded construction. The failure to set forth price and wage guidelines encouraged round after round of inflationary settlements between management and labor. A \$2.5 billion tax cut, which Nixon signed in December 1969, further fed inflation. By 1971 the country was experiencing the worst of all possible worlds: "stagflation." Inflation (5.3 percent in 1970) coexisted with recession (6 percent unemployment). At fault, said Democratic party chieftain Lawrence O'Brien, was "Nixonomics." O'Brien explained, "All the things that should go up—the stock market, corporate profits, real spendable income, productivity—go down, and all the things that should go down—unemployment, prices, interest rates—go up."

NIXON'S SOUTHERN STRATEGY

Most objectionable of all to progressives was the administration's "southern strategy." In its broad outlines this reflected the argument of Kevin Phillips, a Justice Department aide who wrote *The Emerging Republican Majority* in 1969. To Phillips the preeminent need of the GOP was to outflank men like Governor Wallace by 1972. This meant securing the votes of "middle Americans"—southern whites, blue-collar workers, Catholic ethnics, suburbanites, conservatives. It meant stressing the theme of "law and order," discrediting activist students, and paying relatively little attention to the wishes of blacks, Hispanic-Americans, and others who were predominantly Democratic anyway.

This southern strategy helps to explain Nixon's civil rights policies. These were a predominantly conservative mixture of forward and backward movements. To assist blacks, Nixon instituted the so-called Philadelphia Plan, which required unions working on federal projects to accept quotas of blacks as apprentices and to admit them when training was completed. To secure black support, he named James Farmer, a leading activist, as an assistant secretary of HEW. He told Farmer that he wanted to do "what's right" for blacks. "I care," he added. "I just hope people will believe that I DO care."

During the two years that Farmer stayed with HEW, however, he was unable to do much. Like other advocates of civil rights, he confronted the influence of Attorney General John Mitchell, a Nixon law partner who emerged as the strongest figure in the new cabinet. Under Mitchell the Department of Justice attempted (unsuccessfully) to prevent extension of the Voting Rights Act of 1965. He also brought suit to delay school desegregation guidelines in Mississippi. Outraged attorneys in the civil rights division of the Justice Department and HEW protested vigorously. Though the Supreme Court's ruling for desegregation "at once" foiled Mitchell's effort, he had shown the white South that the administration cared.

Mitchell's passion for "law and order" led him into several other blunders between 1969 and 1971. One was his attempt to prosecute antiwar demonstrators. Among the many activists he had arrested were the "Harrisburg Seven," the "Gainesville Eight," and others who were tried in groups. Capping efforts to stifle dissent, Mitchell brought suit in 1971 to stop publication of the so-called Pentagon Papers, a 47-volume, 2.5-million-word summary that documented the escalation of the war in Vietnam prior to 1969. However, the Supreme Court ruled against prior restraint of publication in the press, and lower courts sustained the antiwar demonstrators. The court decisions revealed the continuing independence of the judiciary from executive activity. They suggested also Mitchell's disregard for civil liberties. For a guardian of "law and order" it was a highly controversial performance.

The southern strategy came gradually to dictate the administration's choice of justices to fill vacancies in the Supreme Court between 1969 and 1972. The first nominee, Warren Earl Burger of Minnesota, was a moderate named to replace Chief Justice Warren, who retired after sixteen years on the bench. The Senate confirmed him quickly. Mitchell's next choice was Judge Clement F. Haynsworth, Jr., a South Carolinian. Union leaders, civil rights advocates, and progressives opposed him. Early supporters wavered when they learned of conflict-of-interest charges marring Haynsworth's judicial record. In November 1969 the Senate, including seventeen Republicans, rejected him.

The Senate's action infuriated Nixon, who called the attacks on Haynsworth "brutal, vicious . . . and unfair." His temper high, he carelessly nominated Mitchell's next choice, G. Harold Carswell, a Floridian who served on the court of appeals. Suspecting Nixon's political motives, opponents produced evidence to show Carswell's racial bias. Law professors throughout the country exposed his mediocrity as a judge. Accordingly, the Senate, including thirteen Republicans, rejected him in April 1970. Adhering to the southern strategy, Nixon burst out, "I understand the bitter feelings of millions of Americans who live in the South. They have my assurance that the day will come when judges like Carswell and Haynsworth can and will sit on the High Court."

After circulating the names of other mediocre candidates, Nixon finally searched for qualified nominees who could command congressional support. By 1972 he had named three. The first, Judge Harry Blackmun of Minnesota, held views that resembled Burger's. The second, Lewis F. Powell, Jr., had been a president of the American Bar Association. The third, Assistant Attorney General William H. Rehnquist, was a young Goldwater Republican who was developing a reputation as a thoughtful exponent of conservative jurisprudence. The Senate confirmed all three.

Nixon's actions enhanced his standing in the South. But they antagonized Congress. And they failed to produce a tractable Court. Though the four new appointees often voted together, they showed little disposition to reverse the decisions of the Warren Court, and they did not constitute a majority. In addition to the abortion and Pentagon Papers cases—both of which annoyed the administration—the Burger Court voted unanimously in 1971 that busing was necessary and proper if other means failed to achieve school desegregation. Though later decisions concerning busing left the issue in doubt, it was clear that Burger and his associates would not block the movement for racial justice.

In the next few years the Court continued to antagonize conservatives. In 1972 it held, five to four, that state laws authorizing the death sentence were unconstitutional because they gave too much discretion to judges and juries. The decision did not outlaw the death sentence per se—thirty-two states passed new laws authorizing it by 1975—but it stopped executions for the time being, and it prompted renewed litigation that branded the death penalty unconstitutional "cruel and unusual punishment." The Court also ruled that the government had to get a court order before employing wiretapping against suspected subversives. And in 1974 it ruled, eight to nothing, that Nixon must turn over damning tape recordings to a district court. The President, like many of his predecessors in the White House, experienced the often rugged independence of the judicial branch.

Vietnam, Cambodia, and Laos

Nixon's most divisive policies before 1973 were in the realm where he had seemed so assured: foreign policy. His problem was simple: Vietnamization was not working. As American troops were withdrawn, the North Vietnamese and the Vietcong proved more than a match for the forces of South Vietnam's dictator, Nguyen Van Thieu. To compensate, Nixon authorized unpublicized bombing raids on neighboring Cambodia, which the enemy was using as a sanctuary. These raids, some 3,600 beginning early in 1969, failed to stop the revolutionary forces. Encouraged by the Joint Chiefs, Nixon then sent American troops into Cambodia in April 1970. The fact that the soldiers were invading a nonbelligerent nation did not seem to trouble him. On the contrary, he spoke fiercely. "We will not be humiliated," he explained. "We will not be defeated. If when the chips are down the United States acts like a pitiful helpless giant, the forces of totalitarianism and anarchy will threaten free nations and free institutions throughout the world. It is not our power but our will that is being tested. . . ."

The invasion of Cambodia reduced some of the military pressure on Thieu's forces, and gave Vietnamization a little more time. In this limited sense Nixon and his defenders could call it a success. But in a wider context it was a miscalculation. The invasion failed to drive the enemy out of Cambodia. It further polarized domestic opinion in the United States. Worst of all, the assault dragged Cambodia itself into full-scale civil war, one that tore its society to pieces by the late 1970s.

INTENSIFICATION OF ANTIWAR SENTIMENT

At home Nixon's action prompted stirrings of independence in Congress, which repealed the 1964 Gulf of Tonkin resolution. The invasion also led to tragedy in Ohio. Two nights after Nixon announced his move, students at Kent State University firebombed the ROTC building, causing Ohio Governor James Rhodes to call in the National Guard. For a time it seemed that calm would return. But on May 4 students threw rocks and bottles at the guardsmen, who responded with tear gas. When the soldiers ran out of gas, they retreated nervously up a hillside. They were out of range of rocks, and in no danger. Some of the guardsmen then stopped, turned, and began to shoot. A girl screamed, "My God, they're killing us!" When the firing stopped, four students lay dead and eleven were wounded. The Justice Department, acting under Mitchell's orders, failed to call a federal grand jury to review the tragedy, and it was not until 1974 that eight guardsmen were indicted (and acquitted) on criminal charges of violating, the students' civil rights.

The deaths at Kent State unleashed a torrent of protest, especially on the campuses, which erupted for the third consecutive spring. Within the month demonstrations disrupted more than 400 universities; more than 250 had to be closed down before the end of the semester. By May 9 weekend, some 100,000 students descended on Washington in protest. A week later at Jackson State College (now

Kent State, 1970

Jackson State University) in Mississippi two black students were killed and eleven wounded when police fired indiscriminately into a dormitory. President William J. McGill of Columbia University commented accurately that it was the "most disastrous month of May in the history of American higher education."

Nixon's first reaction was to discredit the students. "These bums . . . blowing up the campuses," he said, ". . . burning up the books, storming about." After the bloodshed at Kent State he commented that the shootings should "remind us once again that when dissent turns to violence it invites tragedy." But the protests worried him, and before dawn on May 9 he got out of bed and stole off to talk to demonstrators camped near the Lincoln Memorial. He intended to be responsive, conciliatory, understanding. But the ensuing dialogue exposed the gulf that separated him from the demonstrators. To California students he talked about surfing; to those from Syracuse he posed questions about the college football team. When he left to eat breakfast in a Washington hotel, he had done nothing to placate his opposition.

The campus disorders also heightened the President's desire to curb dissent. Already he had arranged to tap the phones of thirteen top government officials whom he suspected of leaking stories about the bombings in Cambodia, and of four journalists who had published them. Now, in June 1970, he tried to form a special national security committee composed of top people from the CIA, FBI, and Defense Intelligence Agency, and headed by FBI chief J. Edgar Hoover. The committee was to have the power to engage in electronic surveillance, stage break-ins, open mail, and infiltrate college campuses. Hoover, however, spiked the plan by refusing to serve. Disappointed, Nixon had to put the plan aside for a while.

Instead, he relied on the vitriolic rhetoric of his vice-president, Spiro Agnew, who outdid himself during the congressional campaigning of 1970. Dissidents, Agnew said, were "parasites of passion," "ideological eunuchs," an "effete corps of impudent snobs who characterize themselves as intellectuals." The press was an "unelected elite," a "tiny and closed fraternity of privileged men . . . enjoying a monopoly sanctioned and licensed by the government." Agnew's assaults dovetailed neatly with the southern strategy and appealed to "middle Americans" who disliked the radical students and the "metromedia" of the eastern seaboard. But Agnew was practically threatening the media with censorship. Not since the days of the sedition and espionage acts during World War I had an administration acted so menacingly toward its opponents.

Agnew, however, did little to help the administration. The GOP lost ground in the 1970 elections, and Nixon struggled unsuccessfully against worsening stagflation early in 1971. The press carried alarming stories of drug addiction, desertion, and mutiny among the troops in Vietnam. Courting further confrontations with antiwar spokesmen, Nixon had charges of stealing government property brought against Daniel Ellsberg, a McNamara protégé and Rand Corporation employee who had released the Pentagon Papers to the press. Some of Nixon's aides even drew up an "enemies list." It included such threats to the state as James Reston, Jane Fonda, Barbra Streisand, Paul Newman, and many others.

Nixon compounded his difficulties with yet another adventure in Southeast Asia. This was an invasion of Laos by South Vietnamese troops in February. Its aim, like the assault on Cambodia in 1970, was to cut off sanctuaries and supply routes winding into Vietnam. The incursion was also to display the fighting capacity of the South Vietnamese, who were to go it alone this time. When the attack was over in April, Nixon announced proudly, "Tonight I can report that Vietnamization has succeeded." Press accounts showed otherwise. The enemy inflicted 50 percent casualties—3,800 South Vietnamese killed and 4,500 wounded—in six weeks. Only heavy bombing by the United States—again in a neutral country—prevented still more shocking losses.

Predictably, the invasion of Laos provoked demonstrations. This time the universities were relatively quiet—perhaps because students remembered Kent State, perhaps because protest on the campuses had seemed ineffective in the past. Instead, students and antiwar veterans—by then a growing lobby—headed for Washington. Their protests were nonviolent but disruptive, and Mitchell sent in police, national guardsmen, and army troops. Using truncheons and tear gas, they arrested 12,614 people in four days and penned them in open spaces like Robert F. Kennedy Memorial Stadium. Mitchell said that the government had "stopped a repressive mob from robbing the rights of others." The courts, appalled, threw out the arrests as violations of civil rights. Once again the Nixon administration, which had promised to bring the nation together, had helped to drive it apart.

students protest Laos

The Great Turnabout, 1971–72

In mid-1971 the administration began a turnabout that dramatically improved its fortunes. Nixon began it in July by announcing that he was to visit the People's Republic of China early in 1972. Critics grumbled that the proposed trip was a public relations stunt. Others complained that Chiang Kaishek was being abandoned—indeed, the General Assembly of the United Nations voted three months later to seat Mao Zedong's regime. Still others pointed out that the visit would poison American relations with Japan, the most highly industrialized nation in Asia. But many Americans were as pleased as they were surprised by Nixon's announcement. Kissinger's efforts for détente with the great powers were apparently paying off. The Cold War was thawing at last.

A month later Nixon made an equally dramatic announcement: the New Economic Policy. To improve the nation's balance of payments, he said, the United States would permit the dollar to find its own level—to "float" in the international exchange markets. He also called for a 10 percent tax on many imports, the repeal of important excise taxes, and tax breaks for industries that undertook new investment. To bring inflation to a halt, wages, prices, and dividends were to be frozen for ninety days, and controlled thereafter.

These changes were startling. Permitting the dollar to float in its weakened condition was largely the same as devaluing it. To many Americans this was a rude shock. Establishing control seemed even more incredible, for Nixon, who had served unhappily as a young lawyer with the Office of Price Administration in World War II, had adamantly rejected such a policy earlier in the year. But if Americans were surprised, they were pleased by the administration's show of resolve—and by the gains that appeared to follow. As the dollar declined in value (eventually by about 9 percent), American exports became cheaper, and the balance of trade seemed to improve. Controls temporarily slowed down the rate of inflation. Stock prices jumped encouragingly, until the Dow Jones industrial average broke 1,000 for the first time in history, in November. The President's turnabout seemed to be literally paying off.

It did not last. In the next few months Nixon's economic policy was less assured. The government's wage and price commissions began to give way before the pressure of unions and of business interests. Inflation, which controls had checked, began to accelerate again. Disgruntled, the AFL-CIO refused to cooperate any longer in March 1972. For the rest of the year—indeed for the next decade—the rising cost of living became an increasingly vital concern.

But Nixon's pyrotechnic diplomacy in early 1972 helped conceal the faults of his economic policies. His visit to China in February 1972, though accomplishing little that was concrete, was elaborately staged for the American television audience. It greatly enhanced his stature. His handling of Moscow was also dazzling. When North Vietnam mounted an offensive on March 30, Nixon responded by bombing the North for the first time in three years and by dropping mines in the harbor of Haiphong, a provocative step that not even Johnson had dared to take. Yet the Soviet Union, not wanting to drive the United States and China closer together, posed no objections. On the contrary, it welcomed Nixon with open arms when he

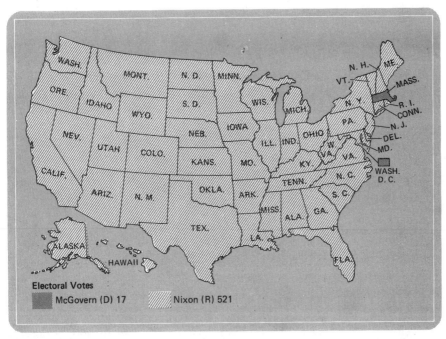

Election, 1972

visited Moscow in May. The trips to Peking and Moscow marked the high points of the Nixon-Kissinger foreign policy.

By this time the President's campaign for reelection was well underway. Here he took no chances. In 1971 he had quietly formed the Special Investigations Unit. It hired "plumbers," outfitted illegally by the CIA, to burglarize the office of Daniel Ellsberg's psychiatrist in an unsuccessful attempt to find compromising evidence. In 1971 Nixon had also formed the Committee to Re-elect the President. CREEP disbursed funds for "dirty tricks" aimed at embarrassing potential opponents like Wallace and Muskie. It arranged to tap the phone of the secretary of Lawrence O'Brien, chairman of the Democratic National Committee. And it collected a record $60 million, much of it in violation of existing laws against corporate contributions to political campaigns.

In mapping out his campaign the President had more than the usual amount of luck. Senator Edward Kennedy of Massachusetts, once the most popular Democratic challenger, had seriously harmed his chances in 1969 when he had driven his car off a bridge on the island of Chappaquiddick near Martha's Vineyard. The crash caused the death by drowning of a passenger, Mary Jo Kopechne. Senator Edmund Muskie, the front-runner early in 1972, was damaged politically by his tearful response to a letter contrived by a "dirty trickster" in the employ of CREEP and published during the New Hampshire primary. George Wallace, who scored well in Democratic primaries in the North as well as in the South and seriously threatened Nixon's chances in November, was shot on May 15 by a deranged white youth,

Arthur H. Bremer. Though Wallace survived, the attack paralyzed him for life and removed him from the presidential race. As it turned out, Wallace's withdrawal practically guaranteed Nixon the election.

The Democratic convention further played into Nixon's hands. It adopted a quota system that favored blacks, women, and young people while lessening the power of labor unions, urban political machines, congressional leaders, and ethnic groups. It thereby alienated the backbone of the Democratic party and exposed the ultimate nominee, George McGovern, to the charge that he (like Goldwater in 1964) was the candidate of a lunatic fringe. As if to ensure McGovern's defeat, the delegates nominated as his running mate Senator Thomas Eagleton of Missouri. Eagleton then disclosed that he had twice been hospitalized for psychiatric care. Under enormous pressure to reject Eagleton, McGovern at first proclaimed his support of the vice-presidential candidate, only to reverse himself and secure Eagleton's withdrawal. R. Sargent Shriver, a Kennedy brother-in-law who had headed the Peace Corps and the war on poverty, took Eagleton's place. McGovern, whose integrity had been a major asset, now struck many people as indecisive and self-righteous.

In an effort to redeem himself, McGovern moved to the attack. He criticized Nixon's handling of the war, which had caused 15,000 American deaths since January 1969. He rapped the administration's economic policies. He charged the President with dropping an antitrust suit against ITT in return for a campaign contribution of $400,000. And he tried to implicate Nixon in a burglary on June 17 of the Democratic National Committee headquarters in Washington's Watergate Hotel.

The Watergate affair, as it became known, deeply worried Nixon, who was told of CREEP's involvement in it. Citing national security reasons, he got Haldeman to stop the FBI from investigating the incident. Later in the campaign he authorized payments of more than $460,000 in hush money to keep the plumbers from implicating higher-ups in the administration. Publicly, he and other ranking Republicans disclaimed any involvement in the affair. Nixon said inaccurately in late August that his counsel, John Dean, had conducted a "complete investigation" that showed that "no one in the White House staff, no one in this administration, presently employed, was involved in this very bizarre incident." Nixon concluded: "What really hurts in matters of this sort is not the fact that they occur, because overzealous people in campaigns do things that are wrong. What hurts is if you try to cover them up."

Americans apparently believed such protestations of innocence. Indeed they had little choice, for the Democrats lacked evidence at the time to implicate the White House in a cover-up. The voters also seemed impressed with Nixon's conduct of foreign policy. Despite the failures of Vietnamization, troop withdrawals were continuing, and casualty lists, which had shown around 300 American deaths per week in late 1968, totaled near zero by September 1972. A month later, on October 26, Kissinger held a televised press conference to announce a breakthrough in the negotiations he had been conducting with the enemy in Paris. "Peace," he declared grandiloquently, "is at hand."

Kissinger's misleading announcement probably added to the large margin of victory for the team of Nixon and Agnew, which took 47 million votes to 29 million for McGovern and Shriver. This was 60.7 percent of the vote, the third highest percentage in modern American history (behind FDR, with 60.8 percent, in 1936, and LBJ, with 61 percent, in 1964). Nixon carried every state except Massachusetts and the District of Columbia, for a margin in the electoral college of 521 to 17. Nixon's critics bravely explained that turnout had been low and pointed out that Democrats still held wide margins in Congress. But it was impossible to deny that the voters had endorsed the President. At least for the time being Nixon was a resounding political success.

Acrimony Again, 1973–75

INTERNATIONAL PROBLEMS

Those who hoped for harmony after the election were immediately disillusioned. Kissinger's forecast of peace, it developed, was inaccurate, primarily because General Thieu refused to agree to the deals the United States and North Vietnam were making without his participation. By mid-December the prospects for peace seemed as remote as ever.

Nixon, safely reelected, reacted sharply by authorizing the heaviest bombing of North Vietnam in the twelve-year history of American involvement in the war. General Alexander Haig, Kissinger's deputy, described it aptly as the "brutalizing" of the north. Some of the bombs hit a hospital in Hanoi; others damaged a camp holding American prisoners of war. The enemy, better defended than in the past, shot down fifteen B-52 planes (each costing $8 million) and captured ninety-eight American airmen in two weeks.

The resumption of bombing, though costly, may have served some diplomatic purposes; two weeks after starting it Nixon announced that peace negotiations were soon to resume. At the same time, he stopped the raids. More important in North

America's Mood:
The Public's View of the Most Important
Problem Facing the Country,
According to Gallup Poll Results,
1969–74

1969	Vietnam
1970	Reducing crime
1971	Inflation
1972	Vietnam
1973	High cost of living
1974	Energy crisis

SOURCE: Adapted from *U.S. Foreign Policy: Context, Conduct, Content* by Marian Irish and Elke Frank. © 1975 by Harcourt Brace. Reproduced by permssion of the publisher.

Desperate Vietnamese refugees try to board an American evacuation helicopter April 1975.

Vietnam's willingness to talk may have been pressure to settle from Russia and China, both of whom were tired of the war. In any event, the negotiations succeeded in establishing a cease-fire beginning January 28. An agreement signed by the United States, North Vietnam, South Vietnam, and the Vietcong's Provisional Revolutionary Government (PRG) decreed that in the next sixty days America would remove its 23,700 remaining troops, and the enemy would return 509 prisoners of war. The future of Vietnam—left vague—was to be determined by negotiations, not by force.

The agreement brought to an end, after twelve years, the presence of American combat troops in Vietnam. In that time the dead included 57,000 Americans, 5,200 allied soldiers, 184,000 South Vietnamese, and an estimated 925,000 North Vietnamese. Approximately five times these numbers were wounded. The total of refugees, and of civilian deaths, in Vietnam, Laos, and Cambodia could only be guessed at—probably many millions. In the face of such statistics it is not surprising that many Americans, relieved at the prospect of withdrawal, did not dispute Nixon's statement that he had brought "peace with honor."

Thoughtful observers knew better. In part because Nixon had secretly assured Thieu of military support in the event of communist gains, South Vietnam refused from the start to recognize the PRG, to consider communist participation in a coalition government, or to work earnestly to restrain its combat forces. Faced with this all-or-nothing attitude, the PRG and North Vietnam pressed on for a military solution, and fighting ravaged the country again. In response America dispatched bombing raids over Laos and sent billions more in military equipment to sustain Vietnamization. For a time in early 1973 Nixon even considered resuming saturation bombing of North Vietnam, refraining only for fear of domestic turmoil. Russia and China, meanwhile, aided Hanoi and the Vietcong.

Whether America learned the correct "lessons" from the war also remains to be seen. World War I, after all, had taught the "virtues" of noninvolvement; World War II had encouraged globalism. By 1973, however, many Americans seemed fairly sure about two things: first, that they could not protect the whole world; and second, that Southeast Asia should fight its own civil wars. Holding to such views, Congress forbade the President to undertake any military action whatever in Indochina after August 15, 1973. It also approved, over Nixon's veto, the War Powers Act of 1973. Henceforth the White House was to give Congress a full explanation within forty-eight hours for the dispatch of American troops abroad. Presidents must withdraw such troops within sixty days unless Congress specifically authorized them to stay. As in 1919, presidential excesses prompted a resurgence of congressional will.

It was too much to expect, however, that the withdrawal of American troops could end the nation's problems. On the contrary, continuing deficits in the balance of payments resulted in further devaluation of the dollar—this time of 10 percent—by February 1973. Rising inflation forced Nixon to reintroduce price controls, first on petroleum products and meat, and then (in June) on all retail prices. The controls lasted sixty days. At the same time, militant Native Americans on the Oglala Sioux reservation in South Dakota reminded Americans of injustice at home. Rising in anger at Wounded Knee, site of a massacre of Indians eighty-three years earlier, they seized eleven hostages and demanded redress of their grievances. Federal authorities responded by surrounding the protesters and blocking the flow of food. Before the siege ended eleven weeks later, outbreaks of shooting had killed one Native American and wounded one FBI man. The protracted confrontation settled nothing of consequence.

Withdrawal from Vietnam also failed to deliver the nation from complicated overseas involvements. These became obvious in October 1973, when Israel and the Arab states went to war again. As in 1948, and 1956, and 1967, the Israelis showed their military superiority. But this time the Arabs inflicted costly losses on their enemies, and it became clearer than ever that the future of Israel depended heavily on continuing American support. In the next two years Kissinger, who became secretary of state in October 1973, shuttled back and forth to the Middle East in an effort to promote some understanding between the antagonists. Though he made progress with Egypt, he found Israel reluctant at first to return territory gained in the 1967 war. He also could not placate the Palestine Liberation Organization, which claimed to represent the million-plus Arabs uprooted from their lands in Israel. Meanwhile the Soviet Union continued to provide arms to the Arabs and to persecute Jews at home. Soviet-American détente was obviously limited.

The Middle East war had the further effect of drawing the often quarrelsome Arab states closer together. Using oil as a weapon, they cut back on exports of oil to their enemies, including the United States. Thereafter, they raised their prices. These actions dramatically exposed the dependence of the industrialized nations on

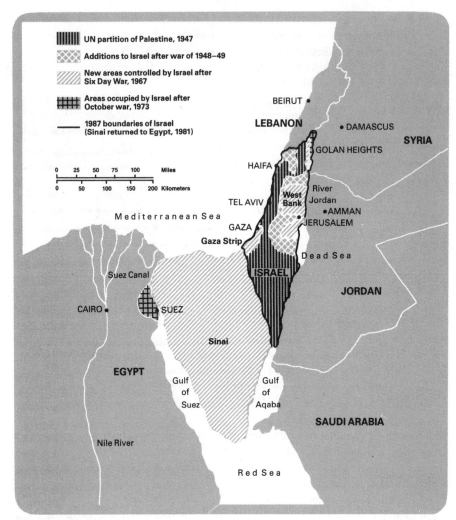

Middle East, 1947–81

oil—the great powers, one observer cracked, were now the United States, Russia, Saudi Arabia, Kuwait, and Abu Dhabi. The increase in oil prices was also followed by the most frightening wave of inflation to date throughout much of the industrialized noncommunist world. Nixon called for voluntary restraint in the use of gasoline and heating oil. But he refused to impose rationing, to investigate high oil company profits, or to develop a long-range policy for the conservation of energy resources. Inflation continued to mount, the stock market to plummet, and the economy to stagnate.

A popular President might have been able to act resourcefully against these problems. But a host of revelations in 1973–74 combined to undermine Nixon's standing. One showed that the CIA had been involved in a military coup in September 1973 that overthrew Chile's Salvador Allende, a popular Marxist leader. Though the CIA denied the charges, other rumors about the agency's excesses placed it also on the defensive. (One such rumor, that the CIA had hired Mafiosi to kill Fidel Castro in 1961, was later confirmed.)

WATERGATE

Charges of corruption further harmed the administration in 1973–74. In October 1973 Vice-President Agnew, champion of law and order, had to resign when it was revealed that he had cheated on his income taxes and had taken more than $100,000 in payoffs from contractors between 1966 and 1972. The IRS then disclosed that Nixon himself owed more than $400,000 in back taxes and penalties. Other critics showed that CREEP had solicited huge corporate campaign contributions, illegal under the 1972 campaign financing law, that the government had spent millions on improvements to the presidential properties in Florida and California, and that the administration had raised subsidies to milk producers, who thereupon gave $527,500 to the Republican party. The trail of corruption surrounding the election was winding dangerously close to the Oval Office.

The President's major problem was the Watergate burglary. Though he did his best to cover up his administration's involvement in the affair, hard-working reporters from the *Washington Post* and other papers gave him no rest. Judge John Sirica of the United States district court of the District of Columbia, which heard the cases of the burglars in early 1973, was especially persistent. Imposing stiff sentences in March, he disclosed a letter from one of the plumbers that implicated higher-ups in the administration. A Senate Select Committee on Campaign Practices, headed by folksy Sam Ervin of North Carolina, then probed the affair more deeply.

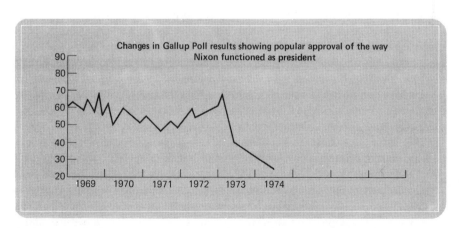

SOURCE: Adapted from p. 104 of *U.S. Foreign Policy: Context, Conduct, Content* by Marian Irish and Elke Frank. © 1975 by Harcourt Brace. Reproduced by permission of the publisher. And from *Gallup Opinion Index*, no. 111, Sept. 1974, p. 11.

Nixon's popularity peaked in late 1969 and early 1973 when 68 percent of respondents approved of his handling of the presidency, and it reached a low of 24 percent shortly before he resigned in 1974.

A series of revelations between April and July of 1973 badly damaged the administration. Patrick Gray, who had been acting chief of the FBI since Hoover's death a year earlier, resigned after admitting that he had burned incriminating documents concerning Watergate and related matters. Evidence linking the White House to the cover-up forced the resignations of Haldeman and Erlichman. In June, White House counsel John Dean testified that the President himself had been involved in the cover-up. And a month later a White House aide revealed that Nixon had taped many of the conversations concerning the affair. This disclosure set off a year-long war in which the Senate, Judge Sirica, and federal prosecutors fought the President for access to the tapes.

In an attempt to promote public confidence in his conduct the President brightened the image of his administration. To head the FBI he picked William Ruckelshaus, an Indianan who then headed the Environmental Protection Agency. To run the Justice Department, the prosecuting arm of the government, he named Elliot Richardson, his secretary of defense. Both men had reputations for courage and integrity. The President even accepted Richardson's choice for a special Watergate prosecutor. This was Archibald Cox, a Harvard law professor. Cox, Nixon said, would have full cooperation from the White House.

When Cox insisted on going to court for the tapes, however, Nixon demanded that Richardson fire him. Claiming executive privilege, the President added that he would personally edit a summary of the transcripts. Richardson refused to do Nixon's bidding and resigned in late October. Ruckelshaus, who had become Richardson's deputy, agreed with Richardson, and was fired. Solicitor General Robert Bork, next in command at the Justice Department, then discharged Cox. In the ensuing uproar, Nixon felt compelled to yield some of the tapes, to name a new special prosecutor, Leon Jaworski of Texas, and to tell the public over TV, "I am not a crook." But he refused to give up all the tapes, and Jaworski, as tenacious as Cox, kept up the legal struggle in late 1973 and early 1974.

During this time the President continued to profess his innocence. On April 29, 1974, he appeared on TV to announce that he was releasing transcripts of the tapes. These, he exaggerated "will at last, once and for all, show that what I knew and what I did with regard to the Watergate cover-up were just as I described them to you from the very beginning." On other occasions he angrily blamed the press for his dilemma and insisted that impeachment, which the House Judiciary Committee began considering seriously in May 1974, would "jeopardize" world peace and endanger the American political system. As if to prove his indispensability, he toured the Middle East and Moscow in June and July. Though he attracted sizable crowds, he accomplished little, in part because the Watergate affair was undermining his effectiveness abroad as well as at home. "Every negotiation," Kissinger said later, "was getting more and more difficult because it involved the question of whether we could, in fact, carry out what we were negotiating."

By this time the pressure on Nixon to release all the tapes was overwhelming. But he had good reason to refuse such requests, because he knew that they offered evidence of his obstruction of justice. Accordingly, he cited "executive privilege" and national security as his reasons for keeping the recordings. His lawyers, none of whom was told the facts, were instructed to resist Jaworski's requests for the tapes and to appeal the matter to the Supreme Court.

On July 24 a unaminous Court gave its answer. It agreed that a President could withhold "military, diplomatic, or sensitive national security material." To this extent executive privilege gained explicit High Court sanction for the first time. But the judges went on to insist that the Court, not the President, had the right to "say what the law is," and that the Watergate affair, a criminal proceeding, did not involve "national security." The claim for executive privilege had to "yield to the demonstrated, specific need for evidence in a pending criminal trial," and the President must turn over "forthwith" the sixty-four recordings demanded by his foes. Judge Sirica could listen to the tapes and release relevant portions to Jaworski, who could give them to Congress.

A few days later the House Judiciary Committee acted against the President by voting to impeach him on three counts. The first, passed twenty-seven to eleven, charged him with obstruction of justice. Nixon, the committee said, had made or caused to be made false statements, withheld relevant and material evidence, interfered with investigations by the FBI, the Justice Department, special prosecutors, and Congress, approved the payment of hush money to witnesses, and lied to the American people. The second charge, approved twenty-eight to ten, accused Nixon of abusing his presidential authority by resorting to illegal wiretapping and by using the FBI, CIA, and Internal Revenue Service against American citizens. The third charge hit him for refusing to turn over the tapes, after receiving a congressional subpoena, to the committee. The committee had deliberated long and responsibly, and its concluding debates, carried on radio and TV, did much to restore faith in Congress as an institution. There was little doubt that the House would endorse the committee's conclusions by wide margins. If the Senate could corral a two-thirds majority for conviction—and that seemed entirely possible—Nixon would have to leave office.

Nixon, trapped, procrastinated until August 5, when he finally released the tapes that proved his involvement in the cover-up. He admitted that he had concealed them, even from his own lawyers, but insisted that he had done nothing to warrant conviction by the Senate. Most senators clearly disagreed. So did the American people, who felt betrayed by the President's lies over the previous twenty-six months. In the next few days Republican as well as Democratic senators indicated they would vote for conviction. Deprived of support, the President resigned on August 9, 1974. Vice-President Gerald Ford of Michigan, whom Nixon had appointed to succeed Agnew earlier in the year, was immediately sworn in as the next president.

Nixon's resignation, while welcomed by many people at home and abroad, enabled him to avoid the Senate trial that might have established clearly the extent of his involvement in the Watergate affair. It also left many questions unanswered. What self-incriminating documents had the administration hoped to steal at Watergate? Would Nixon have been impeached if he had destroyed the tapes, along with logs that showed what they contained? What if some future president, having committed some egregious act, concealed such misconduct by claiming executive privilege based on the existence of "military, diplomatic, or sensitive national security material"? Such questions suggested that future presidents might still find ways of acting above the law. The imperial presidency, which the founding fathers had feared—and which twentieth-century chief executives from TR on had done so

Richard Nixon waves goodbye outside the White House as he boards a helicopter after resigning as president on August 9, 1974.

much to create—might again endanger constitutional processes and lead to paralysis of the state.

Subsequent disclosures did little to dispel such fears. These disclosures revealed a new kind of corruption. The men around Grant, Harding, and other scandal-stained presidents had acted primarily for financial gain. Many of Nixon's criminal subordinates, however, truly believed that their ends—defined as everything from reelection of the President to the maintenance of world peace—justified the means. They had no qualms about subverting democratic institutions and civil liberties. Charles Colson, Nixon's counsel, had exclaimed, "For the President I would walk over my grandmother if necessary." A plumber, Gordon Liddy, added that Watergate was "an intelligence-gathering operation of one group of persons who were seeking to retain power against another group of persons who were seeking to acquire power. That's all it was. It's like brushing your teeth. It's basic." Defending the cover-up, CREEP director Jeb Magruder added that "after the

Democrats nominated Senator McGovern, we felt that we were protecting the honorable peace that the President was bringing to Vietnam. . . . We were not covering up a burglary; we were safeguarding world peace." He concluded, "We wanted to win the election and we wanted to win it big. Just as a corporation wants to dominate its market, our reelection committee wanted to dominate that year's election. . . . We were past the point of halfway measures or gentlemanly tactics."

In the Aftermath of Watergate

The resignation of Nixon brought to the fore problems that excitement over Watergate had helped to obscure. The afflictions that had troubled the nation in the twentieth century—racial injustice, urban blight, economic inequality, sex discrimination, oppression of Native Americans and Hispanics—persisted. So did stagflation, which proved chronic and serious into the early 1980s. In April 1975, the North Vietnamese won their civil war against the South, forcing General Thieu and his supporters to flee. But the ending of Western influence there did not bring peace to Southeast Asia. In the ensuing years, Communist Cambodia fell victim to cruel authoritarianism and famine; Vietnam, too, was revealed as a harsh and repressive state; and sporadic fighting broke out between China, Cambodia, and Vietnam.

Americans worried about the capacity of their new leaders to deal with these problems. In his lengthy political career as a Michigan representative Ford had shown little interest in fighting urban or racial problems. He was largely uninformed concerning fiscal policy. He was handicapped also by his lack of a popular mandate. But he and his new vice-president, former Governor Nelson Rockefeller of New York, were Republicans facing the most aroused and self-assertive Democratic Congresses in recent memory. Thanks to the Twenty-fifth Amendment (1967), which authorized presidents to nominate (and Congress to confirm) vice-presidents, both men were nonelective officials. The United States, which had done so much to advance the cause of political democracy 200 years earlier, had to wait more than two years before being governed by a popularly elected president.

President Ford then compounded doubts about his ability by pardoning his predecessor. He did so, he said, because he wanted people to forget the recent past and because Nixon had suffered enough. A few weeks later, when Nixon almost died after an operation on his leg for phlebitis, Ford's action seemed compassionate. Whether the pardon was proper was another matter. Men like Erlichman, Haldeman, Mitchell, Dean, and Magruder—and many lesser officials—were either in jail or appealing convictions for crimes ranging from perjury to obstruction of justice. These people, like millions of Americans, wondered about the fairness of a system that punished the little fish while the shark got a pardon. Americans found it equally difficult to forget the deceit and hypocrisy that had contaminated governmental institutions since the mid-1960s. As one magazine phrased it earlier, the United States seemed to have swung half circle in the 200 years of its existence: "from George Washington, who could not tell a lie, to Richard Nixon, who could not tell the truth."

As if to register their alienation, the voters showed little interest in the off-year elections of 1974. Democrats gained throughout the nation. But only 45 percent of eligible voters cast their ballots. In a nation supposedly governed by popular majorities, this was hardly encouraging. The turnout of youth was especially poor: only 21 percent of people aged eighteen to twenty bothered to vote. This apparent political apathy (or alienation?) persisted into the 1980s. Indeed, students seemed remarkably quiescent in contrast to a few years earlier. Confronting a sluggish economy, they worried about finding jobs or getting into graduate schools. With the civil rights movement in disarray, and the war in Vietnam a thing of the past, they had fewer causes for sustained protest. The historian C. Vann Woodward commented, "Rarely in history has publicized activism been replaced so rapidly by apparent apathy, student dissent by silence."

Many Americans in the late 1970s and early 1980s shared the students' worries about the future. Though the nation was calmer than it had been in the turbulent years of the late 1960s, no one could be confident that domestic tranquility would last. Some observers feared that the approach of zero population growth, for the first time in American history, signaled not only the end of economic expansion but also a more general loss of confidence. The last frontiers, it appeared, had been conquered; it was time to consolidate and pull back. Others, lamenting the continuing coexistence of inflation and recession, foresaw an apparently irreparable and stagnant economy. Robert Lekachman, a respected economist, wrote, "I think we are entering a long period of slower growth. I take seriously the resource scarcities. We've reached thg end of cheap energy. . . . The prospects for improvement in the American standard of life thus are much less than they've been."

Trend of Inflation, 1967–81				
	CONSUMER PRICE INDEX	DOLLAR'S REAL VALUE	MEDIAN FAMILY INCOME	
			ON PAPER	IN REALITY
1967	100.0	$1.00	$ 7,974	$7,974
1968	104.2	.96	8,632	8,284
1969	109.8	.91	9,433	8,591
1970	116.3	.86	9,867	8,484
1971	121.3	.82	10,285	8,479
1972	125.3	.80	11,116	8,872
1973	133.1	.75	12,051	9,054
1974	147.7	.68	12,902	8,735
1975	161.2	.62	13,719	8,511
1976	170.5	.59	14,958	8,773
1977	181.5	.55	16,009	8,820
1978	195.4	.51	17,640	9,028
1979	217.7	.46	19,684	9,042
1980	247.0	.40	21,023	8,511
1981	272.3	.37	22,390	8,223

SOURCE: Andrew Hacker, ed., *A Statistical Portrait of the American People* (New York: Viking, 1983), p. 159.

Reflecting these doubts, many observers concluded that the nation was becoming a "business civilization" like that of the 1920s: materialistic, hollow, lacking in altruistic values or sense of purpose beyond individual self-aggrandizement. The rise of such a society, critics said, exposed the mixed blessings of modernization, which had unleashed a revolution in expectations along with economic instability and technological progress. Restless, cranky, divided, Americans seemed psychologically unfulfilled and impossible to satisfy.

American foreign policy gave special cause for concern. In 1975 the United States operated a defense budget of $104 billion—an increase of $15 billion over the amount needed during the years of involvement in Vietnam in 1972–74. America also sold arms to more than 130 countries and maintained military commitments to forty nations. Most of these forty were NATO or Latin American countries. Other commitments included South Korea and the Philippines—both repressive states—Japan, Taiwan, Australia, and New Zealand. Two danger zones, West Berlin and Israel, were not covered by treaty but appeared to be integral parts of America's worldwide defense perimeter. With naval vessels circling the globe, warplanes ever in the air, 8,500 strategic nuclear weapons in full deployment, and more than 400,000 troops stationed overseas in the cause of Pax Americana, the once uncommitted United States ran the risk of constant military involvement.

The Ford administration quickly showed its readiness to use part of this formidable arsenal. In May 1975 Cambodia captured the *Mayaguez,* an American merchant vessel sailing near its shores. When the anti-American government of Cambodia was slow to answer United States protests, Ford authorized an attack by 350 marines on Koh Tang, a nearby island where the crew was wrongly believed to be held. The assault, accompanied by bombing in Cambodia, marked a heavy overreaction to a minor incident. It cost the United States some fifteen dead, three missing, and fifty wounded. It was probably unnecessary, for Cambodia was in the process of returning both ship and crew at the time. But many Americans exulted in Ford's show of steel. The incident suggested that they were eager to strike back in order to regain standing in Southeast Asia.

It was nonetheless possible in the mid-1970s to contemplate the future with guarded optimism. Whatever the President's faults, he appeared honest and open. Some people hailed him as a Republican Harry Truman. Ford also proved willing to compromise. When Congress rebuffed his conservative economic policies in late 1974, he reversed himself to favor a multibillion-dollar tax cut, an increase in unemployment benefits, and a Keynesian budget that envisaged a deficit of $52 billion. His turnabout did little to arrest inflation—it may in fact have made it a little worse—and it failed to end the worst recession since the 1930s. Unemployment, hovering at around 9 percent in 1975 (affecting more than eight million people) had not been so high since 1940. Still, Ford's flexibility slightly relieved observers who had feared a return to Hooverism. Congress acted quickly to expand on his proposals.

Americans with a sense of history also recognized that the strife of the immediate past had brought progress as well as pain. The forces of technology, industrialization, and economic growth had made America much richer in 1976 than it had been in 1776, or—more to the point—than in 1940 or 1960. The civil rights revolution had brought the most impressive gains for blacks since emancipation. Supreme Court decisions had broadened the civil rights and civil liberties of the people. The Cold War, with its attendant threat of nuclear catastrophe, had softened. The country's political institutions, apparently so flawed, had remained stable under pressure of war, assassinations, and incomparable presidential abuse. The virtues of a free press, an independent judiciary, and an alert Congress had rarely been so clearly revealed. For all the nation's problems, it had withstood a public airing of its deficiencies that would have disrupted many other countries in the world. For these and some other blessings the United States could take cautious pride in its bicentennial year.

Bicentennial and After: Social Problems

In contrast to some of the bleaker periods of American history, the years from the bicentennial in 1976 into the 1980s offered some grounds for optimism. Public opinion polls revealed that 70 to 75 percent of Americans were happy in their own lives and optimistic about the future as it was likely to affect them personally. These feelings of individual well-being were understandable in a country that had seen real personal income double since the 1940s. The phenomenal increase in educational levels, the prosperity of spectator sports, the enormous sales of VCRs and of compact disk players (in 3 million American homes by 1988), the vogue for blockbuster films, and the growth of the travel business suggested the continuing existence of affluence and leisure time for the favored middle classes.

Thanks in part to expanded research in universities—much of it financed by government—technological and scientific developments promised the conquest of further frontiers in the near future. Scientists attempting to unravel genetic strands of deoxyribonucleic acid (DNA) and to recombine the strands with others were changing the instructions governing living cells; by the 1980s they had succeeded in transferring genes into living animals and in producing test-tube babies. Other scientists were moving ahead rapidly in the field of fiber optics, which some thought could revolutionize the field of communications. Scientists working for the space program succeeded in 1981 in reusing a space vehicle, thus indicating the possibilities of space shuttles in the future. Progress in computer technology was especially startling. In 1970, 16 "bits" (or pieces of information) could be packed on one silicon chip in a computer. By 1985, the capacity of a chip was 250,000 bits. The age of the minicomputer (at no increased cost)—for the home, libraries, stock market, medical services—had arrived.

Optimists could point to a number of other changes that were bettering the lives of Americans in the late 1970s and 1980s. One of these was continuing improvement in the public health—a key measure of a "good society." The death rate declined from 9.5 per thousand people (per year) in 1970 to 8.6 per thousand in 1983. During this era the average life expectancy at birth rose from 67.1 years to 71 for males and from 74.7 years to 78.3 years for females. These changes, in turn, led to the steady aging of the population—from a median age of 28 in 1970 to 31 in 1983 and to 33 in 1992—and to increasing political power for the elderly. Americans over 65 comprised 12 percent of the population in 1985, as opposed to but 8 percent in 1970. Reflecting this "gray power," Congress approved great increases in

	1970 (in millions of dollars)	1979 (in millions of dollars)	PERCENTAGE GROWTH		PERCENTAGE FEDERAL SHARE: 1979
			ACTUAL	ADJUSTED	
Social Security (old-age, disability, survivors)	29,686	102,596	245.6	131.1	100.0
Medicare	7,149	29,155	307.8	164.3	100.0
Public employees retirement	8,659	33,774	290.0	154.8	67.3
Unemployment insurance	3,820	11,313	196.2	104.8	21.7
Workers' compensation	2,950	11,109	276.6	147.7	21.0
Public assistance (including welfare allowances)	9,221	17,299	87.6	46.8	53.1
Public assistance medical services (including Medicaid)	5,213	23,401	348.9	186.3	51.8
Food stamps	577	6,478	1022.7	546.0	100.0
Other health-care programs	5,313	11,628	118.9	63.5	53.5
Medical research	1,635	4,225	158.4	84.6	90.0
Veterans compensation	5,394	9,898	83.5	44.6	100.0
Other veterans services	3,684	10,557	186.6	99.6	92.0
Elementary and secondary education	38,632	77,280	100.0	53.4	8.0
Higher education	9,907	24,111	143.4	76.6	18.7
Housing programs	701	6,226	788.2	420.8	93.2
Child nutrition (including school lunches)	896	3,939	339.6	181.3	85.7
All other programs	12,419	45,344	265.1	141.5	60.8
Total	145,856	428,333	193.7	103.7	61.7

Growth of Government Social Welfare Programs, 1970–79

SOURCE: Andrew Hacker, ed., *A Statistical Portrait of the American People* (New York: Viking Press, 1983), p. 178.

appropriations for social security, which reduced poverty among old people and the disabled. Higher spending for food stamps and for Medicaid (until cuts in 1981) helped alleviate destitution among millions of other Americans. While 32.4 million Americans—nearly one in seven—continued to live in households earning less than the official poverty line in 1986, this statistic represented progress of a sort in a country that had had 40 million designated as poor in 1960. The percentage of people officially defined as poor (cash income of $11,203 for a family of four in 1986) dropped from 21 to 13.6 in these years.

Black Americans, too, had some reason to be encouraged by trends of the period. Various developments stemming from the civil rights movement, including affirmative action programs administered by the federal government, led to remarkable changes in the occupational and economic status of many blacks. "We have a truly visible black middle class," the National Opinion Research Center concluded in 1980. "Twenty percent of blacks earn more than the median white income, and proportionally, the rates of going to college are higher for blacks than for whites."

To sustain this progress, the Supreme Court seemed willing to sharpen the teeth of affirmative action guidelines. In 1978 it considered the suit of Alan Bakke, a white man who had been refused admission to the medical school at the University of California at Davis, where there existed an explicit quota system for admitting blacks and other minority students. The Court ruled in favor of Bakke, who had shown that his examination grades and other intellectual qualifications were superior to those of many blacks who had been admitted. But it did so on the relatively narrow ground that such explicit quotas, when used by state-funded institutions, violated the equal-protection clause of the Constitution. It said that admissions schemes that take race into account as one factor among many, and use informal targets rather than strict quotas, were legal. In the Weber case of 1979 the Court added that private industries were free to apply voluntary racial preference programs in hiring. These decisions seemed to safeguard affirmative action in practice. Conservatives, indeed, accused the Court of sanctioning reverse discrimination.

The promising developments of the period, however, were neither large nor solid enough to satisfy most Americans. Polls showed that while people were optimistic about their own personal futures, the majority were dissatisfied with the way the nation as a whole was going. Contemporary commentators perceived a general malaise in the late 1970s and early 1980s. Some blamed the hangover of Vietnam. "That goddam war really soured the country," one survey researcher concluded. Another social scientist added, "the trauma and scars [of the war] had the same psychological impact on America that the loss of empire had on Britain." Many others blamed the sluggish economy. "I have a growing feeling," one man said, "that we are close to the edge. I don't see how we can continue the way we did in the last ten years—it really scares me."

Others seemed profoundly alienated by what they perceived as the persistent injustice of American society. More than three-fourths of Americans polled in 1977 agreed that "the rich get richer and the poor get poorer." More than 60 percent agreed that "what you think doesn't count any more" and that "most people with power try to take advantage of people like yourself." These figures represented sizable increases over the percentages responding to the same questions in 1972. The responses appeared to reveal a growing gulf between expectations and realities.

Many worried Americans perceived a crisis of social instability—centered, perhaps, in the decay of the nuclear family. Thanks in part to record-high divorce rates (33 percent of first marriages failed during this period, and 40 percent of second marriages), the number of households headed by women rose to nearly 20 percent by 1980. (By 1990 it was more than 24 percent). At that time, some 12 million children under the age of 18 lived in divorced families. A decade later, 20 percent of American children lived in families that were poor. Nearly 50 percent of poor families by 1987 were headed by women, as opposed to 30 percent in 1966. Americans worried also about the continuing liberation of sexual behavior. By the late 1970s more than 1 million couples lived together without the blessing of marriage. Of people aged 18 to 24, 95 percent of men and 80 percent of women acknowledged having indulged in premarital sexual intercourse. The number of legal abortions increased to 1.3 million in 1980—or 350 for every 1,000 live births. The percentage stayed in this range into the early 1990s. Though many people rejoiced

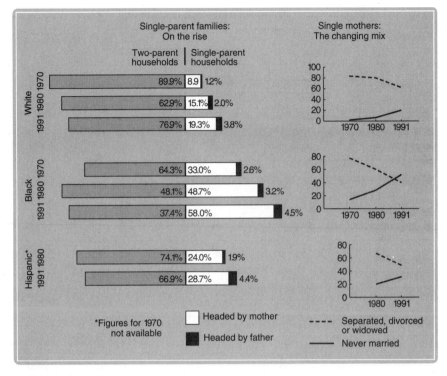

SOURCE: Census Bureau

Number of single-parent families, 1972–1990

at the legalization of abortion, they also worried about the future of family life. Some were convinced that traditional standards of morality were collapsing.

Still more alarming, many people thought, was the violence of American society in the late 1970s and 1980s. During this time the political activist Allard

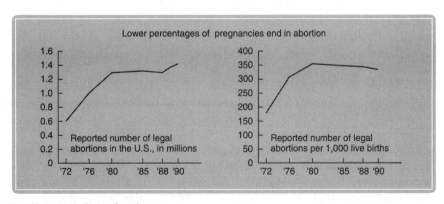

SOURCE: Centers for Disease Control

Reported number of abortions, 1972–1990

Lowenstein and the former Beatle John Lennon were killed. Would-be assassins tried to kill President Ford and wounded President Ronald Reagan. The rate of violent crime in cities with populations over 250,000 had been 300 per 100,000 people in 1960; by 1978 it was 1,100. In 1986 alone, 341 children were shot in Detroit, and dozens killed. Rates of homicide, assault, rape, and robbery were higher in the United States than in other Western democratic nations, the American rate of gun murders was about 50 times as high. Citizens complained that they could not walk about freely on the streets or sit securely in their homes. "They don't just rob you any more," one complained. "Now they gotta beat you up." Calling for tougher measures against criminals, Reagan in 1981 declared that crime was "an American epidemic—it takes the lives of 23,000 Americans, it touches nearly one-third of American households, and it results in at least $8.8 billion in financial losses."

Those who advanced suggestions for coping with violence included advocates of a strict federal gun control law. Such legislation, they argued, might at least impose controls on the sale of handguns, or "Saturday night specials." Led by the powerful National Rifle Association, opponents of such legislation managed to defeat such efforts. Many other Americans demanded tougher treatment of criminals. Reflecting this mood, the Supreme Court edged away from its landmark decisions of the 1960s dealing with criminal justice. In 1976 it held that the death penalty did not violate the Eighth Amendment's ban against cruel and unusual punishment. Executions, Justice Stewart said, were "an extreme sanction, suitable to the most extreme of crimes." By mid-1987, 86 (39 black or Hispanic) inmates had been executed, and 1,911 remained on death rows. Cities also attempted to strengthen their police forces, including SWAT teams specially trained to deal with violent crimes. Such measures, however, remained controversial. Some critics claimed that they facilitated police brutality. Others argued that they did nothing to attack the causes of criminal activity, including poverty and drug addiction. Amid continuing debate over such measures, violence persisted as a serious blight on American society in the 1980s and early 1990s.

The status of African-Americans also gave many contemporaries great cause for concern. Numbering more than 29 million in the total 1987 population of 240 million, blacks seemed to be dividing sharply along class lines. Many of those in the middle classes, and in intact two-parent families, were achieving impressive gains. But nearly 50 percent of black families were female-headed, most of them very poor. Partly for this reason, the gap between overall black income and white income increased after the early 1970s. Poverty afflicted 31 percent of blacks in the late 1980s, many of whom seemed to be mired in a dangerously alienated "underclass." Unemployment among blacks was much higher than among whites; for black teenagers it exceeded 40 percent in some areas. In one such area, the Liberty City ghetto of Miami, rioting broke out in 1980, following the acquittal of four white policemen on charges of killing a black businessman. The riot lasted four days and caused great destruction to property.

Moreover, blacks were not the only group facing severe social and economic problems by the 1980s. Despite court decisions returning land to tribal control, most Native Americans remained as economically deprived and isolated as ever. More than 50 percent were poor on some reservations. Many Puerto Ricans suffered under living conditions in New York City and elsewhere that were as bad or

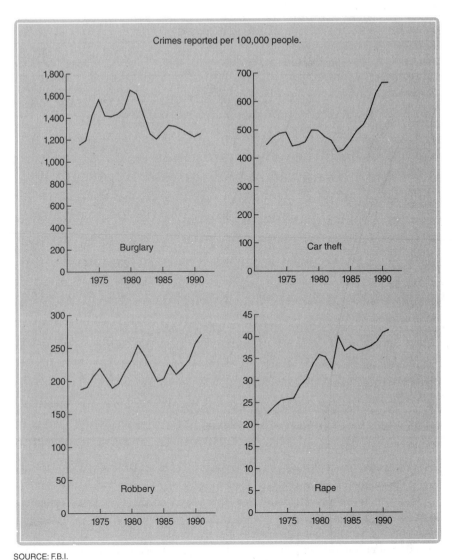

SOURCE: F.B.I.

Crime in America, 1975–1990

worse than those of blacks. Thousands of Puerto Ricans (who were American citizens) shuttled back and forth to their homes on the island. Contemporaries worried also about social conditions arising from the mounting tide of immigration following the Immigration Act of 1965, which widened the gates for many Third World peoples. By 1986 40 percent of new immigrants were Asians (as opposed to 7 percent in 1965). Immigration, much of it illegal, from Latin America grew greatly. The census estimated that the number of Hispanics in the United States increased from around 3 million in 1960 to 24 million in 1992, perhaps a quarter of whom were illegal aliens. This was roughly 9 percent of the population, as opposed to 2

U.S. Population, 1990						
	NON-HISPANICS	BLACKS	HISPANICS	MEXICANS	PUERTO RICANS	CUBANS	CENT. & S. AMERICANS
Population (in millions)	227.4	30.9	21.4*	13.4	2.4	1.1	3.0
Medium household income (in dollars)	30.513	18.676	22.330	22.439	16.169	25.900	23.568
Percent households with income of $50,000 or more	25.4	11.9	13.4	11.6	11.9	19.8	15.7
Percent households maintained by families	69.6	70.0	80.1	81.7	77.8	78.8	82.5
Percent female-headed households	11.4	47.8	19.1	15.6	33.7	15.3	21.5
Percent urban households	72.8	N/A	91.8	90.5	95.2	95.7	97.0
Percent households owning or buying home	65.8	42.4	39.0	43.5	23.4	47.3	22.2
Percent completed high school	80.5	66.7	51.3	43.6	58.0	61.0	60.4
Percent with four or more years of college	22.3	11.5	9.7	6.2	10.1	18.5	15.1
Percent unemployed	6.9	12.4	10.0	10.7	10.3	6.4	10.3
Percent of individuals below poverty level	12.1	31.9	28.1	28.1	40.6	16.9	25.4

SOURCE: Various current Population Reports, 1991 (U.S. Bureau of the Census).

*Not shown in the table are 1.6 million people in the category "other Hispanic."

percent in 1960. Some 28 percent of these people were poor, as opposed to 13 percent of the population at large.

Many Asian immigrants—Chinese, Japanese, Koreans, Laotians, Vietnamese, Cambodians, Indians—moved steadily up the economic ladder in the United States. So did smaller but nonetheless significant percentages of Hispanics, who worked hard at low-paying jobs often rejected by Americans. A much-debated immigration law (Simpson–Mazzoli) that was finally passed in 1986 attempted to alleviate the problems of Hispanics by conferring legal status on many of those already in the United States. A number of Hispanic leaders, however, opposed the law because it also stipulated that employers would be prosecuted for hiring illegal aliens. This provision, the leaders feared correctly, would either prove hard to enforce or lead to discrimination in employment. Indeed, the law was hardly an answer to a basic question: what to do about an accident of geography that has given the United States a border and a coastline thousands of miles long next to some of the poorest areas in the world. Demographers, in fact, estimated in 1992 that Hispanic Americans would account for more than 40 percent of all population growth in the United States in the following 60 years—raising the Hispanic population from 24 million in 1992 to 42 million in 2013, at which point there would be more Hispanics than blacks in the United States, and to 81 million by the year 2050.

Women and the Job Market: Percentage of Jobs Filled by Women
in 1970 and 1986

JOB CATEGORY	1970	1986
Managerial and professional specialty (such as administrators, financial managers, buyers)	33.9	43.4
Professional specialty (such as lawyers, teachers, writers)	44.3	49.4
Sales occupations	41.3	48.2
Administrative support, including clerical	73.2	80.4
Service occupations	60.4	62.6
Precision, production, craft, and repair (such as mechanics)	7.3	8.6
Operators, fabricators, and laborers	25.9	25.4
Transportation and material moving occupations	4.1	8.9
Handlers, equipment cleaners, helpers, and laborers	17.4	16.3
Farming, forestry, and fishing	9.1	15.9

SOURCE: Bureau of Labor Statistics, Census Bureau; and *The New York* Times, July 17, 1987.

Overall, the status of women as a group was better than that of these minorities. The movement for women's rights, indeed, proved considerably broader and more durable than those for black or Native American power. It rested, after all, on changing demographic forces, notably on the continuing movement of women into the work force: by the 1990s, 55 percent of women over age 16 considered themselves in the job market, as opposed to 40 percent in 1966, when NOW had been founded. But it was also clear that much sexual discrimination persisted. In part because many working women held beginning-level jobs, their income on the average was about two-thirds that of men. In 1987 the Congressional Caucus for Women's Issues calculated that the average annual income for female college graduates (in 1984) had been $20,247, while that for the average male high school dropout had been $19,120. Alarmed, advocates of women's rights demanded a host of improvements in the conditions of work, including better provision for maternity leave, higher funding for day care, and legislation making child-care costs tax deductible. In the mid-1980s they began to call for the revamping of pay scales to reflect the "comparable worth" of the work involved. Feminists and others also complained with special bitterness about the withdrawal of federal government financial help for abortions for the poor under the provisions of Medicaid, and about a ban imposed in 1987 on federal aid to family clinics that counseled clients about abortion.

Feminists particularly lamented the failure of the requisite number of states to ratify the Equal Rights Amendment by 1982. The demise of the amendment (which said that "equality of rights under the law shall not be denied or abridged by the United States or by any State on account of sex") revealed the well-organized power of special interest groups. Led by a militant antifeminist, Phyllis Schlafly, opponents of the ERA employed arguments—predicting the introduction of unisex public toilets and of women fighting as combat soldiers—which worried large numbers of women as well as men. Though NOW and other groups continued to press their cause after 1982, the fate of the ERA suggested that the women's movement in the 1980s, like the civil rights movement in the 1970s, might be stalling— at least until the gains of the recent past could be assimilated or institutionalized. The stalling of socioeconomic goals suggested also a further fact of life—that Americans will accept legislation (such as the civil rights acts of 1964 and 1965) that confers legal equality of opportunity on deprived groups, but will balk at efforts to mandate greater equality of socioeconomic condition.

The condition of many workers seemed equally unpromising by the early 1980s. Factory workers showed some signs of rebelling against "blue-collar blues"—the monotony and hectic pace of assembly line work. Some demanded greater control of the work process itself. Similarly, white-collar workers sought to organize unions. The United Federation of Teachers became a potent union in some places, notably New York. The American Federation of State, County, and Municipal Employees emerged as one of the largest in the AFL-CIO. Despite such efforts, unions did not flourish. Indeed, the percentage of nonfarm workers in unions declined from 31 percent in 1960 to 25 percent in 1980 and continued to fall in the 1980s, to 16 percent by 1989. Other indicators—notably a rise during the 1980s of income inequality (by 1990, the wealthiest 20 percent of Americans had 46 percent of personal income, the poorest 20 percent had 4 percent)—revealed that American society was growing more inegalitarian.

THE INSECURE ECONOMY

The status of all these groups—blacks, immigrants, women, workers—and of other, more fortunate Americans depended ultimately on the functioning of the economy. This, however, remained uncertain into the early 1980s. Public opinion polls at the time revealed that Americans worried above all in the postbicentennial years about the future of the economy.

These worries reflected profound general questions about national development. Could economic prosperity—readily assumed by middle-class Americans since the 1940s—be sustained, or had the country at last staggered to its final frontier? Was the nation, indeed the whole Western industrialized world, now engaged in a zero-sum game in which as many were to suffer as to prosper? If the economy was to stagnate, could the United States maintain its dynamic, expansive role in the world?

One especially alarming problem concerned the high costs and threatened shortages of energy sources. Several forces produced this situation, including the policies of the OPEC nations, which quintupled the price of oil between 1972 and 1979. Attempting to cope with these pressing problems, experts called for various solutions. Some insisted that the answer was to develop solar energy. But cheap and effective methods of producing solar energy on a large scale proved elusive to develop. Others hailed the potential of atomic-based power. But a frightening accident at the atomic power plant at Three Mile Island, Pennsylvania, in 1979 dramatized

A cow grazes in front of Three Mile Island nuclear power plant, site of America's most frightening nuclear accident.

the potential dangers involved in the widespread development of such installations. Other experts called for greater production of coal, of which abundant resources remained. Coal, however, had its disadvantages. Some of the cheapest and most available coal had to be strip-mined, savaging the landscape and polluting surrounding streams. Much of this coal burned "dirty," polluting the atmosphere. Attempting to encourage further exploration for energy sources, Congress in the late 1970s instituted a policy of gradual deregulation of natural gas and funded efforts aimed at developing oil from shale in the western mountains. Whether these efforts promised a real answer, however, was debatable. Surely, they were leading to even higher energy costs in the short run. Meanwhile, until oil prices dipped sharply in 1982, the oil companies were reaping record profits. Even by the 1990s the United States had failed to develop a coherent energy policy.

To many observers it seemed that the only long-range answer to the "energy crisis," as it was coming to be called, was conservation. Americans, they pointed out, drove long distances in gas-guzzling automobiles and heated their homes to high temperatures. They consumed much more energy per capita than did people of other nations. As gasoline and oil prices rose in the late 1970s, many Americans began conserving on a small scale. They turned to more fuel-efficient automobiles, and they heeded advice about ways of improving home insulation. But the drive for conservation faded in the mid-1980s, when oil prices declined. In 1987 Congress repealed a "windfall profits tax" that had been imposed on oil companies in 1979. Moreover, old habits did not die quickly, for the exploitation of apparently abundant natural resources, and the attendant comforts that this exploitation made possible, were widely regarded as fundamental to the American way of life. Cutting back on energy, in fact, necessitated sacrifices and sharpened the struggle between groups for slices of a smaller pie. As Arthur Schlesinger, Jr., put it, "Our national development has been premised on the assumption of limitless supplies of low cost energy.

But the age of cheap energy is over. The realization of this fact, as it slowly sinks in, will bring painful readjustments not only in energy policy and in economic management but in our very habits of thought and ways of life."

The most hotly debated economic problem of the late 1970s and early 1980s, caused in part by the higher cost of energy, was inflation. The cost of living doubled between 1968 and 1978 and continued thereafter to rise at an alarming rate until 1982. Interest rates reached record highs (around 20 percent), dampening investment. Worse, rising unemployment accompanied the inflation, and some of the nation's leading industrial enterprises teetered on the brink. Many of the "smokestack industries" in the Middle West seemed especially threatened, creating a "Rust Belt" in the nation's manufacturing heartland. The situation in automobile production was especially alarming. In 1980 the federal government chose to bail out Chrysler Corporation, which lost a record $1.7 billion. General Motors also lost money in 1980—for the first time since 1921. Ford ended the year with a $1.2 billion deficit, as Japan gained huge shares of the American market. A total of 200,000 American auto workers were unemployed in 1980. Perhaps the most frightening aspect of this crisis in American manufacturing was that it stemmed in part from an apparently inexorable decline in productivity increases. This had grown at around 3 percent per year in the prosperous 1960s. After 1973 the rate of increase dropped to virtually zero and lagged badly in comparison to continuing growth in economies such as Japan's and West Germany's.

Frustrated by "stagflation," Americans searched for simple solutions to it. Some, attributing the problem to escalating government budgets at all levels, responded by calling for lids on spending and for tax reductions. In 1978 Californians voted for Proposition 13, which called for dramatic cuts in state taxes. Massachusetts residents demanded reductions in taxes, and therefore in state services, two years later. Partly because of such efforts, government employment—federal, state, and local—declined in 1981, for only the fourth time in modern American history. (The others had been in the recession of 1920–21, in the depression year of 1932–33, and during demobilization in 1945–47.) But these efforts provided no answer to the stagnation of productivity, which appeared to be caused by deeper forces, including reliance on aging plant and equipment and slow rates of spending on capital investment.

Many Americans, fearful of the economic future, acted to maximize their pleasure in the present. "It's important to maintain the quality of life," one mother with four children commented. "I'll continue to dip into savings so we can go on trips and out to dinner." A young worker added, "I may not earn much, but I'm making it count. I'm planning a trip to Central America next month. There's no point in letting money sit in the bank." An executive concluded, "We'll spend money on household furnishings that will increase in value—antiques, lamps, and rugs." Reactions such as these were not possible, of course, for the millions of Americans who lived close to the line of poverty. But they were apparently widespread among the more affluent middle classes. They reflected a sense that the economy would continue to be unsteady and that inflation would remain a permanent part of life. In such a world, they believed, old-fashioned virtues such as frugality no longer applied.

How deep was this pursuit of individual pleasure? One contemporary critic, the historian Christopher Lasch, thought it was pervasive; he said America had

First Person

The symbol of contemporary America is no longer the Statue of Liberty, holding her lamp to beckon the poor of Europe toward the promise of a new life; it is no longer the great white dome of the U.S. Capitol, which promised them democracy, nor even the production line of Henry Ford, which promised them affluence. It is instead the new suburban shopping mall, which promises them—domestic ease.

from Mike Edelhart and James Tinen, *America the Quotable.* New York: Facts on File Publications, 1983.

developed a "culture of narcissism." Other observers labeled the 1970s the "Me Decade." Americans, they argued, showed little interest in social reform; even the campuses remained relatively quiet. Instead, they turned to more solitary pursuits, such as jogging, which enjoyed a phenomenal rise in popularity. (James Fixx's *The Complete Book of Running* sold almost 800,000 copies in hardback between 1977 and 1979.) According to some contemporary critics, Americans became even more obsessed with sexual pleasure than ever, Alex Comfort's illustrated "how-to" book, *The Joy of Sex,* was a best seller, with 1 million hardback copies and 2.4 million paperback copies sold from 1972 to 1979. So were "M's" *The Sensuous Man* (4.5 million paperback copies sold from 1971 to 1979) and Marabel Morgan's *The Total Woman* (2.7 million copies from 1973 to 1979). In fiction, best sellers included Erich Segal's escapist *Love Story* (9.8 million paperback copies), Peter Benchley's *Jaws* (9.2 million copies), and Richard Bach's *Jonathan Livingston Seagull* (7.3 million). *Seagull* celebrated the wonders of individual freedom.

Whether such cultural signs betokened a more hedonistic or narcissistic nation was impossible to prove. (Best sellers, for instance, tend to be escapist in all periods.) Still, it seemed fair to say that middle-class Americans did not want to make major alterations in their life-styles. When Paul Volcker, chairman of the Federal Reserve Board, said in 1979 that the "standard of living of the average American has to decline," his advice fell on hostile ears. Instead, Americans characteristically persisted in believing that some way could be found—must be found—to improve the economy. As one commentator noted, "most Americans would say there is something that can be done about inflation. They don't know what it is, but the notion that nothing can be done—that's un-American. They think the problems can be solved, and they are mad at institutions because they're not solving them." In this somewhat cranky yet not despairing mood, Americans entered their third century of independence. Whether new economic frontiers yet beckoned remained an unanswered question.

POLITICS: FROM 1976 TO 1981

Political developments in any democratic nation ordinarily reflect underlying social realities and attitudes. So it seemed to be in the United States in the years from 1976 into the early 1980s. Beset by economic instability, Americans alternately expected great answers from public officials, then blamed governmental institutions for ineffectiveness. This gulf between expectations and official performance led to increasing dissatisfaction with political leaders, a dissatisfaction that expressed itself by 1980 in an apparently general disillusion with liberalism.

This dissatisfaction was apparent during the 1976 election campaign. President Ford, after barely overcoming a challenge from Governor Ronald Reagan of California for the GOP nomination, seemed doomed to defeat. Though Americans thought him an honest man, they also perceived him as Nixon's appointee and as the man who had pardoned the chief Watergate conspirator. Moreover, Ford seemed prone to careless statements, such as his remark that "there is no Soviet domination of eastern Europe." As the incumbent, Ford inevitably drew criticism for the shaky nature of the economy. In midsummer 1976, few observers gave him a chance in November.

Ford's challenger was a virtual outsider to national politics, Jimmy Carter of Georgia. Carter was a former naval officer, a successful businessman and peanut farmer, and a one-term governor of Georgia. He won his party's presidential nomination easily, in part because he managed to convince voters in primaries that only an outsider such as he could clean up the mess in Washington. "I will never lie to you," he told people who remembered Watergate. Avoiding substantive issues, Carter promised people a "new era of honest, compassionate, responsive government." His appeal rested also on his moderate approach to issues. Democratic leaders recalled the disastrous McGovern campaign of 1972 and yearned for a candidate who was safe. Carter, perhaps the most conservative Democratic presidential nominee since Alton Parker in 1904, appeared to fit the bill. His nomination signaled the disarray and uncertainty of liberalism by the mid-1970s.

The results of the election revealed that voters did not have much enthusiasm for either candidate. There was much talk at the time, in fact, of a "clothespin vote—hold your nose and vote for one or the other." Carter won, but in so doing lost almost all of the huge margin that he had enjoyed in midsummer. He received only 50.1 percent of the popular vote, compared to 48 percent for Ford and 1 percent for Eugene McCarthy of Minnesota, who ran as an independent. Polls revealed that as many as 20 percent of voters made up their minds in the last week of the campaign and that only 40 percent trusted either candidate to "do the right thing most of the time." The turnout, 53 percent of eligible voters, was the lowest since 1948. It appeared that Carter won mainly because he was able to hold onto many traditional areas of Democratic strength in the North and because he regained the South. His appeal to African-Americans, among whom he was especially popular, was perhaps crucial to his cause.

President Carter offered a somewhat contradictory image. As a Southerner and a "born again" Christian who taught Sunday school classes, he represented a growing wave of evangelical Protestantism in America. At the same time, however, he was an efficient, somewhat colorless technocrat—in some ways a characteristic representative of the new South, not the old. Rejecting the aid of old Washington hands, he surrounded himself with advisers from his campaign team, mostly fellow Georgians. He presented a folksy image, appearing dressed in sweaters for TV "fireside chats" to the American people. He also ran a phone-in "talk show" of sorts from the Oval Office of the White House.

Cultivation of the art of public relations, however, could not work wonders in the long run. Indeed, the commentator Eric Sevareid noted as early as 1977 that Carter and his somewhat inbred team might soon lose their appeal. "He has the mind of an engineer," Sevareid said. "He's very bright, has an enormous capacity and is a quick study. He's got a lot of little filing cabinets in his mind that he seems able to use as needed. But he doesn't seem to have much stylistic change of pace, and I fear he will become less and less stimulating."

Sevareid's judgment proved accurate. Lacking special charisma and facing deep problems, Carter compounded his difficulties by refusing to cultivate amicable relations with Congress. He increasingly alienated Democratic liberals, notably Senator Edward Kennedy of Massachusetts, who demanded more resolute federal action to counter the nation's economic and social problems. For these reasons Carter did not succeed in securing passage of measures that he requested, such as comprehensive welfare reform that aimed to set a minimum floor under the income of most American families. During the Carter years, the Democratic Congresses also did not agree on other domestic issues, such as national health insurance (for which Carter and Kennedy offered rival plans) or energy policy. Most damaging, Carter never developed a consistent "game plan" to deal with rising unemployment and inflation. The zero-sum economy, it seemed, was at hand. By 1980 Carter faced sharp criticisms from all sides. The columnist George Will cracked, "Carter has on his desk Truman's sign, 'THE BUCK STOPS HERE.' The resemblance stops there."

Criticisms such as these, while witty, reflect a widespread tendency of Americans to blame their presidents for the assorted ills of society. The reality was that the major issues defied simple solutions. Indeed, they existed in most Western democratic nations in the late 1970s and early 1980s. For all of Carter's limitations—and he was both a poor manager of Congress and an uninspiring, inconsistent leader—he came to office at a time when the presidency as an institution had been badly damaged by Vietnam and Watergate. Unlike Nixon, he could not achieve much by waving the flag. Carter also presided over a badly divided Democratic party and over a political arena dominated by single-interest pressure groups. As the political scientist Richard Neustadt explained in 1980, "The next man's problems will be much like Carter's. Those who put their hopes on 'charismatic' leadership from the United States government, on a par with Roosevelt or Eisenhower, are just heading for disappointment."

In foreign policy Carter scored a few successes, notably the Senate's narrow ratification of a treaty with Panama in 1978. The treaty promised to turn over the Canal Zone to Panama by the year 2000. Carter also sought to regularize relations with the People's Republic of China, which was recognized formally in December 1978. His most notable success was the Camp David accord worked out between Egypt, Israel, and the United States. This accord, for which the patient diplomacy of Carter and his top advisers was partly responsible, resulted in Egypt's recognition of Israel and in Israel's promise to turn over the Sinai to Egypt by 1982. Though subsequent developments (including the assassination of Egyptian leader Anwar Sadat in 1981) reinflamed the area, thereby destroying the "spirit of Camp David," Carter's efforts were impressive at the time. Israel, indeed, later kept its promise concerning the Sinai.

Presidents Sadat and Carter and Prime Minister Begin during signing of Camp David accords

Carter, however, did not succeed in defusing the Cold War. To a limited degree his own policies prevented such a result, for he brought to his public utterances a moralistic element that broke with the *Realpolitik* of Henry Kissinger and that irritated the Soviet Union. In his inaugural address in 1977, the President proclaimed his "absolute commitment to human rights." "Because we are free," he added, "we can never be indifferent to the fate of freedom elsewhere." When Carter then denounced the Soviet Union for its treatment of dissidents like the nuclear physicist Andrei Sakharov, while simultaneously maintaining relatively cordial relations with repressive regimes elsewhere, he annoyed Soviet leader Leonid Brezhnev. Carter nonetheless attempted to develop détente in defense policies, working for Senate approval of SALT II, an agreement that promised to bring about some limitations on the development of nuclear weapons. The Senate, however, was suspicious of the Soviets and refused to approve it. The Soviets then destroyed all chances for détente by invading neighboring Afghanistan in December 1979. Outraged, Carter called the invasion the "most serious threat to world peace since World War II." He then cut off various agreements with the Soviet Union and staged an American boycott of the 1980 Olympics in Moscow. For the remainder of his administration, Soviet-American relations were cold indeed. Détente, never very healthy, perished.

Events in Iran, however, overshadowed all other aspects of America's foreign relations during the last year of Carter's presidency. Early in 1979, revolutionaries overthrew the long-standing, pro-American regime of the shah of Iran. Amid great

Americans from the U.S. embassy in Tehran are held hostage by Iranian students. This photograph was taken on the day the embassy was captured by Islamic revolutionary students and clergy.

instability, Muslim fundamentalists loyal to the Ayatollah Ruhollah Khomeini gained control of the country. When the shah was welcomed to the United States for treatment of cancer (which killed him in 1980), nationalistic Iranians seized the U.S. embassy in Tehran and held 52 Americans hostage. At least one of these Americans represented the CIA. The Khomeini government supported the takeover and refused to free the hostages until America pledged to keep out of Iranian affairs, to return the shah's wealth (given an astronomical value by the Khomeini government), and to unfreeze Iranian assets. Carter refused, and later approved a dramatic airborne expedition to free the hostages. The raid was badly conceived and proved a dismal failure. Appalled, Secretary of State Cyrus Vance resigned in protest, and the war of nerves dragged on through 1980. It was not until the day that Carter left office in January 1981 that America unfroze many Iranian assets, in return for which the hostages were freed, after 444 days in captivity.

The lengthy imprisonment of the hostages deeply angered Americans at home. Frustrated by failure in Vietnam, seemingly unable to control events anywhere abroad. Americans erupted in sharp displays of xenophobia. Texans paraded with pictures of John Wayne and placards reading. "Don't buy Iranian oil." One poster read, "They can take their students and shove them up their pipeline." The *Wall Street Journal* said that Washington should "put obstreperous Iranian students on the next plane for Iran." Other Americans chafed openly at American impotence. "America today needs a tough-talking and tough-acting leader," one exclaimed. "America's strength was built on national pride and morale, and both of these have dropped under the weight of the defeat in Vietnam, the scandal of Watergate, and the catastrophic policies of Jimmy Carter." When the hostages finally came home the nation turned out in an orgy of welcome that contrasted sharply with the neglect shown returning Vietnam veterans a few years earlier. By 1981, the stage was set for a more militaristic, anticommunist, and nationalistic foreign policy. That was the short-run legacy of the trauma of the hostages in Iran.

Suggestions for Reading

Useful starting places for the politics of the Nixon era include Godfrey Hodgson, *America in Our Time* (1976); Otis Graham, Jr., *Toward a Planned Society: From Roosevelt to Nixon* (1976); and Allen Matusow, *Nixon's Economy: Booms, Busts, Dollars and Voters* (1998). Studies of policy include Henry Aaron, *Politics and the Professors* (1978); and James T. Patterson, *America's Struggle Against Poverty, 1900–1994* (1995). For political trends in the late 1970s, see James Duffy, *Domestic Affairs: American Programs and Problems* (1979); Haynes Johnson, *In the Absence of Power* (1980). Gary Fink and Hugh Davis Graham eds., *The Carter Presidency: Policy Choices in the Post-New Deal Era* (1998), on the Carter administration; and Peter Steinfels, *The Neoconservatives* (1979). Books on Richard Nixon include Stephen Ambrose, *Nixon: The Education of a Politician* (1987), and *The Triumph of a Politician, 1962–1972* (1989), a thorough treatment, and Garry Wills, *Nixon Agonistes** (1970). Other books that deal with politics and policies of the 1970s are Leonard Silk, *Nixonomics** (1972); Jules Witcover, *White Knight: The Rise of Spiro Agnew* (1972); Robert S. Ansom, *McGovern* (1972); and Daniel Moynihan, *Politics of a Guaranteed National Income** (1973). On the Supreme Court's important decision regarding abortion, see David Garrow, *Liberty and Sexuality: The Right to Privacy and the Making of* Roe *v.* Wade (1994).

Important books on political trends include Walter Dean Burnham, *Critical Elections and the Mainsprings of American Politics** (1972), a stimulating analysis of twentieth-century developments; Walter De Vries and V. L. Torrance, *The Ticket Splitters* (1972); Samuel Lubell, *The Hidden Crisis in American Politics** (1970); Peter Steinfels, *The Neo-Conservatives: The Men Who Are Changing American Politics* (1979); and David S. Broder, *The Party's Over** (1972); and Thomas and Mary Edsall, *Chain Reaction: The Impact of Race, Rights and Taxes on American Politics* (1991). See also Theodore White, *Making of a President, 1972** (1973); Kevin Phillips, *The Emerging Republican Majority** (1969); and Richard Scammon and Ben Wattenberg, *The Real Majority** (1970). Among the books on Watergate are Carl Bernstein and Bob Woodward, *All the President's Men** (1974), a devastating account by two *Washington Post* reporters; Raoul Berger, *Impeachment: The Constitutional Problems* (1974); Philip Kurland, *Watergate and the Constitution* (1978); Theodore White, *Breach of Faith* (1975); and Stanley Kutler, *The Wars of Watergate* (1990).

Sources for foreign policy include Raymond Garthoff, *Détente and Confrontation: American-Soviet Relations from Nixon to Reagan* (1985), an authoritative book. See also Lloyd Gardner, ed., *The Great Nixon Turnaround* (1973); Morton Halperin, *Defense Strategies for the Seventies* (1971); and Leonard Mosley, *Power Play* (1973), on oil problems in the Middle East. See especially the following: Henry Kissinger, *White House Years* (1979) and *Years of Power* (1982), which are

*Available in a paperback edition.

fascinating memoirs; Seymour Hersh, *The Price of Power: Kissinger in the Nixon White House* (1983), which is very critical; William Shawcross, *Sideshow: Kissinger, Nixon, and the Destruction of Cambodia* (1979), equally critical; and Robert Litwak, *Détente and the Nixon Doctrine* (1984). Books on the Carter years include Gaddis Smith, *Morality, Reason, and Power* (1986), a scholarly study; and Betty Glad, *Jimmy Carter* (1980).

A starting point for studying the 1970s is Peter Caroll, *It Seemed Like Nothing Happened* (1982). Domestic unrest in the early 1970s is the subject of many books, including James Michener, *Kent State: What Happened and Why* (1973); George Jackson, *Soledad Brother: The Prison Letters of George Jackson* (1970); Tom Wicker, *A Time to Die* (1975), on the prison riot at Attica. N.Y., and Robert Wood, *The Necessary Majority: Middle America and the Urban Crisis* (1972). An important book dealing with corporate power is John Kenneth Galbraith, *The New Industrial State** (1971). Other books dealing with social and economic trends include Andrew Levison, *Working Class Majority* (1974); A. M. Josephy, *Now That the Buffalo's Gone* (1982), on Native Americans; Kirkpatrick Sale, *Power Shift* (1975), on the rise of the Sun Belt: and Barry Bluestone and Bennett Harrison, *The Deindustrialization of America* (1982). On immigration see John Crewdson, *The Tarnished Door* (1983); Werner Sollors, *Beyond Ethnicity* (1986); and David Reimers, *Still the Golden Door* (1985). Other broad studies of American society and culture include Charles Silberman, *Criminal Violence, Criminal Justice* (1978); Orlando Patterson, *Ethnic Chauvinism* (1977); Albert Camarillo, *Chicanos in a Changing Society* (1979); Daniel Bell, *The Cultural Contradictions of Capitalism* (1976); Christopher Lasch, *The Culture of Narcissism* (1979); and J. Anthony Lukas, *Common Ground* (1986), a powerful account of race and education in Boston.

Among books that deal with environmental issues are Paul Ehrlich, *Population Bomb** (1968); and Barry Commoner, *The Closing Circle** (1971). See also Emma Rothschild, *Paradise Lost: The Decline of the Auto-Industrial Age* (1973); and Jonathan Schell, *The Fate of the Earth* (1982), a frightening account of the results of nuclear disaster.

Berlin Wall, 1989

7

Republican Years, 1981 – 1992

After losing the 1980 presidential election to Ronald Reagan, Carter announced that he would "avoid any significant action for the rest of my term." A columnist responded, "This is ironic . . . he has been doing just that since 1977."

Though unfair, this response helps explain the decisive victory of Reagan and former Representative and CIA Director George Bush, his running mate, in that election. On the surface a stunning triumph for the Republican party (which even regained control of the Senate for the first time since 1954), and for conservatism generally, the election can more simply be explained as a repudiation of Carter and of Democratic economic and foreign policies. Americans, personalizing their public problems, took out their frustrations on the man, and the party, that had occupied the White House for four years of economic stagnation and overseas difficulties. That interpretation was the view of many political scientists, who stressed the ability of Reagan, a consummate media politician, to exploit Democratic failures, and who rejected the GOP claim that the election represented a sea change in public sentiment. Though Reagan won a large margin in the electoral college, he captured only 51 percent of the voters, 3 percent more than Ford had in 1976. Carter received 41 percent, John Anderson, an independent, got 6.6 percent, and eighteen other candidates divided the remainder among themselves. The election of 1980, like many since the early 1960s, seemed to reflect widespread distrust of both parties. It exposed anew the high expectations of people who at once suspected that politicians could do little and yet blamed them when they did not do much.

Reagan and Congress

As if to confound these pessimists, Reagan took office with a flurry of activity, especially in domestic policy. An ardent New Dealer in the 1930s and 1940s (his father had received assistance from the WPA), he had moved to the right wing of the

---

First Person

Ronald Reagan, Second Inaugural Address

The heart of our efforts is one idea vindicated by 25 straight months of economic growth: freedom and incentives unleash the drive and entrepreneurial genius that are the core of human progress. We have begun to increase the rewards to work, savings, and investment; reduce the increase in the cost and size of government and its interference in people's lives.

Vital Speeches, February 1, 1985, p. 227.

Republican party in the 1950s and 1960s. As a popular governor of California between 1967 and 1975 he had made a name for himself by denouncing governmental interference in the free market. The oldest president in American history (he was 70 when inaugurated in 1981), he often seemed vague and ill-informed on many issues. But he was extraordinarily affable, politically astute, and (as a former movie actor) a "Great Communicator" on television and in personal appearances.

Employing these assets in 1981, Reagan developed remarkable control over Congress, including the nominally Democratic House of Representatives. During the 1981 session Congress approved his requests to cut more than $35 billion from domestic programs, including medicaid, medicare, welfare, food stamps, and public job training and employment. Most of these cuts threatened to harm those most in need and thereby occasioned loud but futile protests from liberals, who were demoralized and disorganized. Congress, going even further than Reagan had requested, also enacted a huge tax reduction of $750 billion over the next five years. Many of these reductions benefited the wealthy, whose top rates decreased from 75 to 50 percent. Their savings, Reagan thought, would promote investment and therefore "trickle down" into the rest of the economy. This "supply-side economics," as it was called, was reminiscent of the conservative fiscal policies of the Coolidge administration.

Congress did not endorse all of Reagan's economic ideas; it refused to consider major cuts in such politically sacrosanct programs as social security. But it did approve his call for dramatic increases in defense spending, which pumped money into the economy. Meanwhile, tough-minded officials of the Federal Reserve Board pursued tight money policies that had been started in the last two years of the Carter administration. These policies resulted in rapidly increasing interest rates, but also curbed inflation. For all these reasons the Reagan administration seemed almost revolutionary in its economic policies. There was talk of a "Reagan Revolution." The new President's performance, said the writer Jeff Fishel, "was virtually unparalleled in the modern presidency."

These actions marked Reagan as decidedly conservative in temper. That was no surprise, for he had campaigned as a political conservative who believed that domestic programs needed to be cut, and that the defense budget required massive infusions of money. Moreover, his economic policies gradually appeared to work. Though the combination of high interest rates and cuts in social programs exacted very great hardships—unemployment exceeded 10 percent in 1982, the highest

Anxious job seekers, New York City, 1982

since 1940—the economy began to recover in 1983. Between then and the end of 1986 more than 11 million new jobs were created in the country. Thanks in part to decreases in the price of oil, consumer price increases leveled off, from a high of 13.1 percent in 1979 to 1.4 percent seven years later. This was the lowest rate of price increases since 1964 (1.2 percent). In 1986 Reagan also secured a major tax law from Congress. Eliminating a number of special tax breaks, the law cut maximum rates from 50 to 28 percent (a few wealthy Americans paid 33 percent), and reduced rates for lower income groups. Many observers, having long despaired at the complexity of America's tax laws, applauded the Presistent's persistent quest for simplification.

Notwithstanding gradual improvements in the economic climate, many observers remained deeply alarmed by federal economic policies. One was his first budget director, David Stockman, who lamented in 1981 that "none of us really understands what's going on with different baselines and such complexity." Stockman complained especially of the power of special interest groups. Tax cuts were possible, he said, because congressmen "got so goddamned greedy that they got themselves way out there on a limb." He concluded, "I have a new theory—there are no *real* conservatives in Congress."

Reaganomics, as critics called it, evoked similar criticisms later in the 1980s. Opponents emphasized that Reagan failed to deliver on his promises to trim the size of government. On the contrary, escalating expenditures for defense, while helping to pull the nation out of recession, contributed to enormous growth in federal spending, which increased from $634 billion in 1981 to more than $1 trillion by 1986. This was 24 percent of the GNP, as opposed to 22.7 percent when Reagan took office. Federal deficits, meanwhile, mounted alarmingly to more than $200 billion a year, the highest in American history. Interest payments on the national debt, $96 billion in 1981, leaped to $140 billion seven years later.

Congress, belatedly trying to reverse these trends, passed the Gramm-Rudman Act in 1985, which mandated a balanced budget by 1991. But the Supreme Court struck down part of the law, and critics predicted correctly that neither Congress nor future presidents would be able to resist the special interests, whose demands were relentless. James Buchanan, winner of the 1986 Nobel prize in economics, explained, "As a structural revolution, Reagan's presidency surely does not qualify. It will leave in place basically the same institutions of politics and bureaucracy that it inherited."

Critics pointed to still other limitations in Reagan's domestic vision. Rising defense expenditures, they said, came at the expense of the minorities, the poor, and the sick. Poverty afflicted almost 33 million people—14 percent of the population—in 1986. Unemployment, though below 6 percent by 1988, continued to be a serious problem. Farmers found it increasingly difficult to compete in world markets; thousands failed in the 1980s. Indeed, all sorts of American exports confronted stiff competition from Japan, South Korea, and other productive nations. By 1987 America's foreign trade deficit, which had been $20 billion in 1980, reached an all-time high of $170 billion.

Critics also deplored Reagan's environmental policies. His first interior secretary, James Watt, strongly opposed many of the environmental regulations that had been approved in the 1970s, notably during the Carter years. America, he said, should "mine more, drill more, cut more timber, use our resources rather than simply keep them locked up." Acting on these beliefs, he opened up federally controlled land to oil exploration by private interests. He blocked further additions to national parks and proposed that up to 80 million acres of federal lands be turned over to private developers by the year 2000. Reagan and Watt also reduced funding for the Environmental Protection Agency and for the Occpational Safety and Health Administration. Scandals involving the EPA resulted in mass resignations in 1983,

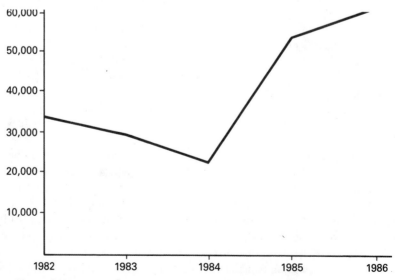

Number of farms that went out of business, were sold, or were foreclosed on, 1982–86

and protests by environmentalists and others led to the departure of Watt himself later in the year. By then, however, liberals were on the defensive. For the time being at least, the Reagan administration had slowed the movement for environmental controls.

Reagan's record in civil rights was equally discouraging to liberals. Like many conservatives, he believed that government should relax its efforts on behalf of blacks and other minority groups. Affirmative action programs, he thought, promoted reverse discrimination. Quotas, numerical goals, and timetables aimed at compensating for previous discrimination ought to be rejected. To achieve these goals the Reagan administration cut funding for the Equal Employment Opportunity Commission and for the civil rights division of the Justice Department. The EEOC filed 60 percent fewer cases by 1984 than it had at the start of the Reagan administration. The Justice Department virtually ceased to prepare suits against segregation in schools or housing. In 1981 it supported a case brought by Bob Jones University against the Treasury Department, which (following previous policy) had refused it tax-exempt status on the grounds that the university discriminated against blacks. Though the Supreme Court in 1983 upheld the Treasury Department, by an 8 to 1 decision, the case made it abundantly clear that Reagan hoped to turn back some of the clock on civil rights. The one dissenter, Justice William Rehnquist, was later elevated by Reagan to the chief justiceship. Like many other "revolutions" that had developed in the turbulent 1960s, civil rights was stymied—as was liberalism in general—in the 1980s.

Social Concerns of the 1980s

Though the future of the economy, the environment, and civil rights remained central concerns in the late 1980s, a range of other sociocultural issues also provoked debate. High among these were questions involving education, religion, and life-styles. All exposed sharp class and cultural conflicts: on many issues America remained a deeply divided society.

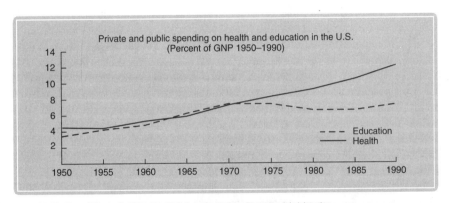

Private and public spending on health and education in the U.S. (Percent of GNP 1950–1990)

SOURCE: U.S. National Center for Education Statistics, Health Care Financing Administration

Loud debates over education revealed the persistence of many older questions. One perennial problem was fairness. As the *New York Times* education editor observed in 1987, "Escalating college costs, without additional financial aid to students, threaten to create two categories of colleges—one for the rich, the other for the rest." At the elementary and secondary level, disorder and drugs virtually overwhelmed schools in many poorer districts.

Another perennial educational issue concerned quality and content. Conservatives, led by Education Secretary William Bennett, demanded that schools and colleges devote more attention to the teaching of traditional values. Ernest Boyer, president of the Carnegie Corporation for the Advancement of Teaching, complained that many universities neglected undergraduate education and catered excessively to the marketplace. A federally sponsored report in 1983 by the National Commission on Excellence in Education concluded that a "tide of mediocrity" was undermining the nation's competitiveness in the world economy. Reports such as this prompted rising state and local spending for the schools, as well as tougher requirements for students. By the early 1990s, however, it was unclear that such measures were making much difference—especially for minorities and poor people in inner cities.

Some of the most divisive debates over education exposed a major development of the 1970s and 1980s: the resurgence of Christian fundamentalism. Those who professed such views were hardly unique to this period, but they became much more outspoken, and they developed unprecedented organizational skills. Though they differed considerably in their theological beliefs, a large majority embraced conservative social and educational opinions. Many rejected Darwinian ideas about evolution and insisted on the teaching of what they called "creation science" in the schools.

The creationists developed strong political lobbies, especially in the South. Taking to the courts, they won a notable victory in 1987 when a federal judge in Tennessee ruled that children might leave the classroom whenever they were offended by anything being read or discussed. The creationists also secured passage of state laws requiring that public schools teaching Darwinian theories of evolution give equal time to creationist science—by which they mainly meant the Book of Genesis. Though the Supreme Court struck down such laws in 1987—holding them in violation of the principle of separation of church and state—the religious Right kept up the struggle. Textbooks reflected the continuing reluctance of publishers to offend the views of militant and well-organized fundamentalists.

The religious Right also revealed its power in the media and in politics. During the 1984 campaign the Reverend Jerry Falwell, one of several "televangelists" who built up well-financed fundamentalist empires, took the lead of the Moral Majority, as it was called, in an effort to advance a range of conservative positions. The Moral Majority opposed the ERA, abortion, welfare, the busing of blacks to schools, affirmative action programs, and modernist religion. They were especially hostile to the Supreme Court, and demanded the restoration of prayers in the public schools. In 1987 they suffered a setback when Jim Bakker, a leading televangelist, was shown to have engaged in extramarital sex and to have enriched himself and his wife, Tammy, with millions of dollars raised during television appeals. In 1988 the Reverend Jimmy Swaggart, another televangelist, was suspended from his ministry following revelations of alleged sexual misconduct. Even these disclosures, however, did not shake the faith of many Americans, especially in rural areas of the South and West, in the agenda of Protestant fundamentalism. As in the 1920s, when Bryan and Darrow had clashed at the Scopes trial, the United States remained a society with profound regional, religious, and cultural divisions.

Life-style and moral issues also evoked intense arguments. One of these, involving the ethics of surrogate motherhood, attracted nationwide attention in 1986–88 when Mary Beth Whitehead, who had contracted to be artificially inseminated, fled to Florida rather than honor her contract to hand over her baby girl to William Stern, the father, and Elizabeth Stern, his wife. Following lengthy and acrimonious legal proceedings, surrogacy contracts for pay were ruled illegal. The Sterns were awarded primary custody of the girl and were permitted to adopt her. The debate over surrogate motherhood, like the issue of abortion, aroused passionate and sometimes unpredictable feelings among feminists, religious leaders, and many others.

The spread of drugs aroused even louder debates in the 1980s. Use of heroin, cocaine, and "crack" seemed widespread, especially among young people in the ghettos. When Len Bias, a twenty-two-year-old University of Maryland basketball star, died of cocaine overdose in 1986, Americans became especially alarmed. President Reagan appeared on TV to announce a nationwide campaign against drugs in schools and workplaces. Nancy Reagan urged America's youth to "Just Say No." Efforts such as these, however, seemed to have little effect. Americans, indeed, were the world's leading consumers of illicit drugs. Use of hard drugs, moreover, was but part of a larger pattern of dependencies. It was estimated that 350,000 Americans died in 1986 of cigarette-related ailments, and that 98,000 more died or were killed as a result of alcohol abuse. As Americans slowly recognized these dangers, they began tightening laws against drunken driving. Grassroots agitation against smoking led to a host of state, local, and federal restrictions on the use of tobacco in public spaces.

No health issue of the late 1980s aroused more fear than the spread of acquired immunity deficiency syndrome, or AIDS. Compared to many other health problems, AIDS was not yet a major killer: some 16,000 Americans died of it between 1981, when it was discovered in the United States, and 1986. But it was apparently spreading rapidly. Federal officials estimated in 1993 that at least 1,000,000 Americans were infected by the human immunodeficiency virus and that some 250,000 people had contracted AIDS. One researcher exclaimed that AIDS, which was always fatal, would "probably prove to be the plague of the millennium." The head of the World Health Organization added, "We stand nakedly in front of a very serious pandemic as mortal as any pandemic there ever has been."

The spread of AIDS proved alarming for many reasons. First, of course, it threatened to become epidemic. Second, in a culture that greatly valued good health and that had exalted the potential of science and technology, it revealed that modern medicine did not have all the answers. Third, AIDS sharpened existing debates over life-styles. While it could be contracted through heterosexual contact and through blood transfusions, it was clear that in the United States, it mainly affected certain homosexuals and drug addicts using contaminated needles. Many Americans were sure that the rise of AIDS was confirmation of the degeneration of society.

The attention given to these ethical and life-style issues inevitably involved political actors. The New Right, indeed, hoped that Reagan would help them promote their agenda. To some degree, he did. Again and again he declared his faith in traditional values. The New Right applauded his positions on abortion, education, censorship, school prayer, affirmative action, welfare, and drug abuse. No American president in the postwar era did more to encourage the resurgence of the religious and political Right.

The Right especially welcomed Reagan's efforts to realign the Supreme Court, which—despite four appointments by Nixon—preserved many of the liberal precedents established during the Warren years. Reagan's first appointment was Arizona judge Sandra Day O'Connor, a conservative. She was the first female justice in U.S. history. When Chief Justice Warren Burger retired in 1986, Reagan

Percentage of Groups Identifying Themselves as Republicans in 1977 and 1987		
	JULY 1977	**JULY 1987**
Percent of total sample	20	30
White	23	35
Black	6	7
Male	19	30
Female	21	31
Northeast	23	32
Midwest	19	31
South	18	29
West	20	28
Liberals	14	19
Moderates	21	29
Conservatives	25	44
18–29 years old	18	29
30–44	19	27
45–60	19	38
Over 64	28	24
Not a high school graduate	18	25
High school graduate	20	30
Some college	20	32
College graduate or beyond	26	34
Protestant	23	33
Catholic	15	26
Income under $12,500		17
$25,000–24,999		28
$25,000–34,999		31
$35,000–50,000		33
Income over $50,000		44

SOURCE: *The New York Times,* July 1987.

named Rehnquist, a Nixon appointee, to the chief justiceship, and Antonin Scalia, a federal judge, to the vacancy. Scalia was widely known for his right-of-center views on most issues. Then in 1987 Reagan nominated Robert Bork, another conservative judge, to replace retiring Justice Lewis Powell. The nomination greatly frightened liberals (and many moderates), who defeated the nomination in the Senate, 58 to 42. A similar coalition then forced the withdrawal of Reagan's next nominee, Douglas Ginsburg. Only in 1988 did the President succeed in replacing Powell, with California jurist Anthony Kennedy. These hotly contested struggles indicated that the Court had become a powerful adjudicator of an accumulating number of sociocultural conflicts in modern America.

Notwithstanding Reagan's efforts to change the Court, he otherwise proved something of a disappointment to the Moral Majority. Too often, the Right recognized, he was unwilling to risk his political popularity by taking exposed positions on inflammatory moral issues. Moreover, the President lacked authority to change much. So the Right remained angry about many trends in American life, and frustrated by their inability to turn back the clock. Abortion was still legal; creationism failed to receive equal time; affirmative action, though sometimes poorly enforced, continued to be the law of the land; criminals (the Right thought) were still being "coddled"; drug abuse seemed to be spreading; AIDS—confirmation of much that they regarded as sinful about American society—threatened (some thought) to become an epidemic. The restlessness of the Right in the late 1980s testified amply to continuing sociocultural conflict in twentieth-century American life.

If conservatives were restless in the 1980s, liberals were close to despair. Their political weakness became especially clear during the 1984 election. The Democrats nominated Walter Mondale, Carter's vice-president, to head their national ticket, and Geraldine Ferraro, a New York congresswoman, as his running mate.

Mondale and Ferraro at the Democratic National Convention in San Francisco, 1984

She was the first woman in American history to be named to the presidential ticket of a major party. Both Democratic candidates waged vigorous campaigns, attacking the Reagan administration for its conservative domestic policies, its hawkishness in foreign affairs, and the low quality of Republican high officials, several of whom had been indicted for corruption. When Reagan appeared vacillating during a nationally televised debate, it appeared that the Democrats might have a chance to unseat him.

In fact, however, the Democrats were badly divided. During an acrimonious primary campaign the Reverend Jesse Jackson developed considerable support among blacks. Moreover, Colorado Senator Gary Hart, who emerged as the leading challenger for the Democratic nomination, subjected Mondale to sharp criticisms — which Republicans later used. In particular, Hart charged that Mondale was subservient to the AFL-CIO and other interest groups that were strong in the party. Ferraro, too, proved a questionable addition to the ticket. Though she was an energetic and articulate campaigner, she was hurt by charges that her husband, John Zaccaro, had engaged in illegal financial practices in New York. Exit polls later suggested that her place on the ticket probably did little to assist the party.

But the biggest problem facing Mondale and Ferraro was the personal popularity of Reagan. Voters remembered the malaise that had surrounded the country in 1980: high inflation, rising unemployment, Americans humiliatingly imprisoned in Iran. Four years later, the economy had rebounded, and the nation seemed more sure of itself in foreign affairs. Reagan, a masterful politician, continued to score well in public opinion polls. Opponents, indeed, dubbed him the Teflon President: No charges seemed to stick to him. The Reagan-Bush ticket swept to an overwhelming victory, taking 59 percent of the vote and carrying every state but Mondale's home base of Minnesota (and the District of Columbia). As in 1980 it remained unclear whether Reagan's triumph represented a major realignment of politics — Democrats in fact recaptured the Senate and controlled a majority of governorships. But there was no denying the fact that the voters had given Reagan a striking vote of confidence. It was equally clear that the Democratic party was fragile and that liberalism, vibrant and promising in the early 1960s, was in disarray. Politically the 1980s was a decade of conservatism.

Foreign Affairs in the 1980s

The Soviet Union, Reagan said in 1982, is "an evil empire . . . the focus of evil in the modern world." He added, "Let us not delude ourselves. The Soviet Union underlies all the unrest that is going on. If they weren't engaged in this game of dominos, there wouldn't be any hot spots in the world." This speech characterized Reagan's ideological view of world politics. Like most of his top advisers, he was an ardent Cold Warrior and an advocate of expanding American influence all over the globe.

This did not mean that he sought always to engage the United States in rash military adventures throughout the world. Like his predecessors, he discovered that many overseas developments were simply beyond the capacity of the United States to influence. During his tenure he dared not send American soldiers to aid anti-Soviet rebels in Afghanistan or to stop the Soviets from imposing a tougher regime in Poland. In 1986 he could not prevent domestic unrest in the Philippines from toppling Ferdinand Marcos, a corrupt tyrant who had long enjoyed support from American politicians.

As ardent right-wingers unhappily pointed out, Reagan also compromised his ideological certitude on occasion. One of his first acts as president was to negotiate a grain deal with the Soviet Union. The deal assisted American farmers, who were desperately seeking overseas markets. Reagan also worked to promote closer relations with the People's Republic of China, thereby antagonizing the pro-American regime in Taiwan. And while he proved cool to arms control, he continued Carter's policy of living up to the terms of the SALT II agreements, even though they had not been accepted by the Senate. In foreign affairs, as in domestic matters, practical political exigencies sometimes tempered Reagan's ideological fervor.

Moreover, Reagan's ideological view of the world seemed to moderate over time. During much of his first term he continued to denounce the evils of world communism, especially in 1983, when the Russians shot down a Korean Air Lines passenger plane that had strayed into Soviet airspace. The incident caused the death of 269 people and inflamed anticommunist sentiment not only in the United States but elsewhere in the West. Soviet-American discussions of arms control in Europe thereupon broke down. Ignoring international demands for a "freeze" on the spread of nuclear weapons, the United States and Soviet Union emplaced intermediate range ballistic missiles on European soil.

In 1984, however, Soviet-American relations began to improve. One reason was the accession to power in the Soviet Union of Mikhail Gorbachev, a younger man who seemed readier than his predecessors to look for détente with the United States. Another was the influence of Reagan's second secretary of state, George Shultz, who replaced General Alexander Haig in 1982. Shultz was a low-key and patient negotiator who generally eschewed extremes of anticommunist rhetoric. A third reason was Reagan himself, who proved more receptive to accommodation with the Soviets than anyone could have imagined a few years earlier. The result of these developments was a series of high-level diplomatic meetings in 1985, followed by a Gorbachev-Reagan summit meeting at Reykjavik, Iceland, in 1986. Though the summit concluded without major agreement, it seemed briefly to promise substantial reduction of nuclear weapons in western Europe. Further talks in 1987 and 1988 indeed resulted in agreement to ban shorter- and medium-range missiles, 2,611 in all. The pact was the first in history to require the destruction of deployed nuclear weapons. It was clear that the Reagan of 1985–88 took a somewhat less ideological view of the world than the Reagan of 1980–84.

Nothing made this shift more clear than Reagan's policies in the Middle East. Here, too, his administration had at first seemed firm and uncompromising. Having come to office on a groundswell of American outrage over the taking of American hostages in Tehran, Reagan proudly emphasized his refusal to deal with terrorists. "No concessions," he said. "No deals." He also broadly defined American interests in the area. Accordingly, he ordered American troops to strife-torn Lebanon in 1982. Their presence angered Moslem extremists, who bombed marine barracks in Beirut in October 1983, killing 240. Reagan pulled out the remaining marines in

Reagan and Gorbachev signing the nuclear arms reduction treaty in Washington, 1987

February 1984, but reiterated his determination to deal severely with terrorists and to isolate the anti-American regime of Iran.

On the surface, Reagan hewed to these stern Middle East policies in his second term. Irritated by the anti-American regime of Libya's Muammar Qaddafi, whom he accused of fomenting terrorism, the President authorized American planes to bomb Libyan installations in 1986. The raids killed an estimated 37 Libyans, including Qaddafi's infant daughter and other civilians. Two American airmen were also lost in one raid. Further expanding American presence in the Middle East, the President ordered American warships in 1987 to escort Kuwaiti tankers in the oil-rich Persian Gulf. By taking this risky move he hoped not only to protect oil shipments from attacks by Iraq or Iran, who were engaged in a bitter war, but also to dramatize the seriousness of America's commitment to Western interests in the region.

In late 1986, however, word leaked out that the Reagan administration had been secretly selling arms to the supposedly hated Iranian regime of the Ayatollah Khomeini. Deeply embarrassed by this disclosure, administration officials offered varied explanations for the sales. Some hinted at first that the sales were part of a sophisticated effort to develop contacts with moderate political elements in Iran. It became clear, however, that Reagan authorized the arms sales in order to satisfy mounting demands at home that he do something to win release of Western hostages held in Lebanon and other undisclosed places in the Middle East. The revelation of the secret arms sales shocked and surprised many Americans, who were forced to conclude that Reagan had given in to terrorism and who complained that he acted without any congressional authorization. Moreover, the deal helped free only two hostages, while more were seized. Relations with Iran grew colder than ever.

These developments shattered Reagan's image as a hard-liner—as a man who did what he said. It was obvious that he was neither so uncompromising an opponent of the Soviet Union nor so determined an antiterrorist as his rhetoric had indicated. Still, his foreign policies in three other regards indicated that anticommunism continued to form the bedrock of his views of the world.

The first involved American policy with regard to dictatorial regimes. Not only in the Middle East but also in many other areas—the Philippines, Chile, South Korea, Angola—the Reagan administration offered support for repressive governments when and if they seemed to stand strongly against communism. This approach to world politics was especially clear with regard to South Africa, where the system of *apartheid,* which brutally excluded nonwhites from basic rights, threatened to provoke civil war. Congress demanded that Reagan take bold steps, including the imposition of economic sanctions, against the South African government. The President, however, vetoed sanctions in 1986. Such measures, he thought, would be counterproductive. South Africa, he also believed, was a bulwark against the spread of communism. Congress then overruled him, and limited sanctions took effect. Still, Reagan adhered to a policy of "constructive engagement" with the South African regime.

The second area concerned defense policies. Though Reagan approved of the ban on short- and medium-range missiles, he did not soften his support of the Pentagon and of the industrial-military complex. He greatly increased spending for counterinsurgency and the navy. Above all, he persisted in backing the expenditure of billions for the so-called Strategic Defense Initiative, a ballistic missile defense system dubbed "Star Wars" by hundreds of doubtful scientists. They argued not only that it might not work but also that it was sharpening Cold War tensions. The Soviets, indeed, maintained that Reagan's insistence on the SDI prevented agreement on reductions in deployment and development of offensive missiles.

It was in the third area—of Central America—that Reagan's fundamentally ideological approach to foreign policy was most clear. In his first term this approach became obvious with regard to El Salvador, which was racked by civil war. Many observers believed that the struggle in El Salvador, like the war in Vietnam, stemmed primarily from internal causes—poverty, political repression, nationalistic hostility to foreign imperialism (mainly American). Reagan, however, was convinced that rebels against the established regime represented Soviet influence. Resurrecting the domino theory, he channeled American military aid to the El Salvador government. In so doing he countenanced barbaric activities of anti-rebel "death squads" throughout the country. Alarmed, Congress stipulated that American aid be cut off unless the government in El Salvador were able to demonstrate improvements in tts handling of human rights. A more moderate government under the leadership of José Napoleon Duarte took firmer control in 1984 and brought some measure of order to the war-ravaged land. For these reasons debate over El Salvador became less contentious during Reagan's second term.

Meanwhile, Reagan's fear of communism in the Caribbean found an outlet in the tiny island of Grenada, where a leftist government friendly with Cuba had taken power in 1983. Reagan reacted sharply, perceiving in Grenada the evil presence of Cuban and Russian influence. He thereupon sent in 2,000 marines, who took the island and installed a pro-American government. The invasion brought joy and pride to millions of Americans, who relished the show of military might on behalf of democracy. Critics, however, emphasized that the invasion cost the lives of 18 Americans, 160 Grenadans, and 71 Cubans. The United Nations condemned the action. Subsequent revelations suggested that there had been no significant communist military buildup on the island.

In Reagan's second term the focus of American attentions in Central America shifted to Nicaragua, where revolutionaries in 1979 had overthrown a long-standing pro-American dictatorship headed by the Somoza family. The Sandinistas, as the revolutionaries called themselves, had at first been accepted by the Carter

A young, U.S.-trained *contra* in Nicaragua

administration, but relations cooled when they curbed civil liberties and moved closer to Castro's Cuba. Opponents of the Sandinistas alleged that the new government was aiding leftist rebels in El Salvador. For these reasons Carter cut off aid to the Sandinistas in early 1981. This was the unsettled state of affairs when the Reagan administration took office.

Reagan's response was to assist rebels against the Sandinistas, whom he considered to be fomenting communism throughout Central America. As early as 1982 the CIA began arming and training counterrevolutionary forces, or *contras,* many of whom had been involved in the Somoza regime. In early 1984 it was revealed that the CIA had mined Nicaraguan harbors and that it had advised the *contras* on how to incite mob violence and assassinate opponents. Disclosures such as these prompted a succession of congressional moves aimed at limiting the flow of American military aid to the *contras.*

Congressional resistance led Reagan and top aides to look for other, secret ways to assist the *contras.* As sensational disclosures revealed in late 1986, the Reagan administration abetted private networks of military aid to the *contras.* More sensational were revelations that profits from sales of arms to Iran had been secretly funneled to arms dealers who, in turn, delivered some $14 million of this money to the *contras.* The Reagan administration, critics pointed out, had circumvented the expressed will of the people as mandated in a series of congressional acts that had curbed aid to the rebels.

News of the secret connection between the Iranian arms sales and aid to the *contras* set off a constitutional controversy reminiscent of Watergate. Most Americans were shocked that Reagan could ever have agreed to any kind of deal with Iran. Other critics were appalled that his administration had circumvented Congress over policy involving Nicaragua. To these critics "Irangate," as it came to be called, seemed even more frightening than Watergate, for it involved central questions of foreign policy making—not just a "two-bit burglary." A special joint committee of Congress conducting widely televised hearings on the affair revealed in 1987 that top Reagan advisers had destroyed documents needed by investigators of the affair

---

First Person

Ronald Reagan on the Iran-Contra Affair

A few months ago I told the American people I did not trade arms for hostages. My heart and my best intentions still tell me that is true, but the facts and the evidence tell me it is not.

. . .

Much has been said about my management style, a style that worked successfully for me during eight years as governor of California and for most of my presidency. The way I work is to identify the problem, find the individual to do the job, and then let them go to it. I've found this invariably brings out the best in people.

Vital Speeches, March 15, 1987, p. 323.

and had deliberately misled the Congress in their use of public funds. In 1988 two of these advisers and two others were formally charged with conspiracy in connection with the affair. A special prosecutor later secured eleven convictions, mostly for perjury, though some of those were overturned on appeal.

These investigations exposed still another disturbing aspect of foreign policy making in the Reagan administration: the nefarious influence of the CIA and the National Security Council within American government. When Irangate first became known, Admiral John Poindexter, head of the NSC, was forced to resign, and Lt. Col. Oliver North, a top aide, was fired. It soon became clear that they, together with CIA Director William Casey, a close friend of the President, had masterminded the deal. Other key officials, including Defense Secretary Caspar Weinberger and Secretary of State Shultz, said they had been informed only belatedly and incompletely about what was going on, and had been ignored when they raised objections. Poindexter and North insisted that Reagan himself was not told of the "diversion" to the *contras* of profits from the arms sales. It was important, Poindexter said, that the President be kept in the dark, so that he would have plausible "deniability" in case news of the secret dealings leaked to the public.

Many informed Americans were hardly surprised by these revelations. Reagan, they emphasized, had always been an unsophisticated, excessively ideological man who saw communists wherever he looked. The CIA, they added, had long exceeded its assigned role of intelligence gathering—witness its direction of coups in Iran in 1953 and Guatemala in 1955. And the NSC had mushroomed in size and importance during the Kennedy-Johnson years and especially under the leadership of Kissinger in the Nixon administration. Shultz was surely not the first secretary of state to be bypassed by the White House and its expanding bureucratic empires.

Still, millions of Americans—many of them previously loyal Reaganites—found Irangate profoundly distressing. Some complained that Reagan, never known as a detail man, entrusted far too much authority to subordinates. Unlike "hands-on" presidents such as Johnson and Nixon, he was a casual and poorly informed administrator. Others, recognizing in the CIA and the NSC an "invisible government," were upset by the repeated evasions of the democratic process. Still others—indeed a majority of Americans polled in 1987—believed that Reagan himself had authorized the entire affair and that he and his aides were engaged in yet another cover-up. All these people perceived a frightening pattern. First the credibility gap over Vietnam. Then lies over Watergate. Then a secret arms deal and surreptitious deliveries of money to the *contras*. Irangate, they said, not only damaged the reputation of the Reagan administration at home and abroad, it also revealed persistent abuse of the nation's constitutional system. Senator Daniel Inouye, co-chair of the congressional investigating committee, concluded that the affair was a "chilling story . . . of deceit and duplicity and the arrogant disregard of the rule of law. . . . It is the story of how a great nation betrayed the principles which have made it great and thereby became hostage to hostage-takers, and, sadly, once the story began to unravel, it became the story of a cover-up, a shredding and altering of the historical record, and of a fall-guy plan suitable for a grade-B movie, not a great power."

As many people noted, it was ironic that these revelations occurred in the bicentennial year of the framing of the Constitution. Americans wondered if the constitutional system could survive many more abuses such as those that had characterized the 1960s, 1970s, and 1980s. Other people, liberals especially, fore-saw little if any likelihood that the government—divided as it seemed to be—would prove capable of coping with a wider range of persistent problems, including continuing racial strife, poverty, and agricultural distress, or of moderating debates over such contentious issues as affirmative action, abortion, and religious funda-mentalism. The Reagan years, it seemed, had perpetuated doubts about the capacity of government to resolve these and other continuing American dilemmas.

Still, it was probably fair to say that for most middle-class Americans, the mid- and late 1980s were personally more satisfying than the 1970s had been. Irangate, though divisive, did not force the resignation of the President. Congress, the courts, the press, and public opinion remained vigorous and alert. Intervention in El Salvador and Nicaragua, while highly controversial, had not escalated into another Vietnam. Relations with the Soviet Union were warmer than in many years. Moreover—and this was a fact of basic, daily importance to ordinary people—the economy of the mid- and late 1980s seemed (stock market alarms of 1987 notwith-standing) healthier than it had been in the scary years of the late 1970s and early 1980s. For all these reasons the mood of much of the nation was relatively optimistic in 1988, the dawn of the Constitution's third century.

Evaluating the Reagan Presidency

When Reagan left office in January 1989, many critics lambasted his performance. The Friends of the Earth, a leading environmental group, accused him of "the worst abuses we've ever seen of public trust and the environment in the history of the Presidency." The executive director of the Leadership Conference on Civil Rights said that he was responsible for "the worst civil rights record of any administration in several decades." Ralph Nader, the consumer advocate, denounced him for lead-ing the nation on a "drunken, world-record spending binge while leaving millions of American workers, consumers and pollution victims defenseless."

Critics were especially unhappy with the long-range legacy of Reagan's regula-tory and fiscal policies. Lax federal oversight of the badly managed savings and loan industry, they said, contributed to widespread S&L failures in the late 1980s. Congress approved an S&L "bailout" in 1989 that was expected to cost taxpayers more than $200 billion over the next thirty years. Another legacy of the 1980s (and earlier) was poor federal upkeep of government weapons manufacturing plants, which had been emitting nuclear poison into the atmosphere. The cost of delayed maintenance of the plants was calculated in 1989 to be an additional $100 billion in the near future.

Bad government management also surfaced in other agencies. Careless lending by the Reagan administration's Farmers Home Administration led to losses esti-mated in 1989 at $22 billion, which taxpayers would have to absorb in the early 1990s. Scandals in the Department of Housing and Urban Development, while less costly (waste of public funds was thought to approximate at least $2 billion), further suggested the laxity of management and the corruption of some high officials in the Reagan administration.

Losses such as these compounded the budgetary expansion and deficit financing that had characterized the Reagan years. Though Congress passed legislation requiring a balanced budget by fiscal year 1993, deficits continued to mount in the early 1990s. Some observers did not worry too much about such deficits, arguing that high levels of federal spending were necessary for a wide variety of purposes and that governmental expenditures stimulated the private sector. But many experts emphasized that deficits of such magnitude cost taxpayers billions to service, drove up interest rates, and damaged the credit of the government. Some predicted the national debt, which exceeded $4 trillion in 1993, could lead to another Great Depression.

Public opinion polls taken in 1989 suggested that many Americans remained highly critical of specific actions and policies of the Reagan administration. Majorities continued to believe that the President had lied when he denied knowing of the connection between Iranian arms sales and aid to the Nicaraguan *contras*. Some Americans simply dismissed the President as a bumbler. "He's like a nice, old uncle," said the liberal historian Arthur Schlesinger, Jr. "He comes in, and all the kids are glad to see him. He sits around telling stories, and they're all fond of him, but they don't take him too seriously."

Nonetheless, critics of Reagan had to concede that he remained extraordinarily popular at the end of his term in January 1989. A *New York Times* poll at that time revealed that 68 percent of the American people (72 percent of whites, 40 percent of blacks) approved of the way he had handled his job as President since 1981. None of the seven previous presidents, dating back to Truman, had reached even 60 percent in comparable polls taken at the close of their administrations. Eisenhower had enjoyed the next highest score, at 59 percent, while Nixon, faced with impeachment, had had the lowest, at 24 percent. The poll further revealed that Reagan was more popular with younger voters than with older ones—a finding that appeared to bode well for the future of conservatism and of the Republican party.

Public opinion surveys also indicated significant changes in popular attitudes toward government. In 1980, the last year of the Carter administration, only 22 percent of people polled had said that they could trust government "most of the time." By 1989, after eight years of Reagan in the White House, the percentage had increased to 38 percent. A total of 48 percent of people in 1989 said that they favored bigger government, compared to only 32 percent eight years earlier. It was indeed ironic that Ronald Reagan, who had consistently proclaimed his hostility to Big Government, had prompted a surge of popular faith in the capacity of the state to deal with public problems.

THE 1988 ELECTION

In 1987, when the protracted presidential campaign began, political pundits found it unusually difficult to predict who might emerge as the candidates in 1988. On the Republican side the contest promised to feature a rugged battle between Senator Robert Dole of Kansas, who had been Ford's running mate in 1976, and George Bush, Reagan's vice-president.

Democrats, meanwhile, appeared to face an exciting struggle involving a large number of possibilities. These included former Colorado Senator Gary Hart, the early front-runner; Senator Joseph Biden of Delaware, head of the Judiciary Committee; Senator Albert Gore, Jr., of Tennessee, a youthful dark horse with strength in the South; Representative Richard Gephardt of Missouri, who focused on trade and tariff issues; Paul Simon, yet another senatorial entrant, from Illinois; the Reverend Jesse Jackson, the charismatic black leader who had sought the nomination in 1984; and Michael Dukakis, who claimed a record of efficiency as the liberal governor of Massachusetts.

Those who anticipated long and closely competitive struggles, however, were rather quickly disappointed. After a slow start, Bush trounced his opponents in the New Hampshire primary, and by April he was assured of the GOP nomination. At the convention that summer he named J. Danforth Quayle, a conservative senator from Indiana, as his running mate.

The Democratic race, too, failed to generate drama. Two of the early favorites, Hart and Biden, virtually self-destructed—Hart because of sexual indiscretions, and Biden because of revelations that he had distorted his record. Gore, Gephardt, and Simon never developed much national appeal. Jackson campaigned impressively, but he did not get much support from party leaders, who feared that America was not ready for an African-American presidential candidate. Well before the Democratic convention it was clear that Dukakis, who was by far the best-funded of the competitors, would get the nomination. As his running mate he picked Lloyd Bentsen, a moderately conservative senator from Texas.

The campaign that followed was both unedifying and unexciting. Dukakis, the first to be nominated, started with an impressive margin in the public opinion polls. But his campaign team was disorganized, and he was a stiff, passionless speaker. His lead quickly evaporated. The Bush campaign staff, by contrast, included seasoned political professionals who developed aggressive television messages. Expenditures for TV, indeed, were enormous, with both candidates attempting to shape images of themselves through the television sets that graced virtually every American home. The outcome of the 1988 campaign, even more than others in the Age of Television, hinged to a considerable extent on the ability of advertising and public relations wizards to convince the public.

In some of his appearances Bush tried to put a little distance between himself and the conservative tenor of the Reagan administration. America, he said, must become a "kinder, gentler nation." Most of the time, however, he attacked liberal ideas. Dukakis, he said, was a soft-headed liberal without backbone on crime. Appealing to superpatriotic sentiments, Bush reminded voters that Dukakis had vetoed a bill requiring Massachusetts teachers to lead schoolchildren in reciting the Pledge of Allegiance. Dukakis retorted that the Supreme Court had ruled such a requirement unconstitutional, but the Republican accusations nonetheless seemed to stick.

The Bush team, emphasizing its toughness regarding crime, called for giving the death penalty to convicted drug kingpins, and denounced Dukakis for having approved a weekend furlough for a black murderer, who thereupon escaped and raped a woman. Liberals retorted that these charges were crude, racist, and largely irrelevant in a presidential election that should have highlighted important national and international issues. Bush, they said angrily, had become "George the Ripper."

Democrats also tried to link Bush to Irangate—as vice-president he attended many important meetings regarding foreign policy. But Bush denied all, and

Dukakis lacked solid documentary evidence to substantiate his suspicions. With this issue proving unproductive, the Democrats seemed ever more on the defensive against an increasingly aggressive Republican campaign strategy.

As expected, Bush won handily in November, taking 53.4 percent of the popular vote and carrying 40 of 50 states. In explaining the result, liberals pointed bitterly to Bush's exploitation of such issues as crime, drugs, the death penalty, and the Pledge of Allegiance, and in retrospect it seemed true that Bush was energized by the mostly favorable popular response that these issues managed to arouse. In contrast to Dukakis he proved a forceful, often negative campaigner.

Election analysts, however, suggested that other forces had important roles. One was electoral geography, especially as it played into the winner-take-all nature of the electoral college system. As in other presidential contests since 1964 the Republican party proved powerful in states west of the Mississippi and among white voters in the South. This reality resulted mainly from the divisive power of race and related issues in American politics. Once the Democratic party had committed itself to a higher degree of racial justice—as it did by sponsoring the historic civil right laws of the mid-1960s—it solidified its hold on African-American voters (Dukakis won 86 percent of them), but it lost white votes in most southern and western states in presidential elections. If it lost a few of the electorally crucial industrial states of the North and Midwest, as the uninspiring Democratic ticket did in 1988, it was virtually doomed to defeat. This was another way of saying that in presidential politics (Democrats gained a few congressional seats in 1988) America seemed to have become an ordinarily Republican nation.

A second force was equally powerful: the peace and prosperity of the later Reagan years. Bush, as Reagan's vice-president, naturally and successfully associated himself with these developments. "Read my lips," he repeatedly told voters: "No new taxes" were necessary to sustain "Republican" peace and prosperity. Otherwise, however, Bush remained deliberately vague on issues, and he received no mandate to do anything as President. Though polls showed little popular enthusiasm for Bush (voter turnout was low, at 50 percent of the electorate), they also indicated that the American people regarded him as the more experienced leader. It remained to be seen whether he could validate this judgment.

Consensus, 1989–90?

Writing in *The New Republic* in May 1989, a columnist perceived that many of the passions that had aroused America since the mid-1960s had finally faded. The Cold War was moderating at last; governmental social programs led to mostly quiet debates; Democrats and Republicans appeared to be moving toward the center on most of the issues. The United States might therefore anticipate a "new era . . . of consensus, conciliation, and compromise, a lot like the 1950s and early 1960s and just as trivial and boring."

There seemed much to commend this observation. Cold War tensions had abated dramatically since the ascension to power of Mikhail Gorbachev in the Soviet Union. In 1989 the Soviets pulled their troops out of Afghanistan, reducing a major irritant to Soviet-American relations. Gorbachev and Bush made modest progress toward mutual reduction of chemical weapons and of conventional forces and weaponry in Europe. Both nations, following agreements made in 1988, began destroying short- and intermediate-range missiles. Bush further helped to defuse foreign policy controversy in the United States by seeming, at last, to accept the end of American military aid to the *contras* in Nicaragua. His administration lent support in early 1990 to the holding there of a democratic election, which resulted in defeat for the Sandinista government.

Bush also generated a large and popular consensus behind his handling of Manuel Noriega, the leader of Panama. Long a CIA informant, Noriega became increasingly authoritarian, as well as openly involved in the international drug trade. In December 1989 Bush resolved to overthrow him and sent in paratroopers to do the job. The mission broke international law, and the fighting resulted in the death of hundreds (some estimates said thousands) of Panamanian civilians. But it caused only 23 American deaths and succeeded in ousting Noriega, who was brought to the United States and charged with drug trafficking. Public opinion polls revealed that 90 percent of Americans enthusiastically supported Bush's actions.

Developments in eastern and central Europe were especially heartening to Americans in 1989–91. Hungary, opening its borders with Austria, permitted thousands of Soviet-bloc refugees to escape to the West. Communist officials in

Ronald and Nancy Reagan

Poland grudgingly agreed to democratic elections, which led to a coalition goernment dominated by the Solidarity party. Most dramatic of all was the tearing down in November 1989 of the Berlin Wall, followed a year later by the reunification of Germany. All these changes were possible because the Soviet Union, increasingly beset with serious ethnic and economic pressures at home, no longer tried to curb dissent in its one-time satellites. Witnessing these historic changes, Americans rejoiced at the victory of democratic values in the world. "The triumph of the Western Idea is total," the columnist Charles Krauthammer exclaimed. European communism, it appeared, was history.

The calming of Cold War rivalry also moderated the bitter debates over defense policy that had divided Americans in the Reagan years. A Gallup poll in mid-1989 found 74 percent of respondents in favor of cuts in appropriations for defense in order to reduce the federal deficit. "It's astonishing how much hostility toward defense there is across the board," one conservative observed in mid-1989, "even among people who describe themselves as staunchly anticommunist."

Reflecting this growing skepticism about heavy defense spending, Bush offered only mixed support for Reagan's Star Wars program. His defense secretary, Richard Cheney, tried to halt funding for development of the Midgetman warhead. Congress cut requests for the B-2 (Stealth) bomber, a sleek, batlike airplane that, if funded at levels recommended by Reagan administration officials, would have cost $530 million per plane, or a total of nearly $70 billion for the 132-plane fleet once claimed by advocates to be essential to American defense. Further cuts in arms spending followed in the next few years, prompting hopes for accumulation of a "peace dividend" that might be spent on alleviating domestic problems.

Most Americans also applauded Bush's handling of tensions in the Middle East that exploded when Iraq invaded neighboring Kuwait in August 1990. Bush skillfully secured international support for an oil embargo, and (with no opposition to worry about from a self-absorbed Soviet Union) set about readying a grand coalition of allied forces for invasion if necessary. Like other world leaders, he was outraged by Iraq's defiance of international law. He also feared that Saddam Hussein, Iraq's dictator, would use his million-man army and arsenal of sophisticated weapons not only to dominate Kuwait but also to intimidate other petroleum-producing nations into setting very high prices on oil. Concerns such as these led the United Nations to demand that Iraq get out of Kuwait by January 15, 1991, or risk attack. Bush then asked Congress for authority to go to war if Saddam defied the resolution. A number of congressmen resisted the effort, arguing that economic sanctions, if given more time, might bring Iraq to heel. But Republicans supported Bush almost unanimously, as did a minority of Democrats, and on January 12 Bush had the authorization he needed.

When Saddam ignored the deadline, aircraft from the United States, France, Kuwait, Britain, and Saudi Arabia retaliated on January 16 with the first of more than five weeks of nonstop bombing raids on Iraq and Kuwait. The attacks destroyed much of Iraq's infrastructure and killed between 25,000 and 130,000 Iraqi soldiers and civilians. Americans, witnessing the attacks on live television, were not able to see much of the killing, but they thrilled to the more impersonal display of modern military technology, including Patriot missiles that knocked down Iraqi missiles aimed at Saudi Arabia and Israel.

General Norman Schwarzkopf

After such ferocious bombardment, the ground war that followed on February 23 was almost anticlimactic. Orchestrated by Defense Secretary Cheney and General Colin Powell, chairman of the Joint Chiefs of Staff, and led in the field by General Norman Schwarzkopf, troops from a multinational force of nearly 700,000 poured into Kuwait and Iraq. The vast majority of them were American, including some 30,000 women. Saddam's forces put up only slight resistance, abandoned Kuwait City, and fell back toward Baghdad. Tens of thousands surrendered. Only 100 hours after the start of the fighting on the ground Bush announced that Operation Desert Storm had liberated Kuwait and that the war was over. Fewer than 150 American soldiers died in the fighting.

In the aftermath of war, a variety of people found fault with Bush's policies. Much of this criticism focused on his actions prior to Iraq's invasion in August 1990. Some noted that Bush (and Reagan before him) had encouraged allies to sell arms and equipment to Iraq, in part to help Saddam in his war with Iran. These had enabled Iraq to develop nuclear, chemical, and biological weapons. The United States, moreover, had approved 771 licenses between 1985 and 1990 that permitted the export of $1.5 billion in advanced equipment to Iraq, some of it useful for military purposes. The Bush administration had also provided Baghdad with $500 million in agricultural credits and failed (critics said) to make it clear to Saddam in the summer of 1990 that the United States would go to war if necessary to prevent an assault on Kuwait. All of these actions, critics charged, had encouraged Saddam to pursue his aggressive policies and to doubt that the United States would retaliate with force.

Other critics faulted Bush's subsequent decisions. A few insisted that narrow economic motives prompted American reaction: "Hell no, we won't go, we won't fight for Texaco." Others denounced the Pentagon's tight control of news reports concerning the fighting. Still others complained that Bush had called off the war too soon. Saddam, though greatly weakened, remained in control of Iraq, and stepped up his persecution of Kurds and other opponents within the country. United Nations inspection teams were repeatedly frustrated in subsequent efforts to ascertain the degree to which Iraq continued to hide and develop nuclear weapons.

Critics, however, were definitely a small minority in 1991. So resounding a triumph, at such modest cost in American life, was extraordinarily popular among the people. When the war was over, 90 percent of Americans thought Bush was doing a good job as President. This was the highest rating any President had received since World War II. Moreover, the war had led to cooperation between Israel and some of its traditional enemies, Saudi Arabia, Kuwait, and Syria, and had tended to isolate the Palestine Liberation Organization, which backed Iraq, from moderate Arabs in the region. Secretary of State James Baker then undertook renewed efforts to resolve some of the differences that had long exacerbated tensions between Israel and its neighbors.

Supporters of Bush's actions rejoiced especially that the United States had demonstrated both the will and the capacity to cooperate with other nations—and with the UN—in opposing armed aggression abroad. Doubts and soul-searching that had prevailed since the Vietnam War could apparently be put away. With the Soviet Union in disarray, the United States now had the potential—or so it seemed in 1991—to promote what Bush and others called a "New World Order" based on American leadership of democracy and prosperity for all.

Though these developments in foreign relations were the most heartening events of the era, debates over economic policies, too, seemed calm compared to those of years past. Economists continued to argue over the precise mechanisms of fiscal and monetary policy, and Democrats and Republicans differed over the amounts to be spent on a range of governmental and social policies. They wrangled especially over ways to improve the nation's patchwork system of medical care, which left more than 35 million people without health insurance. But until late 1990 most of these arguments aroused little of the passion of earlier years. The healer was persisting prosperity. As of late 1990 the economy had expanded consistently for almost eight full years. This was more than twice as long as the average peacetime expansion since 1945. In such an upbeat atmosphere it was hardly surprising that debates over economic policy seemed muted.

Another area of angry debate, environmental policy, also seemed a little less contentious in the early 1990s. Bush, unlike Reagan, seemed concerned about such issues and approved increases in the budget of the Environmental Protection Agency. Though many people were skeptical about the workability of his recommendations to improve air quality by forcing gradual cutbacks on emissions from automobiles and coal-fired power plants, they mostly welcomed passage of the Clean Air Act of 1990, which seemed to offer the best chance for significant federal action since the Clean Air Act of 1970.

As these examples suggest, the potential for "consensus, conciliation, and compromise" in the 1990s seemed considerably enhanced by the moderating presence of Bush. Most Americans thought that he was less dogmatic than Reagan and that he was ordinarily a decent, courteous, and sensible man. The columnist David

Broder wrote, "Bush's instinct is to seek compromise. . . . He is as willing as Eisenhower was to do business with the Democrats on Capitol Hill."

Conflict: The World

Such a rosy perspective was one-sided. It was clear in the early 1990s that serious conflicts continued to threaten the peace of the world and of American society. Many of these conflicts were rooted in deep-seated controversies that seemed beyond the capacity of governmental leaders to control. In the Middle East, hopes for resolution of Arab-Israeli conflict proved overly optimistic, with sporadic violence helping to prevent progress in American-sponsored efforts at mediation. The People's Republic of China remained a tyrannical vestige of world communism. In 1989 it crushed demonstrations in Beijing's Tiananmen Square, killing perhaps 1,000 people. Racial turmoil still threatened to bring about civil war in South Africa. A repressive government in Haiti caused thousands of people to flee toward nearby nations, including the United States, which intercepted them on the high seas and denied most of them entry. Famine caused the death of thousands of people in Somalia, prompting the United States in late 1992 to take the lead in sending a multinational force of soldiers to safeguard the shipping and distribution of food to the Somali people. Animosities between Serbs, Croats, and Muslims from Bosnia and Herzegovina broke up Yugoslavia and led to the fiercest fighting in Europe since World War II. Well-documented reports of atrocities, mainly committed by Serbian armed forces bent on the "ethnic cleansing" of Muslims from large areas of the country, reminded some observers of Nazi crimes.

The situation in the Soviet Union was especially unsteady. Severe economic problems—food shortages, near-runaway inflation—combined with ethnic rivalries to break up the union. In 1990 it imploded, with the Baltic states of Estonia, Latvia, and Lithuania establishing their independence. Ukraine and others also seceded, and in late 1991 the Soviet Union died, replaced by an eleven-republic Commonwealth of Independent States (CIS). Four of these possessed nuclear weapons. Gorbachev, who was nearly toppled by a coup of hard-liners in the summer of 1991, was replaced by Boris Yeltsin, who as the democratically elected president of the republic of Russia in June had led resistance to the coup. Though the budding of democracy was enormously encouraging to the West, Yeltsin and his allies faced formidable political and economic problems that destabilized not only the CIS, but also much of the world around it.

Less dramatic but nonetheless frightening international problems continued to arise from the growth of world poverty. A few have-not nations had or were on the verge of developing nuclear weapons. Many others were defaulting on massive debts to the West. The Bush administration, working with the World Bank and the International Monetary Fund, offered to forgive some of this debt in return for promises of better development policies in the debtor nations. Still, the suffering of billions of poverty-stricken people, many of them bitterly resentful of Uncle Sam, guaranteed the persistence of conflict.

Many Americans, contemplating such problems, remained fervently nationalistic. Expressions of superpatriotism broke out loudly in 1989 in the aftermath of a

A controversial issue: flag burning

five-to-four Supreme Court decision that ruled that constitutional guarantees of free speech extend to people who torch or trample the American flag. A majority of people probably supported the ruling. "I never burned a flag," one man declared, "but I will fight for anyone else's right to do so." But many others reacted furiously. "How does one go about impeaching Supreme Court justices?" one person asked *Newsweek.* Another wrote, "Step on the flag, and you step on American freedom. Burn it, and you destroy our freedom. The flag is a visible sign of something that is invisible."

Bush fanned this patriotic fervor. "The flag," he said, "is too sacred to be abused. If it is not defended, it is defamed." He called for a constitutional amendment allowing states to make flag burning a crime. The House of Representatives also defended the flag, holding an extraordinary all-night session in which congressmen of both parties competed to denounce the Court. Passions soon cooled, but the controversy made it abundantly clear that foreign nations held no monopoly on superpatriotic feelings. Consensus, conciliation, and compromise would always be difficult in such a world.

Conflict: At Home

EDUCATION

During his campaign for election Bush had declared his desire to become the "Education President." Though he offered no concrete reforms at the time, he stimulated renewed debate over the quality of public schooling. Many observers, worried about the loss of America's competitive edge in world markets, saw school reform as a way to stimulate economic growth. Others lamented what one well-publicized report called the recent "flight from the arts and sciences" to business and engineering courses. The percentage of graduate and undergraduate degrees conferred in the arts and sciences fell from 40 percent in 1971 to 25 percent in 1985.

Many large universities also faced serious problems stemming from the influence of big-time intercollegiate athletics. This was a uniquely American phenomenon that grew alarming by the 1990s. The pressure to recruit outstanding athletes, to win championships, and to sell tickets at sports events lowered admission standards, prompted favoritism in the classroom, and brought a corrupting commercial air to academe. Many of the athletes, too, appear to have been used. A 1989 report by the General Accounting Office of Congress revealed that between 1982 and 1987, at thirty-five American colleges and universities, fewer than 20 percent of men basketball players graduated. The graduation rates for football players at these schools were only a little better.

As before, many critics focused on the educational needs of the poor. They demanded more spending for elementary and secondary education, particularly on Head Start to help preschoolers, and on maternal and health care. School reform, said the president of the National Education Association, had been "mostly rhetorical, fragmented, and peripheral." Her comments echoed a major refrain in the debates over education: the persistence of glaring social inequalities in schooling— and therefore in life.

A constant focus of such discontent was the Scholastic Aptitude Test, the predominant college entrance exam in many states. In 1989 African-Americans scored an average combined math-verbal score on the SAT of 737, about 200 points lower than the average score of whites. Test officials explained such differences by maintaining that the tests measured the nature and quality of schooling, not innate ability. High school curricula of African-Americans, they said, were not as strong in college preparatory subjects. Unconvinced, minority leaders denounced the tests as racially biased.

Hispanic leaders, too, were alarmed by recent educational trends. A report by the Department of Education indicated that high school dropout rates for whites and African-Americans in the United States had declined in recent years. But dropout rates among Hispanic students were much higher, and were rising, from 34.3 percent in 1968 to 35.7 percent in 1988. This percentage was almost triple the rate of whites, whose dropout rates fell during those years from 14.6 percent to 12.7 percent, and more than double the rate of African-Americans, whose rates dropped impressively from 27.4 percent to 14.9 percent. With huge increases expected in the numbers of Spanish-speaking immigrant children, and with completion of high school a consistently strong predictor of adult income, statistics such as these boded badly for the economic future of Hispanic-Americans. Education Secretary Lauro Cavazos termed the situation a "national tragedy."

Asian-Americans, too, complained of inequities in a number of educational practices. Chief among these, they thought, were admissions quotas that discriminated against them at a number of leading colleges and universities. The overall performance of Asian-Americans in high schools and on the mathematics section of the SAT was indeed remarkably high. In 1989 they scored an average of 522, compared to 490 by white students who took the test. (On the verbal portions Asian-Americans averaged 408, compared to 445 for whites.) Admissions officials denied the existence of quotas, arguing that their policies sought to attract balanced student bodies and that increasing percentages of Asian-American applicants were being accepted each year. Asian-American leaders disputed such explanations. Quotas, one said, have "clearly risen to the very top of the leadership agenda for Asian-American organizations across the country."

As of 1993 these debates over education had not resulted in major changes. Indeed, arguments mounted over "multiculturalism"—how much attention should curricula give to the experiences and writings of minorities? These controversies exposed the continuing importance of racial and ethnic tensions. They showed also that Americans in the 1990s, as earlier, believed deeply in the relationship between formal education, technological progress, and the socioeconomic advancement of young people. Even if this belief was sometimes naive—to what extent could schools make up for wider inequities in the social structure?—it testified eloquently to the persistence of the American dream of success.

RACE, DRUGS, AND THE CITY

As the dramatic improvement in African-American dropout rates indicated, there was reason to be optimistic about the future of race relations in the United States. Other statistics about race relations also contradicted scare stories in the media. Teenage pregnancy rates for African-Americans were declining rapidly, to about half in 1990 what they had been in 1960. The black middle classes continued to grow, and African-American political leaders gained control of many cities, including New York, Detroit, Philadelphia, and Los Angeles. Their political power was especially impressive on the parts of local level in the South.

Still, three much-discussed concerns at the time underlined the enduring power of racial issues in American society. The first concerned the future of affirmative action programs. In a number of controversial decisions in 1989 a deeply divided Supreme Court seemed inclined to turn back the clock on affirmative action. Employees, not employers, it said, had the burden of proving whether a job requirement screening out women or minorities was necessary (and therefore defensible) for business. This ruling, *Wards Cove Packing* v. *Atonio,* overturned a 1971 Court decision. In another case, *Martin* v. *Wilks,* the Court decreed that affirmative action settlements could be vulnerable to subsequent legal action by disappointed white workers.

These and other cases caused liberals to worry that the conservative judicial appointees of Nixon and Reagan might come to dominate the Court. Justice Thurgood Marshall, one of the liberals, lamented publicly that the decisions "put at risk not only the civil rights of minorities but the civil rights of all citizens." Liberals grew still more alarmed when Marshall and fellow liberal Justice William Brennan stepped down from the Court in the next two years. Bush's first appointee, David Souter, was a little-known New Hampshire judge whose views remained unclear at the time. Bush's second nominee, Clarence Thomas, was a conservative African-American. He was confirmed in 1991, but only after the nation watched sensational televised hearings in which a former employee, Anita Hill, accused Thomas of

First Person

She [Anita Hill] is not an October surprise. The times they are a' changin' and the boys don't get it on this issue. They don't really understand what sexual harassment is and it's not important to them. They tried simply to dispense with her in short order.

. . . It's a male bonding thing. They all think of themselves as potential victims, thinking, "We need to stick together or all these women will come and make allegations setting us up."

Representative Patricia Schroeder (D-Colo.) commenting on the treatment of Anita Hill by the Senate Judiciary Committee, quoted in Maureen Dowd, "7 House Women March to Senate in Attempt to Delay Thomas Vote," *The New York Times,* October 9, 1991, p A1, A16.

sexually harassing her. The mainly partisan confirmation vote in the Senate exposed again a salient fact of contemporary public life: the Court remained a politically charged institution with immense potential for good or ill.

The second concern involved the economic standing of racial minorities. Poverty continued to afflict almost a third of African-Americans—three times the rate among whites. Poverty among Hispanics was almost as prevalent as among blacks. African-American male unemployment remained twice as high as among whites. Given the narrowing of the educational gap between African-Americans and whites since the 1960s, the largely unchanging two-to-one racial unemployment ratio was both puzzling and distressing. Politicians and journalists continued to bewail the rise of a largely black "underclass" in the central cities.

Anita Hill testifies before the Senate Judiciary Committee. Hill claims she was sexually harassed by Supreme Court nominee Clarence Thomas.

First Person

Clarence Thomas, Address to Senate Judiciary Committee

This is a circus. It's a national disgrace. And from my standpoint as a black American, it is a high-tech lynching for uppity blacks who in any way deign to think for themselves, to do for themselves, to have different ideas, and it is a message that unless you kowtow to an old order, this is what will happen to you. You will be lynched, destroyed, caricatured by a committee of the U.S. Senate rather than hung from a tree.

Congressional Quarterly Weekly Report, v. 49, no. 42 (October 19, 1991), p. 3070.

Some liberals explained the puzzle of African-American unemployment by arguing that most of the expansion of jobs was occurring in suburban areas far removed from the ghettos. They added that the weakening of affirmative action programs impeded the socioeconomic mobility of blacks. White racism, while less flagrant than it had been prior to World War II, sustained widespread discrimination in employment, education, and housing.

Other observers were not so sure about the "job mismatch" hypothesis. There was little evidence, they said, to suggest that rises (or falls) in black unemployment rates differed much in the poorest areas from those in the wealthiest ones. They added that most ghetto residents had access to cars and that there were plenty of jobs, though mostly ill-paying, within range of the ghettos. There stalled the debate. In the early 1990s high rates of African-American and Hispanic poverty and

Judge Clarence Thomas emphatically denied any sexual harassment of Anita Hill.

unemployment continued to heighten racial tensions, especially in central cities. In April 1992, when a jury cleared four white Los Angeles police officers in the beating of a black man—a beating that had been videotaped and repeatedly shown to viewers on television—rioting erupted in Los Angeles. It lasted three days and nights, killing fifty-three people and causing damages estimated at nearly $1 billion. It was the bloodiest riot in twentieth-century American history.

The third racially oriented concern was the use and abuse of illicit drugs. From 1988 to 1990 this was probably the most hotly debated problem in the nation. In 1989 Bush called drug abuse, widely associated in the popular mind with minority groups in the ghettos, to be the "gravest domestic threat facing our nation today." He asked Congress to approve appropriations of $7.9 billion, much of it for aid to police departments and expansion of prisons. *Newsweek* wrote that crack, a smokable and highly addictive form of cocaine, was a "catastrophe for the young. . . . Its profits . . . have led or forced thousands of inner-city youngsters into hardcore crime, and many others into addictions from which they may never recover. It has bankrupted parental authority and it is destroying the fraying social fabric of inner-city neighborhoods all over the United States."

Cautious observers urged that such cries of crisis be put in broader perspective. Addiction to nicotine and alcohol—which (like addiction to crack) was hardly confined to the ghettos—continued to be far more widespread and to cause far more deaths than did cocaine. The National Institute on Drug Abuse, while reporting a disturbing increase to 860,000 in the number of "intensive" (weekly) cocaine users, reported in 1989 a 25 percent decrease from 1985 to 1988 in the number of Americans who said that they had casually used illicit drugs in the previous year.

The wave of concern over drug abuse, moreover, was not new in American history. Cocaine and heroin, legal and widely available until 1914, had caused such alarm at that time that they were outlawed by act of Congress. Hysteria over heroin broke out again in the 1950s, and every President from Kennedy on had declared a "war" of sorts on drugs. From 1986 through 1989 the federal government had spent a total of $13.6 billion for drug abuse prevention, treatment, and (mostly) antidrug law enforcement. From this historical perspective Bush's request offered little that was new, either in approach or in level of funding. Far more had been spent each year on the B-2 bomber than on "wars" against drugs.

Still, there was no denying that use of illicit drugs, especially cocaine, was a serious national problem, that it was an important cause of violent crime, or that it afflicted large numbers of people—including an estimated 300,000 babies of addicted women. The problem was especially intense in some of the ghettos.

A minority of experts, recalling the nation's often unhappy experience with Prohibition, suggested legalization of some of these drugs. Other critics emphasized that no amount of police work could cut off the supply and distribution of substances such as cocaine, which was made from a plant that grew like a weed in South America. The effort to do so by the Bush administration, they added, wasted billions of dollars, drove up drug prices, enriched criminal elements, and made a mockery of law enforcement in many ghetto areas. These critics stressed the need to focus on drug education and treatment. This approach highlighted the connection between poverty, desperation, crime, and addiction. Suppliers must be punished, but addiction could not be controlled merely by throwing away the key.

VALUES: WOMEN'S RIGHTS AND ABORTION

The quest for women's rights continued to command substantial support in the early 1990s. Two-thirds of American women, one poll revealed, believed that a "strong movement" was still necessary to "push for changes that benefit women." Debates over women's rights, sexual harassment, and especially abortion, rivaled the issues of race and drugs as key concerns of Americans in the late 1980s and early 1990s.

There was much about the recent American past to gratify advocates of women's rights by 1990. Of women aged 25 to 29, 87 percent were high school graduates—as opposed to 84.7 percent of men in the same age group. Almost as high a percentage of these women (21.9 percent) as men (23.4 percent) had completed a four-year college degree. By 1990, 55 percent of women over the age of 16 were in the work force, as opposed to 40 percent twenty years earlier. They represented almost half of all accountants and bus drivers—largely male preserves in the 1960s—and 20 percent of doctors and lawyers (compared to 7 percent and 3 percent twenty years earlier).

But progress seemed too slow for the majority of activists on behalf of women's rights. Though the median income of women workers had climbed from 62 percent to 70 percent of that of men since the late 1960s, the continuing gap was galling. And sex segregation persisted. Women remained virtually unrepresented in such better-paying, unionized jobs as airline pilots, mechanics, construction workers, and firefighters, a few of the occupations in which women held fewer than 4 percent of the jobs.

Many women especially resented the double load that they were carrying as mothers as well as wage workers. "It's like twenty-four hours a day you're working," one young mother of two complained. "The women work all day and then work at home all night. My day never ends." Women such as she pressured Congress to promote prenatal, postnatal, and day care and leave policies for parents of newborns. Welfare reformers gave renewed attention to European-style family allowances and to tax benefits for families with dependent children. Receptive to such pressures, Congress approved legislation that would have required companies with fifty or more employees to give new mothers twelve weeks of unpaid leave. Bush, however, vetoed the measure as burdensome to business.

First Person

Whenever you are seeking to expand the rights of one group of people, inevitably you're going to have another group crying that their rights are being infringed upon. The problem in the child-killing debate is that the children have no voice. When the abortion industry succeeded in legalizing child killing, there was no group of babies who stepped forward and said, "Wait, we have a right to be alive." It is left to those of us who were already born.

Randall Terry, director of Operation Rescue. Interview with Richard Lacayo, *Time*, October 21, 1991, p. 26.

No issue aroused women (and many men) more passionately than abortion. In a hotly debated five-to-four decision, *Webster* v. *Reproductive Health Services,* the Supreme Court in 1989 upheld a Missouri law that partially restricted abortion. The law barred public hospitals or other tax-supported facilities from sanctioning abortions not necessary to save the woman's life, even if no public funds were spent. Public employees, including doctors, nurses, and other health care providers, were prohibited from performing or assisting in such abortions. Medical tests had to be made on any fetus considered to be at least 20 weeks old. If the fetus were thought to be viable, an abortion might be prohibited.

This was one of the most dramatic, long-awaited decisions in modern U.S. history. Crowds jammed the courtroom and paraded outside the Court building on the day it was announced. When the ruling became known, many "pro-life" groups such as Operation Rescue were delighted. A Catholic archbishop exulted, "The biggest winners today are the tiniest of all—children within the womb." The head of the Planned Parenthood Federation of America countered, "This is a sad day for freedom. Now, a woman's access to abortion will become hostage to geography as states enact a patchwork of laws and regulations aimed at blocking abortions." Justice Harry Blackmun, author of the *Roe* v. *Wade* decision (1973) that had established the right to abortion, dissented sadly: "The signs are evident and very ominous, and a chill wind blows."

Opponents of the decision recognized that it stopped short of overturning *Roe* v. *Wade.* But the ruling made it difficult for poorer women—the people most heavily dependent on public facilities—to gain access to abortion. More worrisome to "pro-choice" people, the decision was expected to encourage other states (some of which had already passed a range of restrictions) to go beyond Missouri's footsteps. Indeed, the court agreed to review the constitutionality of existing state laws mandating parental notice or consent before minors could receive abortions and requiring clinics to be equipped as full-scale hospitals before being allowed to perform abortions in the first three months of pregnancy.

Even fairly calm observers worried about the consequences of the Court's action. They feared that angry debates over abortion would polarize the nation and

First Person

Two choices:

We're out of the kitchen and it is unlikely that we're going to go back; so how do you maintain control over a major segment of the community that has always been controlled? The strong, overarching message is that the best way is by maintaining sexual control.

Reproductive freedom is critical to a whole range of issues. If we can't take charge of this most personal aspect of our lives, we can't take charge of anything. It should not be seen as a privilege or as a benefit, but a fundamental human right.

Faye Wattleton, director of Planned Parenthood. Quoted in Marcia Ann Gillespie, "Repro Woman: Faye Wattleton Maps Strategy," *Ms.,* 18 (October 1989), p. 50.

monopolize public attention. If the court overturned *Roe* v. *Wade,* one columnist predicted, "Abortion will instantly become the biggest issue in the country. It will shape the politics of the new era and give it an ideological edge." Another critic added, "By focusing our attention on abortion, our society will ignore matters which threaten our continued existence as a democracy and our role in world society."

In June 1992 the court tried to quiet these debates over abortion by rendering another highly anticipated decision, *Planned Parenthood* v. *Casey.* By a margin of five to four (the new judges split—Souter in the majority, Thomas in the minority) the justices upheld parts of a restrictive Pennsylvania abortion statute requiring women seeking abortions to wait for twenty-four hours and listen to presentations at medical offices aimed at getting them to change their minds. Teenagers were also required to have the consent of one parent or of a judge. But the Court struck down restrictions that placed an "undue burden" on such women, including a provision that would have forced them to notify their husbands of plans to abort. The decision was frank in its reluctance to overturn *Roe* v. *Wade,* perceiving that such an effort would cause "profound and unnecessary damage to the Court's legitimacy, and to the nation's commitment to the rule of law."

Advocates of choice were immensely relieved by the decision: it seemed unlikely that the court soon would reverse *Roe* v. *Wade.* For the first time in several years the issue faded somewhat from public debate, especially during the presidential campaign of 1992. But the controversy was far from dead, and pro-choice leaders talked of seeking congressional legislation approving abortion. In 1993 a pro-life zealot shot and killed a Florida doctor who performed abortions. The passions aroused on the issue in the 1980s and early 1990s exposed with clarity the magnitude of cultural and religious divisions in American life. These divisions, like others involving race and ethnicity, exposed hostilities that seemed impossible to resolve.

The Election of 1992

Thanks in part to euphoria over American success in the war against Iraq in 1991, few people imagined that President Bush could lose in the 1992 elections. Potential Democratic candidates such as Governor Mario Cuomo of New York, the Reverend Jesse Jackson, and Senator Albert Gore, Jr., of Tennessee declined to run for the nomination. And Bush himself was supremely confident, dwelling throughout 1991 and early 1992 on progress since 1988 in the field of foreign policy. "In the final analysis," he told a group in the Oval Office in June 1992, "people are going to say, 'Who do you want sitting at that desk? Who has the temperament? Who has the experience? Who do we trust?'" He added, "That's why I am going to win this election. You watch."

Bush was correct in his assumption that Democrats would find it hard to attack him on foreign policy issues. Now and again, they did attack—assailing him for what they considered his unfeeling policies concerning Haitian refugees, demanding that he get tougher with the People's Republic of China, calling for firmer stands against Japan and other capitalist powers thought to be guilty of unfair trade practices. Critics also faulted him for being slow to provide the CIS with financial assistance, demanded that he act decisively to curb the atrocities in Bosnia and Herzegovina, denounced his "coddling" of Saddam Hussein before the invasion of Kuwait, and tried (as Dukakis had in 1988) to link him directly to Irangate. But the Cold War was mostly history, arms reductions were continuing, and foreign policy issues were less significant in 1992 than in any presidential election since 1936. (Early in 1993 Bush and Yeltsin negotiated START II, a treaty that promised to reduce dramatically the number of missiles and warheads in each country.)

Despite Bush's apparent invincibility, a number of challengers nonetheless emerged to fight for the major party nominations. One was Patrick Buchanan, a former Nixon adviser who had become a well-known television talk show person-sality. Buchanan, a staunch conservative, was angry that Bush had reneged in 1990 on his call for "no new taxes" made during the 1988 campaign. Buchanan also denounced liberals for being soft on crime and drug enforcement and called for greater pressure on behalf of "family values." By this phrase he and other right-wing leaders meant opposition to a wide range of liberal social policies, including abortion, public funding for day care, and generous welfare payments to single mothers. The Right also denounced efforts by advocates of gay and lesbian rights, who were becoming better organized, to wipe out the many state and federal regulations that discriminated against homosexuals. Among these regulations were provisions banning gays and lesbians from the armed forces. Buchanan made a respectable showing against Bush in the New Hampshire primary early in 1992, but then ran out of money and withdrew. Bush thereafter faced no serious opposition from within his party, which renominated the Bush-Quayle ticket.

Democratic challengers, while slow to enter the race, proliferated by 1992. They included former California Governor Jerry Brown, former Senator Paul Tsongas of Massachusetts, Governor William ("Bill") Clinton of Arkansas, and Senators Paul Harkin of Iowa and Robert Kerrey of Nebraska. Harkin and Kerrey

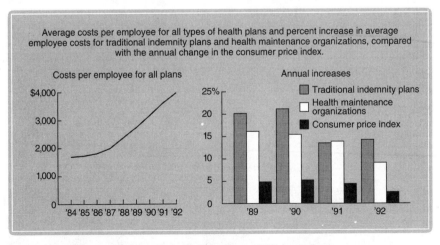

Average costs per employee for all types of health plans and percent increase in average employee costs for traditional indemnity plans and health maintenance organizations, compared with the annual change in the consumer price index.

SOURCE: Bureau of Labor Statistics; Foster Higgins Health Care Survey 1992/Indemnity Plans

Health care costs, 1984–1992

did poorly in primaries and dropped out. Tsongas and Brown scored some successes, but excited little enthusiasm within the party. Clinton seemed highly vulnerable in early 1992, both because of allegations that he had committed adultery and because he had apparently manipulated the Selective Service System to avoid the draft during the Vietnam War. He also had very little experience in the area of international affairs. But Clinton, a former Rhodes scholar, was otherwise a strong and increasingly well-financed candidate—a five-term governor with an obvious relish for campaigning and wide knowledge of domestic policy issues. He sewed up the nomination well before the Democratic convention, where he selected Gore, who was known for his liberal environmental record, as his running mate.

Clinton was less liberal on most domestic issues than Mondale had been in 1984 or Dukakis in 1988, and he planned a strategy aimed at appealing to suburban and centrist voters who had strayed from the Democratic party in previous elections. With Gore, a fellow southerner, he hoped to revive his party in the South. Gore repeatedly accused the Bush administration of bowing to corporate interests that were blocking regulations—the Clean Air Act and other legislation—designed to improve the quality of the environment. Clinton, however, risked the wrath of liberal social reformers by appearing to call for changes in welfare programs that would push people off the rolls and into private employment. While deploring the racial tensions that erupted in the Los Angeles rioting in April, Clinton also denounced racist statements by African-Americans, such as the young "rap" singer Sister Souljah, and kept his distance from such liberal activists as Jesse Jackson. Many African-American leaders were piqued, but Clinton calculated correctly that few would swing to Bush and that moderate white voters would be pleased by his show of political independence.

Bill Clinton and Al Gore

First Person

So if you're sick and tired of a Government that doesn't work to create new jobs, if you're sick and tired of a tax system that's stacked against you, if you're sick and tired of exploding debt and reduced investments in our future, if like the civil rights pioneer Fannie Lou Hamer said, you're just plain sick and tired of being sick and tired, then join with us, work with us, win with us. Together we can make the country we love the country it was meant to be.

Bill Clinton, Acceptance Address, Democratic National Convention, New York City, July 16, 1992, in *Vital Speeches of the Day*, August 15, 1992, pp. 643–44.

Clinton focused above all on domestic issues relating to the economy. Again and again he deplored the gaps in America's health insurance system, as well as the rapidly escalating costs of medical care. He also warned of the deteriorating infrastructure—bridges, roads, airports, urban services—of American economic life. Pointing to huge imbalances in the nation's foreign trade—in 1990 the United States had a trade deficit of $150 billion—he called for greater attention to job training and to public support of investment in important modern technologies. To raise revenue for these items he favored higher income taxes on people earning more than $200,000 a year, though after the election he raised his taxation proposals.

In soft-pedaling volatile social issues such as race while emphasizing economic concerns, Clinton hoped to appeal to the millions of low- and middle-income Americans who had formed the powerful Democratic coalition forged by FDR in the 1930s. In this effort he was aided by the onset of a recession that grew worrisome in 1991–92. Although it was a mild recession in contrast to many in American history, it came at the worst possible time for an incumbent administration. Newspapers carried countless stories of bad economic news: plant closings, bank failures and scandals, rising unemployment (from 5.4 percent in January 1989 to 7.1 percent three years later). In 1991 General Motors posted a record deficit for an American corporation: $4.45 billion. The recession caused striking increases in the number of Americans who had to rely on food stamps and on Aid to Families with Dependent Children, whose rolls leaped by 25 percent, to 13.6 million people, between late 1989 and mid-1991.

What caused these discouraging developments? Bush argued that they were mainly short-run setbacks inherent in the natural functioning of the business cycle. He also blamed the Democratic Congress, which he had battled vigorously during his four years in office. He added that Republican policies had not only pulled the nation out of the much more serious recession that had begun during the Carter administration but had also facilitated great expansion in the number of jobs available. Democrats countered that the recession stemmed in part from the refusal of the Reagan and Bush administrations to recognize the long-term structural forces that were damaging America's international competitiveness. Most of the new jobs, Democrats added, were in the low-paying service sector of the economy.

A highly visible third-party candidate, H. Ross Perot, took issue with both of these arguments. Perot was a Texan who had made billions in computer software and related industries. He was so wealthy that he had no need of campaign contributions, and he spent millions on television advertisements, which were even more important in 1992 than in earlier campaigns. While Perot echoed Clinton's complaints about America's declining competitiveness, he zeroed in on the huge federal deficit, which by late 1992 had boosted the national debt to more than $4 trillion. The cost of servicing this debt ate up more than 20 percent of federal spending and discouraged private investment. The United States, Perot insisted, must figure out ways to control government spending.

Economists divided in their response to these various arguments. While many agreed with Clinton's analysis of problems, they also thought he was vague on policy prescriptions. Was it possible to improve the infrastructure without adding to the size of the deficit? In any event, what mattered was popular opinion, which revealed widespread anger and impatience with Bush. These Americans appeared to share two broad fears. The first was that the United States was in the throes of long-range economic decline. "There is a deep-seated concern out there," the head of the Federal Reserve board said, "which . . . I have not seen in my lifetime." People were worried "about whether the current generation will live as well as the previous one." The second fear was that Bush, ever focused on foreign affairs, did not care about problems closer to home. He seemed to have no domestic policies to combat the economic slide or to prepare for the future. "People don't think Bush is a crook," one observer noted. "They're just not sure what he is doing, and in that case they think he's doing nothing."

Given the solid electoral base that the GOP had enjoyed since the 1960s in presidential elections, especially in the South and the West, it seemed to many political analysts that Bush could have counteracted such popular feelings. Perhaps so. But his campaign lacked direction and consistency, and stridently right-wing orators such as Buchanan dominated the Republican convention. Thereafter Bush oscillated between appeals for restoration of "family values," denunciations of the Democratic Congress, and insinuations that Clinton had been a draft dodger in the 1960s. Republican loyalists in the State Department went so far as to dig into Clinton's passport records for the 1960s, in an apparent (and futile) effort to document that he had applied for British citizenship at the time.

For all these reasons Clinton won comfortably in November 1992. He got 43.7 million votes, or 43.2 percent of those cast, to Bush's 38.2 million, or 37.7 percent. Perot, with a strong showing, attracted 19.2 million votes, or 19 percent. Perot's showing, most analysts believed, reflected the substantial dissatisfaction that Americans felt about politicians from both parties. Fourteen states, indeed, approved ballot provisions setting term limits on members of Congress. Many observers were heartened that the turnout, at 55 percent of eligible voters, was higher than the 50 percent that had turned out four years earlier. But this was hardly an impressive showing. Nor did the election seem to be much of a mandate for Clinton and the Democratic party. Clinton won only 23.7 percent of the eligible electorate, the smallest percentage for a winner since 1824.

When Clinton moved into the White House in 1993, it was therefore unclear whether America's domestic or foreign policies were likely to change very much.

The new administration, like the Democratic Congress, still faced the apparently unmanageable problem of trying to cut back federal deficits while stimulating the economy in both the short and the long run. The new administration also had to contend with many of the same difficult social, cultural, educational, and religious tensions that had confronted its predecessors. It had finally to decide what sort of a role the nation should take in the new and unpredictable post-Cold War world.

Suggestions for Reading
Useful on the Reagan years are Lou Cannon, *President Reagan: The Role of a Lifetime* (1991); Michael Schaller, *The Reagan Record* (1992); Garry Wills, *Reagan's America* (1987); William Pemberton, *Exit With Honor: The Life and Presidency of Ronald Reagan* (1997); Strobe Talbott, *The Russians and Reagan* (1984); Gillian Peele, *Revival and Reaction: The Right in Contemporary America* (1984); Gary Reinhard, *The Republican Right Since 1945* (1983); Isabel Sawhill, ed., *Challenge to Leadership: Economic and Social Issues for the Next Decade* (1988); James Bill, *The Eagle and the Lion* (1988), on Iranian-American relations; and Robert Pastor, *Condemned to Repetition: The United States and Nicaragua* (1988). Books on domestic issues and problems are William Wilson, *The Truly Disadvantaged: The Inner City, the Under-Class, and Public Policy* (1987); Reynolds Farley and Walter Allen, *The Color Line and the Quality of Life in America* (1987); David Ellwood, *Poor Support: Poverty in the American Family* (1988); Bart Landry, *The New Black Middle Class* (1987); Christopher Jencks, *Rethinking Social Policy: Race, Poverty, and the Underclass* (1992); and James Hunter, *Culture Wars: The Struggle to Define America* (1991). Key books on the economy include Frank Levy, *Dollars and Dreams: The Changing American Income Distribution* (1987); Otis Graham, *Losing Time: The Industrial Policy Debate* (1992); and David Calleo, *Beyond American Hegemony* (1987).

Fire engulfs the Branch Davidian compound near Waco, Texas.

CHAPTER

8

Approaching a Millennium: The 1990s

Late in the Reagan years the historian Arthur Schlesinger, Jr., had prophesied, "At some point shortly before or after 1990, there should come a sharp change in the national mood and direction—a change comparable to those bursts of innovation and reform that followed the accessions to office of Theodore Roosevelt in 1901, Franklin Roosevelt in 1933, and of John Kennedy in 1961." The election in 1992 of the young and energetic Bill Clinton—the first member of the post-World War II generation to become President—seemed to promise the onset of progressive reform for which people like Schlesinger had been waiting.

Clinton's Troubles, 1993–1994

This was not to be, for several reasons. For one, conservatives were well aware that Clinton, with only 43.2 percent of the presidential vote, could claim no great mandate for change. They continued to denounce liberal ideas and programs, often seizing on the alleged excesses of liberals and radicals in the 1960s to call for the elevation of moral values and the "slimming down" of the State. The conservative historian Gertrude Himmelfarb asked Americans to rediscover the sense of shame that had energized the Victorians, and to stigmatize such manifestations of immorality as out-of-wedlock pregnancy. Another conservative, Marvin Olafsky, echoed familiar conservative ideas in his widely noted book, *The Tragedy of American Compassion* (1992), by demanding that government should drastically cut back welfare, making it available only for people who could demonstrate that they were truly needy. Newt Gingrich, an influential conservative Republican congressman from Georgia, was a fervent admirer of Himmelfarb and Olafsky. Leading a confident Republican cohort on Capitol Hill, he echoed their drumbeat for the revival of personal responsibility and for the reduction of government social programs.

A second obstacle to the renewal of progressivism was Clinton himself. He had been elected on a centrist platform that aimed its appeal at moderates. Like the conservatives who tried (inaccurately) to paste a liberal label on him, he had his doubts about parts of the liberal agenda. "It's time to honor and reward people who play by the rules." he said during his campaign. "This means ending welfare as we know it." While he tried to expand the role of the government in the area of health care, he continued as President to dissociate himself from the most fervent advocates of change in his party.

Whatever hopes liberals had for dramatic change then evaporated following a series of controversies that left the impression that the new President was both a careless and an indecisive administrator. In early 1993, as Clinton struggled to learn the ropes, this was an essentially accurate perception. Although he lacked experience in the ways of Washington, he chose to surround himself with friends and associates from Arkansas and from his campaign staff. Many of them were young, cock-sure, and dismissive of the advice of seasoned Democratic leaders in Congress and elsewhere. A series of presidential decisions early in his tenure damaged Clinton's popular image—during much of his first term, only around 40 percent of the American people thought well of his performance—and deprived him of the political support that he needed to get things done on Capitol Hill.

The first of these decisions—Clinton's initial public act as President—was his effort to honor a campaign pledge to lift a ban on homosexuals in the military. His decision unleashed vehement criticism from his Joint Chiefs of Staff and from key congressional figures. Polls suggested that the public, too, objected to the change. Taken aback, the President agreed to await results of a study commissioned by the Defense Department. Finally, in July of 1992, he settled for a compromise: military personnel were not to reveal their sexuality, and the military was not to ask them about it. This policy, known as "don't ask, don't tell," satisfied neither side in the contentious debate over the role of homosexuals in American life. Clinton emerged battered from the controversy, which simmered for the rest of his presidency.

In May 1993 the President committed an especially damaging blunder, when he tried to fire the White House travel office staff. They were to be replaced by cronies of Clinton and his wife, Hillary Rodham Clinton. The reason given for the firings was that the staff had mismanaged the office. It quickly became clear, however, that this was a cover for a partisan house-cleaning of experienced employees who had served previous Presidents. Critics, led by Republicans in Congress, assailed the dismissals and coined a new variant on Watergate—this time, "Travelgate." The President had to backtrack, restoring most of those fired, but not before suffering politically as a result of the affair.

Careless staff work also contributed to embarrassments during Clinton's quest to fill the key position of Attorney General. His first two nominations had to be withdrawn after it was learned that they had run afoul of laws concerning the way they paid their domestic help, leaving the Department of Justice without leadership until his third choice, Janet Reno, was finally confirmed in March. Reno ultimately had the longest term of any Clinton Cabinet member, staying at her post well into his second term. She was hardly a valued presidential adviser, however. Throughout her tenure she insisted on maintaining distance from the White House; Clinton was never to have the close relationship with his top legal official that many previous Presidents had enjoyed.

Reno had scarcely taken command when she had to contend with the Branch Davidians, a religious cult suspected of manufacturing illegal automatic weapons on a compound in Waco, Texas. In late February, agents of the Bureau of Alcohol, Tobacco, and Firearms had stormed the compound, hoping to seize the weapons and arrest the Davidians' charismatic leader, David Koresh. Instead, the agents walked into a forty-five minute gun battle that left four agents and two cult members dead. At least fifteen agents were wounded. Koresh and his followers, having stockpiled plenty of provisions in order to withstand a siege of several months, then barricaded themselves inside the compound, leaving Reno and the FBI (which took over the situation in early March) with the task of forcing them out.

There followed a seven-week-long siege in which some 400 FBI agents surrounded the compound with razor wire and tanks. Koresh (who claimed to be Jesus Christ and had nineteen wives) began warning of an apocalyptic end to the standoff. His prophecy came true on April 19, 1993, when FBI agents battered the walls of the compound with tanks and spread tear gas inside. Koresh then ordered his followers to pour gasoline around the perimeter of the compound and to burn it down. More than seventy members of the cult (including Koresh and many of his own children) died in the blaze; only nine followers survived. Reno justified the assault by saying that she had received reports of children being beaten inside the compound. Clinton backed her up, blaming Koresh for the bloodshed. But the carnage at Waco did little to reassure Americans about the new administration's way of doing things. As later violent acts were also to demonstrate, the fate of the Branch Davidians excited murderous outrage among other militant foes of American officialdom.

THE QUEST FOR HEALTH CARE REFORM

No issue of Clinton's first year in office aroused more controversy—or ultimately caused him more political distress—than his quest to reform the largely private system of health care provision in the United States. Such reform, indeed, seemed long overdue; polls suggested that people favored changes in the system. As reformers pointed out, the cost of medical care had skyrocketed—from $250 billion in 1980 to $800 billion in 1993. These expenditures amounted to 13 percent of the gross national product. Other industrialized nations—all of which except South Africa operated governmentally controlled systems—spent less than 10 percent on such care. Yet an estimated 35 million Americans—around 15 percent of the total population—had no medical insurance, and another 20 million had inadequate coverage.

Clinton, an enthusiastic student of social policy, made reform of this state of affairs his top priority. "If I don't get health care done," he said, "I'll wish I didn't run for President." For these reasons he placed his wife Hillary, an experienced attorney, in charge of coordinating the reform. She, in turn, relied on an old friend and public policy specialist, Ira Magaziner, who ignored key senators and experts in the Department of Health and Human Services, where such a reform would normally have gestated. He listened instead to academic "experts" and other so-called "policy wonks," who sat through many long and large meetings. Some of these gatherings brought together more than 100 people, who wrangled far into the night in the treaty room of the Old Executive Office Building. Many who survived these and other meetings concluded that Magaziner (a former Rhodes scholar) and others had managed to create a virtual caricature of the policy-making process. One participant described the effort as the "Road to Nowhere."

The plan that emerged from this procedure in September 1993 struck many people as the very symbol of too much government: a bill of 240,000 words. Ironically, however, it did not call for a government-run "single-payer" system such as the one in Canada hoped for by many liberals. Rather, the complicated plan emphasized "managed competition." It required employers to pay for 80 percent of the costs of their workers' health insurance. Employees would normally cover the rest. (The government was to pay for the insurance of the unemployed and the uncovered.) The plan also called for the establishment of regional insurance-purchasing alliances that were expected to promote greater competition, thereby bringing about a lowering of health care premiums.

Such a proposal predictably aroused fierce opposition, especially from small employers, who claimed that they would be forced out of business; from doctors, who worried about losing their autonomy; and from small insurers, who feared that they would be squeezed out of the action. These powerful interests, which had overcome many earlier efforts for health reform, spent millions of dollars to finance television ads aimed at defeating the administration's initiative. The ads featured "Harry and Louise," a married couple who complained that the plan would create a huge new government bureaucracy, increase their taxes, and limit their freedom of choice. "They [the government] choose," Harry said. "We lose," Louise replied. That this message distorted the proposal did not stop millions of Americans from watching, apparently with approval. On Capitol Hill, meanwhile, Newt Gingrich spearheaded a team of lobbyists, businessmen, and conservative politicians who placed defeat of the plan at the top of their agenda. The Clintons, Gingrich said, "were going against the entire tide of Western history. I mean centralized, command bureaucracies are dying. This is the end of that era, not the beginning of it."

Disinterested observers of the struggles that followed never expected that the Clinton program, buffeted from so many directions, had a decent chance of passage. They were correct, for Congress—though controlled by the Democrats—never showed much enthusiasm for it. Many liberals continued to demand a single-payer plan. After a year of acrimonious debates, the White House and congressional leaders conceded in August 1994 that reform of health care was dead, at least for the time being.

Health care reform, in fact, stayed dead for the remainder of Clinton's presidency, during which time the number of uninsured Americans slowly increased. Health Maintenance Organizations (HMOs) proliferated rapidly by offering large employers cheaper health care packages for their employees. But HMOs, too, became increasingly controversial by the late 1990s, mainly because members accused them of trying to cut costs by denying expensive medical procedures. Meanwhile, the prolonged controversy over reform in 1993–94 left political scars. Having been badly beaten, the President thereafter shied away from proposing large changes, not only in health care but also in other areas of domestic policy making.

Defenders of the embattled President managed to derive a little satisfaction from a few other policy efforts of his first two years. Two nominees to the Supreme Court—federal judges Ruth Bader Ginsburg and Stephen Breyer—were confirmed. Congress approved a law requiring employers to allow workers up to twelve weeks of unpaid leave to deal with family illness or care for newborn babies; established a short waiting period for the purchase of handguns; banned the sale of assault weapons; passed a "motor-voter law" to permit people to register to vote when they applied for drivers' licenses; and set up a modestly funded national service program for young people. In late 1993 Congress enacted legislation to implement the so-called North American Free Trade Agreement (NAFTA), which had been initiated by President Bush. While labor leaders and environmentalists opposed the agreement (they thought it would benefit cheap-labor employers in nations such as Mexico, at major cost to American workers), Clinton and his supporters—many of them Republicans in this case—thought the pact would boost the economy by opening up trade and lowering prices for consumers. In late 1994 Congress also approved a $30 billion package that expanded governmental efforts against crime. In addition, the President succeeded in lifting restrictions on abortion counseling at federally funded clinics.

Most important, Clinton and Congress started a long-run process of deficit reduction by agreeing in 1993 on a package that cut federal spending and increased income and Social Security taxes on the wealthy. The measure, approved without a single Republican vote (GOP legislators demanded further cuts in spending and opposed the tax hikes), was expected to cut the deficit by $500 billion (or 38 percent) over the next four years. This package was a considerable achievement, helping to reverse the high levels of deficit spending that Congress and Presidents alike had approved since the early 1970s.

The Republicans Fight Back: 1994

As Clinton and his supporters prepared for the off-year elections of 1994, they knew they were in for trouble. While nursing wounds inflicted by Congress over issues such as health care, the President had to face damaging accusations from his tenure as governor of Arkansas. He and partners in the so-called Whitewater Development Corporation, which had been formed to promote land deals, were accused of engaging in illegal practices. In January 1994 an independent counsel was named to investigate his and Hillary Rodham Clinton's involvement in this and related business arrangements. Drawn-out, expensive legal conflicts followed, in which Kenneth Starr—named later in 1994 to replace the original independent counsel—dug deeply into these revelations. Starr, a Republican, had been Solicitor General in the Bush administration. In time, he secured the conviction of several people on charges of fraud.

The Clintons also suffered from problems affecting close friends. A former law partner of Hillary Rodham Clinton, Webster Hubbell, whom the President had named to the number three position in the Justice Department, was sent to prison in 1994 for bilking clients and law partners. Another of her former law partners, Vincent Foster, Jr., who served as the President's deputy counsel in 1993, committed suicide. Senate hearings subsequently looked into whether the White House had obstructed probes into the circumstances surrounding his death.

In May 1994, Clinton had to face charges from another quarter. At that time an Arkansas woman, Paula Jones, brought suit against the President, charging him with sexual harassment stemming from an incident alleged to have taken place in a Little Rock hotel room in 1991, when she was a state employee and Clinton was governor. This suit, moving slowly through the courts, seemed to be constantly in

Paula Corbin Jones was allowed to sue President Clinton for sexual harassment that she claimed happened while he was governor of Arkansas.

the news. If polls were to be believed, most Americans did not seem to care very much about the President's private life, but they were clearly saddened by the disrepute that the Jones suit brought to the office of the presidency.

Confronted with so many problems, the Democratic party seemed certain to encounter losses at the polls in the 1994 elections. Republicans in the House of Representatives, indeed, moved to the attack in 1994. Led by Gingrich, they unveiled a so-called Contract with America, which promised "an end to government that is too big, too intrusive, and too easy with the public's money." In an extraordinary show of solidarity, a total of 367 GOP House candidates (the House has 435 members) ultimately promised to support the Contract. At ceremonies in state capitols, county courthouses, and city halls, Republican candidates for state legislatures and local offices made similar pledges.

A glance at some provisions of the Contract offers insight into central tenets of American political conservatism in the mid-1990s. One sought to "discourage illegitimacy and teen pregnancy by prohibiting welfare to minor mothers and denying increased AFDC (Aid to Families with Dependent Children) for additional children on welfare." It also called for a "tough two-years-and-out provision with work requirements [for recipients of welfare] to promote individual responsibility." Another provision, entitled "Taking Back Our Streets," outlined a war against crime that featured "effective death penalty provisions" and higher funding for the construction of prisons.

The Contract also promised that Republicans would bring to a vote an "American Dream Restoration Act." This measure would feature a $500-per-child-tax credit and "American Dream Savings Accounts to provide middle-class tax relief." Another goal was a "Job Creation and Wage Enhancement Act," which would include incentives for small business, a cut in capital gains taxes, and a scaling back of governmental regulations on businesses. A "Common Sense Legal Reform Act" would set "reasonable limits on punitive damages and reform of product liability laws to stem the endless tide of litigation."

While the Contract focused on domestic issues, it included a pledge to advance to the floor of Congress a "National Security Restoration Act." This would assure that no American troops served under a UN command and would increase military funding in order to "strengthen our national defense and maintain our credibility throughout the world."

A highlight of the Contract was a demand for "fiscal responsibility," to be achieved especially by approval of a balanced budget amendment to the Constitution and by legislation that would give presidents "line-item" veto power. Such a power, it was believed, would enable presidents to eliminate wasteful items, or "pork," as it was called, from congressional spending. The goal of such measures was to "restore fiscal responsibility to an out-of-control Congress, requiring them to live under the same budget constraints as families and business." Signers of the Contract intended measures such as these to slash the federal debt.

Democrats (and others) assailed what they considered the demagoguery of the Contract. Why give the high-sounding label "American Dream Restoration Act," they complained, to a modest measure to promote middle-class tax relief? How could Congress cut spending if it increased funding for national defense? Liberals also attacked the meanness they saw in the proposed scaling back of welfare. They

House Speaker Newt Gingrich holds a copy of the Republicans' "Contract with America."

insisted that the Contract offered all sorts of benefits to the wealthy while inflicting suffering on millions of the poor.

Complaints such as these apparently had no effect on voters in November 1994, when Republicans won smashing victories. The GOP took control of both houses of Congress for the first time since 1954, increasing its numbers from 43 to 52 in the Senate and 176 to 230 in the House. It also achieved majorities in seventeen additional state legislatures and captured, for the first time in twenty years, a majority (30 to 19 and one Independent) governorships. Gingrich, who became Speaker of the House, proclaimed happily that the election was "the most shatteringly one-sided Republican victory since 1946." Less partisan observers not only agreed with Gingrich's claim but also believed that the election of 1994 ended the Democratic dominance of Congress that dated from the 1930s. Al From, executive director of the Democratic Leadership Council, said that "the truth of the Democratic party is that there is no party. . . . We have lost the middle class, and instead we have minority voters, a few liberals, and union members. That's it. That's all we have left."

Political Battles, 1995–1998

Confident of popular support, Republicans hastened in early 1995 to enact the Contract—and to set the stage for victory in the presidential election of 1996. Robert Dole of Kansas, the Senate majority leader, was favored to become the GOP presidential nominee in 1996. While more moderate than Gingrich, he, too, aggressively sought to cut back the size and scope of the federal government. Everything from Amtrak to zoological subsidies, Dole said, would face reductions in spending.

At first it seemed that Republicans would achieve most of their goals. The House passed a balanced budget amendment to the Constitution as well as a sweeping package of antiregulatory measures aimed at softening enforcement of environmental, health, and safety laws. Republicans in both houses fashioned a combination of spending and tax cuts that promised to end the federal deficit by the year 2002. In late 1995 Congress agreed on bills cutting back welfare programs and set about reducing the budget for Medicare, the federal program that provided health coverage for most of the nation's elderly. In 1996, Congress approved the line-item veto (enabling Clinton, who signed the bill, to veto 82 provisions in 11 laws, saving some $1.9 billion, by mid-1998). In 1998, however, the Supreme Court, by a vote of 6 to 3, declared that the line-item veto violated the Constitution.

As early as mid-1995, however, the Republican counterrevolution began losing some of its political momentum. Senate Republicans, less conservative than their colleagues in the House, refused to approve the balanced budget amendment. House Republicans (many of whom enjoyed great seniority on Capitol Hill) defeated the Contract's demand for congressional term limits. Moreover, Clinton, shaken by the elections in 1994, followed a moderate course. In his State of the Union message in January 1995 he signified his readiness to accept major changes in welfare. In the spring he accepted Republican initiatives for a balanced budget. By moving to the center, the President obviously hoped to attract voters back to the badly damaged Democratic party.

In late 1995 and early 1996, however, Clinton made it clear that he would go only so far toward accommodating the GOP. When the Congress seemed to threaten Democratic health, education, and environmental programs, he refused to compromise. In late 1995 he vetoed the Republican budget bill. The standoff that followed twice shut down federal government offices. Although Republicans attacked Clinton for causing the standoff, polls in early 1996 suggested that the American people blamed the GOP. Gingrich and his allies, it appeared, had overplayed their hand.

As anticipated, Dole won the GOP presidential nomination in 1996, beating back challenges from more conservative opponents such as Patrick Buchanan, a former aide to President Nixon; Senator Phil Gramm of Texas; and Steve Forbes, a multimillionaire businessman who favored a "flat tax" that would have overturned

At the end of 1995 parts of the federal government were shut down due to a federal budget impasse between President Clinton and the Republican Congress.

the nation's progressive income tax system. Dole named Jack Kemp, a former congressman from New York State, as his running mate. But Dole, a seventy-three-year-old Republican regular who had been President Ford's running mate in 1976, was an uninspiring campaigner and speaker. His central platform, to cut federal income taxes 15 percent across the board, had a superficial appeal, but worried many Americans who wondered how the Republicans could slash taxes, increase military spending, and balance the budget at the same time.

Clinton was hardly a tough target to hit during the campaign. Republicans made much of Whitewater and of the President's alleged womanizing. But he was, as ever, an energetic and often charismatic campaigner, and he seemed much more self-assured than he had been during his error-prone first two years in the White House. Clinton hammered at Republican efforts, as he saw them, to damage popular social policies such as Medicare. Dole, moreover, was afraid to distance himself very far from the Republican Right, which had gained considerable strength in the party. Dole refused, for instance, to disavow GOP allies who opposed abortion. Partly for this reason, a "gender gap" developed, in which women—by a greater margin than men—turned to Clinton. Polls also suggested that many Americans worried that Republicans like Gingrich, given free rein in a GOP administration, would dismantle needed programs. Clinton, like Truman in 1948, probably benefited in 1996 from having resisted the highly partisan Republican congressional majorities that had opposed him since 1994.

At the same time, Clinton solidified his ties with the political center by signing a Republican welfare bill. The aptly named Personal Responsibility and Work Opportunity Act of 1996 ended the sixty-one-year-old AFDC program of public assistance and turned welfare policies over to the states. The law set limits—normally of two years—on the length of time that eligible poor (mostly single women and their children) were entitled to receive federal relief. Thereafter, it was expected that most mothers would work for whatever assistance that states chose to give them. The act also killed many benefits for recent immigrants. Although many liberals were incensed at Clinton for signing the measure, they should not have been surprised: he had long disliked the existing apparatus of welfare. The President, moreover, was probably correct in calculating that the majority of Americans opposed AFDC, which they thought wasted money in support of "lazy, immoral" people, many of them minorities. AFDC, unlike insurance programs such as Social Security and Medicare, commanded little popular backing.

Perhaps the most important asset for Clinton during the 1996 campaign was the state of the economy, which has often been a major determinant of American elections. Since 1992, when President Bush had paid a price for holding office during a recession, the economy had rebounded. Unemployment and poverty rates had fallen; prices had remained fairly stable; overseas competitors such as the Japanese, who had loomed as threats in 1992, were facing a host of economic difficulties by 1996. The healthier economy owed little to presidential policies, but Clinton—like politicians before him—was quick to claim credit for prosperity. A popular refrain that pundits had recited in 1992 said a good deal as well about the results in 1996: "It's the economy, stupid!"

For all these reasons Clinton was easily re-elected. He received 49.2 percent of the vote, to Dole's 40.7 percent. H. Ross Perot, running again (as the candidate of the Reform party), captured 8.4 percent, and many lesser candidates won the remaining 2 percent. Clinton and Gore took the electoral college, 379 to 159 for Dole and Kemp.

Given the swamp into which Clinton and the Democratic party had sunk in 1994, the results of the election of 1996 represented a remarkable recovery. The GOP, in fact, seemed strong only in parts of the South and the West. Democrats were understandably pleased. But it was an unsavory election in many ways, featuring shameless use by both parties of loopholes in laws that were supposed to regulate campaign financing. It was also difficult for Democrats to argue that the President had achieved much of a mandate. As in 1992, he had been elected by a minority of those who voted. Republicans retained control of both houses of Congress. Reflecting widespread apathy, voter turnout was low: 8,275,000 fewer Americans went to the polls in 1996 than in 1992.

In the next two years Clinton moved more cautiously than earlier in the realm of domestic policy. As tax revenues increased, Congress let him have a few small measures that he had promised during his campaign: tax breaks for working fami-

The Numbers Behind a Divided Decision

HOW THE STATES VOTED

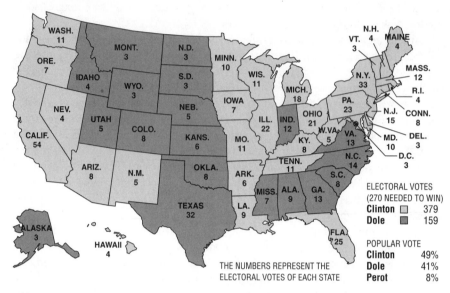

ELECTORAL VOTES
(270 NEEDED TO WIN)

Clinton   379
Dole   159

POPULAR VOTE
Clinton   49%
Dole   41%
Perot   8%

THE NUMBERS REPRESENT THE
ELECTORAL VOTES OF EACH STATE

WHO WENT TO THE POLLS

	CLINTON	DOLE	PEROT	ALL VOTERS
Men	44%	44%	10%	**48%**
Women	54	38	7	**52**
Black	83	12	4	**10**
White	43	46	9	**83**
Democrat	84	10	5	**40**
Republican	13	80	6	**34**
Independent	43	35	17	**26**
Religious right	26	65	8	**16**
Union household	59	29	9	**24**
First-time voter	54	34	11	**9**

WHAT THEY CARED ABOUT MOST

	CLINTON	DOLE	PEROT	ALL VOTERS
Economy, jobs	61%	27%	10%	**21%**
Deficit	27	52	19	**12**
Medicare and Social Security	67	26	6	**15**
Taxes	19	73	7	**11**
Crime and drugs	40	51	8	**7**
Education	78	16	4	**12**
Foreign policy	35	56	8	**4**

SOURCE: *Newsweek,* November 18, 1996.

lies, money for college scholarships, a modest campaign to improve literacy. Most important, he struck a deal with Congress that proposed to balance the budget by 2002. These measures fell far short, however, of inaugurating the new era of progressivism that Arthur Schlesinger and other liberals had dreamed of a few years earlier. George Stephanopoulos, a former Clinton adviser, concluded in 1997: "The last three years [of Clinton's tenure] are going to be largely a rhetorical presidency. Legislatively, it's over."

The President frequently found himself on the defensive. In 1998 independent prosecutors were busy investigating alleged wrongdoing by four of his one-time or current Cabinet members. Republicans in Congress held up many of his nominations for judgeships and key posts in the executive branch. Independent Counsel Kenneth Starr and his staff, continuing their probes into the Clintons' financial dealings, also followed up sensational new allegations concerning the President's sexual behavior in the White House. As before, Americans did not seem ready to repudiate Clinton—indeed, popular approval of his official performance reached new highs in 1997 and 1998. People also recognized that partisan political enemies of the President helped to bolster Starr. But some of the allegations linked Clinton to a possible coverup and obstruction of justice. The long-running investigations did nothing for the image of the presidency and diverted the White House from other business.

In such a battleground of deadlock it was hardly surprising, in 1997, that many people criticized Clinton. One moderate Democratic senator thought the President had given up and was spending too much time on the golf course. He exclaimed, "It's golf, golf, golf, interspersed with politics." An adviser, Richard Morris, added, "Everybody wondered after the election whether he'd go to the left or to the right. Nobody thought he'd go to sleep." A liberal political scientist, Walter Dean Burnham, concluded that Clinton was operating a passive, "finger-in-the-dike presidency." Burnham conceded that Republicans hemmed Clinton in, but added, "I don't think he has a very clear idea of where he wants to go from here."

Whether these criticisms were fair awaits later judgments. The barbs revealed, however, a major fact of American political culture since the early 1960s: the prevalence of widespread disenchantment with political leaders of all sorts. The media, aroused by the "credibility gap" that had widened in the aftermath of Vietnam and Watergate, did much to strengthen such negative attitudes. To heed the media was to believe that an antiestablishment, anti-VIP mood had gripped the nation.

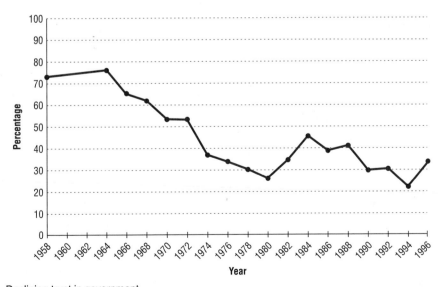

Declining trust in government.

SOURCE: American National Election Studies, 1958–1996, University of Michigan

In the mid-1990s Hollywood, too, joined in. *Primary Colors,* a novel originally credited to an anonymous author (later determined to be the columnist Joe Klein) during the campaign of 1996, centered on an oversexed, charismatic presidential candidate. No one doubted that Klein's amoral protagonist was modeled on Clinton. The book became a best seller and was fashioned into a popular movie two years later. *Wag the Dog,* another Hollywood effort (1997), featured Dustin Hoffman and Robert DeNiro in a satire about a President who had been caught fondling a little girl in the Oval Office. Seeking to keep such a scandal off the front pages, the film president's staff hired "spin doctors" and a movie producer who (among other diversions) proceeded to manufacture stories about a threat of war from Albania. *Wag the Dog* left the impression that war and politics are nothing more than forms of show business.

Impeachment

Clinton's political difficulties in 1997 paled in contrast to the troubles that beset him after January 1998, when apparently reliable rumors leaked that he had had frequent sexual relations in the White House with Monica Lewinsky, a young woman who had served as a White House intern. Moving quickly, Attorney General Janet Reno authorized independent counsel Kenneth Starr, who was still looking into the Clintons' involvement in the Whitewater land deal, to get to the bottom of the Lewinsky-Clinton story.

There followed many months of acrimonious, often sensationally reported accusations and counter-accusations. Clinton ultimately conceded that he had had an inappropriate relationship with Lewinsky, which he acknowledged had been "wrong." It was obvious, however, that he was evasive, clinging to a highly restrictive definition of "sexual relations," which he denied having had with her. But Starr's investigative team (which ultimately spent more than $50 million in its various probes into the President's conduct) arranged a deal with Lewinsky that granted her immunity in return for her sworn testimony. In September 1998 Starr released his report. To the surprise of many observers, it was silent about Whitewater and other alleged presidential excesses (such as his firing in 1993 of employees in the presidential travel office). But the report had much to say about sex in the White House, offering 445 pages of often graphic details concerning ten sexual engagements involving Clinton and Lewinsky.

The scene soon moved to the House Judiciary Committee, which held widely publicized, often televised hearings concerning whether to impeach the President for his part in the scandal. These were highly partisan, with Republicans headed by committee chairman Henry Hyde of Illinois angry both at the president's conduct and at what they thought was his lying about it under oath and his efforts, as they saw it, to obstruct justice. Democrats retorted that what the President had done—or might have done—was tawdry and disrespectful of the dignity of his high office, but that it did not merit congressional impeachment, much less conviction.

As the partisan lines hardened, Congress seemed obsessed with the controversy. Senator John McCain, a Republican from Arizona, complained in October

1998 that "it's never been like this since Watergate in terms of business not getting done." Important national issues—working out a publicly-approved settlement concerning claims against tobacco companies, developing campaign finance reform, regulating managed-care health plans—did not come close to resolution.

When Democratic candidates fared well in the off-year elections of November 1998, it appeared that Clinton would escape impeachment. House Speaker Gingrich, blamed by Republican colleagues for his party's poor showing, announced that he was stepping down from the leadership and would leave the House in 1999. Indeed, the elections confirmed a striking fact that pollsters had repeatedly discovered during the protracted controversy: approval of the President's job performance was higher—at 60 to 70 percent in most polls—than it had been at any earlier time during his six years in office. Americans, it seemed, were considerably less "puritanical" about sexual matters than it had been thought. Although deploring Clinton's personal behavior, they told pollsters that his private flaws should not obscure what they considered to be his successes as President. Clinton's enhanced popularity no doubt stemmed also from his good fortune to be President during a time of considerable economic prosperity.

But Clinton then further angered House GOP leaders by giving cavalier answers to a series of written questions that they had asked him. In retrospect, it appears that he had become overconfident. On partisan votes the committee endorsed four articles of impeachment, and in December the Republican-controlled House approved two of them. One, endorsed by a vote of 228 to 206, accused him of committing perjury in his grand jury testimony about the affair. The other, approved 221 to 212, asserted that the President had obstructed justice in his efforts to conceal the truth. It was only the second time in American history that the House had impeached a President. The first time, in 1868, the Senate (which has the constitutional duty of trying articles of impeachment approved by the House) had fallen one vote short of the two-thirds margin required for conviction.

By early 1999, when the Senate set about its constitutionally appointed task, many Americans—if polls are to be believed—were heartily tired of the drawn-out partisan warfare. As in 1998, they gave strong approval to the President's job performance. Democratic Senators, bolstered by such polls, closed ranks behind their embattled leader. They insisted above all that Clinton's sexual activities—even lying about them—were simply not what the Founding Fathers had imagined to be impeachable offenses. Compared to Nixon's misdeeds in the early 1970s, they said, Clinton's sins were trivial. Republicans, who had a majority of 55 to 45 in the Senate, spoke loyally on behalf of their GOP counterparts in the House.

In the end, the President escaped conviction. Clinton's foes needed two-thirds of the votes, or 67, and they did not come close to getting them. Amid high drama on February 12 (Abraham Lincoln's birthday) 10 Republicans—mostly moderates from the Northeast—broke ranks on the article accusing Clinton of lying under oath, which failed by a vote of 55 to 45. Five Republicans then deserted their colleagues on the article alleging obstruction of justice. The vote on this count was 50 to 50. After 13 months of battling, the war was over.

In the immediate aftermath of the Senate's action, various pundits—journalists, historians, constitutional lawyers—tried to assess the legacy of the struggles. One thing seemed clear: Clinton's historical reputation was almost certain to suffer. It also appeared likely that he could expect little cooperation from a Congress that remained in the control of Republicans, many of whom emerged bitter and angry from the affair. Liberals who yearned for passage of their unfulfilled agenda would have to hope that a Democratic President and Congress would arise from the millennial elections of 2000.

Some experts looking back on the affair tried further to assess the long-term results. Many (mainly those who had defended the President) maintained that the fight had set a dangerous precedent whereby partisan congressmen might resort to the weapon of impeachment whenever they wanted to overturn the results of presidential elections. In such a scenario, something resembling a parliamentary system of government would replace America's constitutional checks and balances. Presidents would hold office only at the sufferance of legislators. Critics of this argument dismissed it as a partisan overreaction. Clinton, they said, had brought his troubles upon himself and deserved to be impeached and convicted. The presidency, they added, had survived many more damaging battles (including the near-impeachment of Nixon in 1974), and had not suffered much from what had happened in 1998–1999. Only in the future, of course, could these much-contested claims be clearly assessed.

Following the battle, both sides seemed relieved that the fighting was over. Or was it? Rumors persisted that Starr's office might decide to bring charges against Clinton after he left office. And Americans continued to show fascination about aspects of the affair, notably the persona of Lewinsky. In March 1999 she appeared on television's "20/20" to be interviewed by Barbara Walters. An estimated 70 million viewers in 33.2 million homes were said to watch all or part of the two-hour program. Although this was a smaller number than had turned on the Super Bowl two months earlier (83.7 million) or the Academy Awards in 1998 (87 million), it was a huge audience. No single-network news program had ever been watched by so many people. ABC charged advertisers up to $800,000, far higher than the usual cost on "20/20," for a 30-second commercial.

Lewinsky, having had her say on TV, then toured Europe to promote a book, *Monica's Story,* about her life. It rose briefly to the top of best-seller lists. Knowledgable observers estimated that she would pocket $600,000 from royalties on the book, another $600,000 for an interview on European TV, and other royalties as additional foreign rights were sold to her book and interviews. These efforts would help pay her legal bills, which (like Clinton's) were huge. They also signified that the wheels of advertising and public relations, so vital to the powerful consumer culture of the 1990s, moved as smoothly as ever throughout the scandal.

INTERNATIONAL CONTROVERSIES

During 1993–94—and later—the President also had trouble developing coherent foreign policies to cope with the post-Cold War world. This was hardly surprising, for he had had little experience outside of Arkansas before entering the White House. Moreover, the new international scene was unpredictable—difficult for even more seasoned experts to deal with. Indeed between 1989 and mid-1998, ninety-eight Americans were killed in attacks by terrorists. Should the United States—the strongest nation on earth—use its power to act as a policeman for a host of good causes, if necessary by dispatching American troops to advance democracy and human rights? Or, learning from its experience in Vietnam, should it be extraordinarily careful before committing American troops abroad? Should the United States maintain and expand the North Atlantic Treaty Organization (NATO)—created in 1949 to promote western interests in the Cold War era—or should it focus more on disarmament and disengagement in Europe? Would it help or hurt the cause of human rights to encourage trade and cultural exchanges with oppressive regimes such as those that dominated Cuba, China, and many other countries? How "isolationist" was the apparently uncertain American public? These and other complex questions aroused sharp debates throughout the post-Cold War years of Clinton's presidency.

At the start, Clinton was resolute in his support of President Boris Yeltsin of Russia, thereby helping a little in the mid-1990s to stabilize the very fragile political situation there. Soon, however, he sought to expand NATO by including Hungary, Poland, and the Czech Republic, thereby unsettling Russian leaders, who still controlled a massive (but carelessly managed) nuclear arsenal. This consisted in the late 1990s of some 7,000 long-range nuclear warheads and 30,000 or so short-range nuclear warheads and fissile cores. Supporters of Clinton's effort argued that NATO expansion, which was popular with arms manufacturers (who would help supply the larger alliance) and with many Americans of east European descent, would promote stability in the area. Critics retorted that expansion would require expenditures of billions of dollars on weapons, revive old Cold War phobias, and possibly drag the United States into fighting—some day in the future—in eastern Europe. "This is really a Marshall Plan for arms dealers," one opponent exclaimed. Following a protracted process the Senate approved the expansion in 1998 by a vote of 80 to 19.

Clinton had to cope with a wide range of other problems that tested Russian-American relations. One centered on the Balkans, where Russia tended to side with Serbs in Yugoslavia, who took aggressive military actions against Bosnian Muslims and Croats. The United States and Russia, meanwhile, continued to engage in overseas arms sales, thereby poisoning international relations. Russia sold arms to Iran, a leading terrorist state, to the Greek Cypriots, and to India. Not to be outdone, Pakistan and Turkey escalated their own arms buildups. In 1998 both India and Pakistan, bitter foes, conducted nuclear tests, which alarmed nations all over the world.

In dealing with other areas, Clinton seemed to vacillate. Having criticized Bush during the 1992 election campaign for sending American troops as part of a United Nations effort to restore order in chaotic and famine-torn Somalia, he reversed himself in 1993, only to face outraged criticism when eighteen of these troops were killed and more than seventy wounded in October during a gun battle with local warlords. Alarmed, the President ordered in reinforcements. Televised pictures of dead soldiers being dragged through the streets of Somalia, however, shook Americans and reinforced feelings, strong since the Vietnam War, that the United States should avoid the role of "international policeman." Later, the troops were removed. But factional and sectarian warfare continued to plague Somalia, which as of 1999 still had no central government.

Clinton's actions regarding Haiti seemed equally irresolute. Only a few days after the killings in Somalia, Haitian demonstrators prevented an American vessel from landing 200 noncombat UN troops on the island. The troops were supposed to

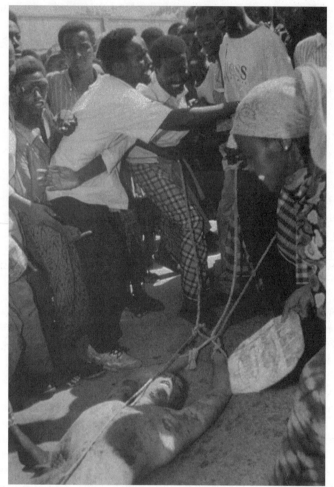

The body of an American is dragged through the dusty streets of war-torn Mogadishu.

facilitate the return to power of democratically elected President Jean-Bertrand Aristide, who had been overthrown in a military coup two years earlier. Embarrassed, the President withdrew the ship carrying the troops. It was not until late 1994, following considerable bloodshed on the island, that the Clinton administration threatened an invasion and aided by a deal brokered by former President Carter, managed to dislodge the *junta* ruling Haiti. With the protection of American soldiers Aristide was reinstalled as President, but instability continued in the poverty-stricken island.

The President found it especially hard to bring American power to bear in the violence-prone Middle East. In late 1993 his administration helped to promote an historic accord between Israel and the Palestine Liberation Organization (PLO). Israel and the PLO recognized each other's right to exist. The PLO pledged to end its holy war against Israel, in return for which the Israelis conceded Palestinian self-rule in the Gaza Strip and Jericho. This was a substantial achievement, and the

School children play in the bombed out remains of the National Library in downtown Sarajevo.

Clinton administration labored patiently and evenhandedly thereafter to secure the rights of both Israelis and Palestinians. Later, however, an Israeli fanatic assassinated the nation's leader, Itzhak Rabin, and extremists on both sides resorted to violence. Then and later, the accumulation of religious hatreds, expressed in bloody conflicts over land and water rights, frustrated the efforts of all people — American or otherwise — to resolve the crisis.

Frustrations also greeted the President's attempts to moderate ethno-religious hostilities in the Balkans. At first, he hoped that diplomatic pressure, reliance on "peacekeepers" from the UN, and economic sanctions might force the contenders — Roman Catholic Croats, Orthodox Catholic Serbs, and Muslims — to agree to peace. These efforts failed, resulting in mass killings and forced evacuations — "ethnic cleansing" — of people in the area. Much of this cleansing was done to Muslims by the Serbs, but Croats, too drove hundreds of thousands of Serbs out of Croatia. Later estimates concluded that 100,000 people had been murdered in the fighting between 1992 and 1995. In August, 1995, Croatian and Muslim armies scored important military victories, and NATO planes launched seventeen days of attacks on Bosnian Serbs. Forced to the defensive, the Serbs agreed to an accord put together at Dayton, Ohio in November 1995. It provided for a cease-fire and, while maintaining Bosnia-Herzegovina as a single state, divided that area into two "statelets," one to be adminstered by Serbs, the other by a Bosnian-Croat federation. The accord further called for the return of refugees to their homes, trials of alleged war criminals, and a gradual reintegration of the two statelets. Clinton sent

20,000 American troops to the area—supposedly for only a year—to help NATO forces implement the accords.

The Dayton accords represented a moderate success for NATO and the Clinton administration. By mid-1999 the cease-fire had held for almost four years with some 7,000 American troops still helping to preserve the peace there. Most of the alleged war criminals, however, remained on the loose, and hundreds of thousands of people dared not return to their homes. Meanwhile, in 1998, historically power-ful tensions in Kosovo, a province within the Serbian republic of Yugoslavia inhab-ited mostly by people of Albanian-Muslim background, broke out into warfare. Leaders of the Kosovo Liberation Army demanded independence, but Serbs cher-ished the region as part of their heritage and tightened their control. By early 1999, observers in the province reported that Serbian military and police forces were en-gaging in widespread ethnic cleansing of the ethnic Albanian Kosovars.

In March 1999 American and NATO leaders, having failed to reach a settle-ment, began sustained air attacks on Serbian troops and installations. These were launched without congressional consent and represented the first NATO assaults on a sovereign nation in the 50-year history of the organization. The attacks, however, did not seem to deter the Serbs, who stepped up their destruction of Kosovar vil-lages. By May 1999 it was estimated that several thousands of ethnic Albanian Kosovars had been killed and that as many as 1.3 million—some two-thirds of the population of the province—had fled their homes, many to the adjacent Yugosla-vian republic of Montenegro and to the neighboring nations of Albania and Mace-donia. These poverty-stricken areas were nearly destabilized, overwhelmed by the masses of people who had landed in their midst.

To many observers the tragic events surrounding Kosovo indicated that American and NATO leaders had done too little and too late. When the air attacks at first failed to discourage the Serbs, some of these observers began to demand that NATO send in ground troops. Other experts disagreed, emphasizing that the fighting in Kosovo was essentially a civil war, and that there was relatively little that outside powers could do as of 1999 to moderate the tensions that had long plagued the region. Committing American ground forces to Kosovo, these observers added, would lead to very high casualties, bog the United States down for years to come in the Balkans, and establish a bad precedent, encouraging other dissident groups, such as 25 million stateless Kurds in the Middle East, to intensify their fights for independence.

One thing seemed clear, however, in mid-1999: even the escalation of air strikes—which until mid April led Clinton to call up more than 30,000 reservists and National Guardsmen, and to seek an emergency appropriation of $6 billion to support military action and aid to refugees—was slow to deter the Serbs. The United States, indisputably the strongest nation on the planet, could not easily en-force its will on the world.

The quest for peace and democracy seemed elusive elsewhere in the world dur-ing the late 1990s. Like other countries, the United States stood aside in 1994 while at least 500,000 people were slaughtered as a result of ethnic fighting in Rwanda. Four years later, on a trip to Africa, Clinton expressed regret that the United States and other nations had done so little at the time. What they might have accom-plished, given the indifference of most Americans and Europeans (or other Africans, for that matter) to events in sub-Saharan Africa, he did not make clear.

Meanwhile, North Korea, the world's last-surviving Stalinist regime, was spending scarce resources on the development of nuclear weapons and ballistic missiles, some of which it was selling to Iran and Pakistan. Its government's mismanagement led to famine at home that killed an estimated 3 million people during the 1990s.

In Iraq, Saddam Hussein not only remained in command, in 1999, killing domestic opponents, but also defied UN inspectors who were supposed to prevent him from manufacturing or possessing nuclear, chemical, and biological weapons. To bring him into line, Clinton in 1997–98 authorized an enormous military buildup in the Persian Gulf. Full-scale war with Iraq seemed certain in early 1998. Clinton's moves, however, aroused opposition at home, from Russia, and from most of his overseas allies, who wondered if fighting could succeed in toppling Saddam—or in replacing him with a more democratic successor. War against Iraq, they predicted, would kill thousands of civilians and inflame anti-American feelings in the Arab world. At the last minute, the UN brokered a face-saving compromise, and Clinton called off the attack. The United States, however, maintained sizable military forces in the area, and in late 1998 and 1999 it launched many air raids blasting Iraqi installations. It also fastened an embargo on Iraq. The result of such reprisals, however, seemed as unproductive as those against the Serbs in Kosovo: in early 1999 Iraq no longer had to worry about inspections of its arms-making activities, and Saddam clung firmly to power.

When Clinton tried more accommodating approaches to oppressive regimes, he also encountered difficulties. A case in point was his experience involving China; he encouraged trade relations between China and the United States in the hope that Beijing, exposed to American ideas and practices, would gradually soften its handling of dissidents at home. The results of this effort, however, seemed modest as of the late 1990s. The Chinese government released a few of its democratic opponents from prison and sent them into permanent exile in the United States; if they returned to their homeland, they would be re-arrested. The Chinese continued to persecute religious minorities—in Tibet as well as at home—and to advance the nuclear weapons programs of Iran and Pakistan.

Neither in 1993 nor later was it possible to discern a clearly articulated global strategy behind Clinton's foreign policies. Many of his moves, moreover—in Haiti, Somalia, Iraq, and Kosovo—seemed to have failed. Some things about his policies, however, seemed clear. First, the United States aggressively assisted American corporations seeking overseas markets. Expansion of world trade became a cornerstone of Clinton's efforts abroad. Commerce, he believed, exposed other nations, such as China, to democratic ways of doing things and promised over time to weaken authoritarian regimes.

The Clinton administration also reduced military expenditures. Manpower in the Army dropped from 2 million in 1990 to 993,000 in early 1998. Still, the United States hardly became isolationist. It remained politically and militarily engaged in many areas of the world—during Clinton's tenure NATO was expanded, and American troops stayed in western Europe and South Korea. They were sent to the Persian Gulf, Somalia, Haiti, and the Balkans. In the summer of 1998, reacting to bomb attacks on American embassies in Kenya and Tanzania, the administration authorized air attacks against alleged terrorists in the Sudan and in Afghanistan.

Polls suggested that the American people continued to be edgy—as they had been since the bloodshed of Vietnam—about such use of the awesome power of the nation in ways that would involve the country in costly military commitments abroad. Without a communist arch-enemy like the Soviet Union to contend with, they did not seek to police the globe. But they seemed cautiously supportive of the Clinton administration's ventures into world politics.

A Nation Divided?

In 1990 the Dow-Jones industrial average, a key measure of stock prices, averaged 2,634. In February 1995 it closed above 4,000 for the first time in American history. A little more than four years later it surpassed 11,000! Thanks in part to the rapid spread of employee pension plans, more than 33 percent of households (as opposed to 10 percent in 1959) had entered the stock market by 1997 and pushed the prices of stocks ever higher. By 1998 Americans had more personal wealth stashed away in the stock market than in their own homes. These fantastic developments promised bonanzas not only to stockholders, but also to all sorts of institutions, such as philanthropic organizations and universities, that depended heavily on charitable contributions.

They also stunned economists, who offered any number of explanations for them. Underlying most of these explanations was a central assumption: the economy, growing by roughly four percent per year between 1996 and 1999, was in much healthier shape than it had been earlier in the decade. Unemployment in March 1999 fell to 4.2 percent, the lowest since 1970. Prices remained stable. Even the federal budget deficit, which had grown enormous (to $290 billion in fiscal year 1992) seemed to be coming under control. Counting social security funds, it showed a modest surplus in fiscal 1998, the first plus since 1969. The Congressional Budget Office then foresaw budgetary surpluses totalling more than $1.55 trillion by 2008.

Much-heralded technological advances accompanied these developments. Pundits celebrated a "Digital Revolution," which they said was replacing the industrial revolution (which in its time had transformed the nation). The microchip, they added, was the dynamo of a new world that would feature low unemployment, negligible inflation, and a "global economy" of lightning-fast decision making. A knowledge-based world, reflected in the extraordinary expansion of computers and, in the 1990s, electronic mail and the Internet, was said to be arriving as a force that would revolutionize the way that institutions did business. Indeed, Smith Corona, a major typewriter company, filed for bankruptcy while shares of companies involved in the "Net" zoomed to unimaginable heights. The dynamic new technological world was expected to transform not only the international economy but also to empower individual people. More than a third of American households in 1998 had personal computers.

One might expect that wonders such as these, hailed as wonders of an ever more prosperous free market in the post-Cold War world, would brighten the American Dream, which by 1992 had faded since the onset of economic gloom of the 1970s. Optimists imagined that prosperity would gratify people, thereby softening the animosities of race, class, religion, and gender that had afflicted American society in the wake of post-1960s backlash. As a new millennium approached, perhaps the United States could rediscover an ideal: *e pluribus unum.*

Children attend computer lab in this Jasper, Alabama public school.

For fortunate people—those who profited from the prosperity of the late 1990s—these were indeed exciting times. Many executives of large corporations did wonderfully well: William Gates, the head of Microsoft, had a net worth in 1998 of $51 billion. The Walton family, which owned Wal-Mart stores, was worth $46 billion. Salaries and bonuses for CEOs in major companies often topped $2 million. "High-end" stores reported record sales. Millions of Americans in the upper-middle classes enjoyed far more comfortable lives than anyone could have imagined in 1970. Their homes contained impressive displays of wealth and gadgetry: huge TV sets, $1,800 refrigerators, marble flooring in foyers and halls, cherry-wood cabinets, Jacuzzi foot baths. Their garages sheltered $30,000 sport utility vehicles and other large, gas-guzzling cars. They dined at high-priced restaurants and vacationed at faraway resorts. Their children attended universities whose costs for tuition, room, and board rose to more than $30,000 a year in the most competitive private institutions.

Farther down the income pyramid, most steadily employed salaried and wage-workers also did as well or a little better in the late 1990s than they had in the 1970s or 1980s. These Americans, too, lived more comfortably than in the past: the median size of single-family dwellings grew from 1,385 square feet in 1970 to 1,950 square feet in 1997. But productivity, aided only slightly if at all by computerization, rose slowly—around 1 percent per year from 1973 to 1998, as opposed to 3 percent per year between 1945 and 1973. Economic growth was much more sluggish over the twenty-five years following 1973—even in the flourishing late-1990s—than it had been in the twenty-five years following World War II. M.I.T. economist Paul Krugman concluded in 1997 that the real income of the median American family rose at most by 35 percent between 1973 and 1997, compared to 100 percent between 1945 and 1973.

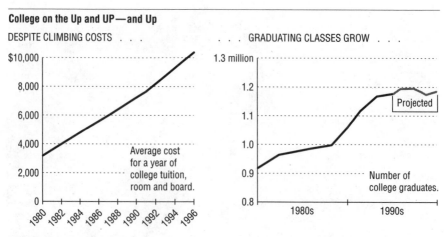

College on the Up and UP—and Up

DESPITE CLIMBING COSTS . . .   . . . GRADUATING CLASSES GROW . . .

Average cost for a year of college tuition, room and board.

Projected

Number of college graduates.

SOURCE: *Department of Education*
The New York Times

Economists generally agreed, moreover, that income inequality had increased since the 1970s, possibly accelerating during the Clinton years. Experts disagreed on the causes of this trend, but often pointed to a long-run structural reality: the stagnation in the number of skilled, fairly well-paying manufacturing jobs relative to growth in less remunerative service work, where wages and salaries often provided lower buying power in 1999 than they had in 1969. The fastest-growing occupations in the 1990s—all offering low or modest pay—were cashiers, janitors and cleaners, salespeople, waiters and waitresses, and nurses. Jobs commanding better-paying salaries ordinarily required higher education or expensive specialized training. A widely reported statistic in the late 1990s dramatized one aspect of inequality: corporate CEOs by that time earned 120 times as much (some economists said 200 times as much) as their workers, compared to 35 times as much in the mid-1970s.

Well-publicized stories of "downsizing" of employees, which highly paid heads of corporations undertook in order to cut costs and toughen competitiveness, may have further sharpened class resentments, not only among blue-collar workers but also among middle managers. AT&T, for example, announced in 1996 that it would let go 40,000 workers, or 13 percent of its employees, in the next three years. Many observers thought that downsizing (which had a long history) improved the international competitiveness of previously inefficient American firms. The frequency of news reports about downsizing, however, caused some popular unease; critics branded the process as a "democratization of insecurity" that was creating a "politics of the anxious middle."

Americans in the 1990s also read about a host of mega-corporate mergers. Between 1995 and 1997, more than 27,800 companies joined hands, completing more mergers than in the entire decade of the 1980s (which had once been considered the high point for corporate combinations). In 1997 alone there were 156 mergers of $1 billion or more in the United States, a number 60 percent higher than in 1996. In 1998, Exxon and Mobil proposed a merger that would have created a new corporation with revenues of $203 billion, the highest in the world. The total value of new mergers during 1998 was $1.68 trillion, or 12 percent of GNP.

The concentration of economic power began to alarm the Clinton administration. In 1998 it instituted anti-trust suits against Microsoft and against Intel, the world's largest maker of computer chips. It did not challenge the mergers, however. As the millennium of 2000 approached, it remained to be seen whether the merger mania would continue.

Another worrisome economic trend that seemed to accelerate in the 1990s was "outsourcing," whereby manufacturers channeled production to lower-paid workers in the South or abroad and discharged long-term workers in the process. Labor leaders bitterly opposed these practices (which also had a long history) and tried to breathe life into the ailing union movement in the United States. In the late 1990s, however, labor unions did not advance: only 14 percent of workers belonged to unions—a percentage far smaller than in most industrialized nations. The percentage of unionized workers in private employment was smaller still, around 8 or 9 percent.

Anguished concerns over job security accompanied these class differences. Hear the words of a fifty-three year-old middle manager in 1997. He had a six-figure income that enabled him and his wife (who also worked) and two children to live comfortably and to own two cars. But he had friends who had lost their jobs, and he was nervous. "I earn more in a month than my dad did in a year," he said. "But I feel my life is more difficult. I don't gamble. I don't have season tickets to the Bulls. How can I earn this much but not have anything left over?" He had trouble keeping up with ever-growing expectations, which had escalated in the postwar era. Like many Americans, he worried about losing ground.

Still farther down the income pyramid, there remained the lowest-paid workers, the underemployed, the long-term unemployed, the disabled, and single parents (mostly women) who were too busy with child care to work on a regular basis. Many of these people subsisted on very little. Amid the general prosperity of the mid- and late-1990s, the proportion of Americans defined by the government as "poor" declined, from approximately 15 percent in 1993 to around 13.3 percent in 1998. This was 35.6 million people, compared to 39.3 million in 1993. The number of people on welfare also fell, from 14.1 million in early 1993 to 7.6 million in March 1999. This was less than 4 percent of the population, the smallest proportion in more than twenty-five years. Although these were heartening statistics, they could not obscure the fact that millions of people in the world's richest nation scrambled for subsistence. Many of these Americans were aged, sick, or otherwise unable to work steadily, yet had no wholly secure governmental safety net to protect them. Some 20 percent of all children—a total of 14 million—lived in poverty, a percentage far higher than in other industrialized nations. Liberals argued that really severe poverty had increased since the 1960s, and they wondered what would happen to the welfare population when the two-year limit on public assistance established by the 1996 welfare law went into effect. Should a recession occur, poverty was likely to increase dramatically.

What these economic indicators revealed was the persistence in the United States of considerable economic divisions. The United States remained a land of opportunity for millions of people in the 1990s; upward socio-economic mobility

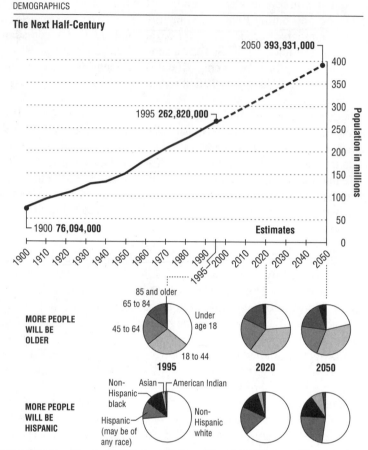

DEMOGRAPHICS

The Next Half-Century

The Census Bureau estimates that the population of the United States will approach 400 million by 2050, and will have larger proportions of both old people and Hispanic people.

SOURCE: *The New York Times*

was still a real possibility. But America also continued to have a less egalitarian income pyramid than most industrialized nations.

RACE AND IMMIGRATION

Divisions of class blended with those of race. The median household income of white Americans in 1998 was $38,972, compared to $25,050 for black households and $26,628 for households of Hispanic ancestry. As in the past, rates of unemployment in the 1990s were roughly twice as high among African Americans and Hispanics as they were among whites. Poverty rates among these minorities (at roughly 27 percent in the late 1990s) were the lowest since the government began measuring poverty in 1959, but remained approximately three times as high as among whites. Rates of out-of-wedlock pregnancy, drug abuse, and violent crime in central

T-shirt vendors hold up shirt models of O. J. Simpson outside of the Los Angeles Criminal Court Building

city areas inhabited by African Americans, while less frightening than they had been during the 1980s, remained staggeringly high in the 1990s.

Tensions between blacks and whites, in fact, seemed, if anything, more pronounced in the 1990s than earlier. An especially sensational manifestation of these tensions surrounded the arrest and trial in 1994–95 of O. J. Simpson, the widely known African American football star and television–film personality. Simpson was charged with the murder in Los Angeles of his white ex-wife and of a young white man. During the long and eagerly watched televised trial that followed, most white Americans were sure that Simpson was guilty as charged. They were shocked and appalled when a predominantly black jury decided otherwise in October 1995. African Americans, by contrast, were said to support the verdict. Some danced in the streets when they heard it.

The Simpson trial exposed with painful clarity the depth of a black-white divide in the United States. Millions of African Americans had climbed into the middle classes and moved to suburbs, most of them segregated by race, by the 1990s. They enjoyed socioeconomic standing and voting rights unimaginable in the days of Jim Crow, and held office in much greater numbers. White Americans, moreover, still supported the historic civil rights acts of the 1960s. But most African Americans who had advanced, like those who had not, looked at the American Dream very differently from the way that whites did. They believed that racial discrimination, especially in housing and employment, was as sharp as ever and that their color deprived them of a host of opportunities.

Other events of the mid-1990s offered further evidence of racial polarization. One was the publication in 1994 of *The Bell Curve,* a much-discussed book by the social scientists Richard Herrnstein and Charles Murray that focused on lower IQ scores among blacks as a primary source of African American poverty. The emphasis in the book on genetic differences between the races aroused furious protests among African Americans and others. A year later Louis Farrakhan, head of the Nation of Islam, staged a so-called Million Man March in Washington. Farrakhan said that the march would be a "holy day of atonement and reconciliation" in which black men would promise to be responsible husbands, sons, and fathers. On other occasions, however, Farrakhan unleashed racist diatribes against Jews—whom he called "bloodsuckers"—and against many other ethnic groups. Given the visibility of people like Herrnstein, Murray and Farrakhan, it was hardly surprising that many students of race relations despaired. Titles of books about race relations published in the 1990s expressed this pessimistic attitude: *Tragic Failure, American Apartheid, Two Nations, Divided by Color,* and *The Coming Race War.*

No racially charged issue of the 1990s aroused more controversy than affirmative action. This approach to race relations suffered some defeats in the 1990s at the hands of the courts, which whittled it back in a number of cases. In 1996 California voters approved Proposition 209, which banned affirmative action in public employment and contracting, and in admissions to public colleges and universities in the state. One result was dramatic declines in 1997–1998 in admissions of blacks and Hispanics to prestigious campuses such as Berkeley, and angry protests from supporters of affirmative action.

The issue of affirmative action in education did not make much difference to the great mass of African Americans (or Hispanics), who did not dream of attending elite universities or graduate schools. But it had symbolic significance for protagonists in the anguished debates of the 1990s. These debates did not always feature blacks against whites—the leader of the drive for Proposition 209 was Ward Connerly, an African American member of the state board of regents. Like many others who opposed affirmative action, Connerly thought that it often discriminated against students (many of whom in California were Asian Americans) who scored well on standardized tests. He also believed that affirmative action stigmatized and patronized African Americans who were admitted to places like Berkeley: white classmates would assume that the blacks had not deserved to get in. Foes of such policies also pointed to the high drop-out rates of African Americans at campuses such as Berkeley. Wouldn't such students be better off if they went to less-demanding institutions? Better yet, wouldn't they benefit most of all from an upgrading in the quality of elementary and secondary schools?

Defenders of affirmative action retorted that it opened otherwise tightly sealed doors that long had barred minority groups from educational opportunities leading to professional and managerial positions. They added that "diversity" was valuable; students learned much from mixing with people of different backgrounds. In 1998 the Association of American Universities, which represented sixty-two of the nation's leading public and private universities, proclaimed that "diversity" was "a value central to the very concept of education." It added, "We are conscious of our obligation to educate exceptional people who will serve all of the nation's different communities."

President Clinton, struggling to improve race relations, offered quiet support for affirmative action, with which all his predecessors since the late 1960s (Reagan and Bush included) had worked. "Mend it; don't end it," he suggested. In 1997 he promoted a "dialogue" on race by naming a panel to hold public forums on racially charged issues. John Hope Franklin, a distinguished historian, headed the group. Opponents of Clinton's efforts, however, protested that Franklin's panel refused to include opponents of affirmative action in their first public session. Franklin retorted that such opponents had nothing to contribute to public understanding of racial issues. Militant supporters of Native Americans, who were not represented on the panel, disrupted a later session. In April 1998, Connerly announced the formation of a rival, conservative panel. Meaningful dialogue over race remained elusive in 1999.

Conflicts over race reflected broader controversy in the 1990s over "multiculturalism." At its starkest, this controversy revived debates that had excited many Americans in the past: should the United States focus on assimilating newcomers into a European/white culture, or should it mainly cherish and celebrate its ethnic and religious pluralism? Battles over these and related issues broke out on a host of fronts. To what extent should schools support bilingual educational programs? Should the curricula in schools primarily explore America's roots in western civilization, or highlight the contributions of other cultures, including those of Africa and Native America? Should English be established as the "official" language of the nation? Should Puerto Rico be admitted to statehood?

The issue of immigration set off many of these battles. In 1965 America had admitted 300,000 legal immigrants; in the early and mid-1990s it admitted 3 to 4 times as many per year. Hundreds of thousands more—no one knew how many—entered every year illegally, mostly in the Southwest. While immigrants remained a smaller percentage of the total population in the late 1990s than they had at the peak of immigration between 1900 and 1914, they tended to concentrate in a relatively few states and cities, and their presence was growing. Some demographers estimated that Hispanics would become 43 percent of California's population and 38 percent of Texas's by the year 2025. It was thought that Hispanics would be 25 percent of the population as a whole by 2050. The majority of new immigrants were nonwhite, non-English-speaking, and unskilled. What would happen to the United States if they continued to arrive in such considerable numbers?

Polls in the 1990s consistently revealed that most Americans liked the immigrants whom they knew, and that they treasured the nation's ethnic diversity and immigrant traditions. After all, the United States was a nation of newcomers. But the polls also showed that a majority of Americans wanted to stem the tide. Large-scale immigration, these restrictionists said, necessitated tax increases to pay for social services, especially for welfare and education. They added that many of the newcomers were willing to work for very little money, thus driving down the wage scales of already badly paid American workers (including millions of blacks). For these reasons, labor leaders, as in the past, were cool to high levels of immigration. Finally, restrictionists argued that heavy immigration threatened cultural peace: the nation, they said, was becoming divided into ever more assertive ethnic interests. "Identity politics" would Balkanize the United States.

Attitudes such as these prompted Californians in 1994 to approve by a 3-to-2 margin Proposition 187, a referendum that stopped state aid, except for emergency hospital care, to illegal aliens. In 1998 Californians voted, 61 percent to 39 percent, for Proposition 227, which called for an end to most state-supported bilingual education programs. Politicians of both parties, not only in California, demanded major strengthening of border controls—and the building of a durable fence—at key points on the Mexican-American line. The welfare reform act of 1996 went further, depriving *legal* aliens of various forms of public assistance. Though Clinton later managed to persuade Congress to restore some of these benefits, fears about immigration, multiculturalism, and the "Balkanization of America" remained strong at the end of the century.

GENDER ISSUES

Debates over gender issues in the 1990s were mild compared to those that featured class, race, or ethnicity. Still, they generated considerable heat. Some of them continued to concern the impact of feminism. On the one hand, statistics seemed to support the aspirations of those who had supported the movement. By the 1990s women had become more successful in politics: 21 percent of state legislators in 1996 were women, compared to 4 percent in 1968. The United States Senate had eight female members; the House of Representatives, forty-eight. A special room was set up near the House floor to help congresswomen who were nursing mothers. Women had won mayoralties in Chicago, Houston, San Francisco, and Honolulu. They registered and voted in record numbers in 1996, helping Clinton to be re-elected.

Women also had become more involved in the world of work outside the home. In 1997, a record-high percentage of more than 60 percent of women aged twenty to fifty-four were either working for pay or looking for work. This figure was almost twice as high as the 32 percent who were in these categories in 1960. Surveys suggested that increasing numbers of men were staying home to be with their children. Although women's wages still lagged behind those of men, most social scientists thought that complex structural forces helped account for the gap. Many women, for instance, took time out to have and to raise children; others preferred to work part-time; millions settled in as second income-earners in two-worker households. Still, some of these female employees were achieving high positions. The number of female executive vice-presidents more than doubled between 1987 and 1997. Some observers thought that the glass ceiling might be cracking. Women, meanwhile, continued to command large power in the consumer culture, making three-fourths of decisions concerning household purchasing.

A key goal of feminism, the right to abortions, seemed constitutionally assured as of the late 1990s. The Supreme Court in 1992 reaffirmed *Roe* v. *Wade,* and Congress in 1994 passed the Freedom of Access to Clinic Entrances Act, which prescribed federal prison sentences for people found guilty of assaults against workers at abortion clinics. But anti-abortion activists refused to surrender, and a minority became more extreme, firebombing clinics and killing five people in 1993–94. Extremists injured six in the bombing of an Atlanta clinic in 1997 and killed one in

Abortion rights advocates and anti-abortion advocates meet to express their opposite views during a demonstration in Washington.

Birmingham, Alabama, in 1998. They were fighting for major stakes: it was estimated that there was an average of 1.5 million abortions performed every year in the United States between 1973 and 1996. The accumulated total in 1996, since *Roe* v. *Wade* in 1973, approximated 34 million.

Religiously motivated people led many of these anti-abortion activities. Many were devout Catholics; many others were conservative and fundamentalist Protestants who, having become bolder in the 1970s, continued to fight against the tides of secularism and liberalism. Beverly LaHaye, a highly organized activist, had founded a key organization of such Protestants, Concerned Women for America (CWA), in 1979. By the 1990s CWA claimed to have more than 600,000 members. Its members opposed abortion, violence on television, pornography, and gay rights. They demanded the teaching of creationism (the Book of Genesis) in the schools. LaHaye exclaimed that "feminism and the sexual revolution are tentacles of the octopus humanism." CWA reflected the considerable visibility of organized conservative religion in the United States in the 1990s.

Other Americans, moreover, were not so sure that feminism made much sense. Some asked what was so wonderful about a movement that sought to help women join men on a slippery corporate ladder. The novelist Norman Mailer quipped in 1998, "You get on the shuttle from Boston to New York, and what do you see? You see a group of women wearing tailored suits, carrying their laptop computers, and they look like the female versions of the men." Some women, too, had second thoughts about parts of the feminist agenda, for the division of labor had not changed greatly in their homes: women still did 87 percent of the shopping, 81 percent of the cooking, and 78 percent of the cleaning. One woman complained, "All that feminism ever got us is more work."

Reflecting doubts such as these, a CBS News poll in December 1997 suggested that only a minority of women (around 25 percent) considered themselves feminists. A majority, while agreeing that the movement had been a good thing, said that they did not feel it had improved their own lives. The poll concluded that most women believed that women who left the home to work were worse as mothers than those who were full-time mothers. (Men thought that leaving home to work made no difference.)

Data such as these tend to ignore, finally, a thirty-year trend that continued until the mid-1990s: the rise of out-of-wedlock pregnancy and single motherhood. By 1996, some 70 percent of black babies and 26 percent of white babies were born out of wedlock. Percentages such as these, which were far higher than in the 1960s and higher than almost everywhere else in the world, attested to the power of a number of postwar forces, notably the sexual revolution. Often, however, it was the young mothers who paid the price for such freedom; unmarried, they received little if any financial support as they undertook by themselves the task of raising children. In 1996 some two-thirds of single mothers with children under the age of six lived in poverty, compared to 9 percent of mothers who lived with their husbands. For the millions of women trapped in the "feminization of poverty," debates over feminism seemed far removed from their lives.

A VIOLENT SOCIETY?

There was yet one more troublesome manifestation of national disunity in the 1990s—one that pitted a wide variety of zealous ideologues and groups in bloody confrontations against authority figures. The first of these battles in the 1990s carried the hatreds of the Middle East to New York City. In February 1993 Islamic militants managed to explode a 1,200-pound car bomb in the underground garage of the World Trade Center, killing six and injuring more than a thousand. Thousands of people in the building had to stumble down more than seventy flights of pitch-black stairs to the street. It was then the most devastating act of terrorism on American soil. Two months later David Koresh and his band of committed Branch Davidians went to their doom. During the 1996 Olympic Games in Atlanta, one person was killed and 100 injured when a bomb blew up at Centennial Park.

Then there was the so-called Unabomber, a mysterious figure who sent homemade bombs through the mail to kill people he had identified as enemies of society. Between 1978 and 1996, when authorities arrested Theodore Kaczynski, the villain of the drama, his bombs killed three recipients and injured twenty-two. Kaczynski,

Rescue workers stand in front of the Alfred P. Murrah Federal Building following the explosion on April 19, 1995, in downtown Oklahoma City.

who had a Ph.D. in mathematics, had abandoned a promising academic career and isolated himself in a cabin in Montana. He hated what he called "organized society in general and the technological establishment in particular." Reading that one of his bombs had blown a man to bits, he wrote in his journal, "Excellent. Humane way to eliminate somebody. He probably never felt a thing. 25,000 reward offered. Rather flattering." Kaczynski later pleaded guilty to the bombings and was sentenced to life in prison.

By far the most horrific act of violence in America during the 1990s occurred on April 19, 1995, two years to the day after the tragedy at Waco. (This was also the 220th anniversary of the battles of Lexington and Concord, which had started the Revolutionary War.) A 4,000-pound truck bomb shattered the Federal Building in Oklahoma City, killing 168 people, including 15 children at an on-site day-care center, and injuring hundreds more. Many Americans assumed that Islamic militants had caused the bloodshed, but it soon became clear that the perpetrators

KEEPING TRACK

Even as Crime Falls, Inmates Increase

Longer prison sentences and an increased use of minimum sentencing
laws are some factors contributing to the increase in inmates.

The crime rate has gone down . . .
Violent and property crimes per 100,000 people.

. . . but the number of inmates continues to rise
Inmates in Federal and state prisons and local jails per
100,000 people on July 1 each year.

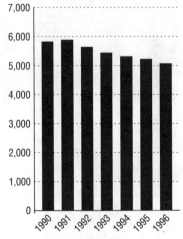

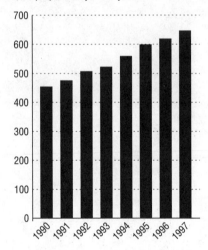

SOURCE: *Bureau of Justice Statistics*
The New York Times

were Americans who had vowed to exact revenge on the government for what
had happened at Waco. One was Timothy McVeigh, an embittered Army veteran of
the Gulf War in 1991 who had joined an apparently growing population of
paramilitary right-wing zealots in the country. McVeigh was later sentenced to
death. An accomplice, Terry Nichols, was found guilty of conspiracy and
manslaughter.

What, if anything, did these bloody events have in common? Can we conclude
that the United States was becoming an ever more violent society? Some pundits
thought so, citing as a cause of such violence the mayhem that Americans, including children, saw on television and in movie theaters. In the 1990s, Americans
tuned into television for an average of thirty hours per week. Many of the movies
employed impressive "special effects" to glorify bloodshed. Widely watched shows
on TV left a message that violence was the way to resolve conflict. The *Jerry
Springer Show,* a popular TV show of the late 1990s, featured cursing and fighting
among guests—men smashing men, women bashing women, women assaulting
men, sometimes even men lunging at women—that erupted when Springer, the
host, induced his guests to talk about their sexual infidelities, many of which were
bizarre in the extreme. There was no doubting the fact that television and movies in
the United States had grown considerably more sexually graphic and violent by the
1990s.

There was also evidence in the 1990s to suggest that right-wing "militia groups," a few of them religious fundamentalists who were deeply alienated from mainstream society, were gaining converts: The Treasury Department estimated that membership in "militia" groups had grown to 40,000 by 1995. The Branch Davidians were one such sect. Another was a group calling itself the Aryan Nation, which was anti-Semitic, racist, superpatriotic, and antigovernment. Members of such groups normally gave avid support to the National Rifle Association (NRA), which proclaimed the constitutional right to bear arms. The NRA claimed a membership in 1998 of 2.8 million people.

It was nonetheless difficult to find causal links between these trends and very different people such as Koresh, McVeigh, and Kaczynski. Religious feelings motivated neither McVeigh nor Kaczynski. Only Koresh relied heavily on guns. Moreover, violent hate groups—the KKK, for example—had long polluted American life. Was American society as a whole more "violent" than it had been, say, in the 1960s when Martin Luther King, Jr., and two Kennedys were assassinated and when race riots tore up scores of cities? Or than in the 1970s and 1980s when rates of violent crime in the cities peaked, then declined significantly during the next ten years?

One can question, too, other pessimistic assessments of American life in the 1990s. To be sure, national politics were uninspiring at best. Leaders of foreign policy struggled, sometimes in vain, to cope with changes in the post-Cold War world. Divisions of class, race, and ethnicity appeared to defy mending. But none of these problems was new. They had long existed, contradicting romantic notions of "good old days" of harmony and national consensus.

Moreover, the media also reported on brighter sides to things. Scientists were proclaiming extraordinary achievements. Hardly a week passed without revelations about new wonder drugs, including the depression fighter Prozac, the sexual potency pill Viagra, and magical elixirs against baldness and osteoporosis. Superdiscoveries promised therapies that in the not-too-distant future would eradicate cancer. Some scientists believed that it might be possible to extend human life indefinitely. A few researchers, excited by the cloning of a sheep, predicted the coming of a laboratory-crafted Designer Man.

While many Americans were properly skeptical about such proclamations, they otherwise had reason to place hope in the future. During the late 1990s most people enjoyed unprecedentedly comfortable lives in an economy that was outpacing all international competitors. Nuclear war, an ever-present fear between the 1950s and the late 1980s, seemed less likely than in the Cold War years. For all their differences, Americans generally managed their conflicts peacefully, and they remained committed to democratic political institutions.

A *New York Times*/CBS poll of teenagers (aged thirteen through seventeen) in April 1998 suggested that young people—a key to the mood of the nation in the future?—continued to be optimistic about a good many things. Most of the teenagers trusted the government, admired their parents, and stated that it was still possible to start off poor in life and get rich. Some 94 percent said that they believed in God. Solid majorities claimed that that they never drank alcohol or smoked cigarettes or marijuana. Roughly 50 percent considered premarital sexual relations to be "always wrong." Statistics compiled by the Census Bureau,

Happy teenagers frolic on the beach.

meanwhile, revealed considerable declines during the 1990s in teenage pregnancy rates.

Was this poll to be believed? Did it suggest that a majority of the American people truly anticipated continuing social and economic progress in the twenty-first century? This was hard to say because people often tell pollsters one thing and do another. The pollsters, moreover, noted that 49 percent of these young people had part-time jobs, 66 percent had television sets in their rooms, and 14 percent had their own phone numbers. Were percentages such as these signs of welcome prosperity, or of perhaps overly materialistic, self-absorbed values characteristic of people who did not much care about the poor, the oppressed, and the sick? No one could tell for certain. As the United States approached the millennium of 2000, the directions it would take in its political, economic, and social life were promising but surely dangerous to predict.

Suggestions for Reading

The following are well-written books that look broadly into American life in the 1990s: Michael Elliott, *The Day Before Yesterday: Reconsidering America's Past* (1996), which looks at expectations in the 1990s from the perspective of the past; Nicolaus Mills, *The Triumph of Meanness: America's War Against Its Better Self* (1997), a highly critical liberal account of United States society in the mid-1990s; Gertrude Himmelfarb, *The De-moralization of Society: From Victorian Virtues to Modern Values* (1995), a conservative's assessment of social trends; Alan Wolfe, *One Nation, After All: What Middle-Class Americans Really Think About* (1998), a survey that emphasizes American tolerance; and Michael Sandel, *Democracy's Dis-*

content: *America in Search of a Public Philosophy* (1996), which explores political ideas from a historical perspective. Samuel Huntington, *The Clash of Civilizations and the Remaking of World Order* (1996), is a broad interpretative account of international relations.

Of the many books concerning President Clinton, two of the best are James Stewart, *Blood Sport: The President and His Adversaries* (1996); and David Maraniss, *First in His Class: A Biography of Bill Clinton* (1995). *Primary Colors* (1996) is a best-selling novel, later made into a movie, that is loosely based on Clinton. It was published by Anonymous, later identified as the journalist Joe Klein.

Widely noted books concerning various problems and issues of the 1990s include Peter Brimelow, *Alien Nation: Common Sense About America's Immigration Disaster* (1995); Vernon Briggs, *Mass Immigration: The National Interest* (1994); William Greider, *One World, Ready or Not: The Manic Logic of Global Capitalism* (1997); Robert Kuttner, *Everything for Sale: The Virtues and Limits of Markets* (1997); E.J. Dionne, *They Only Look Dead: Why Progressives Will Dominate the Next Political Era* (1996); C. Eugene Steuerle, et al., eds., *The Government We Deserve: Responsive Democracy and Changing Expectations* (1998), a collection of essays concerning American politics; Godfrey Hodgson, *The World Turned Right Side Up* (1996), concerning conservatives in the postwar era; David Gordon, *Fat and Mean: The Corporate Squeezing of Working Americans* (1996); and James Fallows, *Breaking the News: How the Media Undermine American Democracy* (1996).

Among the many books concerned with race relations, the following are well worth reading: William Julius Wilson, *When Work Disappears: The World of the New Urban Poor* (1996); John Higham, ed., *Civil Rights and Social Wrongs: Black-White Relations Since World War II* (1997), a collection of essays by leading scholars; Orlando Patterson, *The Ordeal of Integration: Progress and Resentment in America's "Racial" Crisis* (1997); and Abigail and Stephan Thernstrom, *America in Black and White: America Indivisible* (1996), a well-researched historical intepretation of race relations in the United States since the 1940s.

Copyrights and Acknowledgments

For permission to use the selections reprinted in this book,
the author is grateful to the following publishers and copyrights holders:

Photo Credits

 # The Contitution of the United States of America

We the people of the United States, in Order to form a more perfect Union, establish Justice, insure domestic Tranquility, provide for the common defence, promote the general Welfare, and secure the Blessings of Liberty to ourselves and our Posterity, do ordain and establish this Constitution for the United States of America.*

ARTICLE I

Section 1. All legislative Powers herein granted shall be vested in a Congress of the United States, which shall consist of a Senate and House of Representatives.

Section 2. The House of Representatives shall be composed of Members chosen every second Year by the People of the several States, and the Electors in each State shall have the Qualifications requisite for Electors of the most numerous Branch of the State Legislature.

No Person shall be a Representative who shall not have attained to the Age of twenty-five Years, and been seven Years a Citizen of the United States, and who shall not, when elected, be an Inhabitant of that state in which he shall be chosen.

[Representatives and direct Taxes shall be apportioned among the several States which may be included within this Union, according to their respective Numbers, which shall be determined by adding to the whole Number of free Persons, including those bound to Service for a Term of Years, and excluding Indians not taxed, three fifths of all other Persons.][1] The actual Enumeration shall be made within three Years after the first Meeting of the Congress of the United States, and within every subsequent Term of ten Years, in such Manner as they shall be Law direct. The Number of Representatives shall not exceed one for every thirty Thousand, but each State shall have at Least one Representative; and until such enumeration shall be made, the State of New Hampshire shall be entitled to chuse three,

---

* The Constitution and all amendments are shown in their original form. Parts that have been amended or superseded are bracketed and explained in the footnotes.

[1] Modified by the Fourteenth and Sixteenth Amendments.

Massachusetts eight. Rhode Island and Providence Plantations one, Connecticut five, New York six, New Jersey four, Pennsylvania eight, Delaware one, Maryland six, Virginia ten, North Carolina five, South Carolina five, and Georgia three.

When vacancies happen in the Representation from any State, the Executive Authority thereof shall issue Writs of Election to fill such Vacancies.

The House of Representatives shall chuse their Speaker and other Officers; and shall have the sole Power of Impeachment.

Section 3. The Senate of the United States shall be composed of two Senators from each State, [chosen by the Legislature thereof,][2] for six Years; and each Senator shall have one Vote.

Immediately after they shall be assembled in Consequence of the first Election, they shall be divided as equally as may be into three Classes. The Seats of the Senators of the first Class shall be vacated at the Expiration of the second Year, of the Second Class at the Expiration of the fourth Year, and of the third Class at the Expiration of the sixth Year, so that one-third may be chosen every second Year; [and if Vacancies happen by Resignation, or otherwise, during the Recess of the Legislature of any State, the Executive thereof may make temporary Appointments until the next Meeting of the Legislature, which shall then fill such Vacancies].[3]

No Person shall be a Senator who shall not have attained to the Age of thirty Years, and been nine Years a Citizen of the United States, and who shall not, when elected, be an Inhabitant of that State in which he shall be chosen.

The Vice-President of the United States shall be President of the Senate, but shall have no vote, unless they be equally divided.

The Senate shall chuse their other Officers, and also a President pro tempore, in the absence of the Vice-President, or when he shall exercise the Office of the President of the United States.

The Senate shall have the sole Power to try all Impeachments. When sitting for that purpose, they shall be on Oath or Affirmation. When the President of the United States is tried, the Chief Justice shall preside. And no person shall be convicted without the Concurrence of two thirds of the Members present.

Judgment in Cases of Impeachment shall not extend further than to removal from Office, and disqualification to hold and enjoy any Office of honor, Trust, or Profit under the United States: but the Party convicted shall nevertheless be liable and subject to Indictment, Trial, Judgment, and Punishment, according to Law.

Section 4. The Times, Places and Manner of holding Elections for Senators and Representatives, shall be prescribed in each state by the Legislature thereof; but the Congress may at any time by Law make or alter such Regulations, except as to the Places of Chusing Senators.

The Congress shall assemble at least once in every Year, and such Meeting shall [be on the first Monday in December,][4] unless they shall by Law appoint a different Day.

Section 5. Each House shall be the Judge of the Elections, Returns and Qualifi-

---

[2] Superseded by the Seventeenth Amendment.

[3] Modified by the Seventeenth Amendment.

[4] Superseded by the Twentieth Amendment.

cations of its own Members, and a Majority of each shall constitute a Quorum to do Business; but a smaller number may adjourn from day to day, and may be authorized to compel the Attendance of absent Members, in such Manner, and under such Penalties, as each House may provide.

Each House may determine the Rules of its Proceedings, punish its Members for disorderly Behavior, and, with the Concurrence of two thirds expel a Member.

Each House shall keep a Journal of its Proceedings, and from time to time publish the same, excepting such Parts as may in their Judgment require Secrecy; and the Yeas and Nays of the Members of either House on any question shall, at the Desire of one fifth of those Present, be entered on the Journal.

Neither House, during the Session of Congress, shall, without the Consent of the other, adjourn for more than three days, nor to any other Place than that in which the two Houses shall be sitting.

Section 6. The Senators and Representatives shall receive a Compensation for their Services, to be ascertained by Law, and paid out of the Treasury of the United States. They shall in all Cases, except Treason, Felony, and Breach of the Peace, be privileged from Arrest during their Attendance at the Session of their respective Houses, and in going to and returning from the same; and for any Speech or Debate in either House, they shall not be questioned in any other Place.

No Senator or Representative shall, during the Time for which he was elected, be appointed to any civil Office under the Authority of the United States, which shall have been created, or the Emoluments whereof shall have been increased, during such time; and no Person holding any Office under the United States shall be a Member of either House during his continuance in Office.

Section 7. All Bills for raising Revenue shall originate in the House of Representatives; but the Senate may propose or concur with Amendments as on other bills.

Every Bill which shall have passed the House of Representatives and the Senate, shall, before it becomes a Law, be presented to the President of the United States; If he approve he shall sign it, but if not he shall return it, with his Objections, to that House in which it shall have originated, who shall enter the Objections at large on their Journal, and proceed to reconsider it. If after such Reconsideration two thirds of that House shall agree to pass the bill, it shall be sent, together with the objections, to the other House, by which it shall likewise be reconsidered, and if approved by two thirds of that House, it shall become a Law. But in all such Cases the Votes of both Houses shall be determined by Yeas and Nays, and the names of the Persons voting for and against the Bill shall be entered on the Journal of each House respectively. If any Bill shall not be returned by the President within ten Days (Sundays excepted) after it shall have been presented to him, the Same shall be a Law, in like Manner as if he had signed it, unless the Congress by either Adjournment prevent its Return, in which Case it shall not be a Law.

Every Order, Resolution, or Vote to which the Concurrence of the Senate and House of Representatives may be necessary (except on a question of Adjournment) shall be presented to the President of the United States; and before the Same shall take Effect, shall be approved by him, or being disapproved by him, shall be repassed by two thirds of the Senate and House of Representatives, according to the Rules and Limitations prescribed in the Case of a Bill.

Section 8. The Congress shall have Power To Lay and collect Taxes, Duties, Imposts and Excises, to pay the Debts and provide for the common Defence and general Welfare of the United States; but all Duties, Imposts and Excises shall be uniform throughout the United States;

To borrow money on the credit of the United States;

To regulate Commerce with foreign Nations, and among the several States, and with the Indian Tribes;

To establish an uniform Rule of Naturalization, and uniform Laws on the subject of Bankruptcies throughout the United States;

To coin Money, regulate the Value thereof, and of foreign Coin, and fix the Standard of Weights and Measures;

To Provide for the Punishment of counterfeiting the Securities and current Coin of the United States;

To establish Post Offices and post Roads;

To promote the Progress of Science and useful Arts, by securing for limited Times to Authors and Inventors the exclusive Right to their respective Writings and Discoveries;

To constitute Tribunals inferior to the Supreme Court;

To define and punish Piracies and Felonies committed on the high Seas, and Offenses against the Law of Nations;

To declare War, grant Letters of Marque and Reprisal, and make Rules concerning Captures on Land and Water;

To raise and support Armies, but no Appropriation of Money to that Use shall be for a longer Term than two Years;

To provide and maintain a Navy;

To make Rules for the Government and Regulation of the land and naval forces;

To provide for calling forth the Militia to execute the Laws of the Union, suppress Insurrections and repel Invasions;

To provide for organizing, arming, and disciplining the Militia, and for governing such Part of them as may be employed in the Service of the United States, reserving to the States respectively, the Appointment of the Officers, and the Authority of training the Militia according to the discipline prescribed by Congress:

To exercise exclusive Legislation in all Cases whatsoever, over such District (not exceeding ten Miles square) as may, by Cession of particular States, and the acceptance of Congress, become the Seat of the Government of the United States, and to exercise like Authority over all Places purchased by the Consent of the Legislature of the State in which the Same shall be, for the Erection of Forts, Magazines, Arsenals, dock-Yards, and other needful Buildings;—And

To make all Laws which shall be necessary and proper for carrying into Execution the foregoing Powers, and all other Powers vested by this Constitution in the Government of the United States, or in any Department or Officer thereof.

Section 9. The Migration or Importation of such Persons as any of the States now existing still think proper to admit shall not be prohibited by the Congress prior to the Year one thousand eight hundred and eight, but a tax or duty may be imposed on such Importation, not exceeding ten dollars for each Person.

The privilege of the Writ of Habeas Corpus shall not be suspended, unless when in Cases of Rebellion or Invasion the public Safety may require it.

No Bill of Attainder or ex post facto Law shall be passed.

[No capitation, or other direct, Tax shall be laid unless in Proportion to the Census or Enumeration herein before directed to be taken.][5]

No Tax or Duty shall be laid on Articles exported from any State.

No Preference shall be given by any Regulation of Revenue to the Ports of one State over those of another; nor shall Vessels bound to, or from, one State, be obliged to enter, clear, or pay Duties in another.

No Money shall be drawn from the Treasury, but in Consequence of Appropriations made by Law; and a regular Statement and Account of the Receipts and Expenditures of all public Money shall be published from time to time.

No Title of Nobility shall be granted by the United States; And no Person holding any Office or Profit or Trust under them, shall, without the Consent of the Congress, accept of any present, Emolument, Office, or Title, of any kind whatever, from any King, Prince, or foreign State.

Section 10. No State shall enter into any Treaty, Alliance, or Confederation; grant Letters of Marque and Reprisal; coin Money; emit Bills of Credit; make any Thing but gold and silver Coin a Tender in Payment of Debts; pass any Bill of Attainder, ex post facto Law, or Law impairing the Obligation of Contracts, or grant any title of Nobility.

No State shall, without the Consent of the Congress, lay any Imposts or Duties on Imports or Exports, except what may be absolutely necessary for executing its inspection Laws; and the net Produce of all Duties and Imposts, laid by any State on Imports or Exports, shall be for the Use of the Treasury of the United States; and all such Laws shall be subject to the Revision and Control of the Congress.

No State shall, without the Consent of Congress, lay any duty of Tonnage, keep Troops, or Ships of War in time of Peace, enter into any Agreement or Compact with another State, or with a foreign Power, or engage in War, unless actually invaded, or in such imminent Danger as will not admit of delay.

ARTICLE II

Section 1. The executive Power shall be vested in a President of the United States of America. He shall hold his Office during the Term of four years, and, together with the Vice-President, chosen for the same Term, be elected, as follows:

Each State shall appoint, in such Manner as the Legislature thereof may direct, a Number of Electors, equal to the whole Number of Senators and Representatives to which the State may be entitled in the Congress; but no Senator or Representative, or Person holding an Office of Trust or Profit under the United States, shall be appointed an Elector.

[The Electors shall meet in their respective States, and vote by Ballot for two persons, of whom one at least shall not be an Inhabitant of the same State with themselves. And they shall make a List of all the Persons voted for, and of the

[5] Modified by the Sixteenth Amendment.

Number of Votes for each; which List they shall sign and certify, and transmit sealed to the Seat of the Government of the United States, directed to the President of the Senate. The President of the Senate shall, in the Presence of the Senate and House of Representatives, open all the Certificates, and the Votes shall then be counted. The Person having the greatest Number of Votes shall be the President, if such Number be a Majority of the whole Number of Electors appointed; and if there be more than one who have such Majority, and have an equal Number of Votes, then the House of Representatives shall immediately chuse by Ballot one of them for President; and if no Person have a Majority, then from the five highest on the List the said House shall in like Manner chuse the President. But in chusing the President, the Votes shall be taken by States, the Representation from each State having one Vote; a quorum for this Purpose shall consist of a Member or Members from two-thirds of the States, and a Majority of all the States shall be necessary to a Choice. In every Case, after the Choice of the President, the Person having the greatest Number of Votes of the Electors shall be the Vice-President. But if there should remain two or more who have equal votes, the Senate shall chuse from them by Ballot the Vice-President.][6]

The Congress may determine the Time of chusing the Electors, and the Day on which they shall give their Votes; which Day shall be the same throughout the United States.

No person except a natural-born Citizen, or a Citizen of the United States, at the time of the Adoption of this Constitution, shall be eligible to the Office of President; neither shall any Person be eligible to that Office who shall not have attained to the Age of thirty-five years, and been fourteen Years a Resident within the United States.

[In Case of the Removal of the President from Office, or of his Death, Resignation, or Inability to discharge the Powers and Duties of the said Office, the same shall devolve on the Vice-President, and the Congress may by Law provide for the Case of Removal, Death, Resignation, or Inability, both of the President and Vice-President, declaring what Officer shall then act as President, and such Officer shall act accordingly, until the disability be removed, or a President shall be elected.][7]

The President shall, at stated Times, receive for his Services a Compensation, which shall neither be increased nor diminished during the Period for which he shall have been elected, and he shall not receive within that Period any other Emolument from the United States, or any of them.

Before he enter on the execution of his Office, he shall take the following Oath or Affirmation;—"I do solemnly swear (or affirm) that I will faithfully execute the Office of President of the United States, and will, to the best of my Ability, preserve, protect, and defend the Constitution of the United States."

Section 2. The President shall be Commander in Chief of the Army and Navy of the United States, and of the Militia of the several States, when called into the actual Service of the United States; he may require the Opinion, in writing, of the principal Officer in each of the executive Departments, upon any subject relating to the Duties of their respective Offices, and he shall have Power to Grant Reprieves and Pardons for Offenses against the United States, except in Cases of Impeachment.

[6] Superseded by the Twelfth Amendment.

[7] Modified by the Twenty-fifth Amendment.

He shall have Power, by and with the Advice and Consent of the Senate, to make Treaties, provided two thirds of the Senators present concur; and he shall nominate, and by and with the Advice and Consent of the Senate, shall appoint Ambassadors, other public Ministers and Consuls, Judges of the supreme Court, and all other Officers of the United States, whose Appointments are not herein otherwise provided for, and which shall be established by Law: but the Congress may by Law vest the Appointment of such inferior Officers, as they think proper, in the President alone, in the Courts of Law, or in the Heads of Departments.

The President shall have Power to fill up all Vacancies that may happen during the Recess of the Senate, by granting Commissions which shall expire at the End of their next Session.

Section 3. He shall from time to time give to the Congress Information of the State of the Union, and recommend to their Consideration such Measures as he shall judge necessary and expedient; he may, on extraordinary occasions, convene both Houses, or either of them, and in Case of Disagreement between them, with respect to the Time of Adjournment, he may adjourn them to such Time as he shall think proper; he shall receive Ambassadors and other public Ministers; he shall take Care that the Laws be faithfully executed, and shall Commission all the Officers of the United States.

Section 4. The President, Vice-President and all civil Officers of the United States, shall be removed from Office on Impeachment for, and Conviction of, Treason, Bribery, or other high Crimes and Misdemeanors.

ARTICLE III

Section 1. The judicial Power of the United States, shall be vested in one supreme Court, and in such inferior Courts as the Congress may from time to time ordain and establish. The Judges, both of the supreme and inferior Courts, shall hold their Offices during good Behaviour, and shall, at stated Times, receive for their Services, a Compensation, which shall not be diminished during their Continuance in Office.

Section 2. The judicial Power shall extend to all Cases, in Law and Equity, arising under this Constitution, the Laws of the United States, and treaties made, or which shall be made, under their Authority;—to all Cases affecting ambassadors, other public ministers and consuls;—to all cases of admiralty and maritime Jurisdiction;—to Controversies to which the United States shall be a Party;—to Controversies between two or more States;—[between a State and Citizens of another State;][8]—between Citizens of different States,—between Citizens and the same State claiming Lands under Grants of different States, and between a State, or the Citizens thereof, and foreign States, Citizens or Subjects.

In all Cases affecting Ambassadors, other public Ministers and Consuls, and those in which a State shall be Party, the supreme Court shall have original Jurisdiction. In all the other Cases before mentioned, the supreme Court shall have appellate Jurisdiction, both as to Law and Fact, with such Exceptions, and under such Regulations as the Congress shall make.

---

[8] Modified by the Eleventh Amendment.

The trial of all Crimes, except in Cases of Impeachment, shall be by Jury; and such Trial shall be held in the State where the said Crimes shall have been committed; but when not committed within any State, the Trial shall be at such Place or Places as the Congress may be Law have directed.

Section 3. Treason against the United States, shall consist only in levying War against them, or in adhering to their Enemies, giving them Aid and Comfort. No Person shall be convicted of Treason unless on the Testimony of two Witnesses to the same overt Act, or on Confession in open Court.

The Congress shall have power to declare the Punishment of Treason but no Attainder of Treason shall work Corruption of Blood, or Forfeiture except during the Life of the Person attained.

ARTICLE IV

Section 1. Full Faith and Credit shall be given in each State to the public Acts, Records, and judicial Proceedings of every other State. And the Congress may be general Laws prescribe the Manner in which such Acts, Records, and Proceedings shall be proved, and the Effect thereof.

Section 2. The Citizens of each State shall be entitled to all Privileges and Immunities of Citizens in the several States.

A Person charged in any State with Treason, Felony, or other Crime, who shall flee from Justice, and be found in another State, shall on demand of the executive Authority of the State from which he fled, be delivered up, to be removed to the State having Jurisdiction of the crime.

[No Person held to service or Labour in one State, under the Laws thereof, escaping into another, shall, in Consequence of any Law or Regulation therein, be discharged from such Service or Labour, but shall be delivered up on Claim of the Party to whom such Service or Labour may be due.][9]

Section 3. New States may be admitted by the Congress into this Union; but no new State shall be formed or erected within the Jurisdiction of any other State; nor any State be formed by the Junction of two or more States, or parts of States, without the Consent of the Legislatures of the States concerned as well as of the Congress.

The Congress shall have Power to dispose of and make all needful Rules and Regulations respecting the Territory or other Property belonging to the United States; and nothing in this Constitution shall be so construed as to Prejudice any Claims of the United States, or of any particular State.

Section 4. The United States shall guarantee to every State in this Union a Republican Form of Government and shall protect each of them against Invasion; and on Application of the Legislature, or of the Executive (when the Legislature cannot be convened) against domestic Violence.

ARTICLE V

The Congress, whenever two-thirds of both Houses shall deem it necessary, shall propose Amendments to this Constitution, or, on the Application of the

[9] Superseded by the Thirteenth Amendment.

Legislatures of two-thirds of the several States, shall call a Convention for proposing Amendments, which, in either Case, shall be valid to all Intents and Purposes, as part of this Constitution, when ratified by the Legislatures of three-fourths of the several States, or by Conventions in three-fourths thereof, as the one or the other Mode of Ratifications may be proposed by the Congress; Provided that no Amendment which may be made prior to the Year One thousand eight hundred and eight shall in any Manner affect the first and fourth Clauses in the Ninth Section of the first Article; and that no State, without its Consent, shall be deprived of its equal Suffrage in the Senate.

ARTICLE VI

All Debts contracted and Engagements entered into, before the Adoption of this Constitution, shall be as valid against the United States under this Constitution as under the Confederation.

This Constitution, and the Laws of the United States which shall be made in Pursuance thereof; and all Treaties made, or which shall be made, under the Authority of the United States, shall be the supreme Law of the Land; and the Judges in every State shall be bound thereby, any Thing in the Constitution or Laws of any State to the Contrary notwithstanding.

The Senators and Representatives before mentioned, and the Members of the several State Legislatures, and all executive and judicial Officers, both of the United States and of the several States, shall be bound by Oath or Affirmation to support this Constitution; but no religious Test shall ever be required as a qualification to any Office or public Trust under the United States.

ARTICLE VII

The Ratification of the Conventions of nine States shall be sufficient for the Establishment of this Constitution between the States so ratifying the same.

Done in Convention by the Unanimous Consent of the States present the Seventeenth Day of September in the Year of our Lord one thousand seven hundred and Eighty seven, and of the Independence of the United States of America the Twelfth. In Witness whereof We have hereunto subscribed our Names.

Articles in Addition to, and Amendment of, the Constitution of the United States of America, Proposed by Congress, and Ratified by the Legislatures of the Several States, Pursuant to the Fifth Article of the Original Constitution.

AMENDMENT I[10]

Congress shall make no law respecting an establishment of religion, or prohibiting the free exercise thereof; or abridging the freedom of speech, or of the press; or the right of the people peaceably to assemble, and to petition the Government for a redress of grievances.

---

[10] The first ten amendments were passed by Congress September 25, 1789. They were ratified by three-fourths of the states December 15, 1791.

AMENDMENT II

A well regulated Militia, being necessary to the security of a free State, the right of the people to keep and bear Arms shall not be infringed.

AMENDMENT III

No Soldier shall, in time of peace, be quartered in any house, without the consent of the Owner, nor in time of war, but in a manner to be prescribed by law.

AMENDMENT IV

The right of the people to be secure in their persons, houses, papers, and effects, against unreasonable searches and seizures, shall not be violated, and no Warrants shall issue, but upon probable cause, supported by Oath or affirmation, and particularly describing the place to be searched, and the persons or things to be seized.

AMENDMENT V

No person shall be held to answer for a capital or otherwise infamous crime, unless on a presentment or indictment of a Grand Jury, except in cases arising in the land or naval forces, or in the Militia, when in actual service in time of War or public danger; nor shall any person be subject for the same offence to be twice put in jeopardy of life or limb; nor shall be compelled in any criminal case to be a witness against himself, nor be deprived of life, liberty, or property, without due process of law; nor shall private property be taken for public use, without just compensation.

AMENDMENT VI

In all criminal prosecutions, the accused shall enjoy the right to a speedy and public trial, by an impartial jury of the State and district wherein the crime shall have been committed, which district shall have been previously ascertained by law, and to be informed of the nature and cause of the accusation; to be confronted with the witnesses against him; to have compulsory process for obtaining witnesses in his favor, and to have the Assistance of Counsel for his defence.

AMENDMENT VII

In suits at common law, where the value in controversy shall exceed twenty dollars, the right of trial by jury shall be preserved, and no fact tried by a jury, shall be otherwise reexamined in any Court of the United States, than according to the rules of the common law.

AMENDMENT VIII

Excessive bail shall not be required, nor excessive fines imposed, nor cruel and unusual punishments inflicted.

AMENDMENT IX

The enumeration in the Constitution, of certain rights, shall not be construed to deny or disparage others retained by the people.

AMENDMENT X

The powers not delegated to the United States by the Constitution, nor prohibited by it to the States, are reserved to the States respectively, or to the people.

AMENDMENT XI (1798)[11]

The Judicial power of the United States shall not be construed to extend to any suit in law or equity, commenced or prosecuted against one of the United States by Citizens of another State, or by Citizens or Subjects of any Foreign State.

AMENDMENT XII (1804)

The Electors shall meet in their respective States and vote by ballot for President and Vice-President, one of whom, at least, shall not be an inhabitant of the same State with themselves; they shall name in their ballots the person voted for as President, and in distinct ballots the person voted for as Vice-President, and they shall make distinct lists of all persons voted for as President, and of all persons voted for as Vice-President, and of the number of votes for each, which lists they shall sign and certify, and transmit sealed to the seat of the government of the United States, directed to the President of Senate;—The President of the Senate shall, in the presence of the Senate and House of Representatives, open all the certificates and the votes shall then be counted;—The person having the greatest number of votes for President, shall be the President, if such number be a majority of the whole number of Electors appointed; and if no person have such majority, then from the persons having the highest numbers not exceeding three on the list of those voted for as President, the House of Representatives shall choose immediately, by ballot, the President. But in choosing the President, the votes shall be taken by states, the representation from each state having one vote; a quorum for this purpose shall consist of a member or members from two-thirds of the states, and a majority of all the states shall be necessary to a choice. [And if the House of Representatives shall not choose a President whenever the right of choice shall devolve upon them, before the fourth day of March next following, then the Vice-President shall act as President, as in the case of the death or other constitutional disability of the President.][12]—The person having the greatest number of votes as Vice-President, shall be the Vice-President, if such number be a majority of the whole number of Electors appointed, and if no person have a majority, then from the two highest numbers on the list, the Senate shall choose the Vice-President; a quorum for the purpose shall consist of two-thirds of the whole number of Senators, and a majority of the whole number shall be necessary to a choice. But no person constitutionally ineligible to the office of President shall be eligible to that of Vice-President of the United States.

[11] Date of ratification.

[12] Superseded by the Twentieth Amendment.

AMENDMENT XIII (1865)

Section 1. Neither slavery nor involuntary servitude, except as a punishment for crime whereof the party shall have been duly convicted, shall exist within the United States, or any place subject to their jurisdiction.

Section 2. Congress shall have power to enforce this article by appropriate legislation.

AMENDMENT XIV (1868)

Section 1. All persons born or naturalized in the United States, and subject to the jurisdiction thereof, are citizens of the United States and of the State wherein they reside. No State shall make or enforce any law which shall abridge the privileges or immunities of citizens of the United States; nor shall any State deprive any person of life, liberty, or property, without due process of law; nor deny to any person within its jurisdiction the equal protection of the laws.

Section 2. Representatives shall be apportioned among the several States according to their respective numbers, counting the whole number of persons in each State, excluding Indians not taxed. But when the right to vote at any election for the choice of electors for President and Vice-President of the United States, Representatives in Congress, the Executive and Judicial officers of a State, or the members of the Legislature thereof, is denied to any of the male inhabitants of such State, being twenty-one years of age, and citizens of the United States, or in any way abridged, except for participation in rebellion, or other crime, the basis of representation therein shall be reduced in the proportion which the number of such male citizens shall bear to the whole number of male citizens twenty-one years of age in such State.

Section 3. No person shall be a Senator or Representative in Congress, or elector of President and Vice-President, or hold any office, civil or military, under the United States, or under any State, who, having previously taken an oath, as a member of Congress, or as an officer of the United States, or as a member of any State legislature, or as an executive or judicial officer of any State, to support the Constitution of the United States, shall have engaged in insurrection or rebellion against the same, or given aid or comfort to the enemies thereof. But Congress may by a vote of two-thirds of each House, remove such disability.

Section 4. The validity of the public debt of the United States, authorized by law, including debts incurred for payment of pensions and bounties for services in suppressing insurrection or rebellion, shall not be questioned. But neither the United States nor any State shall assume or pay any debt or obligation incurred in aid of insurrection or rebellion against the United States, or any claim for the loss of emancipation of any slave; but all such debts, obligations, and claims shall be held illegal and void.

Section 5. The Congress shall have the power to enforce, by appropriate legislation, the provisions of this article.

AMENDMENT XV (1870)

Section 1. The right of citizens of the United States to vote shall not be denied or abridged by the United States or by any State on account of race, color, or previous condition of servitude—

Section 2. The Congress shall have power to enforce this article by appropriate legislation.

AMENDMENT XVI (1913)

The Congress shall have power to lay and collect taxes on incomes, from whatever source derived, without apportionment among the several States, and without regard to any census or enumeration.

AMENDMENT XVII (1913)

The Senate of the United States shall be composed of two Senators from each State, elected by the people thereof, for six years; and each Senator shall have one vote. The electors in each State shall have the qualifications requisite for electors of the most numerous branch of the State legislatures.

When vacancies happen in the representation of any State in the Senate, the executive authority of such State shall issue writs of election to fill such vacancies: *Provided,* That the legislature of any State may empower the executive thereof to make temporary appointments until the people fill the vacancies by election as the legislature may direct.

This amendment shall not be so construed as to affect the election or term of any Senator chosen before it becomes valid as part of the Constitution.

AMENDMENT XVIII (1919)[13]

Section 1. After one year from the ratification of this article the manufacture, sale, or transportation of intoxicating liquors within, the importation thereof into, or the exportation thereof from the United States and all territory subject to the jurisdiction thereof for beverage purposes is hereby prohibited.

Section 2. The Congress and the several States shall have concurrent power to enforce this article by appropriate legislation.

Section 3. This article shall be inoperative unless it shall have been ratified as an amendment to the Constitution by the legislatures of the several States, as provided in the Constitution, within seven years from the date of the submission hereof to the States by the Congress.

AMENDMENT XIX (1920)

The right of citizens of the United States to vote shall not be denied or abridged by the United States or by any State on account of sex.

Congress shall have power to enforce this article by appropriate legislation.

---

[13] Repealed by the Twenty-first Amendment.

AMENDMENT XX (1933)

Section 1. The terms of the President and Vice-President shall end at noon on the 20th day of January, and the terms of Senators and Representatives at noon on the 3d day of January, of the years in which such terms would have ended if this article had not been ratified; and the terms of their successors shall then begin.

Section 2. The Congress shall assemble at least once in every year, and such meeting shall begin at noon on the 3d day of January, unless they shall by law appoint a different day.

Section 3. If, at the time fixed for the beginning of the term of the President, the President elect shall have died, the Vice-President elect shall become President. If a President shall not have been chosen before the time fixed for the beginning of his term, or if the President elect shall have failed to qualify, then the Vice-President elect shall act as President until a President shall have qualified; and the Congress may by law provide for the case wherein neither a President elect nor a Vice-President elect shall have qualified, declaring who shall then act as President, or the manner in which one who is to act shall be selected, and such person shall act accordingly until a President or Vice-President shall have qualified.

Section 4. The Congress may by law provide for the case of the death of any of the persons from whom the House of Representatives may choose a President whenever the right of choice shall have devolved upon them, and for the case of the death of any of the persons from whom the Senate may choose a Vice-President whenever the right of choice shall have devolved upon them.

Section 5. Sections 1 and 2 shall take effect on the 15th day of October following the ratification of this article.

Section 6. This article shall be inoperative unless it shall have been ratified as an amendment to the Constitution by the legislatures of three-fourths of the several States within seven years from the date of its submission.

AMENDMENT XXI (1933)

Section 1. The eighteenth article of amendment to the Constitution of the United States is hereby repealed.

Section 2. The transportation or importation into any State, Territory, or possession of the United States for delivery or use therein of intoxicating liquors, in violation of the laws thereof, is, hereby prohibited.

Section 3. This article shall be inoperative unless it shall have been ratified as an amendment to the Constitution by conventions in the several States, as provided in the Constitution, within seven years from the date of the submission hereof to the States by the Congress.

AMENDMENT XXII (1951)

Section 1. No person shall be elected to the office of the President more than twice, and no person who has held the office of President, or acted as President, for more than two years of a term to which some other person was elected President shall be elected to the office of the President more than once.

But this Article shall not apply to any person holding the office of President when this Article was proposed by the Congress, and shall not prevent any person who may be holding the office of President, or acting as President, during the term within which this Article becomes operative from holding the office of President or acting as President during the remainder of such term.

Section 2. This article shall be inoperative unless it shall have been ratified as an amendment to the Constitution by the legislatures of three-fourths of the several States within seven years from the date of its submission to the States by the Congress.

AMENDMENT XXIII (1961)

Section 1. The District constituting the seat of Government of the United States shall appoint in such manner as the Congress may direct:

A number of electors of President and Vice-President equal to the whole number of Senators and Representatives in Congress to which the District would be entitled if it were a State, but in no event more than the least populous State; they shall be in addition to those appointed by the States, but they shall be considered for the purposes of the election of President and Vice-President, to be electors appointed by the State; and they shall meet in the District and perform such duties as provided by the twelfth article of amendment.

Section 2. The Congress shall have power to enforce this article by appropriate legislation.

AMENDMENT XXIV (1964)

Section 1. The right of citizens of the United States to vote in any primary or other election for President or Vice-President, for electors for President or Vice-President, or for Senator or Representative in Congress, shall not be denied or abridged by the United States or any State by reason of failure to pay any poll tax or other tax.

Section 2. The Congress shall have power to enforce this article by appropriate legislation.

AMENDMENT XXV (1967)

Section 1. In case of the removal of the President from office or of his death or resignation, the Vice-President shall become President.

Section 2. Whenever there is a vacancy in the office of the Vice-President, the President shall nominate a Vice-President who shall take office upon confirmation by a majority vote of both Houses of Congress.

Section 3. Whenever the President transmits to the President pro tempore of the Senate and the Speaker of the House of Representatives his written declaration that he is unable to discharge the powers and duties of his office, and until he transmits to them a written declaration to the contrary, such powers and duties shall be discharged by the Vice-President as Acting President.

Section 4. Whenever the Vice-President and a majority of either the principal officers of the executive department or of such other body as Congress may by law provide, transmit to the President pro tempore of the Senate and the Speaker of the

House of Representatives their written declaration that the President is unable to discharge the powers and duties of his office, the Vice-President shall immediately assume the powers and duties of the office as Acting President.

Thereafter, when the President transmits to the President pro tempore of the Senate and the Speaker of the House of Representatives his written declaration that no inability exists, he shall resume the powers and duties of his office unless the Vice-President and a majority of either the principal officers of the executive department or of such other body as Congress may by law provide, transmit within four days to the President pro tempore of the Senate and the Speaker of the House of Representatives their written declaration that the President is unable to discharge the powers and duties of his office. Thereupon Congress shall decide the issue, assembling within forty-eight hours for that purpose if not in session. If the Congress, within twenty-one days after receipt of the latter written declaration, or, if Congress is not in session, within twenty-one days after Congress is required to assemble, determines by two-thirds vote of both Houses that the President is unable to discharge the powers and duties of his office, the Vice-President shall continue to Discharge the same as Acting President; otherwise, the President shall resume the powers and duties of his office.

AMENDMENT XXVI (1971)

Section 1. The right of citizens of the United States, who are eighteen years of age or older, to vote shall not be denied or abridged by the United States or by any State on account of age.

Section 2. The Congress shall have power to enforce this article by appropriate legislation.

Presidential Elections, 1900–1932

YEAR	NUMBER OF STATES	CANDIDATES	PARTIES	POPULAR VOTE (IN THOUSANDS)	ELECTORAL VOTE	PERCENTAGE OF POPULAR VOTE*
1900	45	WILLIAM McKINLEY	Republican	7,218	292	51.7
		William J. Bryan	Democratic; Populist	6,356	155	45.5
		John C. Wooley	Prohibition	208		1.5
1904	45	THEODORE ROOSEVELT	Republican	7,628	336	57.4
		Alton B. Parker	Democratic	5,084	140	37.6
		Eugene V. Debs	Socialist	402		3.0
		Silas C. Swallow	Prohibition	258		1.9
1908	46	WILLIAM H. TAFT	Republican	7,657	321	51.6
		William J. Bryan	Democratic	6,412	162	43.1
		Eugene V. Debs	Socialist	420		2.8
		Eugene W. Chafin	Prohibition	253		1.7
1912	48	WOODROW WILSON	Democratic	6,296	435	41.9
		Theodore Roosevelt	Progressive	4,118	88	27.4
		William H. Taft	Republican	3,486	8	23.2
		Eugene V. Debs	Socialist	900		6.0
		Eugene W. Chafin	Prohibition	206		1.4
1916	48	WOODROW WILSON	Democratic	9,127	277	49.4
		Charles E. Hughes	Republican	8,533	254	46.2
		A. L. Benson	Socialist	585		3.2
		J. Frank Hanly	Prohibition	220		1.2
1920	48	WARREN G. HARDING	Republican	16,143	404	60.4
		James N. Cox	Democratic	9,130	127	34.2
		Eugene V. Debs	Socialist	919		3.4
		P. P. Christensen	Farmer-Labor	265		1.0
1924	48	CALVIN COOLIDGE	Republican	15,718	382	54.0
		John W. Davis	Democratic	8,385	136	28.8
		Robert M. La Follette	Progressive	4,831	13	16.6
1928	48	HERBERT C. HOOVER	Republican	21,391	444	58.2
		Alfred E. Smith	Democratic	15,016	87	40.9
1932	48	FRANKLIN D. ROOSEVELT	Democratic	22,809	472	57.4
		Herbert C. Hoover	Republican	15,758	59	39.7
		Norman Thomas	Socialist	881		2.2

(continued)

SOURCE: Adapted from *Historical Statistics of the United States,* p. 682; *Statistical Abstract of the United States: 1974,* p. 422; *and World Almanac: 1988,* p. 320.

* Candidates receiving less than 1 percent of the popular vote have been omitted. For that reason the percentage of popular vote given for any election year may not total 100 percent.

	NUMBER			POPULAR		PERCENTAGE
	OF			VOTE	ELECTORAL	OF POPULAR
YEAR	STATES	CANDIDATES	PARTIES	(IN THOUSANDS)	VOTE	VOTE*

Presidential Elections, 1936-1996

YEAR	STATES	CANDIDATES	PARTIES	POPULAR VOTE (IN THOUSANDS)	ELECTORAL VOTE	PERCENTAGE OF POPULAR VOTE*
1936	48	FRANKLIN D. ROOSEVELT	Democratic	27,752	523	60.8
		Alfred M. Landon	Republican	16,674	8	36.5
		William Lemke	Union	882		1.9
1940	48	FRANKLIN D. ROOSEVELT	Democratic	27,307	449	54.8
		Wendell L. Willkie	Republican	22,321	82	44.8
1944	48	FRANKLIN D. ROOSEVELT	Democratic	25,606	432	53.5
		Thomas E. Dewey	Republican	22,014	99	46.0
1948	48	HARRY S TRUMAN	Democratic	24,105	303	49.5
		Thomas E. Dewey	Republican	21,970	189	45.1
		J. Strom Thurmond	States' Rights	1,169	39	2.4
		Henry A. Wallace	Progressive	1,157		2.4
1952	48	DWIGHT D. EISENHOWER	Republican	33,936	442	55.1
		Adlai E. Stevenson	Democratic	27,314	89	44.4
1956	48	DWIGHT D. EISENHOWER	Republican	35,590	457	57.6
		Adlai E. Stevenson	Democratic	26,022	73	42.1
1960	50	JOHN F. KENNEDY	Democratic	34,227	303	49.9
		Richard M. Nixon	Republican	34,108	219	49.6
1964	50	LYNDON B. JOHNSON	Democratic	43,126	486	61.1
		Barry M. Goldwater	Republican	27,176	52	38.5
1968	50	RICHARD M. NIXON	Republican	31,785	301	43.4
		Hubert H. Humphrey	Democratic	31,275	191	42.7
		George C. Wallace	American Independent	9,906	46	13.5
1972	50	RICHARD M. NIXON	Republican	47,170	520	60.7
		George S. McGovern	Democratic	29,170	17	37.7
1976	50	JIMMY CARTER	Democratic	40,830	297	50.0
		Gerald R. Ford	Republican	39,147	240	47.9
1980	50	RONALD W. REAGAN	Republican	43,899	489	50.8
		Jimmy Carter	Democratic	36,481	49	41.0
		John B. Anderson	Independent	5,719	0	6.6
1984	50	RONALD W. REAGAN	Republican	54,282	525	59.2
		Walter E. Mondale	Democratic	37,457	13	40.8
1988	50	GEORGE BUSH	Republican	47,917	426	53.9
		Michael Dukakis	Democratic	41,013	111	46.1
1992	50	BILL CLINTON	Democratic	43,728	370	43.2
		George Bush	Republican	38,167	168	37.7
		Ross Perot	Independent	19,237	0	19.0
1996	50	BILL CLINTON	Democratic	47,401	379	50.1
		Bob Dole	Republican	39,198	159	41.4
		Ross Perot	Independent	8,085	0	8.5

* Candidates receiving less than 1 percent of the popular vote have been omitted. For that reason the percentage of popular vote given for any election year may not total 100 percent.

Index

319